DOSTOYEVSKY

AN EXAMINATION OF THE
MAJOR NOVELS

COMPANION STUDIES

DOSTOYEVSKY

AN EXAMINATION OF THE MAJOR NOVELS

RICHARD PEACE

Lecturer in Charge of Russian Studies
Bristol University

CAMBRIDGE
AT THE UNIVERSITY PRESS
1971

Published by the Syndics of the Cambridge University Press
Bentley House, 200 Euston Road, London N.W.1
American Branch: 32 East 57th Street, New York, N.Y.10022

© Cambridge University Press 1971

Library of Congress Catalogue Card Number: 77–116838

ISBN: 0 521 07911 X

Printed in Great Britain by
W & J Mackay & Co Ltd, Chatham

CONTENTS

TO MY WIFE, VIRGINIA

PREFACE

There are many good books on Dostoyevsky: his biography; his religious and philosophical ideas; his influence on world literature; the realism, the dramatic qualities of his work; the novels as tragedies; the novels as comedies – all these aspects, and many more, have already been well covered. The intention of the present study is not to do what has already been done, but rather to look closely at the texts of the major novels and see how each functions as a work of art.

After a brief survey of the early writing and an examination of *Notes from Underground*, two chapters are devoted to each of the major novels in turn (*Crime and Punishment, The Idiot, The Devils, The Brothers Karamazov*). The final chapter attempts to draw general conclusions from the evidence which emerges from this examination.

I wish to express my gratitude to Professor Henry Gifford for his wise counsel and ever-patient attention at all stages of my work on this book.

R.A.P.

Bristol, 1970

EARLY WRITING AND 'NOTES FROM UNDERGROUND'

Dostoyevsky is the author of four incomparable novels: *Crime and Punishment, The Idiot, The Devils* (also translated as *The Possessed*) and *The Brothers Karamazov*. Each of these novels repays careful and detailed study; but before we proceed to examine this major body of work, it would be as well to cast a glance over Dostoyevsky's earlier writing, and look, in particular, at *Notes from Underground* – a work which in many respects serves as an introduction to the major novels.

After three o'clock one May morning in 1845, during the period of 'The White Nights' in St Petersburg, two young men in an excited state of mind knocked up a third young man to tell him he was a genius. The sleeper whose greatness was so dramatically proclaimed was Dostoyevsky, and his visitors, Grigorovich and Nekrasov, had just finished reading the manuscript of *Poor Folk*. It is difficult for the modern Western reader to appreciate why this sentimental novel in letters so impressed Dostoyevsky's contemporaries. Yet Nekrasov in recommending the manuscript to the influential critic Belinsky spoke of Dostoyevsky as 'a new Gogol', and here, perhaps, is the clue to the apparently immoderate praise which greeted the first work of this young writer.

To Dostoyevsky's contemporaries *Poor Folk* appeared as a deepening of that 'naturalistic' humanitarian theme which Gogol's story *The Greatcoat* had established three years before. Dostoyevsky presented the plight of an indigent civil servant in St Petersburg without the grotesque embroidery and supernatural accretions so typical of Gogol. Moreover the theme itself had been 'humanised': the civil servant's love for an inanimate object – a greatcoat – had been replaced by his love for another human being – one of society's 'insulted and injured' like himself. Belinsky greeted the manuscript with rapture: the fame of the young man was assured.

Dostoyevsky was lionised in St Petersburg society, and his sudden success seems to have gone to his head. Yet he could scarcely afford to be arrogant; for, apart from the few, no one as yet had seen the proof of his genius: *Poor Folk* was not to be published until the following year (January 1846). The position of a gauche provincial genius whose worth had to be taken on trust by the sophisticated society of the capital was inherently ludicrous, and Dostoyevsky's own lack of self-assurance – the very quality responsible for his nervous overacting of his new role – made him recoil all the more violently before the anecdotes and witticisms which soon began to circulate at his expense.

Turgenev at first had offered the newcomer his warm friendship, but now took a leading part in baiting him. Dostoyevsky had thus good reason to bear a grudge against his brilliant contemporary, and this was to complicate their relationship in later life. But Belinsky himself was growing more critical of Dostoyevsky. He did not like *A Novel in Nine Letters* which his young protégé dashed off in one night, nor did he really understand the new direction Dostoyevsky was taking in *The Double*. As for *The Landlady*, Belinsky condemned it out of hand – and with justice.

Dostoyevsky now seemed to be breaking his ties with all his erstwhile friends and to be making new acquaintances in the circle of an eccentric publicist of revolutionary ideas named Petrashevsky. In 1847 he started visiting Petrashevsky's Friday gatherings, but in Russia the times were hardly propitious for radical sympathies. The year 1848, which was marked by revolutions in Europe, was the signal in Russia for sterner repressive measures at home by an ever vigilant tsar. In the April of 1849 once more Dostoyevsky was awakened in the early hours of the morning. This time, however, the intruders brought him not laurels but a crown of thorns: the tsar's officers had come to arrest him.

The gravest charge that the authorities could find against him was his public reading of Belinsky's now famous letter to Gogol in which both Church and State came under strong attack. Yet within the Petrashevsky circle itself Dostoyevsky belonged to a secret and more radical group, which had acquired a printing press and was planning to disseminate propaganda. He was fortunate that this did not come to light.

After the cruel mock execution, staged so that Dostoyevsky and his fellow Petrashevsky should be reprieved at the very last moment, Dostoyevsky was dispatched to Siberia, at first to the penal settlement in Omsk for four years, and then to serve as a private in the ranks. In all, Dostoyevsky was cut off from the literary and cultural life of the capital for ten years. No other writer has experienced such a long and enforced break between the writings of his youth and those of his maturity.

The works of the young Dostoyevsky, as might be expected, are backward-looking. It is not merely that *Poor Folk* and *A Novel in Nine Letters* are both written in the epistolary convention of the eighteenth century; it is more that, in general, his writing is influenced by the great master of Russian prose of the first half of the nineteenth century – Nikolay Gogol. Yet even here the future Dostoyevsky can be glimpsed. Thus *The Double* (1846), in spite of its debt to Gogol's stories *The Nose* and *Diary of a Madman*, reveals a very Dostoyevskian obsession, as its title alone would suggest. Towards the very end of this pre-Siberian period two works in particular, *Netochka Nezvanova* and *The Little Hero*, show an insight into child psychology and precocious sexuality which look forward to the achievement of the mature novelist. A recurring figure in the writings of this early period is that of 'the dreamer' – *mechtatel'* (cf. *The Landlady, A Weak Heart, White Nights*). The figure, that of a hypersensitive young man who lives in a world of the imagination, may have had some autobiographical significance for Dostoyevsky himself at that period, and if the dreamer, as such, does not survive into Dostoyevsky's mature work, his associated qualities of introspection and idealism have a career all their own in his later writing.

After ten years of banishment Dostoyevsky returned to St Petersburg in many respects a changed man. His ordeal appears not to have engendered bitterness, but rather to have reconciled him to the *status quo*. He had returned only after tireless supplication both by himself and his friends, and he undoubtedly had to tread carefully, particularly as he soon hoped to establish a journal – *Vremya* [*Time*]. Nevertheless, despite many of the attitudes of a reactionary – and these were to become more evident in later years – there was still a revolutionary heart within this ex-convict who was now approaching middle age. Indeed it was this urge to challenge the existing order of things coupled, at the same time, with a need for reconciliation with it which was to provide the questing intellectual dynamism behind all his major novels.

One of the first works which Dostoyevsky published on his return, *Notes from the House of the Dead*, was a literary re-working of his own experiences in the Omsk penal settlement. There are new themes here: crime and the criminal; the nature and effect of punishment; but above all an interest in 'the strong man' – the man of the will. Nevertheless the minor writing of the immediate post-Siberian period reads like a continuation of the younger Dostoyevsky, except that there are signs of an implied rejection of his earlier work. Thus *The Village of Stepanchikovo and its Inhabitants* (1859) is a comic story owing much to the manner of Gogol, yet one of the chief characters, Foma Opiskin (a name derived from *opiska* = 'an error in writing') is a polemical portrait of Gogol himself. This is Gogol, the preacher, towards the end of his life, and it is perhaps significant that Foma Opiskin is the usurper and dead moral authority who has to be driven out of the village of Stepanchikovo, before the true master may come into his own.[1]

In *The Insulted and the Injured* (1861) Dostoyevsky even seems to be turning his irony against himself and his earlier figure of 'the dreamer'. The narrator, Ivan Petrovich, is himself the author of a novel which appears to be strongly reminiscent of Dostoyevsky's own *Poor Folk*. The roué, Prince Valkovsky, not only pokes fun at Ivan Petrovich as a novelist of the 'natural school' (i.e. the followers of Gogol) but jibes at what he calls his 'Schillerism' – the very essence of his quality as a 'dreamer'.

4

That it should be Valkovsky who challenges Ivan Petrovich on this score is significant; for he is the first of Dostoyevsky's purely fictional portraits of a 'self willed man': a figure which is to take over from 'the dreamer' as a central preoccupation in Dostoyevsky's mature writing.

The attack on misapplied idealism is carried on in *A Sordid Story* (1862) which is a comic exposure of paternalistic liberalism. But the real break comes with *Notes from Underground* (1864) – a work which serves as a prelude to the major novels. In its hero the introspection of 'the dreamer' fuses with the cult of the will of the 'strong man' who figures so largely in Dostoyevsky's later writing. But if the introspection of 'the dreamer' has by now turned sour, the *underground man's* cult of his own will is as yet chaotic and lacking in direction.

The whole fabric of *Notes from Underground* is permeated by a spirit of rejection; not least, the author is rejecting his own early work. Thus there are strong indications that in the person of the underground man Dostoyevsky wished to portray a disillusioned idealist from his own generation – the generation of 'the forties'. In an introductory note he describes his hero as: 'A character of the recent past. He is one of the representatives of the generation which is still with us.' The 'Schillerism' of the forties, or in the words of the underground man himself: '"All that is beautiful and lofty", as we used to call it at one time', is a recurrent motif in the work: it still has a claim on this soured idealist.

The rejection of the forties, its romantic idealism and its literary clichés, is particularly prominent in Part II. Here the underground man launches into an attack on romanticism, and makes constant ironic use of the phrase: 'all that is beautiful and lofty' as he picks out the Russian romantics for special condemnation. He accuses them of insincerity, of professing high ideals whilst having their sights firmly fixed on material things (there is even an apparent sneer at Turgenev for having gone off to Germany to preserve his romanticism intact).

The ironic title given to Part II: 'Apropos of Sleet' is intended to suggest the writings of the 'natural school' of the forties

– those followers of Gogol with whom Dostoyevsky himself had been classified,[2] and the first incident which the underground man here relates reads like a pastiche on Gogol's story *The Greatcoat*. Here, as in Gogol, a downtrodden civil servant (the underground man himself) endures privations so that he may have clothes which are better than his means allow (in particular a showy fur for his greatcoat). In both stories clothes are treated as a symbol of human dignity, but in Dostoyevsky's version the sentimentalised submissiveness attributed to Gogol's hero has been replaced by the malicious self-assertiveness of the underground man. Dostoyevsky's hero needs his clothes, not to satisfy the basic demands of everyday existence, but those of his own psychological perverseness: he needs them so that *on one occasion* he may confront as an equal some officer whom he chooses to think has insulted him. The underground man is the very inversion of Gogol's pathetic hero: Dostoyevsky's downtrodden civil servant is not merely a victim, he in turn is a tyrant; he is the underdog in rebellion against the literary cliché which up to now has sought to confine him. He refuses to be treated as an *object*, he too is a *subject* in his own right. After the underground man Dostoyevsky's male representatives of 'the humble and the downtrodden' can never be the same: Marmeladov, Lebedev, Lebyadkin, Snegirev are all his spiritual heirs.

The continuation of Part II (the underground man's encounter with his 'friends') jeers at the noble ideas on friendship current in the forties and culminates in an incident with a prostitute which is an open revision of the verses by Nekrasov which the underground man takes as his epigraph. 'When from the gloom of erring ways' was written in 1846, the year after Nekrasov's 'discovery' of Dostoyevsky himself. Its ideas are thus closely linked to Dostoyevsky's youth. The theme of the redemption of a fallen woman, typifies the 'beautiful and lofty' humanitarian ideals of the forties.

Nekrasov was an idealist, who as a successful literary *entrepreneur* certainly had his sights fixed on material things, and the ironic way in which Dostoyevsky introduces this poem (cf. the bathetic ending 'Etc, etc. etc.' matched again in chapter nine by the comment 'from the same poetry') prepares the reader for a polemical treatment of this 'beautiful and lofty' theme. But the underground man's perverse attempt to rescue Liza is not only a comment on the sentimental humanism of Nekrasov's poem, it may also be taken, in a certain sense, as a revision of the platonic sexual relationship between an older man and a younger girl portrayed by Dostoyevsky in his own *Poor Folk*. Dostoyevsky in renouncing the Schilleresque values of the forties is also renouncing his own youth.

The polemics of *Notes from Underground*, however, are being waged on two fronts: the greater part of the underground man's philosophising is directed against ideas current at the actual time of writing – the ideas of 'the sixties'. These two periods of the 1840s and the 1860s were high points in Russian cultural life. Between them stretched the barren waste of Tsar Nicholas's 'barrack-room régime' at its worst. The difference between the gentle, aesthetically orientated humanism of the older generation and the new stridently utilitarian and 'ethically' preoccupied attitude of the younger men is clearly expressed in Turgenev's novel *Fathers and Children*. Dostoyevsky, who had been whisked away at the height of the forties to return to the new social ferment of the sixties, was able to see the contrast clearer than anyone. The theme of the generations is one which we shall encounter more than once in his later writing.

The chief target of *Notes from Underground* is Chernyshevsky – the then acknowledged leader of the younger generation, who the previous year (1863) had published *What is to be done?* This work claimed to be more than a novel, it was offered as a 'textbook of life' for the author's young contemporaries. In *Notes from Underground* we have Dostoyevsky's reply.[3]

Chernyshevsky saw self-interest as the mainspring for all human behaviour; he preached an ethic of enlightened self-interest which he called 'rational egoism'. The underground man jeers at this self-centred basis for morality:

7

When they prove to you that, in reality, one small drop of your own fat ought to be dearer to you than a hundred thousand of your fellow creatures and that these so called virtues, obligations and other fantasies and prejudices will all come into being because of this – then you must accept it, there is nothing you can do about it, because twice two [equals four] is mathematics. Just you try and object.

(Pt I, Ch. 3)

The brunt of his attack falls on Chernyshevsky's attempt to link egoism to reason; for if, as the underground man argues, the rational faculties constitute a mere twentieth part of man's make up, how then can reason satisfactorily be equated with the whole of man's self-interest? He maintains that there is, in fact, a greater self-interest which the advocates of 'rational egoism' have left out of account. This 'most advantageous of advantages' is the freedom to do exactly as one chooses *even if it means acting against one's own self-interest*. Here, of course, is paradox, but paradox is the natural element of the underground man, and what he seeks to stress is that for man's happiness volitive urges are more important than rational motives. Indeed, inasmuch as the mind may impose restrictions on desires, it curtails man's freedom and prevents him from realising his full potential. But more than this, the values of the intellect are ultimately seen to be anti-human; for the advocates of 'rational egoism' are striving towards what they take to be the ideal of the perfect society, but what, in the estimation of the underground man, is nothing more than the ideal of the ant-heap.

The symbol for this perfect society of the rationalists is a palace of crystal. The symbol is Chernyshevsky's own; for in *What is to be done?* the heroine dreams of visiting the perfect society of the future housed in enormous palaces of glass, which are so wonderful that the Crystal Palace in London is merely a hint at what they are like. London's Crystal Palace also colours Dostoyevsky's attitude to this symbol; he had visited it two years before and had voiced his misgivings in *Winter Notes on Summer Impressions* (1863).[4]

The fact that the perfect society is encased in glass precludes

8

any possibility of real privacy. Moreover the very 'perfection' of the crystal palace is in itself a mark of its non-human quality; for, argues the underground man, human beings hate perfection, hate to achieve their goal. Man not only loves to build, he also loves to destroy, and the nature of the crystal palace is such that all negative responses become virtually impossible:

Perhaps I fear this building because it is of crystal and eternally indestructible, and because it will not be possible to stick one's tongue out at it even surreptitiously.   (Pt I, Ch. 10)

The crystal palace, however, is a symbol for more than the perfect society, it stands too for the triumph of man's reason, for his ultimate ability to comprehend and to codify the whole of creation. Yet in codifying his own irrational promptings man will not so much understand as destroy: he will have substituted reason for desire, and in the words of the underground man: 'who wants to want according to a table?' Human science will end by destroying man himself; for it will reduce him to the function of a piano key or an organ stop. Man will no longer be able to will and to desire, he will only be able to ratiocinate.

Yet this can never be. Rather than be reduced to this, man would choose to go mad so that he might, in some fashion, live according to the dictates of his own non-rational will. A leader would inevitably arise who would be the mouthpiece for man's irrational urges, and he would recommend the destruction of the crystal palace, so that man could revert to the stupid, wayward life he lived before.

The perfection of the crystal palace is, paradoxically, its greatest weakness. Perfection admits of no progression: it is a dead end, a dead formula like $2 \times 2 = 4$. The perfection of the crystal palace would be no advance on the obvious imperfections of that other symbolic edifice – *the underground*.[5] The underground might even be better, argues its inhabitant, for there at least he has means at his disposal for the relief of boredom.

The arguments of the paradoxalist on 'perfection' are basically the same as those he used to attack 'self-interest'. He maintains that perfection is not really perfection if it leaves out of account man's fear of perfection, just as earlier he argues that self-interest is not genuine self-interest if it exclude man's need to act against his own self-interest. In both cases he is attacking glib assumptions about abstract concepts and arguing the cause of human freedom against the restricting categories of facile theorists.

The underground man boasts that he takes to extremes what other people only dare to take half-way, and he has certainly developed the argument on the triumph of human reason to its ultimate point in his symbol of the crystal palace. In much the same way he pushes the counter argument on man's will to its very limits. For the underground man, human desires reach out towards infinity; he refuses to allow them to be thwarted either by the dictates of reason or the laws of the natural world, in spite of the fact that both these forms of restraint appear as intractable as mathematical formulae. The underground man objects to the inevitability of twice two equalling four; he refuses to accept something as humbling to his own ego as 'laws of nature' in the drafting of which he has had no part. The will cannot be reconciled to impossibility merely because it is impossibility, no matter what objections are raised to this by the rationalists:

'Good gracious,' they will shout at you, 'you cannot rebel: this is twice two equals four! Nature does not ask your permission; she has no concern for your wishes, nor as to whether you like her laws or not. You are obliged to accept her as she is, and accordingly to accept all her consequences. A wall *is* a wall etc. etc.'

Good heavens, what do I care for the laws of nature or for arithmetic, when I happen not to like these laws nor the fact that twice two equals four? Of course, I shall not be able to break through such a wall with my head, if, in fact, I haven't the strength to break through, but I shall not be reconciled to it merely because it is a stone wall which is before me and my strength is not sufficient.

(Pt i, Ch. 3)

In the concept of the 'wall' we have another important symbol for the underground man. It stands for the obstacles placed before man's will by the laws of the natural world. The origin of the symbol lies perhaps in a Russian saying. Thus Serge, a negative character in *What is to be done?* defends his own complacency in the following terms:

'You will not break through a wall with your head', we Russians say. We are an intelligent people, Julie. You see how calmly I live, having accepted this Russian principle of ours.

(What is to be done? Ch. I, sect. 2)

The particular 'wall' against which Serge has no desire to try his strength is a flagrant social abuse: the case of a mother trying to sell her daughter. The argument of Chernyshevsky throughout the novel is that 'walls' of this nature are not only capable of being penetrated 'by the head', but they must be completely destroyed, as they are the fabric of a corrupt society. When, however, Chernyshevsky speculates on the power of the human will confronted by the 'wall' of the laws of nature, his conclusions are quite different:

If a certain propensity has not been given by nature, or has not been developed by life, independently of the intentions of the man himself, that man cannot create it in himself by an effort of will.

(What is to be done? Ch. III, sect. 21)

Thus Chernyshevsky and his followers are but timid rebels when compared with the underground man. They merely wish to change that which is susceptible of change – social and political institutions – whereas the underground man wants to change that which is immutable – the laws of nature: he would like the formula $2 \times 2 = 5$ to be a possibility. In the arguments of the underground man the concept of 'revolution' suffers the same sort of development as Chernyshevsky's other ideas on 'self-interest' and 'perfection' – it is pushed to its uttermost limits. Chernyshevsky's revolution is merely directed against man, whereas the underground man is in revolt against God. It is an interesting fact that in Dostoyevsky's later writing the political revolutionary and the metaphysical rebel are never far apart.

The metaphysical revolt of the underground man inheres in

the fact that he himself is aspiring to the condition of godhead: he wishes to push man's capabilities to their very limits. It is characteristic that even at the height of his attack on the triumph of human reason, he feels called on to state that he regards this triumph as possible: 'For it is contemptible and senseless to believe *a priori* that there are certain laws of nature which men will never find out.' (Pt I, Ch. 8.) Thus the underground man will not tolerate any restriction of man's capabilities even if it means the temporary vindication of the power of human reason. Nevertheless it is the will which is the chief vehicle for the underground man's striving towards godhead: it is this alone which he opposes to the stone wall of the metaphysical *status quo*.

Here once more we come up against a paradox; for Dostoyevsky had originally intended that this would-be usurper of God's role should end by proving his own need for God, but by an irony that was to affect his work more than once, these positive religious ideas had to be excised for reasons of censorship.[6] All that remains of this positive argument can be found in Part I, chapter 10. Thus the underground man appears to be on the point of voicing a religious solution to his problems when he says:

Why then have I been created with such desires? Surely I have not been so created merely to come to the conclusion that I have been cheated in the way I was created. Surely the whole aim cannot be in this? I don't believe it.   (Pt I, Ch. 10)

The religious equivocation of the underground man smacks of that dilemma which is to haunt the pages of Dostoyevsky's novels: the claims of man/god versus those of God/man: (man setting himself up as god in atheism as opposed to God coming down as man in Christ).

The underground man is, of course, ill. This is how he introduces himself to the reader in the very opening words of the work. His illness is not merely physical, not merely his liver complaint or his toothache, it is psychological. The fact that he can find pleasure in toothache points to a graver affliction than the toothache itself; for the underground man has strong sado-masochistic tendencies which condition both his 'philosophy' and his behaviour. That hypersensitive awareness which he calls consciousness is the 'retort' which fabricates both his thought and his actions, and 'consciousness', as he himself admits, is the result of suffering: 'But I am convinced that man will never renounce real suffering, that is renounce destruction and chaos; for suffering is the sole cause of consciousness.' (Pt I, Ch. 9.) Here the underground man seeks to ascribe failings which are peculiarly his own to humanity at large, but these are implications which cannot be lightly dismissed: an 'underground man' lurks within each one of his readers.

We have seen that literary polemics lie at the very heart of *Notes from Underground*, but 'fiction', in its widest sense, is a key concept for the work. Dostoyevsky is at pains to tell us in his note of introduction that the work and its author are both complete fiction. But it does not end here: the fictitious author of the fictitious notes feels himself obliged to invent fictitious readers with whom he can enter into conflict. He invents his readers' objections to his own ideas, and the disturbing thing is that his reader has been conceived in his own image as a man who sneers and jeers at the arguments of the underground man in much the same way that he himself ridicules the ideas of his adversaries. Yet the underground man claims that he can invent his readers' words with propriety:

Of course all these words of yours I have just made up myself. This too is from the underground. I have listened to your words there through a chink for forty years on end. I myself have thought them up, for it is only this which could be thought up. It is no wonder that it has been learned by heart and has taken a literary form.

(Pt I, Ch. 11)

By the same rights of 'fiction' which empower the underground man to invent the existence of readers he is also entitled to invent their non-existence:

I am writing for myself alone, and once and for all I declare that if I write as though I were addressing readers, it is solely for the look of the thing, because it is easier for me to write like that. It is a question of form, mere empty form. I shall never have any readers. I have already declared this.   (Pt I, Ch. 11)

The underground man finds it impossible to distinguish between fact and fiction; fact becomes fiction: fiction fact. Thus even the concrete surroundings in which he finds himself assume an abstract quality. For him, St Petersburg is 'the most abstract and contrived city in the world',[7] and his own private quarters in that city he calls his 'underground', by which term he is really referring to his own mental state. Moreover in this 'underground' his chief occupation is the pursuit of fiction. This takes either the form of introspection (the word he himself uses is 'consciousness') or reading.

At home, most of all, I read. I sought by means of external sensations to damp down all that boiled ceaselessly inside me, and as to external sensations, the only possibility for me was reading.   (Pt II, Ch. 1)

He escapes from his underground into the real world merely to commit scandals and to indulge in debauchery, and on such outings he constantly reminds himself that this is reality which he is experiencing, while at the same time acknowledging the literary nature of his actions. Thus when he attempts to have himself thrown out of the window of a billiard saloon he exclaims: 'The devil knows what I would have given then for a real quarrel, a more correct quarrel, a more fitting quarrel, a more, so to speak, *literary* quarrel.' (Pt II, Ch. 1.)

In the incident with Zverkov and his 'friends', we find him wondering whether the loathing he feels towards his fellow men is not in itself derived from books. The state of his clothing fills him with feelings of inferiority. He tries to suppress them: 'Now is no time for thinking, now reality is approaching.' (Pt II, Ch. 3.) But 'fiction' once more gets in the way, and he fears that the effect he will produce will be: 'miserable, not *literary*, ordinary, every day'. (Pt II, Ch. 3.)

His 'unreal' behaviour at the meal itself poisons the atmosphere for himself just as much as for the others, and when he rushes out to follow them he mutters: 'So that's what it is,

14

that's what it is, after all, the contact with reality.' (Pt II, Ch. 5.) Once in the cab he indulges in day-dreams about duels with Zverkov, which, as he himself acknowledges, are influenced by his reading of Pushkin and Lermontov.

At a further point in the narrative his dealings with Liza have a strong 'literary' flavour. Thus when he paints a lurid picture of the fate awaiting her and contrasts this with the happy family life she is missing, her comment is that all this is straight from a book. Later his day-dreams about the delicate amorous relationship between himself and Liza owe much to George Sand,[8] as he is prepared to acknowledge, and his final cruel act of giving her money is described as 'so affected, so contrived, intentionally concocted, bookish' that he himself feels ashamed of it.

His own explanation for such behaviour is that it stems from acute self-awareness, or, as he himself calls it, 'consciousness'. Consciousness produces boredom, and boredom produces eccentricities. Faced with boredom he has to invent life: 'I myself have invented adventures and thought up my life, in order that I might indeed live – no matter how.' (Pt I, Ch. 5.) Perhaps, after all, the adventures which the underground man relates are not to be taken as real events, but merely as figments of his own imagination; for he intimates that, cooped up in his underground, he thinks things up against himself which have never happened, and does so merely on the grounds that such things could happen. In *Notes from Underground* the reader becomes lost in a web of fiction.

But the reader cannot stand aloof. This *literariness* is a vice which the underground man refuses to regard as peculiarly his own: his readers are, after all, cast in his own image:

We have all grown unaccustomed to life. We all hobble along, each one of us, more or less. We have grown so unaccustomed to life even, that sometimes we feel revulsion from real 'actual life'[9] and cannot bear to be reminded of it. We have reached the point where we consider real 'actual life' almost as a service, and we have all agreed to ourselves that it is better to live according to a book.

(Pt II, Ch. 10)

15

The underground man taunts his readers for what he considers to be their pusillanimity before life. Since he, on the other hand, takes everything to extremes he feels that the same charge cannot be made against him:

I, perhaps, turn out to be more alive than you. Look more closely. We do not know where to find life now, nor what it really is, what it is called. Leave us alone without a book and we will immediately become confused, become lost. We will not know what to attach ourselves to, what to hang on to, what to love and what to hate, what to respect and what to despise. (Pt II, Ch. 10)

Thus the underground man ends his tirade against his readers with words that are an indictment of the Russian intelligentsia as a whole. They are fed on abstractions, live in 'abstract' cities cut off from the Russian people; they are, indeed, unable to live at all unless guided by some such 'textbook of life' as Chernyshevsky's *What is to be done?* This is not merely the vice of the men of the sixties, it is a vice inherited from their fathers:

We are born dead, and for a long time now have not been born from living fathers. We like this more and more. We acquire the taste for it. Soon we shall think how, in some way or other, we might be born from an idea. (Pt II, Ch. 10)

This theme of the 'unreal' fathers giving birth to 'unreal' sons Dostoyevsky will take up again in *The Devils*, but here it is the underground man himself who is the representative of 'the fathers', and, as Dostoyevsky reminds us, he cannot stand apart from the social process:

In our society it is not merely that such people as the writer of these notes can exist, they must exist if we take into account those circumstances under which, in general, our society was formed.
(Dostoyevsky's Introductory Note)

The lack of any real grasp on life which so characterises the underground man is not just his own personal vice – it is a national vice too, and by one of the paradoxes so typical of Dostoyevsky's writing, the underground man is both the embodiment of that vice and its most eloquent enemy.

In writing *Notes from Underground* Dostoyevsky seems to have had some analogy with music in mind. In a letter describing his work on the second part he speaks about it as 'a transition as in music',[10] and at the end of the first part the underground man himself seems to anticipate this musical transition when he describes the anecdote he is about to retail as 'an annoying musical motif' which he cannot get out of his mind. The analogy with music has particular relevance for Part i. Here Dostoyevsky was faced with the problem of dealing with the thoughts of a man who has renounced reason, and of presenting them in such a way that his arguments are persuasive and convincing. This problem he appears to have solved by resorting to the devices of music; for in the arguments of the underground man ideas are treated like musical themes: they are introduced, reintroduced, woven into other themes, inverted, restated; and if the general drift of the argument progresses (as indeed it does) this is a movement which is nearer to progression in a musical sense rather than development according to the laws of logic. It would be possible, for instance, to give each of the eleven chapters of Part i a heading to indicate the chief topic upon which the chapter is centred, but this would give no hint of the interpenetration within each chapter of the many and varied motifs which form the basic material of the work.

There is moreover a kind of counterpoint discernible in the duologue between the underground man and his imagined readers. In it can be seen the beginnings of that dialectical method of presenting ideas which is the hallmark of Dostoyevsky the mature artist. Paradox is one of the chief weapons used by the underground man in his fight against reason, and this love for the tension between opposites looks forward to the warring contradictions from which, in the major novels, Dostoyevsky will construct his truths.

Notes from Underground is a rehearsal of many of the themes which will be encountered in the later novels. It is interesting in this respect that the work springs from a desire to do battle with Chernyshevsky; for this same itch to engage in polemics with the radicals conditions each one of the major novels, and the associated theme of the generations is one which we shall meet again more than once.

In attacking the purely rationalist outlook of Chernyshevsky, Dostoyevsky emphasises the contrary principle of man's volitive urges, and so it is that through the obscuring mists of the underground man's 'philosophy' there can be glimpsed the rough outlines of that self-willed hero who was so to obsess the mature artist.

The 'wall', the metaphorical barrier which thwarts man's will looks forward to other such symbolic obstacles in the novels, whereas the symbol of the crystal palace, in its identification with the despotism of the perfect society, is a foretaste of Dostoyevsky's concern with those other man-made tyrannies described on the pages of *The Devils* and *The Brothers Karamazov*.

Finally there is that state of hypersensitive awareness which the underground man calls 'consciousness'. This, as we have seen, links him with the earlier figure of 'the dreamer', but its significance is double-edged. On the one hand consciousness makes the underground man feel superior to his fellow creatures; for he is acutely aware of what they fail to see: on the other hand it is responsible for the worst excesses of his own behaviour, and causes him acute suffering. These two aspects of consciousness have a career all their own in the later novels, and if a tortured sensitivity is a constant trait in Dostoyevsky's characterisation, the positive side of consciousness, the capacity for greater awareness, is destined to become a corner stone in the author's own philosophy.

Of all the major novels *Notes from Underground* throws most light on *The Devils*. It shares with this work a strong polemical element coupled with the theme of the generations. On a metaphysical level, both works explore the idea of the will in collision with the 'wall' of the laws of nature and common sense. But the first of Dostoyevsky's masterpieces, *Crime and Punishment*, also owes much to *Notes from Underground*, and it is to this novel which we must now turn our attention.

18

2

THE ETHICAL REAPPRAISAL: 'CRIME AND PUNISHMENT'

Dostoyevsky originally conceived *Crime and Punishment* as a novel narrated in the first person; it was to have been a 'confession'[1] – the genre he had exploited with such success in *Notes from Underground*. Although Dostoyevsky abandoned his original intention, the two works nevertheless still invite comparison.

If in the person of the underground man the romantic figure of the 'dreamer' has gone sour, then Raskolnikov too in his own way is a soured dreamer – a perverted idealist. In much the same way as the nameless hero of the *Notes* skulks in his 'underground', so too Raskolnikov locks himself up in his 'coffin' of a room, and in both cases hermetic surroundings appear to act as a retort for the distillation of unusual ideas.[2] Raskolnikov and the underground man, each in his own way asserts the primacy of the individual will. The underground man puts forward the concept of the 'wall' as a symbol of everything that thwarts his own will. Raskolnikov sees his will confronted by a similar symbolic obstacle which must be 'crossed over'. He makes the effort and appears to succeed, only to find out ultimately that such obstacles cannot be crossed with impunity.

Both men are offered salvation and regeneration as human beings through a relationship with a prostitute. Once again Raskolnikov takes a positive step where the underground man fails to act; he offers Sonya his love and receives hers in return. Yet it is not merely that Raskolnikov is a more decisive figure than the underground man, there is one quality which quite clearly marks him off from his anti-rationalist predecessor: Raskolnikov is, above all else, a man whose actions are based on cool and calculating reason – he is a member of that same younger generation against whom the underground man is taking up arms.

The polemical intention in both cases is, of course, the same; for if the underground man is the theorist challenging the proposition that man's pursuit of reason can bring him nought but good, then Raskolnikov is the illustration of his argument – he is the living example of the folly of basing human actions on reason and reason alone. Thus the underground man's protest against man's subjugation to the rules of arithmetic and the laws of nature finds its antithesis in the deterministic reasoning behind Raskolnikov's theory on the emergence of supermen:

One thing alone is clear: the order according to which these different categories and subdivisions emerge, must be very precisely determined by some law of nature. This law, of course, is as yet unknown, but I believe that it does exist and that in the future it may indeed become known. The great mass of mankind is material which exists merely so that through some sort of effort, by some sort of mysterious process we know nothing about as yet – the crossing of races and types – this mass may exert itself and ultimately give birth to one man in a thousand who is to some extent independent. A man of even greater independence will be born perhaps out of ten thousand (I am speaking in approximate terms for greater clarity); a man of still greater independence out of a hundred thousand; geniuses from millions; and great geniuses, the crowning glory of humanity, only as a result of many thousands of millions of people. In short, I haven't looked into the retort where all this is taking place, but a definite law undoubtedly must exist, it has to exist; there can be no chance in all this. (Pt III, Ch. 5)

The belief in man's ability to codify the laws of nature; the Darwinian overtones; the mathematical reasoning; even the retort – all these are elements which we have met before in the arguments of the underground man. But these arguments were the very reverse of the thesis Raskolnikov advances above. The underground man rejected the idea that human beings could be mere 'organ stops': Raskolnikov sees men as units in a purely mechanistic formula, and the very same mind which is capable of regarding the mass of humanity as mere material, is also capable of disregarding the human being within a money-lender. There is something inherently paradoxical in Raskolnikov's attempt to ascribe the emergence of the independent will to a deterministic process such as this (it was to similar 'laws of nature' that the underground man sought to oppose the counter-principle of his own will). But Raskolnikov can no more escape contradictions than the paradoxalist himself. Thus though he reduces human beings to statistics in the purely theoretical argument he advances above, when similar statistics could have a bearing on his own family his standpoint then is not much different from that of the underground man. This is what he says about prostitution:

It is essential, they say, that such a percentage should go off every year to wherever it is – to the devil, I suppose, in order that the rest should be kept fresh and unmolested. A percentage. How marvellous indeed these words of theirs are. They are so reassuring, scientific. Once you have said percentage there is nothing to worry about, but if it were another word, then it would be more disturbing perhaps. And what if Dunya should somehow find herself in the percentage, if not in this, then in another. (Pt I, Ch. 4)

The underground man had a strong desire to stick his tongue out at the crystal palace, and Raskolnikov suddenly feels the same urge to 'stick his tongue out' at the police clerk Zametov by taunting him with the revelation of his own coolly calculating, rational behaviour at the time of the murder. In doing so, he is not merely jeering at Zametov, he is 'sticking his tongue out' at reason itself; for his actions were not as rational as he claims, nor are his motives in confessing them now dictated by rational considerations. It therefore seems significant that this act of 'sticking out the tongue'[3] should take place in a tavern called 'The Crystal Palace'.

On leaving 'The Crystal Palace', Raskolnikov bumps into his friend Razumikhin (a name derived from *razum* = reason).[4] He is so annoyed at Raskolnikov's fantastic behaviour that he launches into a tirade strongly reminiscent of the ending of *Notes from Underground*:

I tell you that all of you, every single one of you, are idle chatterers and vain braggarts. The moment you have the tiniest bit of suffering

21

you brood on it like a hen with an egg, and even then you plagiarise from other authors. There is not a sign of independent life in you. You are made of wax. You have buttermilk in your veins not blood. I do not believe a single one of you. In all conditions your first concern is how least to resemble a human being.   (Pt II, Ch. 6)

In the eyes of his friend, Raskolnikov is another underground man whose failings reflect the shortcomings of the Russian intelligentsia as a whole.

The many contradictions surrounding the figure of Raskolnikov (and these must be examined more closely in the next chapter) show that he is no bald illustration of a thesis, but a many-sided human being; with uncanny artistry Dostoyevsky has entered into the innermost depths of his hero's soul. Indeed, many commentators have pointed to the circumstances in which the novel was conceived and deduced that the author's state of mind at the time may not have been greatly dissimilar from that of his hero.

In 1865 Dostoyevsky found himself in desperate straits: his second journal *Epokha* [*Epoch*] proved insolvent and was closed down, and in an effort to raise money Dostoyevsky had concluded an inequitable contract with the disreputable publisher Stellovsky, who by buying up Dostoyevsky's bad debts had contrived to cheat him of the full sum promised. With what remained Dostoyevsky fled abroad to Wiesbaden, where he became so engrossed in gambling that he soon lost all he had.

In the cheap hotel where he was staying the penniless foreigner was allowed tea but refused all food until he had paid his bill. At first he sought to escape from the humiliations to which he was subjected by going out, but fresh air and exercise only stimulated an appetite he could not hope to satisfy. In the end he remained immured in his room.

The offer of a new novel to the publisher Katkov was one of the ways by which Dostoyevsky sought to extricate himself from this intolerable position, and it is tempting to see in *Crime and Punishment* a reflection of the circumstances in which the novel was conceived: the pressing financial plight of its author; his sense of desperation; perhaps even the very thoughts which occurred to him, when in a dingy room, without adequate food, he shut himself away from a foreign and hostile world. The end of the novel seems to strike another autobiographical note: Raskolnikov, like his creator, is sent to Siberia, from which experience he too is to emerge a changed man.

Yet if the novel touches on some of the spiritual experiences of the author himself, it cannot be denied that it reflects more broadly the material conditions of contemporary Russia. The great reforms of the sixties affected the social structure of the country quite fundamentally. Even some of the minor reforms left traces on Russian life which are reflected on the pages of *Crime and Punishment*. Thus in 1863 a different method of controlling the sale of spirits had been introduced with disastrous consequences: instead of curtailing the incidence of drunkeness it actually increased it. By 1865 the results were plain for all to see. It was one of the topics of the day. The social problem of drunkenness is treated by Dostoyevsky principally in the sub-plot of the Marmeladov family, but this theme even ante-dates the main plot of the novel itself. Dostoyevsky, it seems, had thought of it as a separate short story before he incorporated it into the fabric of his novel.

Another, and more major reform, was the complete re-shaping of the legal system (1863–4). In the spirit of this, corrupt detectives of the old régime were replaced by more enlightened criminologists. The figure of Porfiry, it has been argued, is in keeping with these new ideas. These same reforms also resulted in the emergence of a new type of pettifogging legal expert as exemplified in the person of Luzhin.

The contemporaneity of the novel is stressed by Soviet scholars. Grossman even goes so far as to say:

If Stendhal's *Le Rouge et le Noir* was to have been called at first *1830*, because of the way it reflected the intellectual currents and morals of that particular point in time, so *Crime and Punishment* could with equal justification be called *1865*. In spite of Dostoyevsky's own view of its timelessness, it was first and foremost a novel of that actual epoch.[5]

It is indeed as a reflection of 'intellectual currents and morals' that *Crime and Punishment* can lay most claim to the title *1865*. Western critics have tended to examine Raskolnikov's ideas on the division of humanity into 'supermen' and 'lice' out of their contemporary setting, relating them retrospectively to Hegel or even prospectively to Nietzsche.[6] Soviet critics, on the other hand have pointed to their relevance to the time of writing. It is significant that the concept of the 'superman' is identified in Raskolnikov's mind with the figure of Napoleon; for in 1865 there appeared the translation of a book in which Napoleon's actions were justified in much the same terms as Raskolnikov seeks to justify his. *The History of Julius Caesar* by Napoleon III caused quite a stir in St Petersburg. The author divided humanity into 'ordinary people' and 'heroes' and so sought to justify the right to absolute power of such figures as Caesar and Napoleon I; by extension he attributed the same right to himself. As this Napoleonic motive is absent from Dostoyevsky's letter to Katkov outlining the plot of *Crime and Punishment*, it has been suggested that it entered into the novel at a later stage, under the influence of Louis Napoleon's thesis.[7]

All this may well be true, but it should be noted that a polarisation of the human condition similar to the one formulated by Raskolnikov had already been expressed in Dostoyevsky's work the year before. Thus the underground man reveals that he too has dreams of greatness:

I almost believed that I would emerge into the world on a white horse, and wearing a laurel crown. I was not capable even of understanding a secondary role, and this is precisely why, in the real world, I quite meekly occupied the very least of roles. Either a hero or dirt; there was no middle way. (Pt I, Ch. 2)

To this extent the Napoleonic aspirations of Raskolnikov are merely the other face of the underground man's psychology: for him too there can be no middle way, but Raskolnikov presented with the alternative 'either Napoleon or a louse' insists that his choice is Napoleon.

There is, however, another reason given for the murder – a

motive of acquisition. Here, too, critics have seen a French source. The famous passage in *Le Père Goriot* where Rastignac quotes Rousseau's idea on the possibility of getting rich by murdering a Chinese mandarin has been seen as a probable influence conditioning Raskolnikov's attitude to the old woman.[8] This again is quite possible; Balzac meant much to Dostoyevsky. His first literary efforts had been directed towards translating Balzac's novel *Eugénie Grandet*, and at the end of his life he had discussed the moral implications of the Chinese mandarin passage in a rough draft for the speech he delivered at the Pushkin Celebrations in 1880.[9] But there is no need to go so far afield. The letter which Dostoyevsky sent to Katkov, offering the novel and outlining its plot, shows well enough what was in the author's mind:

It is a psychological account of a crime. The action is contemporary. It is set in the present year. A young man, an expelled university student, *petit bourgeois* in origin, is living in extreme poverty. Through the shallowness and instability of his thought he has surrendered himself to certain strange and half-baked ideas which are in the air, and has decided to extricate himself at one stroke from his terrible position.[10]

So once more we are brought back to the Russia of 1865 – to 'certain half-baked ideas *which are in the air*'.

The ideas on which Raskolinkov acts are notions which have a certain contemporary currency. This is emphasised by the fact that he is not the only person in the novel who conceives the crime: in a tavern he overhears a student outlining the very same murder which he himself has in mind. The allegedly humanitarian motives which the student gives coincide largely with Raskolnikov's own. Moreover, he even appears to hint at the 'Napoleonic theme': 'Nature can be corrected and given direction, otherwise we should be overwhelmed by prejudices, otherwise there would not be even a single great man.' (Pt 1, Ch. 6.) The ideas of this student are in no way exceptional; theoretical discussions on these and similar topics seem to be a feature of the day:

Raskolnikov was greatly agitated. Of course, all this was nothing more than those conversations, those thoughts which were most usual and frequent among young people, and which he had heard many times, only in other forms and on other themes.

(Pt I, Ch. 6)

Other members of the intelligentsia do not merely discuss: they act. Razumikhin quotes the case of a lecturer at Moscow University convicted of forgery. He too has a 'social' justification for his crime:

Well how did this Moscow lecturer of yours reply to the question; why he was making counterfeit lottery tickets? 'Everybody is making money in various ways, so I too wanted to get rich quickly.' I can't remember the exact words, but the sense was that he wanted something for nothing as quickly as possible and without work. We have got used to living 'with everything found', to walking about supported by other people, to having our food chewed for us, and when the great hour struck, then everyone showed what he was.

(Pt II, Ch. 5)

The phrase 'when the great hour struck' refers to the major reform of the sixties – the Emancipation of the Serfs (1861). Thus in pointing to the increase of crime among the upper classes, Razumikhin seeks to relate the lack of private moral standards to the existence of the larger social evil of serfdom.[11]

The reappraisal of old ethical standpoints was a salient feature of the sixties. In the Great Reforms official Russia had re-examined many of its long-cherished prejudices and abuses, but it had been far outstripped by the younger generation which had made its own unofficial re-evaluation of what was right and what was wrong. Because these young people challenged values which to the older generation seemed unassailable, and championed those which that generation regarded as extreme, they were accused of having no values at all, and labelled 'nihilists'.

The term was given currency by Turgenev in his novel *Fathers and Children*, but his hero Bazarov was seen as a polemical portrait by the majority of the new men themselves. The philosophy of Bazarov throws but little light on the crime of Raskolnikov, moreover his nihilism is presented as ready formed; it affords few glimpses of the processes which have led Bazarov to his extreme conclusions. In the work of N. G. Pomyalovsky, however, a minor writer of the sixties, the development of nihilistic thought can be traced to the point where its relevance to the crime of Raskolnikov becomes obvious.

Pomyalovsky's first short novel *Bourgeois Happiness* (1860) depicts the awakening of a young plebeian intellectual to the social and economic realities of Russian life. The central situation is not unlike *Fathers and Children*, but the hero, Molotov, is more sympathetic and less extreme than his counterpart Bazarov. In the continuation of the life of his hero (*Molotov*, 1861) Pomyalovsky presents us with an out-and-out nihilist in the figure of Cherevanin. He, like Raskolnikov, spends his time shut up in his room, brooding on ethical problems, and like Raskolnikov, he too conceives of morality in purely rational terms. Cherevanin confesses that 'there are terrible thoughts in the realm of ideas', but appears to be restrained from acting on them by his conscience. Conscience is something which he himself cannot understand: it is beyond the control of his reason.

A more ominous note is struck in Pomyalovsky's last work, the unfinished novel *Brother and Sister* (published posthumously, 1864). The hero, Potesin, thinks that he has been able to find a rational explanation for the irrational prompting of conscience, and that by analysing it he has destroyed it. He plans to turn his nihilism to account and get rich through criminal activity, though, like Raskolnikov, he intends to do good with the money he will get. This is how Potesin justifies himself:

Capital funds lie in their coffers and these are possessions which do not belong to them; they belong to no one. He who has gained possession, keeps possession. It is just the same as unoccupied land; he who puts up the first flag keeps it for himself. If you found treasure buried in the ground by robbers, you would surely have no qualms about taking it? Formerly a robber captain and his band would conduct business with knife and bludgeon, nowadays it is with crude vodka or something of that sort. Formerly they buried the money in the earth, now they hide it in chests. Is taking their money, therefore, not just the same as finding buried treasure?[12]

It is with arguments such as these that Raskolnikov can justify the elimination of an exploiting pawnbroker in order that her ill-gotten gains may be put to better use. These are 'the half-baked ideas which are in the air'.

Pomyalovsky described Potesin as a man of primitive honesty protesting against social evil. The description might also fit Raskolnikov. Yet it is obvious that it is but a short step from social protest to political action. Raskolnikov's ideas on the crimes committed by 'exceptional men' also have their wider political implications:

The crimes of these people, of course, are only relative and they take many forms. For the most part, however, in proclamations of one sort or another they demand the destruction of what is, in the name of something better. (Pt III, Ch. 5)

In 1866, as *Crime and Punishment* was coming out, Dostoyevsky saw dramatic expression given to his worst fears about nihilism: a young student Karakozov made an attempt on the life of the tsar. This act inaugurated an ever-growing use of murder as a weapon of political protest. Raskolnikov's murder is not politically motivated, but the distance between him and Karakozov is not so great. In the novel he himself denies that he is a nihilist (to the police) but Dostoyevsky's contemporaries knew better: Strakhov identified Raskolnikov, as a 'suffering nihilist'.[13]

Raskolnikov, however, is not the only nihilist in *Crime and Punishment*; there is also Lebezyatnikov, a foolish character who acts as the comic foil for the tragic implications behind Raskolnikov's own theories. Many of the ideas of the younger generation were crudely fished from the currents of Western European radical thought, and as if to emphasise this, Lebezyatnikov is presented as one who is not entirely fluent in Russian, although he knows no other language. In this 'non-Russianness' he is linked with Raskolnikov, who is described by his friend Razumikhin as a 'translation from a foreign original'. Lebezyatnikov is linked with Raskolnikov in yet another way: he too, is an admirer of Sonya, but this admiration springs principally from ideological considerations; for he considers her profession to be a protest against the existing conditions of society.

Lebezyatnikov even claims that if he *were* to marry, he would force his wife to take a lover so that he could say to her: 'My friend, up till now I have only loved you, but now I respect you because you know how to protest.' (Pt v, Ch. 1.) This is a parody of the rational sexual relationships advocated by Chernyshevsky in *What is to be done?*, and as we might expect from a character whose name is derived from the verb to fawn (i.e. *lebezyat'*) Lebezyatnikov is an intellectual camp follower who glibly repeats the lessons learned from his master. Thus his advocacy of *communes*, his contention that to kiss a woman's hand is to show her disrespect, and his discussion on the right to enter another person's room: all these are crude echoes of key passages in *What is to be done?*

Yet Dostoyevsky had already noted a split in the ranks of the nihilists. Dobrolyubov was dead, Chernyshevsky in prison, and from 1864 the even more extreme ideas of Pisarev and his journal *The Russian Word* [*Russkoye Slovo*] could claim growing support from the younger generation. True to his character as 'a fawner' Lebezyatnikov reflects this shift towards an even more radical position. Thus he claims: 'If Dobrolyubov rose from the grave I would argue with him', and his contention that the cleaning of sewers is a higher form of activity than the creative process of such artists as Raphael and Pushkin is a clear reference to the extreme anti-aesthetic teachings of Pisarev.

Raskolnikov's ideas, too, are extreme. This indeed might have been Dostoyevsky's original conception of the name (cf. *Raskol v nigilistakh* – 'Schism among the Nihilists', the sub-title of a polemical article in 1864).[14] Certainly, Raskolnikov shares the fashionable mistrust in aesthetic criteria. Musing on his failure at the end of Part III, he uses the word 'aesthetic' in a perjorative sense when he refers to himself as an 'aesthetic louse'. Later he seeks to counter Dunya's horror at the nature of the crime itself by this anti-aesthetic argument:

Ah, so the form was not right, the form was not aesthetically pleasing. Well, I just cannot understand why throwing bombs at people in a well-ordered siege is more respectable from a formal point of view. Fear of aesthetic considerations is the first sign of weakness. Never, never have I been more clearly aware of this than now…

(Pt VI, Ch. 7)

What principally links Lebezyatnikov with Raskolnikov, however, is his belief in the exclusively rational nature of man. According to Lebezyatnikov, madness itself may be no more than some sort of logical confusion, and he quotes the example of a French doctor who cured mental patients by arguing logically with them. Lebezyatnikov's faith in the power of reason is such that he even tries to convince Raskolnikov of the possibility of making a distraught person cease crying by arguing logically and explaining to him that there is nothing to cry about. At this stage in the novel, however, Raskolnikov, against all reason, has just confessed his own logically motivated crime to Sonya. He is unimpressed by Lebezyatnikov's arguments and comments that if this were the case life would be too easy.

By a stroke of barbed irony Chernyshevsky's precept of 'rational egoism' finds its chief exponent in the utterly worthless Luzhin. He is an older man who had been Lebezyatnikov's guardian and now lives with him in St Petersburg. Luzhin is by nature a grasping, self-centred individual; but because of a certain fear of the younger generation he pretends to subscribe to their views. He finds their theory that egoism is the motive force behind all human action highly palatable to his own natural inclinations, and throughout the novel not only his own behaviour but his interpretation of the behaviour of others is firmly based on the principle of personal gain. Thus it is typical that he should ascribe his failure with Dunya to the sole fact that he has not given money.

Luzhin expounds his fashionable ideas during his first meeting with Raskolnikov. He dismisses the 'former' principle of 'love thy neighbour' because of the social results brought about by such a precept, and goes on to expound the 'modern' theory of 'love thyself': 'But science says: "Love thyself before all others; for everything on this earth is based on personal interest".'

The conversation turns to the murder of the old woman and then to a discussion of crime in general, and when in his context Luzhin mentions 'morality' and 'rules', Raskolnikov feels he should be taught a lesson:

'What are you worrying about?' Raskolnikov suddenly interrupted. 'It is the result of your theory.'
'How do you mean, of my theory?'
'Well, if you take everything you have just been advocating to its logical conclusions, it turns out that you can kill people.'

(Pt II, Ch. 5)

Raskolnikov thus reveals the connection between the fashionable ideas of Luzhin and the crime which he himself has committed.

In Luzhin's desire to marry Raskolnikov's sister can be seen a debased version of that perennial cliché (already mocked by Dostoyevsky in *Notes from Underground*) the saving of the fallen woman. Because of the attentions of Svidrigaylov, Dunya does, at first, appear to be such a woman, but it is typical of Luzhin's bourgeois caution that his interest in her dates only from the moment of her rehabilitation (though perhaps he is wishing to perpetuate the myth when he finds accommodation for her and her mother in what appears to be a St Petersburg brothel). Luzhin is convinced that in marrying Dunya he is 'raising her up' to his own level and is thereby performing a feat of gallantry [*podvig*] (cf. Pt IV, Ch. 3), but Raskolnikov challenges his motives, claiming that all he wants is a wife whom he can perpetually nag and bully because she will be eternally grateful to him. Raskolnikov himself provides a further ironic comment on the patronising elements implicit in this noble theme; for in his own relationship with Sonya it is the 'fallen woman' who proves to be the moral superior of her 'benefactor'.

31

In between the publication of *Notes from Underground* and *Crime and Punishment* Dostoyevsky had engaged in open and acrimonious polemics with the nihilists, in particular with the followers of Chernyshevsky, who edited the radical journal the *Contemporary*. The publicists associated with this journal during the early sixties were all materialists, who had been particularly influenced by German ideas in philosophy, science and religion. Chernyshevsky, Dobrolyubov and many others were of clerical origin, but had long since renounced any religious adherence they might once have had. Their spiritual leader was rather Feuerbach, who in his *Essence of Christianity* (the Russian translation of which was dedicated to the Russian seminarists) had substituted for Christianity a religion of humanity. Man, argued Feuerbach, had alienated his own godhead to some non-existent mythical being, but it was man, or rather humanity, that was really god. Man accordingly must assume his godhead. Darwin's theories on the evolution of species seemed to lend substance to these claims by suggesting the future perfectibility of man, and these Darwinian overtones colour Dostoyevsky's most explicit presentation of the 'man-god' theme in the figure of Kirillov in *The Devils*. But the idea of 'man-god' lurks behind the Napoleonic aspirations of Raskolnikov; and is present in all Dostoyevsky's major writing from *Notes from Underground* to *The Brothers Karamazov*.

No discussion in print of the ideas of Feuerbach could be entirely unfettered; thus Chernyshevsky obliquely referred to this apotheosis of mankind as 'the anthropological principle in philosophy'. This is the title of a major essay which strongly argues the 'monistic nature' of man; for in their attack on established religion, the radicals were concerned to show that no part of man's being lay outside his own control; that there was no such thing as an immortal soul, representing a spark of the divine in man's nature. Chernyshevsky saw man as a unity. What were apparently non-material manifestations of man's being could all be explained in terms of matter; for physical and psychical phenomena were not essentially different in their nature. Chernyshevsky sought to prove his point by an analogy drawn from physics: ice, water, steam, although they appear to exhibit different qualities, are nevertheless aspects of the same chemical substance.

The monistic nature of man was one of the central doctrines of the radicals. Such articles as Dobrolyubov's 'The Organic Development of Man in Connection with his Mental and Moral Activities' (1858) attacked the old scholastic division of man into body and soul, on which he himself had been reared in the theological seminary. Monism became the order of the day: dualism was to be denounced in all its forms; for, by extension, ambiguity under whatsoever guise it appeared could not be tolerated by the radicals. Thus Dobrolyubov attacked the liberals for their equivocation on social reform, branding the discrepancy between their words and their deeds as '*Oblomovism*'. Ideal human behaviour, on the other hand, as prescribed by Chernyshevsky in *What is to be done?* is always straightforward, clear-cut and rational – it has that singleness of purpose which befits the monistic nature of man.

In the period following the Crimean War these ideas received such currency, that by 1859 Dobrolyubov could claim:

We thought that we had finished with dualism long ago; we were hoping that the indivisible human being could now be torn apart only in Mr. Kikodze's book on psychology... We thought that it was beneath the dignity of an educated man nowadays seriously to concern himself with the antagonisms between two opposing principles in the world and in man.[15]

But Dostoyevsky who from the beginning of his literary career had been obsessed by the theme of the double, who had dissected the perversity of human nature in *Notes from Underground*, could hardly subscribe to such a view. The supposedly rational behaviour of Raskolnikov, as we have already seen, is full of contradictions; the author emphasises this over and over again in the novel. Indeed Dostoyevsky places ambivalence at the very core of *Crime and Punishment* and in so doing he strikes at the very heart of the theories of the radicals.

3

MOTIVE AND SYMBOL:
'CRIME AND PUNISHMENT'

Crime and Punishment, in as much as it is built exclusively round one character, has all the appearance of a monolith. This is deceptive; for the fabric itself of the monolith is ordered according to a dualistic structure which informs the whole work. Dualism is both Dostoyevsky's artistic method and his polemical theme. Dualism is the 'stick with two ends' with which he belabours the radicals of the sixties; for, in Raskolnikov, Dostoyevsky has chosen one of their number who, like the heroes of Pomyalovsky's novels, believes that he can conceive a crime rationally, justify it rationally and execute it rationally. It is this emphasis on man's rationality which Dostoyevsky attacks. The underground man had claimed that man's rational faculties constitute a mere twentieth part of his whole being: the error of Raskolnikov is that he mistakes the part for the whole.

Raskolnikov forces himself to subscribe to the monistic view of human nature; he tries to believe that he is self-sufficient and self-contained, that he is capable of acting solely according to the dictates of reason with that wholeness of purpose which distinguishes the positive characters of *What is to be done?* Dostoyevsky, on the other hand, exposes the dualistic nature of his hero, reveals that there is something else in Raskolnikov's make-up which runs contrary to his rationalism and which gravely undermines it.

Raskolnikov is not the whole man he takes himself to be: he is 'split in two', as his very name suggests (cf. *raskolot*' – to split). His friend Razumikhin points this out when discussing Raskolnikov's behaviour with his mother: 'It is as though two opposing characters inside him succeed one another by turns.' (Pt III, Ch. 2.) The clue to the nature of these 'two opposing characters' may perhaps be found in the ideas on human nature which Raskolnikov propounds in his article on crime. Here humanity is divided into 'ordinary people' and 'extra-ordinary people'; the first category constituting mere human material for the ambitions of the *heroes* of the second category. This is a division of humanity into submissive and aggressive elements, in which submissiveness is equated with stupidity and aggressiveness with intelligence. In inventing this theory, Raskolnikov has merely externalised his own inner conflict between urges to self-assertion (equated with reason) and promptings towards self-effacement (equated with the non-rational). That this theory does indeed reflect an inner struggle can be seen from the fact that Raskolnikov feels compelled to make a choice, and to seek his identity either as 'a Napoleon' or 'a louse'. These two extremes represent symbolically the poles of his own divided character.

Ambivalence permeates the whole novel. On the very first page we see that Raskolnikov, as he leaves his room with thoughts of the murder of one old woman in his mind, is at the same time apprehensive of another such figure – his landlady. Thus from the very first the reader is made aware of the dis-harmony in Raskolnikov between a ruthless side and a meek side. This dichotomy is present in scene after scene throughout the novel. The behaviour of Raskolnikov is now self-assertive, now self-effacing; now rational, now irrational; now 'bad', now 'good', and his own ambivalence is both reflected and heightened through the characters and situations he encounters.

Thus, broadly speaking, the first part of the novel may be reduced schematically to the following incidents: Raskolnikov visits the ruthless, self-interested Alyona; he next meets the squirming, self-effacing Marmeladov; in a letter from home he reads that the self-sacrificing Dunya has escaped the clutches of the ruthless Svidrigaylov only to fall prey to the equally ruth-less Luzhin; musing on this letter, he sees a libertine ruthlessly pursuing a young girl who is the victim of debauchery: he falls asleep and dreams of a ruthless peasant beating to death his patiently suffering horse; he sees by chance Elizaveta, the self-effacing half-sister of Alyona.

The importance of this interplay of scenes opposing aggression to submission is to be seen in the corresponding shifts of attitude evoked in Raskolnikov himself. Thus his visit to Alyona leaves him feeling that what he contemplates is too terrible ever to be carried out, whereas his encounter with Marmeladov leads him to the conclusion that there is nothing to prevent his doing what he wishes to do. His ambivalent attitude to the suffering of the Marmeladov family is brought out by his instinctive act of self-sacrifice in leaving them money, followed immediately by anger and regret at having done so. The letter from home which throws into relief how closely his own situation parallels that of Marmeladov (i.e. Dunya appears to be about to 'sell herself' in order to support her brother, much as Sonya has become a prostitute in order to support her father) evokes once more an ambivalent response:

Almost all the time he was reading the letter, from the very beginning, Raskolnikov's face was wet with tears; but when he had finished his face was pale and contorted and a bitter, spiteful, evil smile played on his lips. (Pt I, Ch. 3)

In the next scene, with the young girl and the middle-aged libertine, Raskolnikov's first reaction of selfless solicitude suddenly yields place to ruthless indifference; after insulting the rake and giving a policeman money to call a cab for the girl, there is an abrupt change of mood: Raskolnikov suddenly calls out to the policeman to leave the couple alone, as it is none of his business.

The dream of the peasant beating the old nag to death leaves Raskolnikov feeling that he could never murder the old woman; yet he has only to meet Elizaveta to become once more convinced that the murder will be committed. Symbols of aggression evoke in Raskolnikov feelings of submission; symbols of submission bring out his aggressiveness. The coin of Raskolnikov's inner realm, bearing on one side the head of Napoleon, on the other the effigy of a louse, spins in a constant game of 'heads and tails' with his surroundings.

It is by this juxtaposition of opposites that Dostoyevsky clearly indicates the divided mind of Raskolnikov on the question of the murder itself. As we might expect, this is not carried out entirely in the calculated way in which one half of Raskolnikov would have liked. Thus, though many details such as the sling and the pledge have been planned with thought, other details such as the procuring of the hatchet, the knowledge that Elizaveta would be absent, the failure to lock the door behind him – all these are dictated by pure chance. The author comments: 'In spite of the agony of his inner struggle, he could never during all these weeks believe for a single moment in the practicability of his plans.' (Pt 1, Ch. 6.) All these details, then, he had dismissed as trifles worthy of his attention only after he was sure of the main problem. But it is precisely this element of the unplanned, the lapses of the rational mind, which leads Raskolnikov to commit a double murder instead of the single murder he had intended. He forgets to lock the door: Elizaveta comes back.

If we turn once more to the schematic appraisal of events in Part 1 leading up to the murder, the conclusion may be drawn that the characters encountered can be divided roughly into two categories, and that these categories correspond to those put forward by Raskolnikov himself in his article on crime. Thus in the category of the self-assertive we have Alyona, Luzhin, Svidrigaylov; in the category of the self-effacing – Elizaveta, Marmeladov, Sonya, Dunya. If this is true, it follows that these characters may in a certain sense be taken as symbolising aspects of Raskolnikov himself; for we have already noted the relationship between the categories of Raskolnikov's theory and the poles of his own inner conflict.

This interpretation raises the question of the extent to which *Crime and Punishment* may be regarded as a novel in the realistic tradition; for *Crime and Punishment* is widely so regarded. But realism is a term which needs to be defined. If by realism is meant the exposure of the grim reality of social conditions, then it cannot be denied that *Crime and Punishment* is a great realistic novel. The street and tavern scenes showing the tribulations of the poor of St Petersburg; the two sub-plots, one centred on the Marmeladov family, the other on Dunya – all belong to this realistic theme of 'the insulted and the injured'. But if by realism is meant the depiction of reality purged of all fantastic elements, the claim of *Crime and Punishment* to be a realistic novel is more dubious.

But the Russian realistic tradition is frequently associated with elements of the fantastic. This is particularly true of the writings of Dostoyevsky's great predecessor Nikolay Gogol.[1] It is not that the supernatural enters into *Crime and Punishment* in the way that it does say in Gogol's *Greatcoat*, though two of the characters (Sonya and Svidrigaylov) claim to have seen ghosts; nor is it so much the fact that the novel is permeated by that sense of 'mystic terror' described by Ivan Petrovich in *The Insulted and the Injured*; nevertheless in *Crime and Punishment* dream passes into reality, reality into dream, and the supernatural always seems uncannily present even though it may be explained in terms of the real world.[2]

What is truly fantastic in *Crime and Punishment* is the predominance of coincidence. Characters bump into one another in the street or meet one another by apparent chance in taverns.[3] Not only this; many characters are found to be living alongside one another in the most improbable way. Thus Svidrigaylov lodges next door to Sonya; Luzhin lives with Lebezyatnikov who in turn lives in the same house as the Marmeladov family. Moreover, there is the question of the way various characters appear to be related to one another: Luzhin is related to Svidrigaylov (through his wife) and is the former guardian of Lebezyatnikov; Porfiry is related to Razumikhin. Yet these three devices which, for want of better terms, may be branded as coincidence, co-habitation and collateralisation all tend towards the same effect – they draw the characters closer together and in some measure identify them one with another. We are dealing here not so much with the realistic portrayal of character as with its symbolic meaning.

When Raskolnikov exclaims that he has not murdered an old woman: he has murdered himself (Pt v, Ch. 4), he is proclaiming the symbolic truth behind the murder; for his two victims represent the two poles within himself: Alyona –

tyrannical, ruthlessly grasping for herself; Liza – meek, self-lessly doing good for others. It is significant that in Part I, at the end of that sequence of alternating attitudes to the crime, Raskolnikov's determination to commit the murder only becomes finally established when he learns that Elizaveta will not be in the apartment with Alyona. In spite of the strength of his previous doubts, this one overheard piece of information is sufficient to give him the singleness of purpose which he needs. Elizaveta represents the weaker side of himself, and Elizaveta, he now knows, will be absent, therefore nothing can now deter him from his assignation with the stronger side of his nature, represented by Alyona.

But this of course is the mistake of Chernyshevsky and his rationalist followers; man cannot dispose so easily of one side of himself; he cannot exert one side of his nature at the expense of the other, and so Raskolnikov, the would-be rationalist, irrationally *leaves the door unlocked; Liza returns and has to be murdered too.* This is why, throughout the initial stages of the murder, Raskolnikov behaves in the zombie-like manner of a man who is 'only half there', whereas after the arrival of Liza he becomes more aware of the reality of the situation: 'He became more and more seized with panic, especially after this second, quite unexpected, murder. He wanted to run away from there as quickly as possible.' (Pt I, Ch. 7.) Symbolically, Dostoyevsky has shown that it is impossible for Raskolnikov to assert one side of his nature without of necessity involving the other: the murder of Alyona inevitably brings in its wake that of Elizaveta.

It is the realisation, at a deep psychological level, of the full horror of this truth which leads to Raskolnikov's breakdown. But what is significant is that Raskolnikov, with one part of himself, again refuses to face this truth; there appears to be an unaccountable blank in his memory once he allows himself to be dominated again by the ruthless, rational side of his character. For the most part, when discussing his theories and defending his actions, it is only the murder of Alyona which is mentioned: Elizaveta is left out of consideration.

Thus he can even defend the murder of Alyona to Dunya just before he goes to make his official deposition to the police, but in this defence no mention is made of Elizaveta. Even in the penal settlement he is still convinced of the validity of his theories and again maintains that it was no crime to kill Alyona: no mention is made of Elizaveta.

Raskolnikov is first reminded that he has also killed Elizaveta by Nastasya, the servant of his landlady. Nastasya was acquainted with Elizaveta, and whereas Alyona exploited Raskolnikov, gave him little money in return for his pledges, Elizaveta, so Nastasya now tells him, rendered him services – she mended his shirts. Shocked at learning this, Raskolnikov turns over in his bed and pretends to study the wallpaper.

As we have seen, Raskolnikov's landlady is linked with Alyona on the very first page of the novel. Moreover it is at her instigation that Raskolnikov is ordered to the police station to pay a debt. This summons, occurring as it does immediately after the murder, appears almost as some sort of retribution from the grave. In the landlady who persecutes him, and the servant who helps him (and is also a friend of Elizaveta) there may be seen a pale reflection of the Alyona/Elizaveta duality.

A much stronger reflection of Elizaveta, however, is to be seen in Sonya. Not only is she too the friend of Elizaveta, but they share many traits of character in common. Both are alike in their self-effacement, their humility, their kindness. Both are 'fallen women'. Sonya is a prostitute; Elizaveta, we learn, has been many times seduced and seems constantly pregnant. More significantly, however, they have exchanged crosses and are thus in some sense spiritual sisters. Moreover, the New Testament from which Sonya reads to Raskolnikov, and which he later keeps under his pillow in Siberia, was given to Sonya originally by Elizaveta. Raskolnikov himself muses on the similarity between these two women and likens them both to 'holy fools'.[4]

All the evidence suggests that Sonya is a restatement of Elizaveta, and it is significant that, when Raskolnikov confesses to Sonya, it is the murder of Elizaveta which for the first time he has in the forefront of his consciousness. Yet not only is there a restatement of Elizaveta; there is too a restatement of Alyona. Towards the end of the novel Sonya's influence on Raskolnikov is very strong, but there is yet another, and contrary influence on him – that of Svidrigaylov. Broadly speaking, Svidrigaylov belongs to that category of the ruthless, self-interested characters to which Alyona also belongs. Unlike Alyona, however, it is not for profit that he exploits 'the insulted and the injured': it is rather for his own pleasure; he satisfies his lust at their expense rather than his avarice.

The connection between these two characters is stated quite clearly in the novel in a scene which deserves to be examined closely, as it not only points to the link between Alyona and Svidrigaylov, but also emphasises the association of Elizaveta with Sonya, and the symbolic relationship of these characters to Raskolnikov himself.

Raskolnikov, having been accused of the murder by an unknown man in the street, returns to his room and begins to turn over in his mind the question of the murder and the problem of his own position:

'*She*[5] must be the same as me,' he added thinking with effort, as though struggling with the delirium which seized him. 'Oh, how I hate the old woman now. I think I would kill her a second time if she came back to life. Poor Lizaveta, why did she turn up then? It is strange, however; why do I scarcely think about her? Almost as though I did not kill her... Lizaveta! Sonya! Poor and meek, with meek eyes. Dear people; why do they weep? Why do they groan? ... They give all away and look at you meekly and gently... Sonya, Sonya, gentle Sonya.' (Pt III, Ch. 6)

At this point Raskolnikov falls asleep and his threat is acted out in a dream; he attempts to kill the old woman a second time, but she refuses to die. He strikes again and again with his axe, to no avail: the old woman openly mocks him. The bedroom *door comes open*, and the mocking and jeering is carried on by other unknown people. He tries to scream, and wakes up. This is how the scene continues:

He drew a deep breath, but it was strange, it was as though his dream were still continuing: the door was open and on the threshold stood a man completely unknown to him, who was gazing at him fixedly.

The unknown stranger is Svidrigaylov; he is the continuation of Raskolnikov's dream – the old woman who has come to life again; the old woman who refuses to die.[6] To strengthen the links between the dream and the symbol, Raskolnikov is shown as taking some time to convince himself that the dream is not, in fact, continuing. The same fly that was there in the dream is also present in the room when he wakes up, and the detail of the open door (the significance of which has been noted earlier) is a feature common to both the dream and the ensuing reality. Moreover the beginning of Part IV, in which Svidrigaylov reveals himself more fully, re-emphasises the point once more: '"Is this really the continuation of the dream?", once again this thought came into Raskolnikov's mind.'

Not only does this bridge between dream and reality indicate that Svidrigaylov is a restatement of Alyona; it also gives an ironical comment on Raskolnikov's failure ultimately to be like them. This time the duality is a verbal one. Svidrigaylov first appears in the doorway, but then he steps over the threshold and enters the room. This act of *stepping over* is here indicated concretely by the very same verb [*perestupit'*][7] which Raskolnikov had used shortly before to describe his figurative act of stepping over; for in his bout of self-questioning before the dream he had said:

The old woman was only an illness, I wanted to step over as soon as possible... I did not kill an old woman, I killed a principle. It was a principle I killed, but as to stepping over, I did not succeed in stepping over.   (Pt III, Ch. 6)

The musings of Raskolnikov on his ability to step over are vividly illustrated in his dream by his failure to kill the old woman, whereas the ability to do so of the truly ruthless character is emphasised by Svidrigaylov's first action after his intrusion into Raskolnikov's dream: 'Suddenly, but with caution, he stepped over the threshold, and carefully closed the door behind him.'

If, therefore, Alyona and Elizaveta may be taken to represent the two poles of Raskolnikov's own character, this polarisation does not cease on their death; it is restated in the figures of Svidrigaylov and Sonya. Thus it is no accident that Sonya and Svidrigaylov live next door to one another in the same house, just as earlier Elizaveta and Alyona lived in the same apartment.

In the murder of Alyona, Raskolnikov has attempted to assert one side of his character, but has been unable to do so without involving the other side of himself: Elizaveta is murdered too. If murder is the action which expresses his self-assertive side, the other, the self-effacing side, is expressed in action by confession. The scene of Raskolnikov's confession to Sonya is designed to form an exact pendant to the scene of the murder.

The formal arrangement of the two scenes is striking. The murder is preceded by a trial visit to Alyona, during which Raskolnikov promises to come again with a silver cigarette case;[8] the confession is preceded by a trial visit to Sonya during which Raskolnikov promises to come again and tell her who has killed Elizaveta. Both scenes end in a similar way; the murder scene culminates in the ringing of the bell; the confession scene ends with the knocking at the door, which announces the arrival of Lebezyatnikov. Nor is this all; on the subject of the confession Raskolnikov has the same feeling of inevitability that he had experienced over the murder, and there is in both events the same mixture of the premeditated and the unpremeditated: 'He could get nothing out. It was not at all, not at all the way he had intended to confess.'

In fact the whole situation reminds him strongly of the murder:

He felt that this moment was terrifyingly like the moment when he stood behind the old woman and, disengaging the axe from the sling, sensed that there was not a moment to lose.   (Pt v, Ch. 4)

In both scenes Dostoyevsky is making the same point; Raskolnikov, consciously murdering Alyona, unwittingly is forced to kill Elizaveta: Raskolnikov, confessing to Sonya, unwittingly confesses to Svidrigaylov. Just as, in the act of self-assertion, Raskolnikov mistakenly believes that he can involve one side of his personality to the exclusion of the other, so here, in the act of self-effacement, he again tries to involve one side of himself and leave the other out of the reckoning. But the other side cannot be so ignored; *Svidrigaylov is listening to his confession from the other side of the door.*

The fact that Svidrigaylov overhears the confession is again a symbolic statement of the hero's divided psychology. Integration still has to be achieved. Even after the confession, even in the penal settlement itself, one half of Raskolnikov seems still to be convinced of the validity of his theory, convinced that it was no crime to kill Alyona. Yet after the death of Svidrigaylov he does at least round off the confession and make a deposition to the police.

At this point it might be opportune to discuss the role of the police in the novel. Their chief representative is Porfiry, and although it is said that Porfiry represents the new type of investigator resulting from the legal reforms of the sixties, there is nevertheless much in his portrayal which hints at something more than a policeman. Through the insights which the 'two ended stick' of psychology affords him, he appears to know Raskolnikov through and through. Indeed, almost like Providence itself, he appears to know everything. Yet at the same time he is less concerned with apprehending Raskolnikov as a criminal, than with saving him as a human being. There are, in the portrayal of Porfiry, strong elements of some sort of 'secular priest',[9] which can only be explained in terms of the symbolism of the novel. An examination of the significance of the names which the chief characters bear will further clarify this.

The name Porfiry is derived from *porphyra*, the purple cloak which was the attribute of the Byzantine emperors. The full name of Sonya is Sof'ya (Sophia) which evokes the great

Orthodox cathedral of Constantinople – Hagia Sophia (The Holy Wisdom of Orthodoxy). Raskolnikov's name comes from *raskol'nik* – a schismatic or heretic. Svidrigaylov evokes Svidrigaylo, a Lithuanian prince who was active during the fifteenth century – so fateful for the Orthodox world. He may be taken as the barbarian *par excellence*, the perpetrator of cynical sacrilege for the goal of self-interest.[10]

Thus on a symbolic level it can be seen that Porfiry is the representative of the temporal power of Orthodoxy, whereas Sonya represents its spiritual power. Both are striving to bring back Raskolnikov, the schismatic, to the true fold, but they are opposed in their efforts by Svidrigaylov, the barbarian who profanes what is holy to achieve selfish ends.

There is yet another character in the novel who serves to reinforce this interpretation of Raskolnikov as the schismatic. Mikolka, the peasant house-painter, is obviously to be taken as a shadowy *double* for Raskolnikov himself. Thus not only is he arrested instead of Raskolnikov on suspicion of the murder, but the psychological evidence which would seem to vindicate him (i.e. his laughter and high-spirits immediately after the murder) is used by Raskolnikov as a means of throwing suspicion away from himself: on the occasion of his first visit to Porfiry Raskolnikov teases Razumikhin so that he may enter Porfiry's apartment laughing and in obvious high spirits.

Porfiry's attempt to play off Mikolka against Raskolnikov ends with Mikolka's false confession; and the explanation which Porfiry gives for this phenomenon is that Mikolka wishes to take on suffering because he is a schismatic – '*On iz raskol'nikov*'. The form in which this is expressed is worthy of note.

But Mikolka does not represent only the 'confessional' side of Raskolnikov. Connected with the name Mikolka is a hint of the same duality which plagues Raskolnikov himself; the peasant who beats the horse to death in Raskolnikov's dream is also called Mikolka. It is perhaps significant too that, just as there had been these painters in the house at the time of the murder, there are also painters present when Raskolnikov returns to the scene of the crime and seems driven to display his guilt.

Religious significance permeates the novel. Some commentators, for example, point to the trinitarian symbolism in the three windows in Sonya's room.[11] Sonya, too, lives with the Kapernaumov family – a name derived from the Capernaum of the New Testament. It is, however, in the theme of Lazarus that the positive religious meaning of the novel resides. Sonya's reading of the story of the resurrection of Lazarus has a great effect on Raskolnikov, and we are told that the New Testament (originally Elizaveta's) which he has with him in the penal settlement, and which is principally responsible for his own 'resurrection', is the same New Testament from which Sonya had read to him the story of the raising of Lazarus. Even before the reading of this story, Porfiry had challenged him on his faith in it, and Raskolnikov had replied that he believed literally in the raising of Lazarus.

However, Dostoyevsky had to sacrifice much of his original intention in the scene where the story is read (Pt IV, Ch. 4), a scene which he himself regarded as the high point of the novel. A prostitute reading holy scripture to a murderer was considered too provocative an incident by his publisher, Katkov, and reluctantly Dostoyevsky had to abandon his original intention. This explains why the theme of the raising of Lazarus is not as fully developed in the novel as its author undoubtedly would have liked.

It may at first sight seem strange that Raskolnikov, who commits a particularly vile murder, should be identified with religious heresy, but the sense in which he is a heretic may be shown by an analysis of the motives which inspired the crime. Here we come up against duality once more. The murder itself, as events turn out, becomes a double murder; but the crime even in its original conception was twofold – murder plus robbery.

More significant still is the fact that Raskolnikov gives two distinct motives for his crime; on the one hand he alleges that his motive was to obtain money for himself and his family: on the other hand, he talks about the crime as an exercise in self-knowledge. For the first explanation to hold, true murder is unnecessary; robbery alone would have sufficed, or even the crime of counterfeiting, which serves in the novel as a commentary theme for Raskolnikov's own crime.

This motive, however, is not quite what it seems: it is not a straightforward question of personal gain. Raskolnikov justifies himself on social grounds; the murder of Alyona, in itself, is seen as the elimination of a social evil; whilst the appropriation of her wealth has the aim of righting social injustices. Although in Raskolnikov's scheme for the righting of social wrongs charity appears to begin at home (he himself and his immediate family are to be the prime beneficiaries of Alyona's wealth) the implications behind such charity are nevertheless much wider; for Raskolnikov believes that by using the money for good deeds he can thereby cancel out the bad deed of murder. The motive is, therefore, in essence a social one, in spite of its personal implications: it is the application of Luzhin's theory of 'enlightened self-interest'.

It is the second motive, however, which is really the personal one; for according to this explanation Raskolnikov is trying to define his own nature, trying to find out whether he is a Napoleon or a louse. This motive, as we have already seen, goes back to Raskolnikov's article on crime; therefore, although it is in essence a personal motive it cannot be divorced entirely from social implications.

The social motivation for the crime links Raskolnikov with the heroes of Pomyalovsky's novels, with the nihilists, among whose ranks Dostoyevsky had already observed a schism. In a social context, Raskolnikov is an extremist and a fanatic, who when faced with a *wall* of accepted social morality *steps over* it, in order to better himself, his immediate family and humanity in general.

The personal motivation for the crime, on the other hand, points to the rebellion of the underground man, to the deification of man's will in his striving towards godhead; for Raskolnikov, in his assault on the wall, is measuring against it the strength of his own will. To this extent he is a rebel in a religious sense; a heretic who believes that the unlimited powers of godhead reside in himself. Indeed, when he is in the penal settlement, Raskolnikov has a dream of a disease sweeping Europe through which men become 'possessed', and each one regards himself as the bearer of truth. The implications behind this dream are those of heresy, and its specific relevance is for Raskolnikov himself.[12]

There are, therefore, in Raskolnikov two types of rebel: a social one and a religious one, and both are linked to schism. There is, of course, no fundamental incompatibility between the two motives he alleges; for it is quite feasible that he could have intended to show himself a Napoleonic man by the same act that benefited others. Yet, despite this, there appears to be a real sense of dichotomy in the mind of Raskolnikov himself. During his confession to Sonya he alleges now one motive, now the other. But there are flaws in both explanations.

If he murdered for money, why was it that he showed so little interest in his acquisitions both at the time of the murder and afterwards? On the other hand, if he were genuinely trying to prove himself a Napoleonic man, can he seriously equate the murder of some pitiable old woman with the grandiose exploits of Napoleon? Even more fundamental is his own recognition that a Napoleon would not have had the doubts about his actions that he himself has had. The mere fact that he had to prove himself shows that he secretly had doubts about his being a Napoleonic man, and this alone shows that he was not entitled to commit the crime.

Once more we return to the idea that the ambivalence of Raskolnikov's character precludes that singleness of purpose which marks out the Napoleonic man from the rest of humanity. Raskolnikov in his confession to Sonya shows himself aware of this. Even before committing the crime he had sensed that the weakness implicit in his self-questioning gave him no right to attempt it, that by asserting one side of his nature at the expense of the other he was dooming himself to failure. The crime, therefore, assumes the nature of an exercise in self-deception masquerading as an act of self-knowledge.

When taxed by Sonya, he is unable in the last analysis to put forward either of these two alleged motives as the real reason for the murder; he falls back on the idea that the murder is in some sense symbolic, claiming that he killed himself (or even, as earlier, a principle) and not an old woman; she was killed, he claims, by the devil. If he *is* to accept full responsibility for the murder, the only explanation he seems able to offer is that he killed for himself; an explanation which seems to exclude any rational motivation but appears rather to indicate some irrational need to kill for its own sake. In the last analysis Raskolnikov is just as perplexed about his motive for the murder as is the reader.

We have seen that Raskolnikov's failure to achieve his ends is brought about because of the opposing characters within himself. But the process of writing with Dostoyevsky is a process of the splitting and subdividing of idea cells; Svidrigaylov and Sonya, although representing poles of Raskolnikov's character, nevertheless undergo the same sort of polarisation themselves.

At first sight it might appear that Svidrigaylov has no philanthropic side to his nature at all; no other interests but the interests of self. He appears to be a man who can 'step over' with impunity. He has led a life of debauchery; is reputed to have seduced a fourteen-year-old deaf mute, and by this act to be responsible for her suicide; it is also held that he bears some measure of guilt in the death of one of his servants; and he is accused of having poisoned his wife. On all these scores he appears to have a clear conscience.

Yet all these deeds are of a different order from that of the central crime of the novel, in that the reader is given no definite proof of their reality: all Svidrigaylov's crimes belong to a penumbra of hearsay and rumour which surrounds him up to, and even after, his first appearance in the novel. It is the symbolic act of stepping over Raskolnikov's threshold, bringing him out of this shadowy land of imputation into the action of the novel itself, which marks the beginning of Svidrigaylov's growing ambivalence.

Thus, at this very first meeting with Raskolnikov, he shows that he has a human flaw: he is in love with Raskolnikov's sister; and he himself presents us with a possible ambivalent interpretation of his behaviour towards her, by asking whether he is really to be considered a monster or a victim. The philosophy of out-and-out humanism which he expresses in the Latin tag, *nihil humanum*, might seem to permit him everything, but it also makes human weakness possible – Svidrigaylov is in love.

Whatever Dunya's attitude to Svidrigaylov may be (and there are indications that she is not entirely unresponsive to his advances), Svidrigaylov is determined to pursue her by all the means within his power. He attempts bribery, blackmail and in the last resort violence, but Dunya draws out a revolver and fires twice at her would-be seducer. The first bullet grazes his scalp, the second shot misfires, and then, although there is yet a third bullet in the chamber, she throws the revolver away. Svidrigaylov attempts to embrace her, but realising in despair that she does not love him,[13] and that for once in his life he is powerless – powerless to compel her love – he lets her go.

After this scene, Svidrigaylov seems a changed man; he openly acknowledges another side to his character. Thus he calls on Sonya and confirms the arrangements he has made to take care of the remaining members of her family (arrangements which had been first mooted as part of his campaign to win Dunya). He then calls on his sixteen-year-old fiancée and leaves her a present of fifteen thousand roubles (Svidrigaylov's wealth had originally been the lure for this fresh young victim).[14]

He takes a room in a shabby hotel, which in its cramped poverty is reminiscent of Raskolnikov's room, and through a chink in the wall he witnesses a squalid scene of aggression and submission, symbolically recalling the dilemma which haunts Raskolnikov and which now appears to be affecting Svidrigaylov himself. His last action in leaving this room is a futile attempt to catch a fly; the motif of the fly links Svidrigaylov's departure from the pages of the novel with his first appearance in the room of Raskolnikov.

During his brief stay in this room, Svidrigaylov is haunted by dreams which reflect the ambivalence of his relations with women. Thus he thinks of Dunya and falls asleep to dream of a mouse which torments him. His second dream is of the four-teen-year-old girl for whose death his 'love' has been responsi-ble, and his third dream is even more striking; he comforts a five-year-old girl who turns out eventually to be a child prostitute. The central dilemma behind all these dreams is whether the lover is a tyrant or a victim.

The night culminates in his suicide with the revolver loaded with Dunya's one remaining bullet; as Dunya cannot feel sufficiently strongly for him even to kill him, Svidrigaylov is reduced to completing the attempt himself and thus turn murder into suicide. The gun which he uses in this act recalls in the chain of its provenance the New Testament instrumental in resurrecting Raskolnikov; for the revolver is not merely Dunya's, it had come originally from Svidrigaylov's wife, and his relations with her have the same ambiguity as his relations with Dunya (in his marriage and subsequent incarceration in the country was Svidrigaylov his wife's victim, or in the circumstances of her death did he play the role of a monster?). The choice of surroundings for his suicide symbolises the nature of his inner dichotomy. Svidrigaylov shoots himself in front of a tiny Jew in a soldier's greatcoat and an Achilles helmet, and commits an act of self-immolation before a symbol of his own personal tragedy; for in the figure of the Jew wrapped up in the soldier's greatcoat, we have one of the persecuted dressed up as one of the persecutors. This idea is further reinforced by the detail of the Achilles helmet, and by the fact, too, that this incongruous figure is itself referred to as 'Achilles'. Here we have an obvious reference to the hero who is apparently un-vanquishable, until his one fatal flaw has been discovered. Svidrigaylov commits suicide because he realises that the question he first put to Raskolnikov has been answered: he is *both* monster and victim, *both* oppressor and oppressed.

If the fate of Svidrigaylov shows that ruthlessness has its weaknesses and its unexpected philanthropy, the way of Sonya, the way of self-effacement, is also seen to have its pitfalls. The dark side of humility is foreshadowed in the person of Marmeladov. He is a weak, submissive character who is responsible for much human suffering; for it is he who must be blamed for the plight of his wife and family. Confession, which for Raskolnikov is the symbolic act of self-effacement, has become for Marmeladov a subtle weapon of aggression. Those who listen to Marmeladov's words of self-denigration feel more uncomfortable than Marmeladov himself; they themselves in some underhand way are being attacked.[15] It may be objected that Marmeladov is not genuinely humble, that he is merely a caricature of humility, but no such criticism could be levelled at his daughter, Sonya, yet the humility of Sonya is shown to have its dark side too.

Raskolnikov does not react uncritically to the influence of Sonya; he points out the flaws in her attitude to life. His objections are that by her very humility, by her very submissiveness, Sonya is vulnerable, and that this does not merely affect herself; for since she is the breadwinner, her family must suffer through her vulnerability, as it had suffered through the shortcomings of her father.

Raskolnikov's point is proved when Luzhin nearly succeeds in having Sonya arrested on a trumped-up charge of theft. Sonya's submissiveness reveals itself as powerless in the face of active evil. She is only saved from prison by the intervention of forceful characters – Lebezyatnikov and Raskolnikov. The fact that Sonya would suffer is not the point. If she were unable to earn money, argues Raskolnikov, the innocent victims of her plight would be her younger brothers and sisters as well as her consumptive step-mother. Although Sonya's submissiveness in the face of Luzhin's active malice does not, in the event, have this effect, the threat is nevertheless there, and it is this incident which comes as the last straw to break her step-mother's long overburdened sanity.

But it is in a second way that the submissiveness of Sonya must be held partly responsible for the death of Katerina Ivanovna and the degradation of her children. Sonya's inability to cope with Luzhin's malice causes her to flee in distress to her room. Raskolnikov follows her there in triumph ('What will you say now, Sof'ya Semyonovna'); for he is seeking to convince himself that his own way of providing for his family, by sacrificing others, is correct; whereas Sonya's way of doing so, by sacrificing herself, is wrong. He thinks that his criticism of her humility has now been fully vindicated by the plot of Luzhin, but at the same time he also tells her of the effect that this incident has had on Katerina Ivanovna.

On hearing of this, Sonya's first impulse is to go to the aid of her step-mother, but Raskolnikov for motives of his own (the confession), prevails on her to stay. Once again, through her submissiveness, Sonya must be held in some measure responsible for the suffering of others; for had she asserted herself against the arguments of Raskolnikov and gone to take care of her step-mother, the harrowing sequence of events leading up to the death of Katerina Ivanovna could have been avoided. Even if the death itself were inevitable, the degradation imposed on the children before her death could have been prevented by the presence of Sonya, and the greatest crimes for Dostoyevsky are always those committed against children.

It is as though Dostoyevsky is forcing a parallel between Sonya's sin of omission and Raskolnikov's crime of commission, when he makes Raskolnikov put the choice to her of either allowing Luzhin to live and carry on with his underhand deeds or letting Katerina Ivanovna die. Sonya refuses to make the choice, but in reality she has already chosen; the very submissiveness which prevents her from defending herself against Luzhin, also prevents her from denying Raskolnikov's right to keep her from her step-mother's side in time of need. Therefore because she is prepared to allow Luzhin to go on living and commit his vile deeds, she is also prepared to let Katerina Ivanovna die.[16] In the very scene where Raskolnikov yields to the promptings of his own weaker side, Sonya in staying to listen to this confession is also unwittingly culpable herself; active guilt and passive guilt are dovetailed together.

Svidrigaylov, the dark antithesis of Sonya, is the unseen

witness both of Raskolnikov's confession of action and also of Sonya's failure to act. By way of stressing Sonya's culpability, Svidrigaylov mysteriously turns up at the death of Katerina Ivanovna, and by quoting back to Raskolnikov his own words on the choice between the life of Luzhin and the death of Katerina Ivanovna, he indicates in one sentence that, not only has he heard the confession, but that he also understands the implications of the death of Katerina Ivanovna for Sonya. Then, as if finally to drive the point home that Sonya's submissiveness has failed to provide a safeguard for her family, it is Svidrigaylov, of all people, who offers to look after them.

These implications behind Sonya's own position during the confession scene would seem to weaken the case for confession itself, and it is only much later that Raskolnikov makes his deposition to the police. Yet neither the confession nor the deposition shows true repentance. Genuine repentance does not come in the novel, not even in the Epilogue; it is a process destined to take seven years after the closing scene of the novel, and could, as Dostoyevsky comments, form the theme for a new novel. It is important to bear these facts in mind; for it is commonly held that the ending of *Crime and Punishment* is unconvincing, that the reader does not really believe in the rehabilitation of Raskolnikov. It is perhaps true that the Epilogue is not written with the same intensity as the rest of the novel, but this should not lead us to assume that the resurrection of Raskolnikov is unconvincing. The Epilogue does not deal with this resurrection: it only marks the beginning of the road.

To regard the hero's rehabilitation as improbable is perhaps to suffer from the same partial blindness that affects Raskolnikov himself: i.e. to disregard the 'Elizaveta' in his make-up. Raskolnikov is not morally corrupt in the normal sense: on the contrary, it is possible to compile an impressive list of his 'good deeds'. Thus, though in a state of penury himself, he gives money away to the needy on various occasions: once to the Marmeladov family; another time to the policeman to whose care he entrusts the drunken girl; yet again to a prostitute in the street. His charity is also stressed by Razumikhin; at the university he had supported a consumptive fellow-student; and later, when the young man had died, he had also taken upon himself to support his father. Nor is his philanthropy lacking in personal valour; even his landlady gives evidence that he had once rescued two small children from a burning apartment, and had himself been burned in the process. Indeed one reason for his crime is, paradoxically enough, his compassion for the 'insulted and injured'.

Yet if the two sides of Raskolnikov's character are ever to be integrated there is a genuine need for contrition. The need to confess, which Raskolnikov feels, may be taken as an urge towards contrition; throughout the course of the novel Raskolnikov has many promptings to confess. Such promptings occur from the very first. Indeed, immediately after the murder he thinks of kneeling down in the police station and blurting out the truth. In his dealings with the police, the idea of confession haunts him more than once; thus to Zametov, the police clerk, he makes a mocking, false confession, and later he even feels prompted to go back to the scene of the crime, and arouse suspicion there by his strange behaviour. Yet most surprising of all is the claim he makes to Sonya, that when he had first heard about her through her father, he had resolved there and then to tell her about the murder. This can only mean that he had thought of telling Sonya about the murder even before it had been committed. The two elements which mark his divided psychology are discernibly associated with one another even prior to their expression in action. Indeed, as might be expected, it even appears that the idea of confession is, in a certain sense, simultaneous in conception with the plan of murder itself; for Raskolnikov claims that he had first discussed the possibility of the crime with another Sonya-like figure, his ailing sweetheart, the landlady's daughter, who has died before the action of the novel begins.

Although this need for confession is fundamental to Raskolnikov's nature, and has resulted in his telling Sonya about the murder and in his ultimate deposition to the police, nevertheless he himself knows full well that confession is not the same as contrition. Even when he has taken on his suffering, and is a convict in the penal settlement, he says how happy he would feel if he could only blame himself for what he has done. That he cannot do so is because, as yet, he has not managed to resolve the conflict within himself; the self-assertive side of Raskolnikov's character, although its position is now undoubtedly weaker, is making its last stand.

The reconciliation of the two opposing elements within Raskolnikov will result in the resurrection that Dostoyevsky prophesies for his hero. The self-assertive side will not be eradicated: its energies will be fused with the gentle, self-effacing qualities of the other side. A new Raskolnikov will emerge to fulfil the exhortation of Porfiry, that he must be a sun for all to see. The beginnings of this integration are discernible in the Epilogue: 'Life had taken the place of dialectics, and something else, completely different, had to work itself out in his consciousness.' The inevitability of this change can be seen by tracing Raskolnikov's development through the Epilogue.

Isolated from the other prisoners through his pride, there is only one person to whom he can turn for help, who represents something other than the hard conditions of the penal settlement; that person is, of course, Sonya. Although all the other prisoners like Sonya, there is still a part of Raskolnikov which struggles against her; but his own intolerable position as an outcast among the outcasts is brought home to him when some of the other convicts attempt to murder him on the grounds that he is an atheist. He falls ill, and in his weakened physical state dreams of a disease sweeping Europe from Asia. This dream is an allegory, which shows Raskolnikov what would happen if everybody were to set himself up as a prophet of some 'new truth'; the relevance of this for Raskolnikov's own theories is obvious.

But Sonya, too, has fallen ill, and is no longer able to see him. First he realises that he misses her; then when next he sees her he realises that he loves her. This sudden love for Sonya is not something unexpected or fortuitous; the foundations have been laid long ago in the novel – it is, if anything, overdue.

Raskolnikov's love for Sonya, and the echo she awakens in the humble side of his nature, is the corner-stone on which he may build the edifice of a new Raskolnikov. Through his love for Sonya he comes to the New Testament, given to him by Sonya and in turn given to her by Elizaveta. Nor is this new-found religious belief entirely unexpected; throughout the course of the novel Raskolnikov gives many indications of his adherence to Christian belief. Thus during his first visit to the Marmeladov family he asks Polechka to pray for him; a request which he repeats to his mother before he goes off to Siberia, and he asserts his faith quite strongly during his first interview with Porfiry.

His love for Sonya, his new-found religious faith, the discipline of the penal settlement – all these are weapons against Raskolnikov's pride and self-assertion. If, however, doubt is still felt on the probability of Raskolnikov's 'resurrection', it should be remembered that at the end of the Epilogue he still has seven long years of suffering ahead of him in which to work out his salvation; and the author himself had direct experience of the way the Russian penal settlement could change a man.

Crime and Punishment is often described as a 'psychological thriller'; this description is quite accurate, but it is a 'thriller' in which suspense is created not through the attempts to detect the culprit, but through the culprit's own wayward efforts to resist detection. Here the reader himself is put in the position of a murderer, and follows with a disturbing degree of self-identification the inner struggles of a psychologically tormented personality.

In this sense *Crime and Punishment* is a 'psychological thriller' at a much deeper level. Behind the story of murder, confession and moral rehabilitation lies an exploration, through symbol and allegory, of the divided nature of the hero; an exploration in which the other characters surround the central figure like mirrors reflecting and distorting aspects of his own dilemma. It is a measure of the greatness of Dostoyevsky that these characters can at the same time stand on their own; for they have individuality in their own right.[17] Moreover symbol and allegory are so skilfully fused into the narrative that their presence, far from exerting a deadening influence, or reducing the novel to a mere mechanical abstraction, enriches and further deepens the significance of the work. *Crime and Punishment* is, above all, an extremely readable novel.

4

THE TRIUMPH OF AESTHETICS:
'THE IDIOT'

In February 1867 Dostoyevsky married Anna Snitkina, and in April took his wife abroad. In all they were to spend some four years wandering about Europe; the first major novel to come from this period of voluntary exile was *The Idiot*. Work on this novel cost Dostoyevsky much anguish, and his original drafts are strikingly at variance with the novel as we know it in its final form.[1] He had in fact arrived at an impasse, from which his work could only be saved by the sacrifice of one of his most cherished ideas. This much he himself confesses in a letter to his niece:

The idea of the novel is my old favourite idea, but so difficult that for a long time I did not dare attempt it; and if I have attempted it now, it is really because I found myself in a desperate situation. The chief idea of the novel is to depict *the positively good man* [*polozhitel'no prekrasnyy chelovek*]. There is nothing on earth more difficult than this, especially nowadays. All writers who have set about depicting the *positively* good have always fallen short, not only our own writers but even the Europeans, because this is a task which is infinite. The good [*prekrasnoye*] is an ideal, and both our ideal and that of civilised Europe is far from having been worked out. There is only one positively good figure on earth and that is Christ. The appearance of this immeasurably and inexhaustibly good figure is, of course, nothing less than an endless miracle [...] Don Quixote alone of all good figures in Christian literature is the most finished, but he is good solely because at the same time he is comical. Dickens's Pickwick (an infinitely weaker conception than Don Quixote, but still immense) is also ludicrous and succeeds only because of this. Compassion is aroused for the good man who is ridiculed and does not know his own worth, and therefore sympathy is aroused in the reader. This arousing of sympathy is indeed the secret of humour. Jean Valjean is also a powerful attempt, but he evokes sympathy because of his terrible misfortune and the injustices of society towards him. In my novel there is nothing similar, absolutely

59

nothing, and therefore I am terribly afraid that it will be a positive failure.[2]

This letter we may take as expressing Dostoyevsky's aim in writing the novel. But if here he is trying to portray 'the positively good man' why should he imply that such a man is an idiot?

One answer to this question may be that the 'idiocy' of the central character is Dostoyevsky's solution to a difficult artistic problem: it is the flaw in the make-up of 'the positively good man', which makes his presentation credible; for in the passage above, in his discussion of other virtuous heroes in literature, Dostoyevsky seems to be suggesting that the reader will believe in the moral superiority of such an exemplar of virtue only if he is allowed by some device such as laughter or pity to establish his own sense of superiority over him. The 'idiocy' of Myshkin could therefore be a kind of periscopic device which allows the reader to look down on an image of virtue which in reality is far above him.

The idiocy of Myshkin is attested not only in Dostoyevsky's choice of title for the novel, and the details he furnishes of Myshkin's mental state both before and after the action of the novel proper, but also in the opinions expressed by the other characters with whom the prince comes into contact. There is scarcely one of these who at some stage in the novel does not brand him as an idiot.

Yet the author himself, in his introductory remarks to Part III, provides a hint that lack of intelligence may perhaps be ascribed not so much to Myshkin, as to those who fail to understand him:

Almost always at the beginning of their career (and very frequently even at the end) inventors and geniuses have been considered in society as no more than fools – this is of course a most commonplace observation, only too well known to everybody.   (Pt III, Ch. 1)

One by one, characters who call Myshkin an idiot are forced to the realisation that he has an intelligence which no idiot could possibly possess. Ganya, Keller, Ippolit all feel bound to reassess their unflattering view of Myshkin, when faced with evidence of the prince's penetrating insight into human nature. 'You notice what other people can never notice', Ganya tells him; and Myshkin himself is well aware how he is misjudged by those who surround him. He frequently thinks to himself: 'Here they are thinking of me as an idiot; but I am, for all that, intelligent, and they don't suspect it.' (Pt I, Ch. 6.)

This discrepancy between, on the one hand, apparent intelligence, and, on the other, imputed idiocy is explained by Aglaya as the difference between a chief form of intelligence and a secondary form:

Although you are indeed not well in your mind [...] nevertheless your chief mind is better than theirs, all of them, it is such that they cannot have even the slightest conception of it. Because there are two minds: the important mind and the unimportant mind. That is so isn't it?   (Pt III, Ch. 8)

This paradox of the intelligent idiot is presented to us from the very beginning of the novel. In the scene where Myshkin introduces himself to the Yepanchin family, he is identified not only as an idiot but also as a philosopher:

'That is all philosophy', remarked Adelaida, 'You are a philosopher, and have come to teach us'.
'Perhaps you are right', said the prince, smiling, 'I am perhaps indeed a philosopher, and, who knows, it could be that I have in fact a new idea to teach. This could well be, it is true, it could well be.'
                                                      (Pt I, Ch. 5)

Yet if the prince is cast in the role of philosopher, he is nevertheless strangely reticent about his philosophy:

There are ideas, there are high ideas, about which I must not begin to speak, because I will undoubtedly make everyone laugh. Prince Shch. reminded me of this very fact just a moment ago...I am unable to make fitting gestures; I have no sense of proportion; the words I choose are wrong, and do not correspond to the ideas, and this is debasing for these ideas. And therefore I have no right... moreover I am suspiciously sensitive...   (Pt III, Ch. 2)

The occasions on which Myshkin expresses his 'high ideas' in the novel are far from numerous, and when they do occur they are not necessarily reported in detail by the author:

He became talkative, and this had not happened again since that very morning, six months ago, when his first acquaintance with the Yepanchins had taken place. After his return to St Petersburg he had been noticeably and intentionally reticent; and quite recently before everybody he had confessed to Prince Shch. that it was necessary for him to restrain himself and keep quiet, because he had no right to debase his thought by expounding it himself. Throughout this evening, he was almost the only person who spoke. He related a great deal, and answered all questions in detail, clearly and gladly. But there was no hint of anything like nice conversation in his words; they were all such serious, even at times such complicated thoughts. The prince even expounded some of his views; some of his own innermost observations, and it would all have been ludicrous perhaps, if it had not been so 'well expounded', as everyone, who heard him, later agreed. (Pt IV, Ch. 5)

This passage shows that it is not merely Myshkin who is reticent about his ideas: the author, too, seems loath to have him expound them on the pages of the novel.[3] Thus the important heart-to-heart talk which takes place in Moscow between Myshkin and Rogozhin is merely referred to, not described; and if we are to find clues to Myshkin's philosophy, these are to be seen in sayings attributed to him by other characters, perhaps even more than in what he says himself. There are, in particular, two striking aphorisms which are ascribed to the prince: 'beauty will save the world'; and 'humility is a terrible force'.

The phrase 'beauty will save the world' rings out as an elevating assertion, but its meaning is obscure; it smacks of mysticism. One explanation of the phrase might be sought in the nature of Myshkin himself as *the positively good man*; the beauty which 'will save the world' might be the prince's moral beauty – the beauty of the example of the positively good man. This interpretation seems to be further strengthened by the fact that the term: '*polozhitel'no prekrasnyy chelovek*', which is usually rendered as 'the positively good man', is in fact couched in the language of aesthetics (i.e. *prekrasnyy* = fine, beautiful). Moreover the terminology of aesthetics permeates Dostoyevsky's letter to his niece, quoted above. Here the phrase '*prekrasnoye yest' ideal*', which was translated as 'the good is an ideal' could also be rendered as: 'the beautiful is an ideal'; for the word, *prekrasnoye* is the standard term in aesthetics for 'beauty'.[4] The Russian language, by confusing two concepts, allows Dostoyevsky to press aesthetic criteria into service as a substitute for the criteria of ethics; beauty, he appears to be saying, is a *moral* force of such power that it can save the world.

But the implications of beauty as a moral force go beyond the mere depiction of Myshkin as 'the positively good/beautiful man'. The nearest the prince comes to an explanation of the saving power of beauty is at the evening gathering at the Yepanchins, when he proceeds to break one by one the prohibitions which Aglaya has placed on his behaviour. On this occasion he pours out all his cherished ideas, irrespective of the effect he is creating, and it is perhaps significant that the reason he gives for this sudden unwonted loquaciousness is the stimulation of beauty; for he tells the old man who is listening to him with curiosity: 'I started speaking because you are looking at me in such a beautiful way [i.e. *tak prekrasno*]; you have a beautiful face [*prekrasnoye litso*].'

Aglaya has forbidden him to talk about beauty saving the world; nevertheless he appears to touch on this theme at the end of his tirade:

Listen, I know it is no good speaking: it is better simply to set an example, it is better simply to begin. I have already begun and... and is it really possible, in fact, to be unhappy? Oh what sort of grief, what sort of trouble can I have, if I am capable of being happy? Do you know, I do not know how one can pass a tree and not be happy that you see it; speak to a man and not be happy that you love him? Oh! I just cannot express... and how many things at each step; such beautiful things, which even the most despairing of men finds

63

beautiful. Look at a child; look at God's sunset; look at the grass as it grows; look into eyes which look at you and love you!

(Pt IV, Ch. 7)

The opening of this passage explains why it is that, in the novel, Myshkin gives no full exposition of the theory that beauty will save the world: 'I know that it is no good speaking: it is better simply to set an example.' The statement, of course, supports the idea that it is the beauty of the example of 'the positively good/beautiful man' which will save the world. Yet the emphasis on beauty in this passage is placed elsewhere: it is placed on the visual beauty of the external world; a beauty which is such as to induce a state of happiness in even 'the most despairing of men'. This is not a moral beauty perceived by the mind: it is a purely physical beauty perceived by the eye; nevertheless the implications of Myshkin's incoherent argument are that the true appreciation of physical beauty can lead to a realisation of moral beauty – that the example of moral beauty which Myshkin strives to set is intimately connected with his perception of the external beauty of the world around him.

Writing earlier of beauty, and in particular of the Apollo Belvedere, Dostoyevsky had speculated:

Who knows, perhaps a kind of internal change takes place in man at the impact of such beauty, at such a nervous shock; a kind of movement of particles or galvanic current that in one moment transforms what has been before into something different, a piece of ordinary iron into a magnet.[5]

For Dostoyevsky, therefore, beauty may have power to alter men radically, and as Myshkin suggests, it should bring them happiness and a sense of harmony.

But the true appreciation of the visual beauty which surrounds man depends on his own ability to look. The problem is even more acute for the artist attempting to capture the external world in his art. When Adelaida, the painter, asks the prince to give her a subject for a picture, his advice is simple: 'look and paint'. Yet it is this very ability 'to look' which Adelaida confesses she lacks, and she attributes Myshkin's ability 'to look' to his residence abroad. From the prince's reply we see once more how closely connected are the ability to look and the ability to be happy:

'I do not know. It was just my health I improved there. I don't know whether I learned how to look. But I was very happy there all the time.'

'Happy! You know how to be happy?' cried Aglaya, 'then how can you say that you have not learned how to look? You have more to teach us.' (Pt I, Ch. 5)

This ability to see beauty in everything about him implies Myshkin's acceptance of the world with all its imperfections. This is the charge which Aglaya throws at him shortly after the passage quoted above, when she says:

'With your quietism one could fill a hundred years of one's life with happiness. Show you an execution or show a little finger, you would from both of them equally draw a praiseworthy thought, and would even remain happy. One can get through life living like that.' (Pt I, Ch. 5)

Although Aleksandra, later in the scene, shows doubts about this charge of quietism, it is nonetheless obvious that the phrase: 'beauty will save the world' in no way contradicts the other of the phrases attributed to Myshkin: 'humility is a terrible force'. If it is to be the moral beauty of the prince's example which 'will save the world', then undoubtedly one of the chief attributes of this moral beauty is humility; it is a quality which Myshkin shows time and time again throughout the novel. His two aphorisms, therefore, are mutually complementary.

The idea of humility as a terrible force smacks of paradox, but the nature of Myshkin too is paradoxical, and the identification of humility with power is reflected in his very name; his christian name, Lev, means 'lion', whilst the surname, Myshkin, obviously derives from *mysh'* [mouse]. Consonant with this is Myshkin's social position; for he is a destitute 'idiot', who is in reality a prince. Both his name and his social status are essential attributes in the portrayal of Myshkin, and they suggest that he himself is the embodiment of the terrible power of humility – that the mouse is really the lion; that the least of mortals is really the first.

At the same evening gathering at the Yepanchins, where the prince touches on his ideas on beauty, he also tries to 'teach' his paradoxical ideas about humility. As a prince of ancient line he appeals to his 'peers' to retain their social superiority through humility; 'Let us become servants in order to be superiors' (Pt IV, Ch. 7).[6]

Myshkin himself makes no social distinctions; at the beginning of the novel we find him conversing with one of the Yepanchins' lackeys as freely and open-heartedly as he is later to do with the masters themselves. It is rather the lackey who appears embarrassed at this disregard for social conventions – not Myshkin:

It might have seemed that the prince's conversation was extremely unaffected, but the greater its simplicity, the more it became absurd in the present situation, and the experienced valet could not but sense that what was completely fitting for a relationship of man to man was not at all fitting for the relationship of visitor to *man*.

(Pt I, Ch 2)

There is here a conscious pun on the double meaning of 'man' (man in the sense of 'human being' and man in the sense of 'servant': i.e. *cheloveka s chelovekom* and *gostyu s chelovekom*). This is a linguistic ambiguity which bears a direct relationship to the theme of the 'terrible power of humility', in as much as it seems to offer the possibility of identifying 'man' with the role of a servant. The word 'man', used in an emphatic way, will recur at certain key points in the novel as an appellation for Myshkin.

Thus at the first meeting of Myshkin and Nastasya Filippovna, it is significant that she mistakes him for a servant and throws him her furcoat; whilst at their second meeting she takes her leave of him with the following words: 'Goodbye, Prince, I have seen a man for the first time.' Here Nastasya Filippovna seems to be acknowledging that the role of servant, which she at first mistakenly ascribed to Myshkin, is after all the true 'man'; for the behaviour of the prince during their second meeting suggests self-sacrifice in her service.

The phrase: 'humility is a terrible force' is ascribed to Myshkin by Ippolit in his 'Necessary Explanation'. It is this confession which constitutes the main counterblast to Myshkin's philosophy of humility. Nevertheless, after reading it, Ippolit prepares himself for his attempt at suicide by embracing the prince. He looks long into his eyes, and proclaims: 'I am saying goodbye to Man.' The word this time has a capital letter (Pt III, Ch. 7).

'Man', as it is used here, seems to have almost a religious flavour, and, indeed, all aspects of the portrayal of Myshkin are heavily charged with religious significance. Thus the prince's 'idiocy' is not only a novelistic device which renders virtue more convincing, it is also the expression of a religious concept dear to the Russian people: the concept of *yurodivyy* or 'holy fool'. It is in this role that Myshkin is identified by Rogozhin at the beginning of the novel: 'You turn out, Prince, to be a real holy fool, and God loves such as you.' (Pt I, Ch. 1.) A sentiment which is endorsed by Lebedev. But there are indications that not only does God love Myshkin; he has actually sent him to help others. In the next important scene in the novel, the prince's meeting with the Yepanchin family, both the general and his wife conclude in their own way that Myshkin has been sent by God for their own particular benefit.

In this scene, too, the theme of beauty, which, as we have seen, is closely connected with visual appreciation and the fine arts, is first identified with Myshkin through the way in which he chooses to recommend himself; he writes out various samples of beautiful handwriting[7] to the delight of the general, who exclaims: 'My dear chap, you are not just a calligrapher, you are an artist.' (Pt I, Ch. 3.) The first example of Myshkin's artistic calligraphy has religious significance: it is a studious imitation of the signature of Igumen Pafnutyy. The prince gives other examples of his penmanship, but that the initial signature of Pafnutyy is meant to have more than passing significance can be seen from the ensuing encounter with the general's wife and daughters. On introducing the prince to them, Yepanchin mysteriously mentions the igumen once more, and Myshkin is called on to explain:

'The Igumen Pafnutyy in the fourteenth century', the prince began, 'he was in charge of a monastic retreat on the Volga, in what is now the Province of Kostroma. He was well known for his holy life. He went to the headquarters of the Tartars, helped to arrange the affairs of the time, and put his signature to a certain document. I have seen a copy of this signature; I liked the hand, and I learned it. When, just now, the general wanted to see how I write in order to place me, I wrote several phrases in various hands, and amongst them 'the Igumen Pafnutyy appends his hand', in the Igumen Pafnutyy's own handwriting. The general liked it very much and that is why he recalled it just now.'

'Aglaya', said Mrs. Yepanchin, 'remember: Pafnutyy, or better still make a note of it. Otherwise I always forget...' (Pt I, Ch. 5)

So the beautiful signature of a priest who strove to save Ortho-dox Russia from the pagan Tartars is scrupulously imitated by Myshkin, the 'holy fool', who proclaims that beauty will save the world. It is with this beautiful signature that he is first introduced to the Yepanchin family, and they, as we shall see, are closely connected with the theme of beauty in the novel.

In this same scene there is yet another religious symbol, with which the prince seeks to identify himself – the lowly ass, present at Christ's birth, and chosen by him for the triumphant ride into Jerusalem. The ass might be taken as an emblem of Myshkin's 'idiocy', but it is also a symbol for triumphant humility; a concrete expression of the second aphorism attributed to the prince: 'humility is a terrible force'. It is the braying of an ass which, like a clarion call, awakens the prince from the spiritual darkness of his early years:

I completely awoke from this darkness, I remember, one evening in Basle, on my entry into Switzerland; and what awoke me was the cry of an ass in the town market. The ass impressed me terribly, and for some reason or other I liked it extraordinarily; and along with this it was as though everything suddenly cleared in my head...

From that time on I have been terribly fond of asses. They strike some sort of sympathetic chord within me. I began to enquire about them because I had never seen them before, and I immediately became convinced that it was an extremely useful animal, hard working, strong, patient, cheap, long suffering; and through this ass I suddenly began to like the whole of Switzerland, with the result that my former despondency ceased. (Pt I, Ch. 5)

Moreover, this symbol of humility is linked with the concept of 'man'; for the prince goes on to defend the ass in these somewhat strange terms: 'All the same, I stand up for the ass; an ass is a good and useful man.'

Everything in the delineation of Myshkin indicates the attributes of a Christ-like figure. The prince is 'the positively good man'; and Dostoyevsky in a letter to his niece stresses that there is only one 'positively good man' – Christ. Myshkin is 'man'; he, like Christ, is Man apotheosised, and his other title of 'prince' serves too to link him with Christ, The Prince of Heaven. The beauty which 'will save the world' suggests the divine beauty of the Saviour, and the humility which 'is a terrible force' seems to express the paradox of Christ's mission on earth: he chose death on the cross to found his church: he chose the ass as a symbol of his triumph.

As we have seen, the evening gathering at the Yepanchins is the only point in the novel where Myshkin attempts to teach his twin doctrines of beauty and humility. This scene we can refer to as 'The Teaching of the Elders'[8] (the childlike qualities of Myshkin are stressed throughout, and before the scene Aglaya had been concerned about the impression he would make, rebuking the prince for his schoolboy's vocabulary). There is, however, yet another important idea which Myshkin preaches on this occasion:

What is necessary is that, in opposition to the West, there should shine forth our Christ, whom we have preserved, and whom they do not even know. We ought not to fall slavishly for the baited hook of the Jesuits, but to stand before them, holding out to them our own Russian civilisation. (Pt IV, Ch. 7)

The concept of 'the Russian Christ' is one close to Dostoyevsky's heart. It is a figure embodying great humility and beauty, which Dostoyevsky took to be the true idea of Christ, preserved in the hearts of the Russian people alone: the spirit of Russian civilisation.[9] If Myshkin is a Christ-figure, he is above all 'the Russian Christ'.

Having thus far stressed the positive side of the portrayal of Myshkin, as the embodiment of 'the Russian Christ', who preaches that 'beauty will save the world', and that 'humility is a terrible force', we must now concede how little of this positive side is fully realised in the novel itself. After finishing *The Idiot* Dostoyevsky wrote to his niece:

I am not pleased with the novel. It has not expressed even a tenth part of what I wanted to express, although, all the same, I will not renounce it. I still love my *idea* even though it has failed.[10]

The novel, it must be admitted, smacks strongly of failure. The final scene of the watch over the body of Nastasya Filippovna by Rogozhin and Myshkin and the prince's ensuing idiocy marks the failure of a great idea; but it does not, it must be stressed, mark an artistic failure; for this ending is one of the most powerful and evocative scenes which Dostoyevsky ever wrote. Indeed, *The Idiot* presents us with a typical Dostoyevskian paradox: as a novel it is an artistic success; while as a vehicle for the great idea, the portrayal of 'the positively good man', it is a failure. But failure at this level does not imply failure at the level of art; for in the novel's structure, even in its very conception, the failure of the 'idea' is implicit from the outset. It is, on the contrary, a mark of Dostoyevsky's greatness, of his artistic and intellectual honesty, that the novel ends as it does; in a lesser writer the novel would have failed with the triumph of the 'idea'.

If the final and complete idiocy of Myshkin marks the ultimate stage in the failure of the 'idea', it must nevertheless be borne in mind that this idiocy is an integral part of Dostoyevsky's conception of the character; it is a flaw in the make up of 'the positively good man', the presence of which is constantly emphasised throughout the novel. Moreover, the murder of Nastasya Filippovna, which is the cause of Myshkin's return to darkness, is no fortuitous and unexpected dénouement; at the beginning of the novel, even before he had met her, Myshkin predicts to Ganya the possibility that Nastasya Filippovna will be murdered.

The physical manifestations of Myshkin's idiocy are epileptic fits (one of the many autobiographical elements which Dostoyevsky has woven into the fabric of this novel).[11] Two of these occur in the course of the narrative, and are of great importance as dramatic expressions of the failure of the great idea. The first fit is connected with the prince's suspicions of Rogozhin; and the second concludes his 'Teaching of the Elders' – it interrupts his discourse on beauty.

That Myshkin falls into a fit as soon as he begins to expound his ideas on beauty is a symbolic expression of his own inability to live up to these ideas. But there is even greater significance than this in the connection between his philosophy of beauty and the curse of his epilepsy. The prince's ideas on beauty owe their very origin to his abnormal condition; they are glimpsed during that almost mystical state of mind, which accompanies the aura before the onset of the fit itself. This much becomes apparent from the record of Myshkin's own thoughts leading up to the first fit:

He mused, incidentally, on the fact that in his epileptic state, there was one stage almost before the very fit itself (if it occurred whilst he was awake) when suddenly, amidst his depression, amidst his spiritual gloom and feeling of being hemmed in, it was as though, at moments, his brain would leap into flame, and in an extraordinary burst all his life forces were at once tensely alert. His feeling of being alive and his self-awareness increased almost tenfold during these moments which lasted for the duration of lightning. His mind and his heart were illuminated by an extraordinary light. All his agitation, all his doubts, all his worries were as though pacified instantly, were dissolved into some kind of higher calm, full of clear, harmonious joy and hope, full of understanding and of knowledge of the final cause. But these moments, these flashes, were merely a premonition of that final second (never more than a second) when the fit itself began. This second was, of course, unbearable. Cogitating on this moment in retrospect, after his return to normality, he frequently said to himself that all these stabs of lightning, these flashes of a higher self-awareness and self-consciousness, and hence of a higher state of being, were nothing more than illness, nothing more than the breaking down of a normal state, and, if this were so, then this, far from being a state of higher being, must on the contrary be ascribed to the very lowest of states. However, he arrived, for all that, at a very paradoxical conclusion: 'What does it matter that it is illness?' he decided finally. 'How does it affect the matter that this is an abnormal state of tension, if its result, if this moment of sensation, recalled and examined later in a state of health, reveals itself as the highest degree of harmony and beauty, gives a hitherto unheard-of and undreamed-of feeling of completion, of a sense of proportion, of reconciliation and of an ecstatic, prayerful fusion with the very highest synthesis of life?' These vague expressions seemed to him quite comprehensible, although they were too weak. That it was, in fact, 'beauty and prayer'; that it was, in fact: 'the highest synthesis of life', he could have no doubt, could not even entertain the possibility of doubt. For these were no visions which he dreamed at that moment, like those from the effects of hashish, opium or alcohol, which, because they are abnormal and unreal, debase the intellect and distort the soul. He could reason sanely about it at the end of his state of illness. These moments were nothing less than an unusual effort of self-awareness, if one had to express this state in a word. That is self-awareness and at the same time self-perception to the very highest degree of immediacy.   (Pt II, Ch. 5)

The description continues, but enough has already been quoted to show that Myshkin is here talking about a mystical experience which it is virtually impossible to put into words. However, the words which he does choose are significant: 'harmonious joy and hope'; 'harmony and beauty in the highest degree'; 'a sense of proportion, of reconciliation'; 'beauty and prayer'; 'self-awareness and at the same time self-perception to the very highest degree of immediacy'. These categories of attempted description are not independent of one another, and although Myshkin attempts to sum up his experiences in one word: 'self-awareness', this poor epitome must comprise all the other qualities he lists. The same would be true if he had chosen any of the other categories in his description to act as an epitome of the whole. If, accordingly, we shift the centre of focus from 'self-awareness' to that of 'beauty', it follows that all the other qualities he speaks of are also implied in 'beauty' as it is conceived of here.

Thus harmony is a concomitant of beauty (and we know how closely Dostoyevsky himself identified the two).[12] Beauty also implies joy, and here we are reminded of the prince's conversation with the Yepanchin sisters on the ability to look and the ability to be happy. Beauty brings a sense of proportion and reconciliation; in other words it points to the quietist strain, which Aglaya thought she detected in Myshkin's philosophy: the reconciliation which is expressed in Myshkin's maxim that humility is a terrible force. This state, too, is one of 'beauty and prayer'; it is an 'ecstatic, prayerful fusion with the highest synthesis of life'. Beauty thus has religious overtones, which recall those present in the portrayal of Myshkin and which are consonant with his mission in the novel. Finally this beauty is 'self-awareness'; this is how he would choose to sum it up, if he had to do so in one word. It is a state of heightened awareness, in which Myshkin is extremely conscious of being alive. It is, indeed, just such a state of increased perception under the mystic impact of beauty, which Myshkin is preaching in the scene of 'The Teaching of the Elders', and it is very revealing that here his exhortations to look, to appreciate the beauty of the external world and so be happy and reconciled to everything, are interrupted by an epileptic fit. These words are thus more than an incoherent attempt to explain his maxim: 'beauty will save the world'; they are more than a brave effort to formulate a doctrine based on the mystical insight described above – they are words spoken during this experience itself; *for at the very moment of speaking* (Pt IV, 7), *the prince is passing through the phase of the aura preceding his fit.*

Myshkin's teachings on beauty, harmony, reconciliation are vitiated from the very outset; they are the product of an abnormal state of mind induced by illness. Yet in spite of this, there is affirmation; for the nature of the experience is such that the prince is prepared to discount the fact that its origins lie in illness. This is, in part, the key to the portrayal of Myshkin in the novel; it helps to explain why on the one hand the prince is the embodiment of great hopes and ambitions, and on the other a figure of failure. The 'idiocy' of Myshkin is an essential trait in the conception of the character: from it springs both his triumph and his defeat.

The beauty which will save the world is only grasped in his abnormal mental state, and therefore Myshkin, in spite of his claim to be 'the positively good/beautiful man', is by no means an incarnation of beauty himself. External beauty should lead to inner harmony, according to the implications of Myshkin's own teachings; yet neither of these qualities are truly his own. Physically the prince lacks grace; his movements are often represented as clumsy, and at the beginning of the novel (both on his first arrival in St Petersburg, and on his return from Moscow) the inelegant cut of his clothes is stressed. Indeed, Aglaya refuses to marry him because of the ridiculous exterior he presents to the world: 'Could one possibly marry a ludicrous character like you? Just you look at yourself in the mirror, the way you are standing at the moment.' (Pt III, Ch. 2.) Myshkin himself acknowledges that he lacks the very qualities which he seeks to extol:

I am always afraid of compromising my thought and my *chief idea* by my ludicrous appearance. I have no grace of gesture. My gestures are always the opposite of what they should be, and this evokes laughter, and cheapens the idea. A sense of proportion is also lacking, and that is very important, it is even the most important of all...

(Pt IV, Ch. 7)

Moreover, for all the calm which he appears to possess, he is aware of his lack of inner harmony: 'Recently the prince was accusing himself of two extremes: of an unusual, "senseless and persistent" trustfulness; and at the same time of a "gloomy and base" suspiciousness.' (Pt II, Ch. 11.) These two extremes are reflected in the two fits which occur in the novel; for the first fit is linked with his suspiciousness over Rogozhin; the second with his trustfulness before the 'elders'. Once more we return to the paradox that the very epilepsy, which yields the prince his insight into perfect harmony, is also responsible for the disintegration of his own personality.

The state of harmony and beauty, which Myshkin glimpses in his moment of heightened awareness before the epileptic fit, is a vision like that of the Holy Grail; it is the quest for this beauty which occupies him throughout the novel. He is therefore cast in the role of a knight, and is identified with the figure projected by Pushkin in his poem, 'The Poor Knight'. It is Aglaya who interprets the poem for us:

It is not stated in these verses what exactly the ideal of the 'poor knight' consisted in, but it is obvious that it was some sort of bright image; 'the image of pure beauty.' (Pt II, Ch. 6)

The identification of Myshkin with 'the poor knight' is apt on more than one count: the theme of humility is present in the very appellation: 'poor knight'; and the device, 'A.M.D.' (*Ave Mater Dei*) which he bears on his shield is in keeping with the religious overtones surrounding the prince in the novel. But in order to see how closely the portrayal of Myshkin follows the parallel of 'the poor knight', we must examine the poem more fully:

There lived on earth a poor knight of a simple and taciturn nature. His appearance was pale and gloomy, but his spirit was bold and direct. He had a certain vision, which was incomprehensible to the mind, and its impression cut deep into his heart. From that moment on with soul aflame, he did not look at women, and right up to the grave did not wish to utter a word to any one of them. He fastened a rosary round his neck instead of a scarf, and did not lift the steel vizor from his face before anyone. Full of a pure love and true to his sweet dream, he traced on his shield 'A.M.D.' in his own blood. And in the deserts of Palestine, whilst the paladins charged into battle over the crags, loudly calling the names of their ladies, he in wild zeal cried out: 'Lumen coeli, Sancta rosa', and his threat vanquished the muslims like thunder. Returning to his distant castle, he lived in strict seclusion. Still silent, still sad, he died as one insane.

The poem throws much light on the image of Myshkin. The vision which the mind could not grasp, but which cut deep into the heart of 'the poor knight' is the vision of beauty glimpsed by Myshkin before his epileptic fit. The silence and refusal to lift the vizor find their parallel in the prince's reticence about his 'chief idea', it explains why he is so loath to discuss what is 'incomprehensible to the mind'. The refusal to have dealings with women is not to be taken literally, but is valid for Myshkin in as much as he himself tells Rogozhin and Lebedev at the opening of the novel, that because of his illness he has no knowledge of women (Pt I, Ch. I) and later confesses to Ganya: 'I am not able to marry anyone; I am ill.' (Pt I, Ch. 3.)

Yet there *is* an ideal of womanhood before 'the poor knight'; for the device on his shield is an invocation to the Virgin Mary. These letters are traced in his own blood – they hint at the tortured relationships of Myshkin with the feminine incarnations of beauty in whom he seeks his ideal. Moreover, Aglaya (one such incarnation of beauty) reads the poem out aloud and substitutes for 'A.M.D.' the letters 'N.F.B.': the initials of her rival.

In the poem the 'poor knight' invokes his ideal of 'pure beauty', and vanquishes the unbelievers in the deserts of the Holy Land, just as Myshkin on his return to Holy Russia tries to vanquish the philistinism around him, under the banner of his 'idea'. But there is the same sense of failure, both in the quest of 'the poor knight' and that of Myshkin; the knight returns to his distant castle and dies insane, just as the prince at the end of the novel is once more in Switzerland in a state of idiocy.[13]

Despite all these similarities there is one obvious difference between the two figures: the knight has but one 'ideal of pure beauty'; the prince has two – besides the initials of Nastasya Filippovna, his shield could also bear those of Aglaya. The ideal of 'the poor knight' is the Virgin and she alone: that of

Myshkin is at one and the same time a virgin (Aglaya) and a fallen woman (Nastasya Filippovna). Myshkin himself seems to regret the simplicity of former ages when he says to Ippolit:

Then people were somehow or other men of one idea, but now they are more highly strung, more developed, more sensitive. In some way or other they are men of two ideas, of three ideas, at once. Present day man is broader, and, I swear to you, it is this which prevents him from being such a unified man as in those times.

(Pt IV, Ch. 5)

These ideas on the broad nature of man seem to look forward to Dmitri Karamazov, who is confronted by a similar dichotomy of the aesthetic ideal.[14] Myshkin too, like Dmitri Karamazov, seems aware that man can be motivated at one and the same time by the conflicting ideas of 'the Madonna' and of 'Sodom'; for when Keller makes a confession to him, the prince realises that his motives for doing so were at the same time both high-minded and base:

'Two thoughts came together. This very frequently happens; it is constantly happening to me. But I think that it is not a good thing, and do you know, Keller, I take myself to task for this more than for anything else? It is just as if, just now, you had related to me my own self. From time to time, it has even occurred to me to think that all people are like this', the prince continued very seriously, truly and deeply interested, 'so that I almost started to justify myself, because it is terribly difficult to struggle with these *double* thoughts; I have experience of it. God knows how they come, and how they are born' [...] The prince was looking at Keller with intense curiosity. The question of double thoughts had obviously occupied him for a long time.

(Pt II, Ch. 11)

It would seem quite consonant with the broad nature of modern man that the prince, troubled as he is by double thoughts, should also be tormented by a double vision of beauty, but whether this ambivalence corresponds to Dmitri Karamazov's division of the ideal of beauty into the ideal of the Madonna and the ideal of Sodom is another matter. On a superficial level the purity of Aglaya is contrasted with the fallen state of Nastasya Filippovna, and Nastasya Filippovna herself seems to interpret the difference between them in this light. Towards the end of Part I she shouts out to the guests assembled in her apartment that she has been Totsky's mistress, and tells the prince that it is Aglaya whom he needs rather than herself; for she (Nastasya) will only destroy him. She also accuses her other suitor, Ganya, of having overlooked Aglaya, and draws the general conclusion:

'Associate either with dishonourable women or honourable ones – there is only one choice; otherwise you will undoubtedly come to grief. See how the general is staring, with his mouth agape.'

'This is Sodom, Sodom', the general kept repeating, shrugging his shoulders. (Pt I, Ch. 16)

But in fact the difference between Aglaya and Nastasya Filippovna is not as simple as this: it is not a straightforward contrast between virtue and sin. There is more which unites these two heroines than separates them; and far from one of them representing the ideal of the Madonna, and the other the ideal of Sodom, each in herself represents this divided ideal; for in each of these characters the 'Madonna' of external beauty is at odds with the 'Sodom' of spiritual chaos.

If Aglaya and Nastasya Filippovna are to be taken as incarnations of an ideal of pure beauty towards which Myshkin is striving, then *their* beauty, it must be stressed, is merely physical: it is, once more, the beauty which reveals itself to the eye; and the impact of their beauty on Myshkin is nearer to that of a work of art. Thus Myshkin's first encounter with the beauty of Nastasya Filippovna is through her portrait: it is not through seeing her in the flesh. The effect of the portrait on Myshkin is immense, and he is drawn to it a second time: 'It was as though he wanted to solve the riddle of something concealed in this face, which had struck him a moment ago.' (Pt I, Ch. 7.) This enigma, which the beauty of Nastasya Filippovna presents, is implied too in the epithet, 'ambiguous' [*dvusmyslennyy*] which is frequently used to describe her. But a riddle lurks too in the beauty of Aglaya. When, on first meeting her, Myshkin is

78

asked to give his opinion of her from her face, he confesses that it is difficult to do so, because 'beauty is a riddle'.

This first meeting with Aglaya follows immediately after Myshkin's acquaintance with the beauty of Nastasya Filippovna, as captured in her photograph, and not only is this portrait reintroduced into the ensuing scene with Aglaya, but the theme of the representation of reality in art and the ability to look is, as we have seen, a major topic of conversation. Moreover, as if to complete the parallel, the face of Aglaya, too, can at times assume the quality of a portrait for Myshkin:

At times he would suddenly begin to look closely at Aglaya, and for five minutes together he would not tear his gaze from her face. But his gaze was more than strange; it seemed as though he were looking at her as though at an object situated two versts away from him, or as though at her own portrait, but not at herself. (Pt III, Ch. 2)

The beauty of both these women is therefore presented as that of a beautiful object: a portrait divorced from the personality of the subject, and when Myshkin attempts to comprehend the essential being behind the beautiful exterior, he arrives in both cases at a riddle. Beauty, truly comprehended according to Myshkin's mystical insight, should also be harmony and happiness; but both these women, beneath their exterior of beauty, are in a state of chaos and unhappiness. Of Aglaya her mother says:

I myself am a foolish woman with a heart but no mind, but you are a foolish woman with a mind, but no heart; both of us are unhappy; both suffer. (Pt I, Ch. 7)

The suffering and unhappiness of Nastasya Filippovna are even more obvious. However, unlike Aglaya, though she may have a great heart, her mind seems lacking. Throughout most of the novel her sanity is called into question, and her lack of spiritual harmony can erupt into acts of violence, as when she lashes her detractor with a whip 'at the music'. The setting of this scene 'at the music' is significant, for once again the arts are used as a symbol of beauty; and it is against a background of external harmony that the inner disharmony of Nastasya Filippovna manifests itself so glaringly.

But the violent impulses of Aglaya, for all her 'mind', seem hardly less irrational. She confesses to the prince that she has some thirty times thought of poisoning herself to punish her family, and rumours circulate that she has ordered Ganya to burn his finger in a candle. However, when the children come to the house with an axe and a hedgehog, it is not the axe (the instrument of destruction) which she chooses to send to Myshkin but the hedgehog; an 'allegory' which seems to suggest that her spines are merely for defence.

There is much which links these two women, and they are closely associated in Myshkin's own mind. The same device of identification through dreams which we have seen in *Crime and Punishment* operates here too. Thus Myshkin, keeping his appointment with Aglaya on the little green bench, falls asleep to dream of Nastasya Filippovna. The dream is interrupted by Aglaya, and Myshkin on awakening cannot distinguish between the dream and reality. This same dream recurs before he opens the letters of Nastasya Filippovna to Aglaya, and the letters themselves are compared to a dream; for they are not those of a rival but of a lover.

But for all that these two women are identified with each other in Myshkin's mind, it remains true that they are individual and apart; for the ideal of beauty which shines before the prince is not only imperfect – it is divided. At this point it is essential to examine what each of these two women represents in the novel. It may be simpler to begin with Aglaya.

The name, Aglaya, is that of one of the three Graces of mythology. The name means 'beauty', 'brightness'. In the novel Aglaya is one of three sisters, all of whose names begin with the letter A. They are closely connected with the arts; thus Adelaida paints and Aleksandra plays the piano. But the two elder sisters look upon Aglaya as something special: 'Amongst themselves, with absolute sincerity, they forecast the destiny of Aglaya to be not just a destiny, but a possible ideal of earthly paradise.' (Pt I, Ch. 4.) That this destiny might come about through marriage with Myshkin is underlined by the author himself; for when Aglaya asks the prince if he is seeking her hand in marriage, she explains to the family: '"An exceptional moment in my destiny is being decided" (Aglaya expressed herself exactly like this)'. (Pt IV, Ch. 5.) The parenthesis is Dostoyevsky's.[15]

One of the ideals of beauty before the prince is, therefore, that of 'paradise on earth', a harmony in purely human terms, a socialist utopia. Thus there are no religious overtones in the depiction of Aglaya; her beauty is non-Christian, and the only attribute which associates her at all with the divine (leaving aside her ultimate lapse into Roman Catholicism) is the name Aglaya which points to the pre-Christian classical world with its political ideal of the republic.

Political considerations predominate in the portrayal of Aglaya. Her mother fears that she is a nihilist and is leading her other daughters astray; at one stage she even cropped her hair short, as if to identify herself with the close-cropped nihilist girls of the sixties. Indeed commentators have seen a prototype for Aglaya in Anna Korvin-Krukovskaya,[16] a young girl with nihilist leanings, in whom Dostoyevsky took a very serious interest for a short time before his second marriage.

Aglaya tells Myshkin that she has read all the banned books, and wants to devote herself to something useful, not spend her life going to society balls; the moral charge which she throws at her rival, Nastaya Filippovna, is that she does not work. To Myshkin she suggests that they both devote themselves to education, which again was one of the social tasks which the 'nihilists' of the sixties set themselves.

When it is announced that the 'nihilists', who are championing the rights of Burdovsky, are waiting to see the prince, it is Aglaya who suggests that he should hear what they have to say, although when they have finished she is disgusted with them. It is Aglaya, too, who restrains her mother, when she is about to strike Ippolit, one of the most outspoken of the 'nihilists', and Ippolit himself obviously regards Aglaya with some degree of veneration, for he wishes his confession to be sent to her after his death. Aglaya even believes it possible that his reason for attempting suicide was to induce her to read it.

These would seem to be the implications behind the projection of Aglaya as an ideal of beauty, but from the outset her beauty is compared with that of Nastasya Filippovna. When he first meets the Yepanchin family the prince is asked to comment on Aglaya's beauty, and he says: 'Almost like Nastasya Filippovna, only the face is quite different.' The beauty of Nastasya Filippovna is certainly different from that of Aglaya: there is behind it a power which recalls Myshkin's phrase that beauty will save the world. Adelaida, on seeing the portrait of Nastasya Filippovna, exclaims: 'Such beauty is a force...with such beauty one could overturn the world.' Later in the novel Nastasya Filippovna herself takes up this remark: 'I heard that your sister Adelaida said about my portrait at that time, that with such beauty one could overturn the world. But I have renounced the world.' (Pt III, Ch. 10.)

There is indeed something unworldly about this portrait as it is first described to us:

A woman of unusual beauty was depicted in the portrait. She had been photographed in a black silk dress of an extremely simple and elegant cut. Her hair, which was apparently dark brown, was arranged simply, in a homely fashion. The eyes were dark and deep, the forehead pensive; the expression of the face revealed passion and perhaps a certain haughtiness. She was somewhat thin in the face, perhaps even pale...   (Pt I, Ch. 3)

The black dress; the simplicity; the pale thin face with its dark, deep eyes, and pensive forehead – all point towards the type of beauty associated with an icon. It is the expression of the face which contradicts this general impression, and it is this which strikes Myshkin again when he looks at the portrait for a second time:

This face unusual for its beauty and for something else, something indefinable, struck him even more forcibly now. It was as though in this face there was immeasurable pride and disdain, almost hatred; and at the same time there was something trustful, something marvellously frank and ingenuous. These two contrasts aroused a feeling almost of compassion when one looked at these features. This dazzling beauty was almost unbearable; the beauty of the pale face, the almost hollow cheeks and the burning eyes. It was a strange beauty! (Pt I, Ch. 7)

Now, as if to confirm the icon-like qualities of the portrait, the prince's reaction is to kiss it.

It seems to Myshkin that he has seen this face before; that the portrait is calling him. Nastasya Filippovna too feels that she has seen Myshkin before – it is as though there is a mystic bond between them. There is indeed; for the relationship between them is that of Christ and 'the fallen woman'. The portrait of Nastasya Filippovna is not the 'icon' of the Madonna: it is that of Mary Magdalene, of whom the forerunner in the novel is Marie, the poor 'fallen' peasant girl, whom Myshkin 'resurrected' in Switzerland. The parallel between the relationship of Myshkin to Nastasya Filippovna and that of Christ to 'the fallen woman' is made explicit by Radomsky: 'The woman was forgiven in the temple, just such a woman, but she was not told that she deserved honour and respect of all kinds.' (Pt IV, Ch. 9.)

But Nastasya Filippovna, for her own part, has a different conception of Christ; again it is an image of beauty in pictorial terms. In one of those strange letters written to her rival, Nastasya Filippovna claims that after meeting Aglaya, she conceived the subject for a picture: Christ alone with a child. Why her meeting with Aglaya should inspire such a picture becomes obvious from the words she addresses to her rival immediately after the description of this picture: 'You are innocent, and in your innocence lies all your perfection.' (Pt III, Ch. 10.) For Nastasya Filippovna, Christ is the lover of innocence. This is why she attempts to engineer the marriage of Aglaya to Myshkin: she deems herself, 'the fallen woman', to be unworthy of him.

But it is Aglaya, who in a fit of pique, reminds the prince that his role is to 'resurrect' Nastasya Filippovna:

So go on, sacrifice yourself; it suits you so well! For you are such a great benefactor. And do not call me 'Aglaya'. Even a moment ago you called me just 'Aglaya'...You must, you are committed to resurrecting her. You must go off with her again, in order to calm and soothe her heart; for you really love her!   (Pt III, Ch. 8)

The possibility of resurrection is implied in Nastasya Filippovna's very name; for Anastasiya (Nastasya) means 'the resurrected woman'; 'the woman returned to life'. But in contrast to Aglaya, who, as we have seen from the passage above, is addressed by Myshkin simply as 'Aglaya', Nastasya Filippovna is always given her patronymic: 'Filippovna' (the feminine of Filippov). This adds a new dimension to the nature of Nastasya Filippovna's fall; for Filippov was the semi-legendary founder of an extreme sect of heretics within the Orthodox fold: the sect of the *Khlysty* or Flagellants. It is significant that after the incident with the whip [*khlyst*],[17] Myshkin is troubled by dreams of Nastasya Filippovna as 'a sinner'.

We have now arrived at an interesting interpretation of the double ideal of beauty, which confronts 'the poor knight'. On the one hand stands Aglaya, one of the three Graces, indeed the Grace of Beauty herself; she is a 'possible ideal of earthly paradise', but this secular beauty is tainted by the ideas of nihilism. On the other hand stands Nastasya Filippovna, whose beauty has strong religious overtones; but she is a 'fallen woman' who has to be resurrected, and her sin is not merely that of the woman in the Temple: there is in her fall a taint of heresy. Here Dostoyevsky is presenting us with a parallel, which we have seen before in *Crime and Punishment*; for in Myshkin's double ideal of pure beauty, nihilism is set alongside schism [*raskol*]: those two apparently diverse elements which meet symbolically in the figure of Raskolnikov.

That the linking of Nastasya Filippovna to the Russian schismatics is in no sense fortuitous can be judged from her close identification with Rogozhin. Indeed, at the end of Part I she brands herself before the assembled company as 'Rogozhin's woman' [*rogozhinskaya*], a term which she seems to equate with her 'fallen' state. But what does Rogozhin represent?

Rogozhin is usually taken as the embodiment of brute physical passion. Critics who interpret the character in this way are basing themselves on Dostoyevsky's own notes, in which he asserts that there are three kinds of love in the novel: (1) Rogozhin – loved based on *strast'* [passion]; (2) Ganya – love born of money; and (3) the prince – Christian love.[18]

But to interpret the word '*strast*'' in the sense of physical passion is obviously wrong. When the prince visits Rogozhin in his house, he is told by Rogozhin of the words uttered by Nastasya Filippovna on seeing the portrait of his father. She accuses him of strong 'passions': 'Everything in you is passion [*strast'*]; you take everything to the point of passion [*strast'*].' (Pt II, Ch. 3.) Here the word '*strast*'' is nearer to fanaticism; for Nastasya Filippovna is talking of the type of life led by Rogozhin's father, with his strong interest in the Russian schismatics at their most fanatical: 'You would settle down in this house, like your father, with your Castrates, and perhaps in the end you yourself would go over to their faith.' (Pt II, Ch. 3.) The Castrates were an extreme development of the sect of the Flagellants whose asceticism led them to believe that the kingdom of heaven could only be achieved through castration.

Rogozhin is very strongly identified with the sect of the Castrates; so the notion that he represents sensual passion in the novel is, to say the least, bizarre. His Christian name, too, suggests the very contrary (Parfen is the Greek *parthenos* = virgin).

Nor in his dealings with Nastasya Filippovna is Rogozhin motivated by sensual passion; his behaviour, however, does reveal fanaticism with strong religious overtones. When he is alone with Nastasya Filippovna in Moscow, we learn that the only physical contact between them is that Rogozhin beats her; and this is followed by a period of one and a half days spent on his knees before her, fasting and repenting. Indeed Nastasya Filippovna seems specifically to be denying any carnal element in their relationship, when she defends herself before Aglaya by asking 'Am I a loose woman? Ask Rogozhin; he'll tell you.' (Pt IV, Ch. 8.) Moreover, when at the end of the novel Nastasya

Filippovna goes to live with Rogozhin in his house, it is not as a bridegroom that he receives her, but as her murderer. The love of Rogozhin for Nastasya Filippovna is not a sensual love: it is a fanatical love; and like all fanaticism it distorts and kills a great ideal.

Rogozhin, who in both speech and attitude represents demotic Russia, is the embodiment of a strain of religious fanaticism, peculiar to the Russian common people. His surname links him with the schismatics; for *Rogozhniki* or *Rogozhskoye soglasiye* was the name given to a sect of Old Believers in Moscow, who were associated with the Rogozhskoye Cemetery.[19]

Rogozhin himself, although a native of St Petersburg, is connected with Moscow in the novel. It is to Moscow that he first runs off with Nastasya Filippovna, and in Moscow, too, that he has his heart-to-heart talks with the prince. Certain details of the murder of Nastasya Filippovna are based on a contemporary crime, which had taken place in Moscow; this explains the prince's comment in the final scene: 'It is like it was in Moscow.'[20] But even more appropriate is the fact that Rogozhin's name links him both with the schismatics and with a cemetery: death is his role in the novel. Ippolit says of Rogozhin: 'his house made an impression on me; it is like a cemetery'. Nastasya Filippovna, too, is adversely struck by the house and has the feeling that there might be a body hidden under the floorboards. The house, indeed, does become a sort of cemetery when at the end of the novel Nastasya Filippovna lies there dead, watched over by Rogozhin and Myshkin.

The nature of Rogozhin's house is such that the prince can tell instinctively whose house it is merely from the façade. This is described as arid, forbidding and sterile, and a significant feature is that the ground floor is occupied by a money changer's shop kept by a Castrate, who also rents the top floor. This house, linked as it is with the sect of the Castrates, Myshkin sees as symbolising the whole of the Rogozhin family: 'Your house has the physiognomy of all your family, and of all your Rogozhin way of life.' Rogozhin replies: 'This house was built by my grandfather. Castrates have lived here from the beginning – the Khludyakovs, and they are still our tenants even now.' (Pt II, Ch. 3.) The house does indeed reflect the Rogozhin family; here gloom, fanaticism and sterility seem uppermost. The idea of celebrating a wedding in this atmosphere seems macabre; thus the prince asks about a portrait of Rogozhin's father:

'He was surely an Old Believer?'
'No he went to church, but it is true that he said that the Old Faith was more correct. He also had great respect for the Castrates. This was his study. Why did you ask about the Old Faith?'
'Will you celebrate your wedding here?'
'Y-yes, here', replied Rogozhin almost starting at the unexpected question. (Pt II, Ch. 3)

Sterility and religious deviation can be sensed in the other occupants of the house. Semyon Semyonych, Rogozhin's brother, lives in a separate wing (it is emphasised that he is a widower) and of him Rogozhin relates:

At night, my brother cut off the solid gold tassels from the brocade pall of my father's coffin, saying: 'What a lot of money they're worth.' For that he could go to Siberia, if I chose, for it is sacrilege. (Pt I, Ch. 1)

Rogozhin's mother too lives in this house, and in a state of religious idiocy spends her time reading the Lives of the Saints.

But this house is like a cemetery in yet another important respect: it is a shrine for a dead Christ. In the picture gallery of Rogozhin's father there hangs a copy of Hans Holbein's *The Entombment of Christ*; a picture in which Christ is depicted as irrevocably dead. It is Ippolit who describes the painting for us:

In this picture Christ is depicted taken straight from the cross. I think that usually it has been customary for artists to depict Christ, whether on the cross or not, with a hint of unusual beauty still in his face. This beauty they strive to preserve even alongside the most terrible sufferings. But in Rogozhin's picture there is no hint of beauty. (Pt III, Ch. 6)

So in Rogozhin's house the prince, who proclaims that beauty will save the world, is confronted with the Saviour of the World devoid of beauty. Art, the vehicle for beauty, has in this picture destroyed beauty. Myshkin had told the artist, Adelaida, to look and paint; later he will tell 'the elders' to look and see beauty; but in this picture the gaze of the artist has revealed something far from beautiful. There is perhaps, after all, another way of looking than that extolled by Myshkin in the scene of The Teaching of the Elders; and so at the conclusion of that scene, at the words: 'look into the eyes which look at you and love you', Myshkin falls into a fit, as he had done earlier when Rogozhin had seemed about to murder him. For there are other eyes: the penetrating eyes of Rogozhin, his spiritual brother, which follow him with suspicion everywhere he goes. The counter-principle to Myshkin's ideas on beauty is embodied in Rogozhin himself: the owner of this ugly, forbidding house with its Castrates and its dead Christ. Even in spite of the prince's attempts to enlighten Rogozhin with the beauty of Pushkin, Rogozhin can only destroy beauty; and Nastasya Filippovna, the ideal of beauty which is before him, will be murdered at his hands in this very house.

But the beauty which this picture destroys is the beauty of Christ, and in the novel the picture is the symbolic centre of a dilemma: belief or unbelief in God:

'I have been wanting for a long time to ask you, Lev Nikolayevich, whether you believe in God or not?' Rogozhin suddenly spoke, going on for a few more steps.

'How strangely you ask...and look at me', the prince remarked involuntarily.

'I like to look at that picture', muttered Rogozhin after a short silence, as though he had forgotten his question.

'At that picture!' the prince suddenly cried out, struck by a sudden idea, 'at that picture! From that picture a man might lose his faith.'[21]   (Pt II, Ch. 4)

However, Rogozhin in asking the prince about his belief in God is perhaps concerned about belief less as a personal issue, than as a national problem; for he goes on to ask Myshkin about the state of faith inside Russia. To this question the prince replies by telling him of four encounters he has had whilst travelling about the country.

The first of these concerns an atheist whom Myshkin met on a train. He found that the arguments of the atheist on religion were off the point; nor could the atheist understand what Myshkin was trying to tell him.

The second is an incident which had happened in a hotel where Myshkin was staying the night. Two peasants getting on in years had spent the previous night there. One of them had a silver watch on a pearl chain, which was coveted by the other to such an extent that:

He took a knife, and when his friend had turned away from him, stealthily approached him from behind, and took aim. He raised his eyes to heaven, crossed himself, and mumbling to himself this bitter prayer: 'Lord forgive me for the sake of Christ!' finished off his friend at one stroke, like a sheep, and took out his watch.

(Pt II, Ch. 4)

It is Rogozhin who points to the significance of these two stories:

'I like that. No, that's best of all!' he cried convulsively, almost choking. 'One does not believe in God at all, and the other believes so much that he kills people with a prayer.'

The first story, therefore, depicts the atheist; the second – the religious man turned fanatic; and in this story Rogozhin recognises something typically Russian, and something of his own: 'you couldn't have thought that up'. he exclaims.

In the next story, Myshkin relates how he was stopped by a drunken soldier, who attempted to sell him the tin cross from his neck, passing it off as a silver one. Myshkin bought it, knowing full well its value, put it on, and the soldier ran off, undoubtedly to get drunk on the money. But the prince is not prepared to judge him too rashly: 'I will wait before condemning this seller of Christ.'

Such tolerance seems justified by the next encounter, which serves not only as a commentary on the incident with the soldier, but also on the two preceding stories. Myshkin meets a young peasant woman with a baby at her breast, and she tells him that just as a mother rejoices when she sees the first smile of her child, so God rejoices when he sees a sinner sincerely praying to him on his knees. Myshkin comments that this woman has uttered a profound religious truth, and who knows but that this woman was not the wife of the very same soldier who 'sold his Christ'.

It would seem that this one encounter with the peasant woman has justified to Myshkin the religious nature of the Russian people:

> The essence of religious feeling cannot be made to fit in with any kind of reasoning, with any kind of misdeeds or crimes, with any form of atheism. Here there is something quite different, and which will always be eternally different. Here there is something over the surface of which atheism of all types will always slide; it will always miss the point. But the chief thing is that you will notice this clearest of all, and soonest of all, in the Russian heart, and there is my conclusion! It is one of the first of my conclusions which I bring from our Russia. There is something to be done, Parfen! There is something to be done in our Russian world. Believe me! (Pt II, Ch. 4)

Myshkin is about to leave when he is called back by Rogozhin:

> 'Lev Nikolayevich!' shouted Parfen from above, when he had reached the first half landing, 'The cross what you bought from the soldier, have you got it on you?'
> 'Yes. I have got it.' The prince stopped again.
> 'Show it to me up here.'
> 'Another new whim', he thought, went up stairs, and brought out his cross to show him, without taking it off his neck.
> 'Give me it', said Rogozhin.
> 'Why surely you...' The prince would have liked not to part with the cross.
> 'I shall wear it, and I shall take off my cross for you. You wear it.'
> 'You want to exchange crosses? All right, Parfen, if that is the case, I am glad. Let us become brothers!' (Pt II, Ch. 4)

Thus by this ceremony of the exchanging of crosses Myshkin and Rogozhin become identified as spiritual brothers, and

Parfen takes the prince to his mother's apartment to receive her blessing.

But Rogozhin's interest during this little scene seems to be concentrated more on the nature of the cross he is to receive than on the actual exchange itself. Rogozhin wishes to wear the cross of the 'seller of Christ';[22] he seeks to identify himself with the soldier in the third of Myshkin's stories. In his words at parting he seems to be identifying himself too with a figure in Myshkin's second story – the peasant murderer: 'Never fear! Although I have taken your cross, I will not cut your throat for your watch.' By the word, 'watch' Rogozhin obviously has in mind Nastasya Filippovna for he adds: 'Well take her then, if fate decrees! She's yours! I surrender her! Remember Rogozhin!' Yet in their next encounter Rogozhin seems far from willing to surrender Nastasya Filippovna, and almost takes on the role of the peasant murderer: he is on the point of cutting Myshkin's throat for 'the watch'.

The religious significance of Rogozhin in the novel is thus clear: he is the dark side of the Russian religious temperament, with its Castrates and Flagellants, its fanaticism and violence. Although Rogozhin is the symbolic brother of the Russian Christ, he is nevertheless joined in brotherhood through his self-identification with the 'seller of Christ' – it is a relationship as uneasy as that of Cain to Abel.

Of the four stories which Myshkin tells in answer to Rogozhin's question on the state of faith in Russia, only one substantiates the claim of the Russian people to be a godly nation. Yet in spite of this, during the scene of 'The Teaching of the Elders', the prince asserts his idea of nationalistic Christianity:

'He who has no native soil beneath his feet has no god.' This is not my expression, it is the expression of a certain merchant, an Old Believer, whom I met when I was travelling about. It is true, he did not exactly express himself like this; he said: 'he who has renounced his native land has renounced his god'. Just think, with us even highly educated people have joined the sect of the Flagellants. Yes, but why then are the Flagellants worse than nihilists, Jesuits, atheists? They might even be more profound. That is what anguish leads to! Open up before Columbus's companions, thirsting and feverish, the coast-line of the 'New World'; open up for the Russian the Russian 'World'. Let him search for this gold, this treasure hidden from him in the earth! Show him, in the future, the renewal of all humanity and its resurrection, achieved alone, perhaps, by the Russian idea, by the Russian god and Christ, and you will see what a powerful, truthful, wise and gentle giant will grow before an astonished world; astonished and afraid, because they expect from us only the sword, the sword and violence; because they cannot imagine us without barbarity, judging us in their own likeness. This has been the case up till now, and the more it goes on, the more it will be so. And...

(Pt IV, Ch. 7)

At this point the prince breaks a fragile symbol of beauty – the Chinese vase.

Earlier, when Myshkin had been disturbed by the destruction of Christ's beauty, depicted in Rogozhin's picture, he had countered by asserting his faith in the religious nature of the Russian people ('There is something to be done in our Russian world'); but here, whilst making a similar assertion, he himself is cast in the role of the destroyer of beauty. Moreover, this clumsy act introduces a sudden comic note of bathos, which seems to undermine the validity of the serious ideas which he is in the middle of expounding; like the fit which is to follow, this too is an expression of the flaw inherent in the prince's 'philosophy'.

At the beginning of this speech Myshkin had been talking about the 'passionate' nature [*strastnost*'] of the Russian character. The Russians, he says, become fanatical and are unable to take half-measures in their beliefs. Yet in expounding his own beliefs it is his own impassioned nature, his own *strastnost*', which causes him to break the vase:

All this feverish tirade, all this flood of passionate [*strastnyy*] and turbulent words and exalted ideas, as though jostling one another in confusion and jumping over one another, all this foretold something dangerous, something special in the mood of the young man, who had suddenly got himself worked up for no apparent reason. (Pt IV, Ch. 7)

Earlier in the novel Myshkin had taken himself to task for his lack of restraint, considering it his chief weakness, and here it is his 'passion' which leads him to break the Chinese vase. A similar lack of restraint is, of course, noticeable in Nastasya Filippovna, whose 'passion' had revealed itself from the first in her portrait; but above all this element of *strast'* links him with Rogozhin, the embodiment of fanaticism, in whose house the beauty of the image of Christ is shattered, destroyed not only in his picture, but also by the perversion of Christianity practised by the Castrates who live there. For if the beauty 'which will save the world' is 'the Russian idea, the Russian god and Christ' by which 'the renewal of humanity and its resurrection' will be achieved, there is also another side of the Russian religious temperament: the fanaticism exemplified by Rogozhin. It is therefore significant that the Chinese vase is broken at the very point when the prince begins to talk about what the West expects from Russia.

But the flaw goes deeper than this; the very idea of a peculiarly national type of Christianity, of a 'Russian god and Christ', linked closely with the Russian soil was, as Myshkin here implies, suggested to him by an Old Believer:[23] it is in itself heretical; hence the immediate mention of the sect of the Flagellants, who believed in many reincarnations of Christ. The idea of the Russian Christ, like the idea of 'beauty' to which it bears a close relationship, is doomed in the moment of its conception by the very circumstances which engendered it. The prince's idea of 'beauty' is doomed, as we have seen, because it is the product of an elevating mental aberration: the aberration which lies behind the concept of 'the Russian Christ' is schism, and the Russian schism implies flagellation, castration and fanaticism.

Yet in spite of all this the prince declares his faith in the religious mission of the Russian people; and there is perhaps hope even for Rogozhin – for both he and the prince are in love with the same ideal of beauty, even though the ideal be a fallen one. Thus Myshkin tells Rogozhin what Nastasya Filippovna has apparently told him earlier: that it is his love for her which prevents him from becoming completely like his father.

Myshkin tries to educate him towards the natural spirit of beauty by reading the whole of Pushkin with him in Moscow;[24] Nastasya Filippovna inspires him to read the history of his own nation: Solovev's *History of Russia*. When Myshkin discovers this book in Rogozhin's home, he believes that this might be the beginning of a new attitude towards Nastasya Filippovna, that Rogozhin's love for her might be approaching the nature of his own love – that this might be the beginning of pity. He is, of course, wrong; for it is from the pages of this book that Rogozhin takes the knife to stab her; from Russian history Rogozhin drawn not pity for the unresurrected ideal but the instrument of her destruction.

It has been noted that the murder of Nastasya Filippovna by Rogozhin has much in common with Othello's murder of Desdemona: Dostoyevsky's rough drafts for this scene also bear this out.[25] If the author had the death of Desdemona in mind when writing this powerful ending to his novel, it is clear that the motive for the murder is not jealousy on the part of Rogozhin (who anyway is as close to his rival, Myshkin, during this scene as at any time during the novel) but something else: it represents the failure of a great ideal; for this is Dostoyevsky's own interpretation of the death of Desdemona – disillusionment with an ideal – a view which he stated more than once.[26]

Nastasya Filippovna represents a great but elusive ideal, which shines before Myshkin – a Russian religious ideal, tainted alas by schism and fanaticism. The mission of Myshkin is to resurrect this ideal and by its beauty save the world. The contest for this beauty is carried on between Myshkin, the positive aspect of the Russian religious temperament, and his 'brother', Rogozhin, who represents the dark side of the Russian religious mind. But it is an unequal contest; from the very first Myshkin has a premonition of her fate, and on the very point of marrying the prince, Nastasya Filippovna runs away with Rogozhin, soon to lie dead in his house with its Castrates and its 'icon' of a dead and unbeautiful Christ. It is significant that when Myshkin comes to this house to find her, his call is answered by Pafnutyevna, the companion of Rogozhin's mother: the name recalls the Igumen Pafnutyy, with whose signature Myshkin had recommended himself at the beginning of the novel. But this 'daughter of Pafnutyy' is linked with the state of religious idiocy of Rogozhin's mother, and with the house which has become a cemetery for the great ideal. Myshkin's religious mission has thus failed, and he himself will soon be in a state of idiocy, watching over the body of Nastasya Filippovna, and linked in her death with his fanatical 'brother', Rogozhin.

Dostoyevsky, in the letter to his niece quoted at the beginning of this chapter, had written: 'Beauty [*prekrasnoye*] is an ideal and both our ideal and that of civilised Europe is far from having been worked out.' If Nastasya Filippovna is 'our ideal', Aglaya stands for the secular 'ideal of civilised Europe' – the political and utopian thought of the West which had already taken root in Russia. Myshkin, who has come from Europe to discover Russia, is drawn irresistibly towards Nastasya Filippovna; but she, aware of her own imperfections, directs his attentions towards Aglaya. Yet it is only after the prince has suffered at the hands of Nastasya Filippovna in Moscow (where Rogozhin is a constant shadow), that he acts on her suggestion: he writes to Aglaya offering her his friendship. Nevertheless, Myshkin is still drawn to Nastasya Filippovna, and when he is put in the position of having to choose between these two women, it is on Nastasya Filippovna that his choice appears to rest, though ultimately he is to lose them both.

Aglaya, too, ends in failure: from the novel's conclusion we learn that she has gone abroad, married a worthless Polish *émigré*, accepted the Roman Catholic faith, and become a member of a committee for the restoration of Poland. Thus all the negative tendencies of Aglaya's nihilism have become realised: she has cut her self off entirely from Russia; is devoting herself to anti-Russian political activity, and has accepted the Catholic church, which according to Myshkin is the father of Socialism[27] (both believe in 'heaven on earth'). The general pronouncement on Russians abroad, with which Aglaya's mother concludes the novel, serves as an epitaph on the delusions of her own daughter:

All this life abroad, and all this Europe of yours is just fantasy, and all of us abroad are just fantasy. Mark what I say. You yourself will see.

Thus both ideals of beauty have failed, brought down by destructive elements within their own composition. But beauty, as Myshkin reminds us, is an enigma; there are at least five facets of this enigma presented in the novel.

First there is the *mystical insight*: beauty as perceived by Myshkin in the aura preceding his fits. But this is not only beauty; it is also harmony; it is also happiness; it has, moreover, religious implications.

Secondly there is the *philosophy*. From the mystical insight, Myshkin appears to draw his teaching of 'looking': beauty, he seems to argue, lies all around, and can induce in the mind of the awakened perceiver a sense of harmony and happiness.

Thirdly there is the *incarnation*; for Myshkin as the positively good/beautiful man is himself a would-be embodiment of spiritual beauty.

The fourth and fifth aspects of this enigma are the *ideals*: on the one hand that of Nastasya Filippovna – a beautiful woman who also represents a national religious ideal, which might bring beauty, harmony and happiness to mankind; on the other hand there is Aglaya – a secular, political ideal, which again might bring man beauty, harmony and happiness.

It is not entirely unexpected that beauty for Dostoyevsky should, in the final analysis, assume either religious or political overtones; for the slogan attributed to Myshkin is: 'beauty will save the world', and there is behind this some hint of an ideal capable of leading man to paradise. Moreover there is in Dostoyevsky's thought an intimate connection between beauty perceived by the eye, and man's living in a state of harmony. This is most strikingly exemplified by the role played in his writing by one of his favourite paintings: Claude Lorrain's *Acis and Galatea*, which he sees as some sort of pledge that man can live in a state of harmony and happiness. This picture is interpreted in this light in both *Stavrogin's Confession* and *A Raw Youth*, and it obviously inspires the depiction of 'heaven on earth' in yet a third work: *The Dream of a Comic Man*. Significantly, perhaps, in all three the harmony is ultimately marred.

But it is the same interrelation of visual beauty and utopian allegory, which is presented to us in the figures of Nastasya Filippovna and Aglaya. Behind the external beauty of these two women (beauty which is likened to that of a picture) there is concealed a tentative promise of universal harmony: a world saved either by a national religious ideal, or by an ideal which is secular and political.

Yet all five facets of beauty which the novel presents are in the end flawed and imperfect; thus it is significant that the picture which is the symbolic heart of the work is Hans Holbein's *The Entombment of Christ*.

But is the novel entirely negative? When Myshkin is asked by Rogozhin about the state of faith inside Russia, he replies by telling his four stories. Yet only one of these gives an affirmation of true faith: this is the story of the peasant girl with the baby at her breast. The novel too seems to reflect the preponderance of the negative; both of Myshkin's ideals of beauty fail; but there is, nevertheless, another female character in the novel who represents yet a third ideal of beauty. Her name is Vera – the Russian word for faith; and she too, like the peasant girl of Myshkin's story, carries a baby: the baby's name is Lyubov' – the Russian word for love.

In Vera Lebedev and her baby sister, Dostoyevsky seems to be presenting us with an allegory based on Myshkin's fourth story, showing the intimate connection between love and faith. The author stresses that Vera and the baby are closely associated; for instance we read: 'At that moment Vera with the baby in her arms, as was customary for her, came out of the room on to the terrace.' (Pt II, Ch. 6.)

Vera, although apparently a minor character, is always presented very positively, and in a way which links her closely with Myshkin. Thus she does not always appear with the baby in her arms; after the reading of the 'The Poor Knight' by Aglaya, she enters the room bearing, not the baby, but the complete works of Pushkin. The national poet, as we have seen, has great importance for Myshkin, for not only is he himself identified with a figure in one of his poems, but we know too that the prince read through the whole of Pushkin with Rogozhin in an attempt to educate him aesthetically.

Moreover, Vera Lebedev shows traits of character which Myshkin himself prizes, and which seem lacking in the ideals of beauty to whom he is attracted. Thus she shows serenity and compassion, expressing sympathy for characters who are wayward and not readily likeable: she reminds her father that he is keeping the nihilistic friends of Burdovsky waiting in vain; she intercedes with Myshkin on behalf of Ippolit.

Her intercession for Ippolit, although unnecessary, is nevertheless in keeping with the behaviour of Myshkin himself; that her actions are in the spirit of the prince's own teachings is further underlined by the fact that at the very time of her intercession she is giving practical expression to another of Myshkin's precepts: she is with a servant, working as a servant, cleaning the terrace.

Such activity is typical of Vera. Unlike Nastasya Filippovna or Aglaya she brings not chaos but order. On two occasions the prince finds her tidying up. Here (the first time), it is after the chaos of his birthday celebrations, and not only is she the bringer of physical order, she also gives spiritual comfort to Myshkin, who is tired after the harrowing incidents of the long night; her words seem like an affirmation of faith in Myshkin as the perceiver of beauty: '"And although you are tired", she laughed, half turning in order to leave, "you have marvellous eyes at this moment, happy eyes".' (Pt III, Ch. 9.) But at this point Myshkin's appreciation of the true worth of Vera seems shortlived; for his mind is preoccupied with Nastasya Filippovna and Aglaya: '"What a wonderful girl", thought the prince, and immediately forgot about her.'

When later he has been deserted by both Aglaya and Nastasya Filippovna, Vera Lebedev again brings him consolation. This time she has been clearing away the remains of the prince's abortive wedding feast; Myshkin now openly expresses his regard for her:

And finally, when she had fully opened the door to go out, the prince stopped her yet a third time, took her by the hands, kissed them, then kissed her herself on the forehead, and with an 'unusual' expression on his face, said to her: 'Until tomorrow'.

(Pt IV, Ch. 10)

The words: 'until tomorrow', refer to Vera's promise to wake the prince early so that he may set out unhindered to search for Nastasya Filippovna. The secret of the prince's final quest is entrusted to Vera alone. This much the author underlines by the words with which he chooses to end the chapter: 'It turned out, therefore, that at that moment he had found it possible and necessary to tell her alone that he was setting out for the city.'

Once again Vera Lebedev comes into the prince's thoughts, as he is sitting in his hotel room, after his initial failure to find Nastasya Filippovna in St Petersburg, and it seems appropriate that at this crisis in the relationship of Nastasya Filippovna and Myshkin, the role of Vera Lebedev should assume such prominence; for the two women invite comparison. The virgin with a baby in her arms ('In place of a mother, but no more than a sister', Lebedev is quick to explain) is not only *Faith* nursing *Love* – she is, too, an obvious madonna figure, and as such is a direct comment on the unrealised potentialities of the portrait of Nastasya Filippovna. There is something terrifying in this portrait, and once more it is the eyes which are symbolic. Thus Myshkin confesses to Radomsky:

'You do not know, Yevgeniy Pavlovich', (he lowered his voice mysteriously) 'I have never said this to anyone, not even Aglaya, but I cannot bear the face of Nastasya Filippovna... Just now you said the truth about that evening gathering at Nastasya Filippovna's, but there is one thing which you have left out, because you did not know it: I looked at *her face*! I couldn't bear it that very morning even, in the portrait... Vera, that is Vera Lebedev, has quite different eyes. I fear her face!' he added with exceptional terror.

(Pt IV, Ch. 9)

The beauty of Vera, the true faith, is after all quite different from that of Nastasya Filippovna, the bride of schism. Myshkin expresses his love for Nastasya Filippovna as though at a remove: he kisses her portrait (with Aglaya he merely kisses her letter) – but with Vera Lebedev, he kisses her hands, then kisses 'her herself' on the forehead.

But if Vera Lebedev is the third ideal: the true ideal of Faith nursing Love, it must be admitted that this is an ideal which is very sketchily put forward. What is interesting too, is that she is the daughter of Lebedev, and therefore her origins point to the same dichotomy which the double ideal of Aglaya and Nastasya Filippovna presents; for in Lebedev are embodied both religious fanaticism and a sneaking regard for nihilism. On the one hand, Lebedev prays for the soul of Mme Dubarry and has earned the reputation of a 'professor of Antichrist' because of his ability to interpret the Apocalypse: on the other hand, he is secretly proud of his nihilistic nephew, and even corrects the article which the nihilists write to 'expose' Myshkin.

Vera Lebedev thus bears a relationship to both the 'ideals of beauty' which are before Myshkin; in her person there is a faint ray of hope not only for the success of these two ideals, but also for a positive ending to the novel itself. It is only to be expected that she should reappear in the Conclusion.

Here we learn that Vera is so overwhelmed by grief at what has happened to the prince, that she falls ill. She is informed about the state of the prince's health by letters which Radomsky sends to her from Switzerland. Through these letters, it is hinted, a love relationship is developing between these two.

So Radomsky seems to become almost some sort of substitute for Myshkin himself. In the novel he has had the role of the reasonable man who explains everything, and is the mouthpiece for some of the author's own ideas. In his mouth such ideas are not compromised, for he has the grace of gesture which Myshkin himself lacks.

This is the nearest approach to a positive ending which the novel offers us: the future seems to lie with Radomsky, Vera Lebedev and Myshkin's own youthful disciple, Kolya Ivolgin.

THE CONDEMNED MAN:
'THE IDIOT'

So far we have looked at *The Idiot* as an elaborate allegory. The names of characters; the obvious use of symbols; the nature of certain incidents which seem charged with special significance – all lead us inevitably to this view of the work. *The Idiot* is not the most readily comprehensible of Dostoyevsky's novels, but it is, of course, much more vivid and alive than its reduction to an allegory might suggest. Nevertheless it is essential to examine the allegorical skeleton of the work, in order to see why its living flesh takes the forms that it does.

It is, moreover, salutary to dwell on the structure of Dostoyevsky's novels, as the allegation is often made that his writing lacks form. Yet the immense amount of effort which Dostoyevsky put into the numerous versions and drafts of the novel before he arrived at his ultimate conception of the work hardly suggests that he was slipshod in his preparations. There are perhaps two distinct processes at work in his creative activity: there is the architectural conception, which involves the ordering and structuring of ideas and scenes; and there is, at the same time, a kind of spontaneous growth (one often feels – explosion) which springs from the very process of writing itself.

In *The Idiot*, for example, the impression is gained that a character like Ganya Ivolgin was originally cast for a more important role in the novel than is ultimately the case: the reverse seems true of Ippolit Terentev, who in the second half of the novel suddenly assumes great prominence. The author himself is aware of this tendency of his characters to go their own way, and feels called upon to comment on it. Thus he says of General Ivolgin:

However much we have tried, we have nevertheless been faced with the necessity of devoting a little more time and space to this secondary character in our tale, than we had up till now proposed.

(Pt IV, Ch. 3)

A positive feature of such spontaneity in the creative process is the communication of greater freshness and immediacy; in a Dostoyevsky novel there is an ever present feeling that the unexpected lurks on the very next page.

But the fact that there is a sub-structure of allegory in *The Idiot* raises the same question that was posed by *Crime and Punishment*: to what extent is Dostoyevsky a realistic writer? One character in the novel who above all others tries to present invention as fact is General Ivolgin, and his absurd reminiscences throw the problems of reality and fiction into sharp relief, not only for other characters, but even for the author himself. Thus when the prince takes up one of Ivolgin's remarks on the way that authors distort reality, these words read more like Dostoyevsky's own defence of *Crime and Punishment*:

I know of a certain murder which was committed for a watch.[1] It is now in the papers. Had a writer thought it up, the experts on national life and the critics would immediately have cried out that it was improbable; but reading it as a fact in the papers, one feels that it is precisely from facts such as these that one learns about Russian reality. (Pt IV, Ch. 4)

Much the same idea had been put forward earlier in the novel by Lebedev, and again it had been prompted by the fantastic stories of General Ivolgin:

For my own part I will remark that almost any kind of reality, even though it may have its immutable laws, is almost always improbable and unlikely; and the more real it is, even, the more improbable it often is.[2] (Pt III, Ch. 4)

Thus through the mouths of two of his characters Dostoyevsky appears to be conducting a defence of the realism of his own art, along the lines that 'truth is stranger than fiction'. In the second half of the novel it is indeed noticeable that such a defence is being carried on; here there is a marked intrusion of the author into his own novel as a commentator on the problems of reality and fiction. Part III opens with a preamble by Dostoyevsky in which 'Russian reality' is once more to the fore; it is a disquisition on the supposed absence of practical people in Russia. Much more relevant to his own methods of characterisation, however, is the introduction with which he thinks fit to open Part IV. Here the problems involved in depicting the 'ordinary man' in literature are discussed:

So, without going into deeper explanations, we will merely say that in the real world, the typicality of characters is, as it were, watered down; all these Georges Dandins and Podkolesins[3] do exist in reality, and are scurrying to and fro, and running about before us every day, but in a diluted state, as it were. Finally, asserting for the sake of the whole truth that even a Georges Dandin in his entirety, as he was created by Molière, can also be encountered in the real world, although rarely, we will finish our discussion, which is beginning to become like a critical article in a journal. (Pt IV, Ch. 1)

This argument on the 'watering down of typicality' in the real world does not seem entirely consonant with the ideas put forward by Myshkin and Lebedev that 'truth is stranger than fiction': but there is a common purpose behind both lines of thought – each in its own way serves to justify any heightening of reality, any 'concentration of typicality', which the reader might detect in Dostoyevsky's own writing.

As the apologist of his own art, the author is present in the second half of the novel not merely in the guise of omniscient interpreter; he can, too, assume a 'brazen naivety' (the expression is his own) as though he is absolving himself from all responsibility for events which are as inevitable, and yet as inexplicable, as real facts, and which thus lie beyond his own control – even beyond his own comprehension:

Two weeks have passed since the event related in the last chapter, and the situation of the characters of our tale has changed so much that it is very difficult for us to embark on the continuation, without special explanations. However, we feel that, as far as this is possible, we must confine ourselves to a simple presentation of the facts without special explanations, and this for a very simple reason: namely that we ourselves have difficulty in explaining what happened in many instances. Such a warning must seem very strange and unclear to the reader. How can one relate something, about which one has no clear understanding or personal opinion?...

(Pt IV, Ch. 9)

One good reason why certain events in the novel may seem inexplicable (even to the author himself) lies in the fact that the motivation of Dostoyevsky's characters depends for the most part, not so much on rational considerations, as on other, 'psychological', factors. Dostoyevsky has, of course, long been hailed as the pre-Freudian master of psychological perception. In another of his asides (in which once more he claims it to be more expedient to confine himself to a simple presentation of events) the author comments:

Let us not forget that the reasons for human actions are immeasurably more complicated and varied than we explain them as being in retrospect; and rarely are they precisely delineated.   (Pt IV, Ch. 3)

Yet much of the 'inexplicable' behaviour of the characters is credible in terms of their own psychology; and in the course of the novel various psychological insights are vouchsafed which go a long way towards explaining the more extreme behaviour which some of them exhibit. At the end of Part I, for example, Ptitsyn comments on the self-laceration to which Nastasya Filippovna has subjected herself before Totsky (Afanasiy Ivanovich) and the assembled guests:

'Do you know, Afanasiy Ivanovich, it is like what is said to happen in Japan', remarked Ivan Petrovich Ptitsyn. 'There the injured party, so they say, goes to the one who has wronged him, and says to him: "You have wronged me, and because of this I have come to rip open my belly before your eyes", and with these words he does indeed rip open his belly before the eyes of the one who has wronged him, and feels, I suppose, great satisfaction, just as though he had in fact revenged himself. The world has some strange people in it, Afanasiy Ivanovich!'   (Pt I, Ch. 16)

With disarming naivety Ptitsyn has confided his observation to the person for whom, above all others, it has most relevance.

A similar piece of paradoxical 'psychology' is put forward

jokingly by Radomsky, only to be taken up fervently by Lebedev as a serious insight: 'in human beings, the law of self-
destruction and the law of self-preservation are of equal
power'. In the context of the prince's birthday party, where the
assertion occurs, it would seem to have relevance for Ippolit,
who, as Lebedev himself suspects, has already planned to commit suicide; but its implications are yet wider: it sheds light
on the attitude of Nastasya Filippovna to Rogozhin. In the same
scene Lebedev tells his story of the penitent monk-eater, and
from this delightfully irreverent piece of nonsense draws the
moral that in human beings the need for repentance is an overwhelming force. Lebedev himself turns this need for repentance
into a psychological weapon against his friend General Ivolgin
by refusing to acknowledge the latter's many bungling but
discreet attempts at repentance in the incident with the stolen
wallet. But yet again this psychological truth has relevance for
Nastasya Filippovna too; for much of her irrational behaviour
can be attributed to her overpowering need for contrition.

Indeed, despite the overtones of allegory, the triangular
relationship of Myshkin, Nastasya Filippovna and Aglaya is
entirely credible in psychological terms: Myshkin is motivated
by sympathy for Nastasya Filippovna, but she is torn between
feelings of her own guilt and promptings towards revenge on a
world which has wronged her; Myshkin offers her a new life,
but she deems herself unworthy of him, and ultimately chooses
her own destruction at the hands of Rogozhin. It is in these
terms that Myshkin explains her behaviour to her rival, Aglaya:

This unfortunate woman is deeply convinced that she is the most
fallen, the most sinful of all earthly beings [...] Oh, she constantly
cries out in frenzy that she regards herself as guiltless, that she is the
victim of a debauchee and a villain; but whatever she tells you, you
must realise that she is the first not to believe what she says, and that,
on the contrary, she believes with all her heart that she herself is
guilty [...] She ran away from me; do you know why? Merely to
prove to me that she was a worthless woman; but the most terrible
thing in this is that perhaps she herself did not know that she wanted
to prove this to me alone. She ran off because inwardly she felt that

she had to do something shameful, in order then to say to herself: 'You have just perpetrated a new act of shame, you must be a worthless creature.' Oh, perhaps you cannot understand this, Aglaya, but do you know that in this constant awareness of her shame there is perhaps some terrible and unnatural enjoyment for her, as though it were revenge on someone. At times I brought her to the point where it seemed that she again saw light around her, but immediately she would once more grow so indignant, that she would bitterly accuse me of elevating myself above her (when such a thought never entered my head) and finally she bluntly announced to me, as regards my offer of marriage, that she did not demand arrogant compassion, or help, or 'raising up to his level' from anyone.

(Pt III, Ch. 8)

Aglaya's relationship with the prince is to some extent conditioned by her earlier rivalry with Nastasya Filippovna over their common suitor, Ganya Ivolgin; for after the discrediting of Ganya, his role as a 'bone of contention' between the two women is taken over by Myshkin. Aglaya's behaviour seems just as capricious as that of her rival, and at first she too refuses Myshkin's hand, excusing her provocative behaviour as that of 'a spoilt child'. There is, indeed, in Aglaya something of the perversity of a spoilt child, but at the same time there is in her love for the prince an element not unlike the quality of Myshkin's own love for Nastasya Filippovna: there is sympathy for 'the insulted and injured'. Varvara Ivolgin points to this mixture of perversity and compassion in the character of Aglaya, when she tells her brother:

She would turn away from the most eligible of suitors, and would run off gladly to the garret of some student or other to starve to death – that is her dream! [...] The prince lured her by the fact that in the first place he did not lure her at all, and secondly by the fact that he is an idiot. The mere fact alone that because of him she can now sow confusion in her family, that is what appeals to her now.

(Pt IV, Ch. 1)

But some aspects of the psychological depths of both women seem difficult to explain in terms of the logic of the everyday real world; at one point, in order to give at least *some* explanation, the author falls back on the logic of dreams. This is what he says about the letters of Nastasya Filippovna to Aglaya:

These letters too were like a dream. Sometimes you have strange dreams, impossible and unnaturalistic ones. On waking you remember them clearly and are surprised at a strange fact. You remember, first of all, that your reason did not desert you through all that long, long time when you were surrounded by murderers; when they cunningly deceived you; concealed their intention and behaved towards you in a friendly way when, in fact, they had a weapon at the ready, and were merely waiting, for some sign. You remember how cunningly you finally deceived them, and hid from them. Then you guessed that they knew every detail of your deception, and were only pretending that they did not know where you were hidden. But you were wily and deceived them again. You remember all this clearly. But how, at the same time, can your reason be reconciled to the obvious absurdities and impossibilities which also crowded your dream? One of your murderers turned into a woman before your eyes, and from a woman into a cunning, vile, little dwarf; and you immediately accepted all this as an accomplished fact, almost without the slightest trace of bewilderment, and precisely when your rational faculties, on the other hand, were at a very high pitch of concentration, showing exceptional powers of cunning, insight and logic? When you have awakened from your dream, and have returned completely to the real world, why is it that almost every time you feel (and sometimes the impression is unusually powerful) that in your dreams you have left behind something which has an unsolved significance for you. You smile at the absurdity of your dream, yet at the same time feel that all this weft of absurdities contains an idea – a real idea; something which pertains to the actuality of your life; something which exists in your heart, and has always existed there. It is as though through this dream you have been told something new and prophetic; something you have been expecting. The impression is a strong one, it may bring either joy or pain, but what it consists in, and what you have been told – all this you can neither understand nor remember. After reading these letters the effect was almost the same.   (Pt III, Ch. 10)

One may ask in what way this passage helps to shed light on the letters of Nastasya Filippovna to Aglaya. One approach to the problem might dwell on the strong homosexual element in the letters themselves and see a reflection of abnormality in the inversion of sexes described in the dream (another explanation of Nastasya Filippovna's feelings of guilt!), but perhaps, after all, there is no need to look further than Myshkin's own explanation for the perversity of her behaviour. The logic behind the symbols in the dream here described does indeed seem to be one of inversion (a murderer becomes a woman, who in turn becomes a vaguely ominous dwarf); but what this sequence suggests is a typically Dostoyevskian alternation between aggression and submission, which is in keeping with Nastasya Filippovna's desire for revenge on the one hand, and her pangs of guilt on the other. The 'dream-like' quality of these letters is to be seen in the light of such an inversion: in them a rival speaks, not with hostility and abuse, but with admiration and love amounting to self-abasement.

This long digression on dreams has, however, even greater significance. Dreams always bulk large in Dostoyevsky's novels, and perhaps part of the secret of the strange power of his art lies in its closeness to the world of dreams; for the reality of a Dostoyevsky novel is not, after all, the reality of everyday life with its 'watered down typicality' – it is rather a heightened reality, in which actions and relationships seem often more symbolic than naturalistic; yet we, like the dreamer in the digression, 'immediately accept all this as an accomplished fact, almost without the slightest trace of bewilderment'.

In the dream here described, four main elements may be discerned: the threateningly violent, cat-and-mouse 'plot'; the fluidity of shapes and concepts; the high-pitched concentration of the rational faculties; and the impression, on reflection, that all this has some unrevealed significance. This could be a description of one of Dostoyevsky's own novels. Indeed, it might be said that in the typical Dostoyevsky novel the central figure is plunged into 'the dream' of the plot, in which the dominant incidents reflect violence, subterfuge and a feeling of foreboding. In this 'dream' he is confronted by strange transformations – the identification of character with character

– and by concepts which shift into their opposites: all of which in some enigmatic way seems charged with special significance for him. But yet there is another level too, a level of reality at which 'reason does not desert him throughout all that long, long time' – a level at which intellectual argument is often carried on at a 'high pitch of concentration'. As a broad analogy this is true for Raskolnikov in *Crime and Punishment*, for Myshkin in *The Idiot*, and for Stavrogin in *The Devils*.[4]

Dostoyevsky's novels, like many of his characters, are 'broad'; they operate on many levels, and the structure of *The Idiot* can accommodate a host of opposites: realism and allegory, reason and the irrational, virtue and vice, comedy and tragedy. This 'broadness' can be seen reflected, as it were in microcosm, in the figure of Lebedev; he above all other characters in *The Idiot* exhibits that fluidity of concepts which is such an integral part of a Dostoyevsky novel. With Lebedev religiosity can yield place to a sneaking admiration for the nihilists, even to active participation in their schemes; blatant lies can be accommodated with profound truths; self-abasement is mingled with arrogance; crude buffoonery is compatible with acute psychological perception; comedy turns into tragedy. Indeed this logic of inversion can be seen even in Lebedev's attitude to his own name, which he tells the prince is 'Timofey Lukanovich': his real name, as his nephew is quick to point out, is Lukyan Timofeyevich.

The role of Lebedev is that of the 'go-between'; he links all the various groups of characters in the novel, and in particular his presence as a 'hanger on' both in Rogozhin's company and amongst the friends of Burdovsky helps to establish a parallel between these two contrasted forms of extremism; in this capacity he is supported by Keller. But, above all, Lebedev is an intermediary between the realism of the novel and its allegory. On the one hand he is a man of the times, whose values seem firmly rooted in the 'real' world, and he is one of the few characters in the novel for whom evidence of earning a living is provided. Exploiting the boom in litigation which occurred as a result of the law reform in 1864, Lebedev has turned himself into a lawyer. His attitude, here again, is 'realistic'; thus his nephew chides him, because in a recent case he chose to defend a money lender rather than his destitute victim, since the money lender offered him fifty roubles.

Yet, on the other hand, Lebedev is an idealist with a passion for eschatology; and the materialism of contemporary life, of which he himself is so much a part, he seeks to condemn on the authority of the Apocalypse. We have already seen that in *The Idiot* pictures assume an allegorical importance for many of the characters; Lebedev, too, presents us with a pictorial allegory; he interprets the growing railway network of Europe as the Star of Wormwood which falls on the springs of life – it is 'a picture, an artistic impression of the materialistic tendency of the age'.

If the dream discussed above holds good as an analogue of the typical Dostoyevsky novel, it should come as no surprise that echoes of that most portentous of all literary dreams, The Revelation of St John the Divine, reverberate on the pages of *The Idiot*. Moreover it is an interesting fact, in view of the religious aura which surrounds her, that Nastasya Filippovna shares Lebedev's enthusiasm for the Apocalypse. Both of them concur in their interpretation of a passage which is of some consequence for the *allegory* of the novel as a key to contemporary *reality*:

She agreed with me that we have reached the third black horse and the rider holding a pair of balances[5] in his hand, as everything in the present age is by measure and by treaty, and everyone looks only for his rights. (Pt ΙΙ, Ch. 2)

This interpretation seems to point to the commercialism of the age, and in the novel this certainly has its representatives in such figures as General Yepanchin, Ptitsyn, Ganya Ivolgin and even Lebedev himself; but there are more outstanding representatives of this 'age of the balances' and they are of a different order: these are the 'nihilists' – the young men who champion the rights of Burdovsky.

In Russia, in the 1860's, life had become a sort of court room; not only had the legal profession itself assumed new prominence after the reforms, but ordinary people were tempted to take the law into their own hands. This preoccupation with rights, with measuring and judging, was the ruling passion of the younger generation. Lebedev's words: 'everyone looks only for his rights' point, therefore to the excessive 'ethical' preoccupation of his age; and Radomsky, the spokesman of sanity in the novel, underlines how closely the behaviour of the champions of Burdovsky conforms to Lebedev's interpretation:

Everything which I have heard from your comrades, Mr. Terentev, and all that you yourself have expounded just now with such undoubted talent boils down in my opinion to the theory of the triumph of rights, before all else, even to the exclusion of everything else, and even perhaps before looking into the question of what rights themselves consist in.   (Pt II, Ch. 10)

Much the same preoccupation with 'rights' (though in an extreme form), we have met before in the law student Raskolnikov. In *The Idiot*, the champions of Burdovsky are his spiritual brothers. Dostoyevsky had sought to prove that the figure of Raskolnikov was no fantasy, but could be justified in fact, by pointing to the murder of a money-lender by a student, Danilov, which was committed when *Crime and Punishment* was still coming out.[6] In the continuation of Radomsky's argument, the connection between the ideas of Burdovsky's champions and those of Raskolnikov is established by reference to this same Danilov:

There could be a jump straight from this to the rights of force; that is to the rights of the individual fist, and of personal desires.

there is no great distance from the rights of force to the rights of tigers and crocodiles, and even to those of Danilov and Gorsky.

The crime of Danilov, and by implication of Raskolnikov, is therefore seen as a logical outcome of the younger generation's preoccupation with rights. The reference to Gorsky strengthens the argument;[7] this eighteen-year-old youth had murdered six members of a certain Zhemarin family, for reasons which, Dostoyevsky considered, were inspired by nihilism.

Earlier in the novel Lebedev had introduced his nihilistic nephew as 'allegorically speaking the future murderer of a future second Zhemarin family'. Gorsky is constantly referred to in the novel, and in a way which widens the scope of the argument, by suggesting that nihilistic ideas have spread even to the very courts themselves. Thus Mrs Yepanchin takes up Radomsky's remarks on Gorsky's trial, and in so doing strikes somewhat the same apocalyptic note as Lebedev in his interpretation of the age:

If, as you yourself said a moment ago, Yevgeniy Pavlovich, a counsel for the defence declared in court that when one has motives of poverty there is nothing more natural than to kill six people, then indeed the last hour has come. I have never heard of such a thing. Now everything is clear to me. And this stammerer, do you think he would not commit murder? (she pointed at Burdovsky who was looking at her in extreme perplexity). I am prepared to bet that he would commit murder. Perhaps he will not accept your money, your ten thousand or so; and perhaps he will not accept it on grounds of conscience. But he will come at night and murder you; will take it out of your coffer; will take it then on grounds of conscience. That in his reckoning is not dishonourable; that is 'the prompting of noble despair'; that is 'negation'; devil knows what it is, for him. Phew! Everyone has turned himself inside out; everyone has turned himself upside down. A young girl grows up at home; suddenly in the middle of the street she jumps into a carriage: 'Mummy, the other day I married so and so Karlych or Ivanych, Goodbye!' Do you think it is a good thing to behave like that? Does it merit respect? Is it natural? Is this Women's Rights?   (Pt II, Ch. 9)

At the end of this passage Mrs Yepanchin is parodying an incident in Chernyshevsky's novel: *What is to be done?*, and for her all these phenomena – the words of Gorsky's defence counsel, the behaviour of Burdovsky, the novel by Chernyshevsky, the rights of women (in which her own daughters are implicated) – all these are of a piece; they reflect the obsession of the younger generation with 'the triumph of rights'.

In the Burdovsky affair itself, the prince has refrained from wholesale condemnation of the younger generation, but at a later stage, Radomsky once more brings up the words of Gorsky's counsel, and asks Myshkin a question which he claims he has specially prepared for him: 'This perversion of ideas and convictions, the possibility of such a warped view in this matter, is this a special case or is it general?' (Pt III, Ch. 1.) The prince is now forced to admit that this is not a particular case, and a little later Radomsky seeks to extend its typicality by asking a second question: how it was that the prince did not notice the same perversion of ideas and moral convictions in the Burdovsky affair?

Thus Burdovsky and his friends are presented as a phenomenon characteristic of the age, which at its most extreme produces Danilovs, Gorskys and Raskolnikovs. The champions of Burdovsky in pursuing their 'theory of the triumph of rights before all else' rush to pass judgement on Myshkin out of hand; in them can be seen the chief embodiment of Lebedev's age of the balances,[8] in which 'everyone looks only for his own rights'.

In the light of this, the prince's assertion that beauty will save the world can be seen in a new perspective; for the ideologues of this 'triumph of rights' – Chernyshevsky, Dobrolyubov and Pisarev – had attacked the role of the aesthetic as a guiding principle in life: even as a guiding principle in art itself. Pushkin, in particular (whose importance for Myshkin is obvious), had come in for strong censure from the younger generation, who sought to substitute their own *ethical* criteria for life and literature in place of the *aestheticism* of the national poet and the older generation; indeed Pisarev had gone so far as to pronounce the destruction of aesthetics. It is obvious, then, that through the figure of Myshkin, Dostoyevsky is seeking to attack his younger contemporaries by inverting their values; for their 'triumph of ethics' he is substituting 'the triumph of aesthetics': beauty will save the world; and Myshkin, the bearer of the aesthetic message is thus Dostoyevsky's own positive reply to the ethically preoccupied Raskolnikov.

In *The Idiot* the conflict between these two opposing principles finds its concrete expression in the Burdovsky sub-plot.

Here the ethical preoccupation of the younger generation is in collision with the aesthetic values of the older generation, but, pre-eminently, with those of Myshkin himself. In spite of the crude attempts of the 'nihilists' to assert the rights of Burdovsky it is the prince who through his magnanimity, his beauty of spirit, emerges as the moral victor; whereas the defeated Ippolit can only deride his opponents for their aestheticism:

You all hate Burdovsky, because, in your opinion, his attitude to his mother has been ugly and inelegant. Isn't that so? Isn't that so? For all of you terribly love external beauty and elegance of form. That is all you will stand up for. Isn't that true? (I have suspected for a long time that that is all you will stand up for).   (Pt II, Ch. 10)

Moreover, that Myshkin's assertion: 'beauty will save the world', is to be taken as a direct challenge to the values of his age may be seen later in the novel, when, during the celebrations on Myshkin's birthday, Lebedev challenges 'all atheists' to tell him 'with what they will save the world?'

The friends of Burdovsky judge the prince and condemn him before they know the full facts; the danger of judging people is brought home to Myshkin early in the novel. He is here speaking to Ganya:

'I will never consider you a rogue from now on', said the prince. 'I had quite thought of you, a while ago, as a villain; now you have suddenly reassured me to the contrary. Here is a lesson: do not judge without experience.'   (Pt I, Ch. 11)

It will be seen from this that Myshkin does not appear to rule out all judgement – only rash condemnation not based on experience. The champions of Burdovsky condemn the prince before they know the truth of the matter; yet to pass judgement, even when guided by the truth, can be unjust. This is a second lesson which Myshkin learns after he has told Aglaya about Ippolit's attempted suicide:

I think that all this is very bad of you, because it is very crude to look at a human soul and judge it as you judge Ippolit. You have no tenderness, just stark truth; therefore it is unjust.   (Pt III, Ch. 8)

These words of Aglaya obviously make a strong impression on Myshkin:

A few moments ago you suddenly said something very intelligent; you said about my doubts on Ippolit: 'here there is just stark truth, therefore it is unjust'. I shall remember this and think about it.

This is some measure of the difficulties confronting Myshkin in his desire to avoid judging, and throughout the novel the all-forgiving tolerance of the prince is constantly being tried. On two occasions he is forced to intervene physically in other people's affairs, in order to prevent further violence, and on one occasion he even loses his temper (this is with Lebedev when he suggests the opening of Aglaya's letter). Nor again is his tirade against Roman Catholicism consonant with his own ideas on humility and compassion; and when later, in *The Brothers Karamazov*, Dostoyevsky sought to portray the confrontation between the real Christ and the ideas of the Roman Church, he did not make Christ rail against the Grand Inquisitor – he had him kiss him!

It is because of 'passion' like this that Myshkin breaks the Chinese vase, and it seems that there is something of the vase's fragility in human relationships. Thus great tact is called for in handling General Ivolgin:

Excusing himself, the prince hastened to sit down, but felt in some way strangely timid, just as though his guest were made of china and he were constantly afraid of breaking him. (Pt IV, Ch. 4)

Later the prince's attempts to show understanding and sympathy for Ippolit meet with this comment:

Because of the naivety with which you refused to agree with me, I understand that you are now trying to console me. Ha, ha! You are a complete child, prince. But I notice that you are always treating me as though I were a china cup. Never mind, never mind, I am not angry. (Pt IV, Ch. 5)

We have already seen that Aglaya reproves Myshkin for judging Ippolit in his *truthful* but *unfair* account of Ippolit's actions, but earlier in the novel, Myshkin himself had pleaded with Radomsky for a more tolerant attitude towards Ippolit's behaviour, insisting that he wanted to forgive as well as to be forgiven; for this he is rebuked by Prince Shch.:

Paradise on earth is not easily achieved; but, for all that, you seem to be counting on paradise. Paradise is a difficult thing, prince, much more difficult than your own good [*prekrasnyy*] heart realises.[9]

(Pt III, Ch. 1)

Paradise on earth is the ultimate goal of the 'triumph of rights' for which Ippolit has set himself up as spokesman; but it is a theme which, as we have seen, is also connected with Aglaya. The words of Prince Shch. may be read as a warning on the difficulties he will encounter in dealing with the nihilistic temperament; for Aglaya too, like Ippolit, indulges in hasty judgements and petulant criticism and it is the behaviour of Aglaya which presents Myshkin with one of his greatest challenges.

On first meeting Aglaya, Myshkin had declined to express an opinion on her character, saying that it was difficult to judge beauty. But judgement can not be avoided; he is present at the confrontation of Nastasya Filippovna and Aglaya, and when his 'Judgement of Paris' appears to have gone against Aglaya the effect on her is overwhelming. Radomsky reproves the prince in words which suggest that once again he has broken a fragile and priceless object:

But you really ought to have understood how serious and how strong the feelings of this girl were...towards you. She did not wish to share you with another woman. And how could you, how could you cast away and break such a treasure! (Pt IV, Ch. 9)

By using such symbols of aesthetic fragility to describe Myshkin's attitude to the other characters, Dostoyevsky seems to be emphasising the difficulties inherent in the prince's attempt to see beauty in his fellow creatures and to preserve it; not to weigh them in any balances. Non-judgement can in itself be a form of judgement, which can threaten the fragility of such beauty. So it is, that in refusing to be critical of General Ivolgin's incredible stories the prince provokes him to hostility:

That very evening he received a strange note, which was short but decisive. The general informed him that he was breaking with him for ever, that he respected him and was grateful to him, but that he would not take 'marks of sympathy lowering to the dignity of a man already beset by enough misfortune' even from him.   (Pt IV, Ch. 4)

The same is true for Ippolit, who resents being treated as a china cup; but the outcome for Aglaya is even more devastating: the treasure is shattered through the prince's futile attempt to avoid judgement.

Thus Myshkin's aesthetic attitude to human relationships is ultimately found wanting. In the last chapter we saw how closely his ideas on beauty were connected with his epilepsy, and how their insubstantiality was expressed through the onset of the second fit; but the first fit, too, has great symbolic importance for the prince's outlook on life – it marks a crisis of 'judgement'. The whole scene deserves close attention.

Hanging over the events which culminate in the second fit there is that symbol of aesthetic fragility – the Chinese vase; there is another such symbol in the scene of the first fit: a symbol of judgement. This is 'The Scales', a hotel in St Petersburg which is mentioned both at the beginning and at the end of the scene. Significantly, perhaps, it is not the prince's own hotel but that of Kolya Ivolgin: a figure who links the ideas of Myshkin with the younger generation; for the prince is in a state of mind in which he cannot refrain from passing hasty and sweeping condemnations.

The mood begins as one of suspiciousness:

It suddenly happened that he consciously caught himself in the act of something, which he had been doing for a long time, but which he had not noticed until that very moment. For several hours now, even while he was at 'The Scales', perhaps even before he had gone to 'The Scales', he had from time to time suddenly begun looking round about him, as though seeking something. Then he would forget to do so for as long as half an hour; then suddenly look round uneasily and search about him.   (Pt II, Ch. 5)

This mood soon passes into one of outright judgement; dark

unformed suspicions about Rogozhin and 'the Russian soul' become confused with Lebedev's nephew and the way in which his uncle had introduced him as an allegorical second Gorsky:

And what a disgusting, smug pimple that nephew of Lebedev's was! But what am I saying? (the prince's musings continued). Of course it was not he who killed those beings, those six people. It is as though I have got it all muddled. How strange it is! My head seems to be going round and round.

At this point positive values reassert themselves; for he continues:

And what a sympathetic, charming face Lebedev's eldest daughter has; the one who stood with the baby. What an innocent almost childish expression she had, her laughter too was almost like that of a child! It was strange that he had almost forgotten this face, and only now recalled it.

So the faith represented by Vera Lebedev is easily forgotten, and Myshkin feels guilty about these hasty condemnations, which seem to have suggested themselves to him against his will, like the whisperings of an evil demon:

But why had he taken it on himself to pass such final judgements on them, he who had only appeared that day? Why was he pronouncing such condemnations?

Yet it is not only Lebedev's nephew who is confused with Gorsky; in the prince's mind the two extremes of nihilism and religious fanaticism become equated in a common identification with this same murderer:

But if Rogozhin were to commit murder, he would not kill so senselessly. There would not be that same chaos: a weapon ordered to specification from a drawing, and yet six people laid low in a state of complete mental confusion! But had Rogozhin ordered a weapon to specification from a drawing? … He had a … but … was it cut and dried that Rogozhin would kill?! The prince suddenly shuddered. 'Is it not a crime, is it not wicked of me to make such a supposition with such cynical frankness!' he cried out, and a flush of shame immediately covered his face.

Then once again, as after the musings on Lebedev's nephew, more positive ideas strive to reassert themselves:

No Rogozhin was slandering himself. He had a great heart which could suffer and feel compassion. When he learned all the truth, and when he was convinced what a pathetic creature this afflicted, half-crazy woman was, would he not then forgive her all the past, and all his sufferings? Would he not become her servant, her brother, her friend, her providence? Compassion would teach even Rogozhin and bring him to his senses. Compassion is the chief and perhaps the sole law of existence for the whole of humanity. Oh, how unforgiveably, and how dishonourably, he had wronged Rogozhin! No, it was not a case of 'the Russian soul is a dark mystery', the darkness was in his own soul, if he could imagine such horror.

But it is not merely the prince's words which betray a lack of trust in Rogozhin; his actions, too, reveal suspicion. In the scene of the exchange of the crosses he had reproached Rogozhin for not believing in him when he was not with him; now it is rather the prince who does not believe in Rogozhin, and this lack of belief pushes Rogozhin to give substance to the prince's fears. It is because Myshkin thinks of Rogozhin as a murderer, that Rogozhin acts like one; in spite of the assurance he gave Myshkin after the exchange of the crosses, Rogozhin assumes the role of the peasant who murdered his friend for his watch; but at the moment when the knife is about to strike, Myshkin cries out: 'Parfen, I don't believe it', and falls down in a fit: the tragedy is averted.

In discussing the attempted murder later with Rogozhin, the prince admits that he shares responsibility:

If you had not been in such a state then that you could only think of one thing, perhaps you would not have raised your knife against me. Right from that very morning, as I looked at you, I had some premonition of it. Do you know what you were like then? Perhaps the thought had occurred to me even as we exchanged crosses. Why did you take me to see your mother? Did you believe that you could restrain your hand because of this? But you cannot really have thought so. Perhaps you just had a feeling, the same as me; we both of us merely had a feeling. But if you had not raised your hand against me as you did (which God averted), what would I have seemed to you now? For, all the same, I did suspect you of it. We share the guilt. It's as simple as that! (Pt III, Ch. 3)

By inwardly judging Rogozhin, the prince has really condemned himself; and the murder, which his own suspicions would have provoked, is forestalled by that other death – his epileptic fit: the prince's inability to live up to his great ideas thus finds its expression in the return of his epilepsy.

It is in ways such as this that Dostoyevsky explores one of the central themes of the novel: that of judgement and condemnation, and its development proceeds according to the logic of inversion, and the fluidity of concepts which characterise the progress of a dream. The active principle of judging is only one aspect of this theme, but it is more in keeping with the passive mood of the prince's 'philosophy', that his chief preoccupation should be not so much with those who judge, as with those who are judged. At the beginning of the novel, Myshkin is the *ingénu* newly arrived in Russia, who sees everything with fresh eyes; yet although his conversation with the Yepanchins' footman reveals that he has been struck by the *ethical* preoccupation of those who surround him ('They talk a lot about courts here now'), this observation merely serves as an introduction to one of the prince's major obsessions – the plight of the condemned man.

Thus the existence of the condemned man haunts the novel almost from its opening pages; and in the ensuing scene with the Yepanchin sisters the theme is taken up again and further developed. Here Myshkin dwells on the state of mind of the condemned man. He relates the experiences of a 'friend', who had been condemned to death only to be reprieved at the very last moment; in particular he is interested in the thoughts which went through the head of this man during what he imagined were the last moments of his life:

He said that those five minutes seemed to him an endless period, an enormous wealth. It seemed to him that in those five minutes, he would live through so many lives, that for the time being there was no point in thinking about the final moment ... (Pt I, Ch. 5)

This sudden, acute perception of the value of time, which the death-sentence has brought him, appears to loom larger in the mind of the condemned man than the execution itself, and anger at his inability to act on this insight seems to overcome even the fear of death:

Apprehension in face of the unknown, and a feeling of revulsion at this new thing which was about to be, which was almost upon him – this was terrible, but he said that nothing was harder for him to bear at that moment than the constant thought: 'What if I do not die! What if life is returned; what an eternity! And all that would be mine! I would then turn every minute into a whole age. I would not let anything be lost. I would put every minute to account. I would not let anything be wasted in vain.' He said that in the end this idea filled him with such bitterness, that he wanted them to shoot him as quickly as possible. (Pt I, Ch. 5)

In this account of the man reprieved at the very last moment, Dostoyevsky is, in fact, describing his own experiences;[10] just as later in the novel he will again put into the mouth of Myshkin an analysis of his own state of mind during the aura preceding the epileptic fit. There is, moreover, a certain parallelism between these two accounts; for the epileptic fit, in itself, has something of the nature of death (a comparison which Dostoyevsky seems to invite by making Myshkin fall into a fit when Rogozhin raises his knife to kill him).[11] In both these accounts, the nervous tension before the inevitable black-out produces a state of heightened awareness, in which reality is perceived in such an intensely vivid way that it amounts to a mystical experience capable of profoundly affecting the outlook of the mind which has undergone it. From both these states of heightened awareness a message may be drawn: from the aura before the fit – a philosophy of perceiving the beauty of the world; from the last moments of the condemned man – an appreciation of the value of time. Both these conclusions are essentially the same in character; for they point to the fact that man is not aware of what he has, be it the concrete surroundings of the world in which he lives, or the abstract element of time which conditions this living.

Yet just as Myshkin's ideas on the true appreciation of beauty are, in the last analysis, found wanting, so too these ideas on the true appreciation of time do not stand up to the pressures of life: the condemned man, returned to the world of the living, is unable to realise that insight which his terrible experience had afforded him. When Aleksandra asks the prince whether his friend was able to profit from his agonising illumination, he replies:

'Oh, no. He himself told me. I have asked him about it. He did not live like this at all, and many were the minutes he wasted.'

'Well then, there's the proof of experience for you. It seems in reality that you cannot live "putting each minute to account". For some reason or other it is impossible.'

'Yes, for some reason or other it is impossible', replied the prince, 'I myself thought so ... But all the same I somehow cannot believe it.'   (Pt I, Ch. 5)

But there is in the novel another account of the thoughts which occur to a man when he is faced with the prospect of certain and imminent death; this is contained in Ippolit's 'Necessary Explanation'. Before deciding to read it Ippolit casts a lot – a 'psychological trait' which he thinks will interest the prince: 'Make a note of it, Prince, remember it; for I believe you are collecting material concerned with capital punishment.' (Pt III Ch. 5.) In this way the 'Necessary Explanation' is linked with Myshkin's earlier conversations at the house of the Yepanchins on the psychology of the condemned man. Indeed, Ippolit more than once specifically refers to himself as a 'condemned man'; for instance he declares:

Let him, into whose hands my 'Explanation' falls, and who has enough patience to read it, let him consider me as a madman, or even as a school-boy, but more to the point, as one condemned to death; who, quite naturally, has come to think that all people apart from him do not value life sufficiently, have grown accustomed to spending it too cheaply and too lazily, that they unscrupulously abuse it, and are all, therefore, to a man, unworthy of it.[12]   (Pt III, Ch. 5)

Unlike Myshkin's friend, judgement has been passed on Ippolit not by man but by nature; yet his state of mind is much the same, and his conclusions on the value of life seem to echo those of Myshkin's friend on the value of time.

Nevertheless, Ippolit has more control over time than the man facing the firing squad – he can end time by an act of his own will: he plans suicide. When the prince suggests that it would be better for him to read his 'Explanation' on the following day, he replies in the words of the Apocalypse: 'Tomorrow "there will be time no longer".' It is significant that Myshkin had used this phrase too – to describe the moment of his fit:

'At that moment', as he once said to Rogozhin, in Moscow, during their meetings there, 'at that moment, it is as though I began to understand that unusual phrase: "that there should be time no longer".' (Pt II, Ch. 5)

And now Ippolit turns to the prince with a question, as though the Angel of Death might have relevance for him too:

But do you remember, Prince, who it was who pronounced: 'that there should be time no longer'? It was pronounced by the great and almighty angel in the Apocalypse. (Pt III, Ch. 5)

The apocalyptic note is carried on in the 'Explanation' itself; for the manuscript is adorned with a big red seal to communicate a sense of mystery, and the first of the incidents it describes, the dream of the 'scorpion', seems to take up the following passage from the Apocalypse:

And to them it was given that they should not kill them, but that they should be tormented five months: and their torment was as the torment of a scorpion, when he striketh a man.

And in those days shall men seek death and shall not find it; and shall desire to die, and death shall flee from them.

(Revelations ix. 4–5)

Ippolit too is a man tormented by the 'scorpion'; he too seeks death, but cannot find it – his attempt at suicide fails. But there is more significance than this in the dream of the 'scorpion': through that fluidity of concepts, which we noted earlier, it can be seen to have relevance for Myshkin himself.

In Ippolit's dream he is alone in a room with this terrifying creature:

It was like a scorpion, but not a scorpion – more loathsome and much more terrifying; more terrifying because, I believe, there are no creatures like it in nature, and because it had come to visit me on purpose, and because in this very fact there was some sort of mystery.

(Pt III, Ch. 5)

Ippolit is filled with horror, and finds that there is nowhere in the room where he can escape from the monster. Yet it seems that the 'scorpion', although poisonous, inspires terror in Ippolit alone:

My mother and some friend of hers came into the room. They began to try to catch the reptile. They were calmer than I was, and were not even afraid. But they did not understand anything.

Nevertheless, the 'scorpion' does appear to inspire terror in an animal, for when Norma (the Newfoundland terrier which had died some five years previously) is called in, she is prepared to do battle. The outcome remains indecisive for although Norma has crushed the shell of the monster, she has also received a poisonous sting in the mouth, and at this point Ippolit wakes up:

Suddenly Norma squealed pitifully; the reptile had somehow managed to sting her tongue. Squealing and howling, she opened her mouth in pain, and I saw that the reptile, for all its cracked shell, was still wriggling in her mouth, and from its half-crushed body was exuding on to her tongue a quantity of white juice, like the juice of a crushed black beetle ... Then I woke up and the prince entered.

The name of the dog seems symbolic;[13] and the battle between the long-dead Norma and the 'scorpion' may be taken as a dream representation of the struggle between normality and disease. This has obvious relevance for the plight of Ippolit; but the fact that the dream ends abruptly with the entry of Myshkin, seems to extend the implications of Ippolit's dream to the prince himself; indeed the detail of the white juice on the tongue of 'normality' has much more relevance for Myshkin's disease of epilepsy than it has for Ippolit's consumption. Once more, as with the phrase: 'that time should be no more' the condition of Myshkin is being compared with that of Ippolit. The prince's own musings at the end of this scene provide confirmation of these hints.

In Ippolit's eyes, it is nature which has condemned him, and yet it is nature whose beauty he is enjoined to admire by his would-be benefactors. He turns on them with the following words:

What use to me is your nature, your park of Pavlovsk, your sunrises and your sunsets, your blue sky and your smug faces, when all this feast which has no end began with the fact that it considered me, me alone, superfluous? How does all this beauty concern me, when every moment, every second, I must recognise, am now forced to recognise, that even this tiny fly, which is now buzzing near me in a ray of sunlight, even that participates in all this feast and choir; it knows its place; it loves it and is happy, whilst I alone am an aborted existence, and it is only through cowardice that I have not wished to understand this until now! (Pt III, Ch. 7)

These words constitute a strong attack on Myshkin's teachings on beauty; yet, strangely enough, they are also Myshkin's own words. It is after Ippolit's unsuccessful attempt at suicide, when the prince is alone in the park in the early morning, that the truth of this is borne in on him:

Above him in a tree a bird was singing, and his eyes began to search for it among the leaves. Suddenly the bird started up from the tree, and at that moment, for some reason or other, he remembered 'the little fly' in 'the warm ray of sunlight' about which Ippolit had written that even 'it knew its place, and had a part in the general choir, but that he alone was but an aborted existence'. This phrase had struck him at the time, and he remembered it now. A long forgotten recollection stirred within him, and suddenly became clear.

It was in Switzerland during the first year, even during the first months, of his treatment. At that time he was still completely like an idiot; he could not even speak properly; at times could not even understand what was required of him. Once he went into the mountains on a clear, sunny day, and walked about for a long time with a certain tormenting thought in his head, which would not take substance. Before him was a brilliant sky; below there was a lake, and round about stretched the bright horizon, whose edge had no end. He looked for a long time in anguish. He remembered now how he had stretched out his hands towards that bright, endless blue, and had cried. What tormented him was that he was a complete stranger to all this. What sort of feast was this? What sort of great eternal holiday which had no end, and towards which he had been drawn for a long time now, ever since childhood, but in which he could in no way take part? Each morning there rose the same bright sun; each morning there was a rainbow on the waterfall; each evening the highest of the mountain peaks, snow capped there in the distance, shone at the sky's edge with a purple flame. Each 'little fly, which buzzed round him in the warm ray of sunlight, participated in all this choir; knew its place; loved it and was happy'. Each blade of grass grew and was happy; and everything had its course; everything knew its course: it departed with a song, and with a song it arrived. Alone he knew nothing; understood nothing, neither people nor sounds – a stranger to everything and an aborted existence. Oh, at that time, of course, he could not speak in these words and frame his questions; he suffered in mute silence. But it seemed to him now, that even then he had said all this – all these very words; and that the reference to 'the little fly', Ippolit had taken from him himself, from the words and the tears that had come to him then. He was convinced of this; and, for some reason or other, his heart beat at the thought.

(Pt III, Ch. 7)

Thus Myshkin can see himself in Ippolit: something which once more emerges when shortly afterwards he recounts Ippolit's attempt at suicide to Aglaya:

'He wanted to meet people for the last time, and earn their respect and their love. These, of course, are very good sentiments, only for some reason it all turned out wrong, perhaps because of illness and perhaps because of something else! For some people everything always turns out well, for others extremely badly.'
  'You added this about yourself, didn't you?' Aglaya remarked.
  'Yes, I added this about myself', the prince replied, not noticing any malice in her question.

(Pt III, Ch. 8)

Ippolit regards himself as condemned by nature, and the same is true for the prince: it is always possible that the state of idiocy which blotted out his earlier years could once more return. This, he realises, is the dark threat behind that wonderful moment before the fit: 'stupor, spiritual gloom, idiocy stood before him clearly as a consequence of these elevated moments'. Although, when speaking of his fits on another occasion, Myskhin merely describes himself as: 'wronged by nature', the truth is that he has been condemned; for nature returns Myshkin to his former state of idiocy, even before she takes the life of Ippolit.

But the prince also identifies himself in his illness with another of the 'nihilists' – Burdovsky:

I myself was in such a state too before leaving for Switzerland. I mumbled disjointed words in the same way; you want to express yourself, but cannot. I can feel great sympathy, because I myself am almost the same. I can say this therefore!   (Pt II, Ch. 8)

Burdovsky is an obvious brother-figure for Myshkin, in that he claims to be the son of Myshkin's benefactor, Pavlishchev (though, in reality, he is just another of the philanthropist's protégés). Through Pavlischev they share a common brotherhood in misfortune; for this 'father-figure', as Ganya Ivolgin has discovered: 'felt all his life a special sort of attraction and tenderness towards everything which was persecuted and wronged by nature, particularly if this concerned children'. (Pt II, Ch. 9.) But the incoherence of Burdovsky makes him unsatisfactory as the nihilistic 'brother-figure' for Myshkin, and this role, of necessity, devolves on Ippolit, who is not lacking in words, and who, indeed, seeks to defend the interests of Burdovsky as 'my neighbour' (Moy blizhniy i.e. 'one who is close to me').

Ippolit's reading of his 'Necessary Explanation' and his attempted suicide occur at a moment of great significance for Myshkin. The occasion is the party called to celebrate his birthday; but this is no ordinary birthday, it seems as though it is intended to mark the birth of a new Myshkin. Thus in inviting his 'brother', Rogozhin, to the celebrations, the prince says:

'I do not want to meet my new life without you, because my new life has begun! Do you know, Parfen, that my new life has begun today?' (Pt III, Ch. 3.) The festivities have already started without them, and when they arrive, Myshkin seeks to be congratulated first of all by Vera Lebedev, who underlines the special significance of the day in her congratulations:

The prince noticed the tender, affectionate glance of Vera Lebedev, who was also hastening to make her way to him through the throng. He stretched out his hand to her first before anyone else. She flushed with pleasure, and wished him a 'happy life *from that very day*'.

(Pt III, Ch. 4)

The next person to greet him is Ippolit, who says that he has been waiting for him specially, and is glad to see him so happy. But Ippolit has his own reasons for saying this; when, a little later, he expresses satisfaction that Myshkin's birthday falls on that very day, and hints that he might have a present for him, we know that he is hinting darkly at his 'Explanation' and his suicide. Ippolit is glad that at that very moment when the prince feels himself reborn into a new and happy life, he will be forcibly reminded of his other self – the condemned man.

The theme of 'the condemned man', in its many varied manifestations, represents a strong counterblast to Myshkin's 'philosophy'. It vitiates his ideas on happiness and beauty, on humility and the role of man as a servant.

As we have seen, Myshkin acknowledges Ippolit's words about 'the feast of life' as his own; and yet these ideas stand out in direct contrast to the affirmation of the power of beauty which the prince is later to make in the scene of 'The Teaching of the Elders' (there are common elements in the three passages: i.e. 'trees', 'sunsets', 'blades of grass'), and it is significant that immediately after this affirmation, Myshkin will reveal himself as 'the condemned man' by falling down in a fit. But even earlier in the novel the theme of 'the condemned man' had cast its shadow over his ideas on 'happiness and beauty': both are inextricably bound together in the scene of Myshkin's acquaintance with the Yepanchin sisters. Thus, quite pointedly, Aglaya asks the prince how he can claim to have spent all his time in Switzerland happily, if, as he says, he has witnessed an execution; and when he is asked by Adelaida to give her a subject for a painting, he suggests, as though in reply to Aglaya's charge of quietism, a subject which reflects, not his own world-saving ideas on beauty, but all the grim realism of the last moments of the condemned man – 'The Head and the Cross'.

The theme of 'the condemned man' also constitutes an attack on the prince's ideas on humility. Thus Ippolit is not prepared humbly to accept his lot; indeed he sneers at Myshkin:

who in his Christian conclusions is bound to arrive at the happy thought that it is really much better that you are dying (such Christians as he always arrive at that idea; it is their favourite hobby-horse).   (Pt III, Ch. 7)

The humble behaviour of the prince in the Burdovsky affair also infuriates Ippolit, as does the forgiving way in which his friend Kolya tries to treat him, under the influence of Myshkin's ideas. Whereas the prince puts forward the idea that human beings must be one another's servants, Ippolit thinks rather that they have been created to torment one another.

Ippolit's contempt for the humble of this world is shown particularly in his dealings with Surikov – the pauper who lives in the apartment above. In Ippolit's eyes, this 'most humble of creatures' is responsible for his own plight; he even tells him as much, on the tragic occasion when Surikov shows him the body of his baby, who has died from the cold. Although Surikov is deeply insulted, and turns him out of the room, he is nevertheless still formally polite to Ippolit whenever he meets him. Ippolit comments: 'If he despised me, then it was in his own fashion: he humbly despised me.' Humble submissiveness, for Ippolit, is not a virtue: it is nearer to being a vice:

Know that in shame, in the consciousness of one's own worthlessness and ineffectuality, there is a boundary beyond which a man cannot go; from that point on he begins to feel an enormous pleasure in his very shame ... Well, of course, humility is a powerful force in this sense, I grant this, although not in the sense in which religion takes humility as a force. (Pt III, Ch. 7)

Such is the abject state of Surikov's mind, that even if he had money, he would not know how to use it. Ippolit dreams that Surikov has suddenly become a millionaire; he does not know what to do with his money, and constantly fears that it will be stolen. Finally he decides to hide it in the ground, but Ippolit, in the dream, ironically suggests that rather than bury all this gold to no purpose, it would be better to melt it down, and bury it as a coffin for his dead child. Surikov accepts this plan with tears of gratitude in his eyes, and sets about doing as he is advised.

Ippolit's attitude to Surikov may seem hard and unfeeling, but his standpoint is that of 'the condemned man', who, because of the sentence passed on him, is acutely aware of the value of time – the value of life itself:

I could not understand, for example, how these people who have so much life, were not able to become rich (moreover I do not understand this even now). I knew one pauper, who, as I was told later, died from starvation, and I remember that it made me furious. If it had been possible to restore this pauper to life, I think I would have had him executed. (Pt III, Ch. 5)

In spite of Ippolit's strictures on humility, he is nevertheless prepared to help those who have suffered wrong. Behind both his championship of Burdovsky and his efforts to rehabilitate the doctor there is, of course, the same 'theory of the triumph of rights', but there is also a certain ambiguity of motive. Even in the Burdovsky affair his aims are not entirely devoid of Christian overtones:

I got carried away and insisted on the rights of Burdovsky, 'My neighbour'; and dreamed that they would all suddenly open their arms and embrace me, and ask my forgiveness, and I theirs. (Pt III, Ch. 5)

These overtones are even more pronounced in the incident with the doctor.

This account, occurring immediately after the episode with Surikov, does much to undo the bad impression left on the reader by Ippolit's cynicism over the dead child; but there is irony here: the person he chooses to help is one who cannot help him – a doctor.[14] The irony, however, goes deeper than this; for his act of philanthropy merely reinforces the sense of his own helplessness. Ippolit extols the value of individual acts of charity, in that they bring benefit to the giver as much as to the recipient; they link him with another human being:

You will, without doubt, come to look on your work in the end as a science. It will absorb all your life; is capable of filling it entirely. On the other hand, all your thoughts, all the seeds you have scattered, and which perhaps you have already forgotten about, these will take on substance and grow. A man who has taken from you will give to another; and how do you know what part you will play in the future solution of human destinies? If your knowledge and a whole life devoted to this work, raises you finally to the point where you are capable of broadcasting an enormous seed, of leaving an enormous thought to the world as its heritage, then, etc. etc. I said a lot then.   (Pt III, Ch. 6)

These words, in spite of the self-deprecatory bathos of the ending, sound more like those of Myshkin than of Ippolit; but their soaring ambition is brought abruptly back to earth by his friend Bakhmutov to whom they are addressed: 'And to think, hearing you say all this, that it is you who have been denied life!' Once more Ippolit is brought up against the blank wall of his condemnation: his activity, even as a force for good, is strictly curtailed – he has only enough time left to indulge in minor acts of charity. This too has relevance for Myshkin; for he, above all, is projected as the philanthropist and the 'sower of seed' – a role which, because of his 'condemnation', he is never destined to achieve.

For all Ippolit's flirtation with Christian humanitarianism, his basic preoccupation is still that of 'rights'. Frustrated in his attempts to do good, because of his condemnation, Ippolit sees that this same condemned state can, on the contrary, provide him with cover for doing evil:

I acknowledge no judges over me and know that I am now outside
the power of any court. Not very long ago I was amused by the
proposition that if I suddenly took it into my head to kill whoever I
liked – kill ten people at once, or do something absolutely terrible:
something regarded in this world as the worst possible crime, well,
now that torture has been abolished, what an awkward position I
would place the court in, seeing that I have only one or two weeks
left.   (Pt III, Ch. 7)

Thus, as with Raskolnikov, an obsession with ethical questions
can lead ultimately to thoughts of crime; a preoccupation with
'rights', as Radomsky asserts, can result in acknowledging the
'rights' of force. (Radomsky even forsees that Ippolit could end
up as the criminal Lacenaire.[15]) When faced with the great
wrong of his condemnation, Ippolit can only defend his rights
before the rights of those who seek to judge him:

Who, and in the name of what right, and for what motive, would
think to dispute now my right to these two or three weeks left to me?
What concern is it of any court, and who is it exactly who requires,
not only that I should be sentenced, but that I should stoically live out
the time which remains in moral rectitude? Does in fact anyone
really require this? For morality's sake?   (Pt III, Ch. 7)

   Ippolit's preoccupation with rights colours the whole of his
'Explanation', and here his anguish arises not so much from
fear of death as from his torment of doubt over the ethical
bases of life: the *fact* of his condemnation does not appear to
cause him as much suffering as the *reason* for his condemnation.
He suggests as much in his account of the 'scorpion':

I was terribly afraid that it would sting me; they told me it was
poisonous. But most of all I was tormented by the question: who
had sent it into my room; what did they want to do with me; and
what was the mystery behind it?   (Pt III, Ch. 5)

Ippolit makes his attitude to religion and divine justice clear in
a passage which constitutes his most eloquent rebuttal of
Myshkin's ideas on humility:

Religion! I grant that there is such a thing as eternal life, and perhaps always have granted it. Let us allow that consciousness has been kindled by the will of a higher power; let us grant that consciousness has cast an eye on the world and said: 'I am'; and let us grant that consciousness has suddenly been ordered by this higher power to perish, because, for some reason or other up there, this is necessary; what this reason might be is not explained. Let us allow this; I grant all this. But once again the eternal question arises: why, in such a case, is my humble resignation to this fact necessary? Surely I can simply be just devoured without my being asked to praise that which has devoured me? It surely cannot be that someone will take offence, because I do not want to wait two weeks? I do not believe it. It is much more to the point to suppose that my insignificant life, the life of an atom, is needed at this point for the fulfilment of some sort of general harmony at large, for some plus or minus or other, for some contrast or other, etc. etc., just exactly as every day the sacrifice is required of the lives of a great many beings, without whose death the rest of the world would not be able to continue (although it must be noted that this idea in itself is not a very magnanimous one). Let us grant all this. I will agree that otherwise, that is without the continuous devouring of one another, it would not be at all possible to construct a world; and I am even prepared to concede that I do not understand anything about the ordering of the world. But, on the other hand, this is what I do know for a certainty: if once I have been allowed to be conscious of the fact that 'I am', then what do I care that the world has been faultily constructed, and that otherwise it could not continue? In view of this, who is it who will judge me, and for what? Whatever you say, all this is impossible and unjust.

(Pt III, Ch. 7)

This is a powerful attack on divine justice from the standpoint of 'the condemned man'. But although Ippolit here talks of 'a higher power', he does not talk explicitly of God, and perhaps he is prepared to acknowledge no higher power than nature; a nature from which godhead itself cannot escape. Thus earlier in the novel he has exclaimed:

'Yes, nature is full of mockery! Why does she', he continued with sudden fervour, 'Why does she create the best of creatures, only later to jeer at them? She has contrived it, that the only being who has been acknowledged on earth as perfection – she has contrived it, that having shown him to mankind, she has then destined him, him above all, to utter words, which have caused so much blood to flow, that had it all flowed at once, man would undoubtedly have drowned.'

Thus, in Ippolit's view, the spiritual message of Christ has been condemned by nature, just as later, when describing the impression left on him by Rogozhin's picture, he sees the body of Christ as subjected also to her laws:

Then the idea comes to you, in spite of yourself, that if death is so terrible, and the laws of nature are so strong, how can one overcome them? How can one overcome them, when even he now has not overcome them? He who during his life conquered nature itself; he to whom she herself submitted: he who cried out: 'Talitha cumi!' and the maiden arose: 'Lazarus come forth!' and the dead man came forth. When one looks at this picture one has the impression of nature in the form of some huge, implacable and dumb beast; or more accurately – it is strange but it is much nearer to the point – in the form of some enormous machine of the latest construction which, quite senselessly and with an unresponsive lack of feeling, has seized, crushed to pieces and swallowed up a great and priceless being; a being which in itself is worth the whole of nature and all her laws; worth all the earth which indeed has been created perhaps solely for the coming of this being. It is as though it is precisely this idea about the dark, insolent and senselessly eternal force to which all is subjected, which is being expressed in this picture; the idea is communicated to you, even in spite of yourself.

(Pt III, Ch. 6)

From this it appears that although Ippolit and Myshkin have been condemned by nature, it is a condemnation which they share with an even greater figure: Christ himself! The *failure* of Myshkin, then, reflects the 'failure' of Christ; for the laws of nature have jeered at Christ's ideas, and *his* body too has been subjected to their brute chaotic forces. Yet in spite of this preponderance of the negative, there is in the message of Christ, as in that of Myshkin, something positive, which is still capable of triumphing. Ippolit continues:

134

Those people gathered round the body (of whom not one is shown in the picture), they must have experienced terrible grief and confusion during that evening, which, at one blow, had crushed all their hopes and almost all their beliefs. They must have dispersed in the most appalling terror, even though each one bore within himself an enormous idea, which now could never be wrested from him.

These musings on Rogozhin's picture come to Ippolit in a dream state of semi-delirium, in which concepts become confused:

But at times it seemed to me as though I could see this eternal force, this dark, dumb and unresponsive being, in some sort of strange and impossible shape. I remember that someone seemed to lead me by the hand; and, holding a candle, he showed me some sort of huge, re-pulsive tarantula, and began to assure me that this was that same dark, unresponsive and all powerful being; and he laughed when I showed indignation. (Pt III, Ch. 6)

Thus Rogozhin's picture leads symbolically to the image of the tarantula; but this in turn is superseded by an apparition of the owner of the picture himself; for at this very point Rogozhin appears to enter Ippolit's room and take up a seat under the lamp which is burning before the icon.[16]

The logic at work here is that fluidity of concepts so typical of dreams. Rogozhin, whose picture of the dead Christ had prompted Ippolit's musings on the dark eternal force of nature is thus identified with that force itself, and this is in keeping with his role in the novel; for Rogozhin is not only an agent of destruction, he is also linked quite specifically with the failure of 'the Russian Christ', with the failure of Myshkin himself. But Ippolit cannot decide whether it really is Rogozhin who is sitting under the lamp, or whether it is a ghost. This possibility brings us back once more to the idea of Rogozhin as the bringer of death; for Ippolit explains a belief he holds, that to see a ghost would mean he would die on the spot.

Ippolit and Rogozhin are two opposites; this is Ippolit's own conclusion:

There was such a contrast between us, that it could not but com-municate itself to us both, particularly to me. I was a man whose days were numbered, and he a man living life most fully and directly, living each minute without any concern for 'final conclusions', figures or anything which did not bear on that ... on that ... well, on that which he was mad about. (Pt III, Ch. 6)

Ippolit is 'the condemned man', the ailing, questioning intellectual, a nihilist and admirer of Aglaya: Rogozhin, on the other hand, is 'the executioner', the robust 'man of nature', a man of deeds not words; he is the religious fanatic, the pursuer of Nastasya Filippovna. In speaking of this contrast, Ippolit comments: '*les extrémités se touchent*'; here as elsewhere in Dostoyevsky's novels the religious fanatic and the nihilist are found side by side, but the real point of such *contiguous polarity* lies in its relevance for the central character. The relationship of Rogozhin and Ippolit to the prince is more than that of two contrasted 'brothers': these characters are potential aspects of Myshkin himself.

Ippolit's words on the contrast between himself and Rogozhin are reminiscent of the contrast which the underground man draws between himself, as the product of a retort, and the simple, direct man of action, who springs from 'the bosom of nature'. It is striking that Ippolit exhibits many of the characteristics of the underground man. The confessional style of the 'Explanation' is in itself reminiscent of *Notes from Underground*, with its mixture of philosophising and anecdote, its love of paradox and its pervasive tone of malice. Moreover both 'authors' have a similar attitude to their writing: the underground man refuses to cross out his bad witticisms just to spite himself; Ippolit, too, refuses to cross out:

I think that I have just written down a lot of terribly stupid things, but I have no time to correct it. I have stated this already. Moreover I am purposely binding myself to correct not a line in this manuscript, even if I notice that I am contradicting myself every five lines. (Pt III, Ch. 5)

It is, however, not merely a question of style. Of the anecdotes which Ippolit recounts, the first (the incident with Surikov) is worthy of the underground man himself; and the second (the

136

episode with the doctor) reflects much the same ambiguity of motive in an act of philanthropy as was present in the underground man's attitude to Liza. Again, the relationship between Ippolit and his old school 'friend', Bakhmutov, is not unlike that between the underground man and Zverkov.

Like the hero of *Notes from Underground*, Ippolit is the product of a retort, a victim of cloistered consciousness:

Do you know, I am not yet eighteen: I have lain so much on this pillow, I have looked so much through this window, and I have thought... about everybody, that...   (Pt II, Ch. 10)

All that Ippolit can see through his window is the blank wall of the house opposite – Meier's wall.[17] This for him becomes a symbol, much as for the underground man the symbol of the 'wall' represents the physical limitations placed on man by nature. But both are rebels; both rail against the laws of nature; both refuse to submit (yet both concede that there is a paradoxical pleasure to be found in the humiliation of submissiveness). The underground man refuses to yield to the 'wall', merely because it is a wall and he has not the strength to overcome it: Ippolit, too, refuses to submit, and like the underground man he opposes to the barrier of 'the wall' the counter principle of his own will:

The final explanation: I am about to die, not because I am in any way incapable of bearing these three weeks. Oh, I would have enough strength for that; and, if I wanted to, I could be sufficiently consoled by the mere consciousness of the wrong done me: but I am not a French poet and I do not want such consolations. Finally there is a temptation: nature by its three week sentence has curtailed my activities to such an extent, that perhaps suicide is the only act, which I can still manage to begin and to finish according to the dictates of my own will. It may even be that I want to avail myself of the last possibility of action? A protest is often a great thing.   (Pt III, Ch. 7)

But if the 'wall' for the underground man is a symbol for the insuperability of 'laws of nature' in general, with Ippolit the metaphor is more precise: not only is Meier's wall a real one, but, on a symbolic level, it represents the insurmountable blankness of his own looming death.

As regards life, however, Ippolit is at one with the underground man in placing emphasis on process rather than conclusion. The hero of *Notes from Underground* contends that life is like chess, which one does not play for its ending but for the game itself; so too Ippolit maintains:

The important thing is life; it is in life alone, in the process of discovering, a process which is endless and eternal: the actual discovery is not the important thing at all. (Pt III, Ch. 5)

If Ippolit looks back to the underground man, he also looks forward to Kirillov in *The Devils*, and to Ivan in *The Brothers Karamazov*. Like Kirillov he chooses suicide as an act of will to defy death itself; like Ivan Karamazov he voices telling criticism of divine justice and the ordering of the world. Ippolit is, therefore, an important character in Dostoyevsky's fiction, but it must be admitted that he is a very trying one. He is the dying man who never dies, but constantly dangles his plight before the other characters as a reproach for their good fortune in being healthy and alive. This lack of tact in refusing to die annoys Ganya Ivolgin:

And tell me, please, why he does not die! He promised to go on living for only another three days; but he has started to get fat here! His cough is ceasing; he himself said, last night, that he had not been coughing blood for two days. (Pt IV, Ch. 1)

Ippolit, too, is conscious of such criticism: 'Everybody is furious because I do not die, but, on the contrary, seem better.' Yet it is not merely the characters of the novel who wish secretly for the death of Ippolit; the reader, too, if he is honest, is also annoyed that Ippolit is still encountered, perversely alive, right up to the very conclusion of the novel. Ippolit is, indeed, a tiresome character, and Dostoyevsky, by alienating that sympathy from him which he so much merits, forces the reader to condemn him. This is a device worthy of *Notes from Underground* where, on the last pages, the underground man presents himself as the moral superior of his readers. It is the ultimate irony of Dostoyevsky's treatment of the theme of the condemned man – the reader too has been made to judge and condemn, unless, like the prince, compassion has prompted him to utter the only words which can be uttered: 'Pass us by, and forgive us our happiness.'[18] (Pt IV, Ch. 5.)

THE PAMPHLET NOVEL:
'THE DEVILS'

In the summer of 1869 the Dostoyevskys found themselves in Dresden. This period of voluntary exile was to last another two years, but throughout all their European peregrinations Fedor Mikhaylovich never lost sight of what was happening in Russia. There the summer of 1869 was marked by political unrest, particularly among the students of the Petrovskaya Agricultural Academy in Moscow. Anna, in her memoirs, relates how these events provided Dostoyevsky with the idea for a new novel:

Fedor Mikhaylovich, having read various foreign newspapers (much appeared in them which did not appear in the Russian ones) came to the conclusion that in the near future political disturbances were about to flare up in the Petrovskaya Agricultural Academy. Fearing that my brother, through lack of years and weakness of character, might take an active part in them, my husband persuaded my mother to send him to stay with us in Dresden. Fedor Mikhaylovich had always liked my brother and was interested in what he was doing; was interested in his acquaintances and in the life and ideas of the student world in general. My brother enthusiastically told him everything in detail. It was from this that Fedor Mikhaylovich conceived the idea of depicting the political movement of the time in one of his novels, and of taking, as one of the chief heroes, the student Ivanov (under the name of Shatov) who was later to be killed by Nechayev. My brother spoke of this student Ivanov as an intelligent person, remarkable for his firmness of character, who had radically changed his former convictions. How deeply shaken my husband was when he learned later from the papers of the murder of Ivanov.[1]

Thus in its original conception *The Devils* was to have been a 'pamphlet novel' [*roman pamflet*] directed against the revolutionaries. Dostoyevsky was working on at least ten plans for such a novel up to the September of 1870, but the work refused to take shape until finally there came a new plan and a new central figure. In a letter to Strakhov of 21 October 1870 Dostoyevsky writes:

There has emerged a new figure with a claim to be the real hero of the novel. So that the former hero (a curious figure, but certainly not deserving the name of hero) has receded into the background.[2]

This 'new figure' of whom he speaks is Stavrogin, and with his advent the work has ceased to be purely a pamphlet novel; for Stavrogin is connected with a completely different plane of ideas.

After finishing *The Idiot* Dostoyevsky had originally conceived an idea for a new novel to be entitled 'Atheism'. This later developed into an ambitious plan for 'The Life of a Great Sinner', a work which he never wrote but which was to furnish material for his last three novels (*The Devils*, *A Raw Youth*, *The Brothers Karamazov*). It is from the unwritten pages of 'The Life of a Great Sinner' that Stavrogin has come to enrich the significance of the pamphlet novel.

The origins of *The Devils* and the way the novel developed under Dostoyevsky's pen reveal quite patently the double warp around which most of his major writing is woven: on the one hand polemics against the nihilists; on the other the exploration of religious and philosophical problems. Unfortunately it was this last aspect of *The Devils* which ran into difficulties. In Part II (between Chapters 8 and 9) Dostoyevsky had originally intended to have a chapter entitled 'At Tikhon's', but this included 'Stavrogin's Confession' which the publisher, Katkov, refused to print even in the toned-down version finally submitted by Dostoyevsky. Thus a key passage for an understanding of Stavrogin is excluded from most editions of the novel.

Yet what was a loss for one strand of the novel resulted in a gain for the other; for Dostoyevsky was able to profit from the delay in his writing to incorporate into his work factual details culled from the extensive newspaper reports of the trial (from

July to September 1871) of the murderers of Ivanov – the so-called Nechayevists. The novel, therefore, was published, with gaps, over a period of two years.

Although the two strands of the novel are closely interwoven at nearly all points, it is necessary to examine *The Devils* as a 'pamphlet novel' before attempting to assess the new dimension which the figure of Stavrogin brings with him into the work. The pamphlet novel is centred on the Verkhovenskys, father and son. The name is significant (*verkhovenstvo* means 'supremacy') and in one of his notebooks Dostoyevsky explains that the father 'throughout the entire novel is engaged in continuous altercation with his son over the question of supremacy'.[3] Such 'vying for supremacy' is to be taken in an ideological sense; for the Verkhovenskys are the representatives of two warring generations. The novel, then, is a revision of Turgenev's *Fathers and Children*, a work which the elder Verkhovensky criticises for its failure to depict the younger generation as it really is:

I don't understand Turgenev. His Bazarov is a fictitious character the like of which does not exist at all. They themselves were the first to repudiate him at the time, as a complete freak. That Bazarov is a vague amalgam of Nozdrev[4] and Byron. C'est le mot. Yet look at these same people closely; they roll about and squeal with joy like puppies in the sun. They are happy; they are conquerors. In what sense are these people like Byron ...? (Pt II, Ch. 1, 2)

Turgenev presents his conflict as the mutual incomprehension of two generations, and this theme, as we have seen, is present in *The Idiot*; but in *The Devils* Dostoyevsky goes further: his thesis is not merely that the men of the forties do not understand the younger generation of the sixties, it is that they are responsible for them – they are their intellectual fathers. Thus Dostoyevsky's Nechayev is not the son of an artisan, as Nechayev was in real life; he is the son of an intellectual of the forties. This father-figure himself (Stepan Trofimovich) comes into early conflict with the new generation when, at the beginning of the sixties, he goes to St Petersburg with Stavrogin's mother in a vain attempt to re-establish his reputation. His conclusions on 'the great idea which has become the plaything of stupid children' are that the young people have taken the ideas of his own generation to an unjustifiable extreme. Later in the novel this theme is made more explicit in Stepan Trofimovich's strictures on Chernyshevsky's *What is to be Done?*:

I agree that the author's basic idea is right ... but this makes it all the more terrible; for it is our idea, no one else's but ours. We were the first to plant it, to raise it, to prepare it. After us, what could they say that was new? But Good Lord! the way all this is expressed, the way it is distorted, the way it is mangled ... Was it towards conclusions such as these that we were driving? Who can recognise our original idea in this? (Pt II, Ch. IV, 2)

An important clue to the figure of Stepan Trofimovich is provided by the notebooks for *The Devils*. Here he was first called 'Granovsky'. T. N. Granovsky was an influential historian and liberal *Westerniser*, who reached the height of his fame with a course of public lectures which he gave at Moscow University (1843–4). Dostoyevsky drew on a recently published biography[5] of this famous professor to furnish details for his portrait of the representative of 'the fathers'. Both are historians and men of letters; Granovsky was a poetically gifted orator; Stepan Trofimovich, too, shows this same love of words, and in broad terms the two have much in common. Thus Granovsky, although not a true believer, could not go all the way with Herzen, when, under the influence of Feuerbach, he denied the immortality of the soul; it was on this issue that relations between the two became strained.[6] Stepan Trofimovich has a similar ambiguous attitude to religious questions:

'I do not understand why they always represent me here as an atheist', he would say sometimes. 'I believe in God. *Mais distinguons*. I believe in him as a being conscious of himself only in me.'
(Pt I, Ch. I, 9)

This is a comic parody of the humanistic elements in Granovsky's religious outlook. But this equivocation holds out a hope for the future. Stepan Trofimovich ultimately becomes a positive figure with a religious message; yet here again, as with Granovsky, it is the immortality of the soul which is the important issue: 'If there is a God, then I am immortal. *Voilà ma profession de foi.*'

Although the portrait of Stepan Trofimovich is derived largely from Granovsky, Dostoyevsky is nevertheless at pains to dissociate his comic character from the eminent scholar.[7] Stepan Trofimovich, we are told, is merely trying to emulate 'a certain immortal professor' when he uses a university chair to try out his 'eagle's wings'. Indeed it was at a dinner given in honour of Granovsky that Stepan Trofimovich last met his rival Karmazinov. The narrator himself says that Stepan Trofimovich was a less important figure, but nevertheless some people thought he was almost the equal of Chaadayev, Belinsky, Granovsky and the early Herzen. The names in this list are significant; for all of them are associated with the westernism in vogue in the forties. Here is the real clue to the portrayal of Stepan Trofimovich – he represents a generalised portrait of the liberal westerniser of the forties, and when Lyamshin chooses to caricature him at the house of the governor, he does so under the title 'A liberal of the forties'.

The westernism of this generation has cut them off from the Russian people; such at least is the opinion expressed by Shatov when he harangues his former mentor:

All of them, and you along with them, were unable to see the Russian common people. Belinsky especially ...

But not only were you unable to see the people, your attitude to them was one of loathing and contempt, as is shown by the mere fact that under the term 'the people', you imagined for yourselves only the French people, and only the Parisians at that, and you were ashamed that the Russian people were not like them'.[8]

(Pt i, Ch. i, 9)

The elder Verkhovensky can hardly utter a sentence without breaking into French, and this is a parody of the prose style of the men of the forties (at times Stepan Trofimovich sounds like exaggeratedly bad Herzen): it is the mark of his westernism. Moreover some of Stepan Trofimovich's utterances in themselves are so extreme that they more than corroborate the words of Shatov. Thus Stepan Trofimovich not only contrasts French intelligence with Russian laziness, but even concludes that the Russians should be exterminated for the good of humanity. Stepan Trofimovich is indeed cut off from his own people, and at the end of the novel he will set out on a symbolic search to find them.

The professed 'liberalism' of Stepan Trofimovich is also presented ironically. The central issue here is the liberation of the serfs: Stepan Trofimovich drinks toasts in honour of the great day, but in reality he is frightened of it; he even tries to go abroad to escape its consequences. When there are minor peasant disturbances, and, in the heat of the moment, troops are sent in, it is Stepan Trofimovich who declares in the club that more troops are needed. His own serf, Fedka, he has sold off into the army in order to cover a gambling debt.

Stepan Trofimovich's claim to be a great scholar and intellectual leader is equally dubious. He has been living for years on the false and cherished illusion that he is a man under police surveillance, regarded by the authorities as a dangerous disseminator of disaffection. His efforts at scholarship are all in the past; and, although he has many projects in hand, he spends his time mostly in talking, drinking and playing cards; nor is he above taking a volume of De Tocqueville into the garden when his real intention is to read a light popular novel. Despite all this, he can still say of himself that for twenty years he has been beating the tocsin with a summons to work.[9]

One of the most ironical features of Stepan Trofimovich's existence is that he is really a hanger-on, a sponger, an ageing cultural gigolo who depends for his comforts on his ability to stay in favour with Stavrogin's mother. His Christian name and patronymic suggest the ironic incongruity between his pretensions to intellectual glory (Stepan = a wreath)[10] and the reality of his social position (Trofim = a ward or nurseling). In his polemical assessment of the typical liberal of the forties,

Dostoyevsky seems almost at one with that spokesman of the younger generation, Dobrolyubov, who analysed such liberalism in his influential essay 'What is Oblomovism';[11] but Dostoyevsky goes on where Dobrolyubov could not follow – the younger generation in its turn falls victim to his polemical pen.

In Petr Verkhovensky we have Dostoyevsky's portrayal of Nechayev, but just as the father has only token identity with Granovsky, so too the son's identification with Nechayev is little more than emblematic. The Nechayev of real life was far more sinister than the somewhat clownish figure presented by Petr Verkhovensky in the novel, and his social origins were quite different. Nechayev was the son of a house-painter; he was born in 1847 in the industrial centre of Ivanovo. In 1865 he moved to Moscow, and the following year to St Petersburg, where he attended university lectures and became involved in revolutionary activity. The year 1870 was forecast by many revolutionaries (Nechayev among them) as a critical year for the régime: it would mark the end of the nine-year period allotted to the full implementation of the liberation of the serfs, and final decisions on the peasants' tenure of land would have to be made. With the possibilities of the year 1870 in mind, Nechayev decided to seize his opportunity. Having been arrested in student disturbances, he tried to create the impression among student leaders in St Petersburg that he had been taken off to the redoubtable Peter Paul Fortress, as an important political detainee; instead he travelled to Geneva where he issued a proclamation boasting of his escape from that fortress.

His reasons for this deceit were masterly, if unscrupulous, and they set the key for all his subsequent behaviour. In the student political movement of the time Nechayev was as yet a nonentity, and if he were to have any influence on the events of the predicted upsurge in 1870, he had but a year in which to establish himself as a leader. He saw a situation ripe for exploitation; the older revolutionary leaders were *émigrés* living for the most part in Switzerland; in Russia itself their prestige was immense, and yet there was little or no direct contact between them and the nascent revolutionary movement at home. The gulf of mutual ignorance was a challenge to Nechayev's considerable gifts as a confidence trickster. The veteran revolutionary Bakunin was only too pleased to believe that, in the person of Nechayev, he was dealing, not only with a representative of the Russian revolutionary movement, but with a leader of such standing that the government had thought fit to incarcerate him in the dreaded Peter Paul Fortress; and his claim to have escaped from the prison, instead of making Bakunin wary, only induced him to venerate this young man all the more. Indeed Bakunin was so anxious to bring the Russian revolutionary movement under his own influence, that he created 'The World Revolutionary Alliance' with a Russian section, and issued Nechayev with a document certifying that he was 'Representative No. 2771'. This was just what Nechayev wanted: he now had impeccable credentials to present to the student community at home, a document which would assure him of obedience; the make-believe world of the veteran Bakunin now lent false substance to the empty claims of Nechayev.

Bakunin was not the only one to be impressed by Nechayev. Ogarev, the close friend of Herzen, dedicated a laudatory poem to this incredible young man under the title 'The Student'. This poem is parodied in *The Devils* as 'A Noble Character' ['*Svetlaya lichnost*''] – verses which are supposed to have been written for Petr Verkhovensky by Herzen himself.

In the August of 1869 Nechayev returned to Russia, and immediately set about organising political activity at the Moscow Agricultural Academy, an institution at which, as we have seen, Dostoyevsky's young brother-in-law was a student. Nechayev's aim was to form revolutionary cells each of which would comprise only five members; the leader of each cell would himself be an ordinary member of a higher cell, and the four remaining cell members were each charged with the formation of other cells in which they, in turn, would act as leaders. So the process would go on. A cellular structure such as this offered the advantage of a wide base for recruitment, whilst at the same time it restricted the effectiveness of police penetration.

It is doubtful whether there existed any other groups of five apart from the one which came to light in the Moscow Agricultural Academy. Ivanov, one of the members of this cell, refused to give the movement (i.e. Nechayev) his blind obedience, and, in November of 1869, Nechayev induced the other members of the cell to murder him. These unfortunate participants in the murder were arrested, whilst Nechayev himself escaped abroad to resume his émigré life in Switzerland.

In the absence of the principal defendant, and the failure of all attempts to apprehend him, the trial of the Nechayevists was delayed until July 1871, but in the meantime accounts of the activities of Nechayev were published in various newspapers, and it was on these that Dostoyevsky could draw for his portrayal of Petr Stepanovich. When eventually the trial did begin, it coincided with the return of Dostoyevsky to Russia, and in writing Parts II and III of *The Devils* Dostoyevsky had at his disposal detailed material provided, for once, by the Russian press itself; for officialdom had decided that the proceedings should be staged as a show trial, and that the newspapers should be allowed to carry full and detailed reports.

One of the incriminating documents brought forward as evidence against the Nechayevists was 'The Catechism of the Revolutionary',[12] which had been written by Bakunin in collaboration with Nechayev. In this can be seen the inspiration for certain aspects of the behaviour of Petr Verkhovensky in Dostoyevsky's novel. Thus the 'Catechism' states that the true and natural revolutionary in Russia is the peasant brigand; in the novel it is the peasant Fedka, the escaped convict and robber, who is one of the chief instruments for the execution of Verkhovensky's schemes. Again one of the aims of the 'Catechism' is the discrediting of established authority, and a method advocated for this is blackmail: 'If possible get hold of their dirty secrets; make them our slaves.' It is not difficult to see in this exhortation the source for Verkhovensky's treatment of the Governor Von Lembke; why he seeks to appropriate the governor's untalented literary efforts and his compromising collection of revolutionary pamphlets. Petr Verkhovensky's false courtship of Von Lembke's wife, on the other hand, seems to derive from another of the 'Catechism's' commands: that the professional revolutionary should conspire with ambitious politicians and liberals, pretend to follow them only to get control of them and compromise them.

The control of others through the ferreting out of their 'dirty secrets' was practised by Nechayev himself not only against his enemies but against his friends. When Bakunin was absent from his apartment, Nechayev went through his papers, until he had found something which could compromise him should the need arise. Relations between the two men grew very strained.

In August 1872 the Swiss police arrested Nechayev and he was extradited by the Russian authorities as a common criminal. He stood trial in January 1873, and was condemned to twenty years' hard labour, followed by exile in Siberia for life. The terms of this sentence were never carried out, instead he was taken to the Alekseyevskiy Ravelin, the most impregnable part of that same Peter Paul Fortress, from which, four years earlier, he had boasted an escape. So it was that Nechayev appeared to have vanished from the face of the earth; for the inmates of the Alekseyevskiy Ravelin lost name, identity and all contact with the outside world; the gaolers of this forgotten part of the prison were not even allowed to utter a word to their prisoners.

It is a mark of the strength of character and personal magnetism of Nechayev that his behaviour did not alter one degree under these apparently inhuman conditions; indeed he set about little by little, and by the methods he had always used, to impose his will on his gaolers. Ultimately he succeeded in organising them into revolutionary groups, much as before in his earlier dealings with the students of the Moscow Agricultural Academy. Such was Nechayev's success that in 1879 he contrived, through the agency of these same gaolers, to smuggle out a message to the revolutionary group operating under the name of 'The People's Will', asking them to effect his escape.

It seemed almost that he was within an ace of accomplishing the empty boast by which he had embarked on his political career, but the leaders of 'The People's Will' would not endanger their main plan, the assassination of Alexander II, in order to rescue a man, who, once free, would ruthlessly set about the destruction of their own movement. Indeed, the realisation of their prime objective hastened Nechayev's fate; for after the assassination of Alexander, the conditions of Nechayev's confinement became even more intolerable, and he died of scurvy the year after the death of Dostoyevsky himself.

It is obvious from this brief biography that Nechayev was a man of quite different calibre from the caricature presented by Dostoyevsky in the figure of Petr Verkhovensky. The Nechayev of real life was undoubtedly a man of magnetic personality – a man of iron will who challenged conventional morality. Such a figure was bound to fascinate Dostoyevsky, and there was a danger that under his pen Nechayev could turn into something of a sympathetic character – could become another Raskolnikov. There was, moreover, the added danger of some degree of self-identification with Nechayev; for apart from the odd coincidence that his own mother's maiden name was Nechayev, Dostoyevsky had himself engaged in revolutionary activity as a young man, and had suffered for it in the ten years spent in Siberia. This parallel must have been clear to Dostoyevsky; for in *The Writer's Diary* in 1873 he was to claim that he himself was an old *Nechayevist*.[13] It was inevitable, therefore, that Dostoyevsky should be dissatisfied with the numerous plans for the work purely as a pamphlet novel. The solution to his problems only came with a new plan and a new hero.

Stavrogin is Dostoyevsky's most ambitious attempt at the portrayal of 'the strong man'. It is as though the author has distilled off into this character all the magnetism and strength of will of the Nechayev of real life, and having done this, he is now able to deal with his fictional portrait of Nechayev in a purely polemical way; for what remains is unpleasant dregs. Petr Verkhovensky is ill-mannered, insolent, peevish and petty-minded in his ruthlessness, but above all he has been given one characteristic which was completely alien to the Nechayev of real life – he is clownish. Petr Verkhovensky is undoubtedly a sinister clown, but clown he nevertheless is; for in order to deal with Nechayev in a way which would exclude his own latent sympathy for such a 'self-willed man', Dostoyevsky had to deck him out in motley.

Thus in the creative process which produced this novel, Petr Verkhovensky and Stavrogin began as a *double*. In Stavrogin the potential of a saint is combined with all the dark strength of will of the criminal: he is a figure from high tragedy. In Petr Verkhovensky, on the other hand, can be seen all the petty tyranny and spleen of a comic caricature: he is the wicked, spiteful doll in a puppet show.

This other charismatic self is absolutely necessary for the political ends of Petr Verkhovensky. Stavrogin is his untainted ideal, and when he suspects that Stavrogin himself might not be equal to his high destiny, he turns on him in anger: 'All right, I am a clown, but I do not want you, my more important half, to be a clown.' (Pt III, Ch. III, 2.)

Yet although Petr Verkhovensky (who appears to have respect for no one) shows such veneration for Stavrogin, this does not prevent his attempting to gain power over his idol by seeking to compromise him in the murder of his wife. Verkhovensky, for his own part, wishes to dispose of Marya Lebyadkin, because she is an embarrassment to what he sees as the heroic pretensions of Stavrogin; she is also an obstacle in his attempt to unite Stavrogin with the rich heiress, Liza Tushina. Marya's brother must be disposed of at the same time, for in a letter to Von Lembke he has threatened to inform on the political activity of Verkhovensky himself. So once more in Dostoyevsky's treatment of the Nechayev affair we come up against the phenomenon of the double: Nechayev had only instigated one murder, but Petr Verkhovensky is responsible for two such crimes, one of which, in itself, is a double murder. This doubling of basic figures is typical of Dostoyevsky's writing.

Stavrogin, as we shall see, brings into the work a new plane of ideas, indeed comes out of another novel, but this is not to say that he has no place in the pamphlet novel. It is a measure of the integrated structure of *The Devils*, that Stavrogin is at one and the same time an important figure in the 'fathers and children' theme of the political novel, while on another level he is the centre of 'the great sinner' theme of the metaphysical novel.

As with Stepan Trofimovich and Petr Verkhovensky, indications of the sociological significance of Stavrogin are clearly given in the text. Stavrogin, we learn, had a promising career before him as an officer in a guards regiment, but he had the habit of picking on people and insulting them merely for the pleasure of doing so. As a result he fights two duels over issues in which he is in the wrong. One of his opponents is killed, the other is crippled; and for this he is reduced to the ranks and sent to a place of exile where he is to serve in a simple army regiment. This could very well be the biography of Lermontov, and Stavrogin's mother who seeks to explain his behaviour in terms of 'a demon of irony' (a phrase with a strong Lermontovian resonance) intercedes for her son, much as Lermontov's grandmother had interceded for him. Certain incidents ascribed to Stavrogin (e.g. knocking people down with his horses; insulting a society lady in public[14]) read like more specific references to Lermontov's hero Pechorin, and it is not surprising that, for his amorous activities Liputin should brand him: 'Pechorin devourer of hearts'.

Yet the real function of these references to Lermontov is to connect Stavrogin with a general social phenomenon rather than with any particular person; there are also similar references to Pushkin,[15] and Stavrogin is compared to the Decembrists in general. Thus Stavrogin's behaviour in his duel with Gaganov is seen as consonant with the mores of the guards officers of the 1820s, and the narrator himself compares Stavrogin to M. S. Lunin (referred to as L-n in the text): a Decembrist renowned for his incredible acts of bravery. Yet in comparing their common quality of 'spleen' [*zloba*] the narrator also draws a distinction:

As regards spleen, of course, we have moved on since L–n, even since Lermontov. There was, perhaps, more spleen in Nikolay Vsevolodovich than in both of them put together, but this spleen was cold, calm, and, if it is possible to say this, *rational*.

(Pt I, Ch. v, 8)

In the figure of Stavrogin there is, then, a résumé of the type of the 'Byronic nobleman' of the twenties and thirties, but at the same time he is the last of a line: he is, in the words of Shatov, '*posledniy barich*' – 'the last of the noblemen's sons'.

The Soviet critic L. Grossman has argued that there are many points of similarity between the portryal of Stavrogin and the biography of Bakunin himself.[16] Indeed Bakunin, earlier in his life, had received a slap in the face from Katkov (the very person who was now publishing Dostoyevsky's novel) and like Stavrogin, he had refused to avenge it, even though he was a renowned dueller. Katkov had also thrown the jibe of 'Castrate' [*skopets*] at Bakunin, for in spite of his many amours and his debauchery, the veteran revolutionary was reputed to be sexually impotent. In *The Devils* the same jibe seems to be cast, in an oblique fashion, at Stravrogin. The occasion is Petr Verkhovensky's visit to Stavrogin after the incident of the slap in the face which he has received from Shatov. Petr Verkhovensky, taking his leave, cannot resist the opportunity for Parthian shafts:

'However, good-bye. You look rather green.'
'I have a fever.'
'I can believe it. You had better lie down. By the way, there are Castrates here in the district. They're curious people. However, of that anon.'

(Pt II, Ch. I, 3)

At first sight these words might not appear particularly significant, but taken in context the impression is different. The whole of this scene is permeated by innuendo (thus Petr Verkhovensky obliquely suggests a deal with Fedka over Marya and Liza) and shortly before this apparently inconsequential reference to the Castrates Petr Verkhovensky had knocked down one of Stavrogin's books: a 'Keepsake' (an album with illustrations [of beautiful women]) entitled *The Women of Balzac*. Thus the immediate shift from an observation on Stavrogin's complexion to a remark on the presence of Castrates reads like a comment on his interest in pretty women; for the Castrates were easily identifiable by their drawn and pallid features.

Moreover, when Petr Verkhovensky has arranged the deal which he hints at in this scene, and has procured Liza for Stavrogin, he again casts aspersions on Stavrogin's virility:

'Just imagine, as soon as you came out to me, I guessed from your face that you had had a "misfortune", even, perhaps, a complete failure, eh? Well I will bet', he shouted, almost choking with delight, 'that you spent the whole night sitting side by side on two chairs in the drawing room, and wasted all the valuable time arguing on some lofty and noble theme.'   (Pt III, Ch. III, 2)

On this occasion the insinuations of Petr Verkhovensky are backed by the testimony of Liza herself. She tells Stavrogin quite plainly of her own disillusionment with the night they have spent together, and compares him to a cripple for whom she refuses to act as nurse.

The imputed impotence of Stavrogin is no mere frill: it is, as we shall see, something which is central to the novel; nor is the reference to the sects without significance for a fuller understanding of what Stavrogin himself represents. But if the 'impotence' of Stavrogin links him with Bakunin (and in view of the latter's association with Nechayev such a supposition is not unreasonable) it is nevertheless the nature of Stavrogin's 'impotence' which marks him off from the veteran revolutionary; for the 'impotence' of Stavrogin is a spiritual state – he is 'neither hot nor cold'; whereas Bakunin himself was, above all else, an enthusiast, and it is the quality of enthusiasm which Stavrogin appears to envy in Petr Verkhovensky.[17]

Just as Stavrogin brings another plane of ideas to the pages of the 'pamphlet novel', so too his sociological significance, within the pamphlet novel itself, is on a different scale of time; for if this 'last of the noblemen's sons' is to be taken as an updated representative of the Byronic figures of the twenties and thirties (even, indeed, if he is to be identified more closely with Bakunin) his sociological role can only be fully integrated into the novel through the operation of a double chronological perspective. Stavrogin and Petr Verkhovensky are represented as young men of the same age; Pechorinism thus appears to be running in parallel with nihilism. Even if Stavrogin is identified with Bakunin the problem still remains, for Bakunin was not the equal in years of Nechayev, he was, in fact, of the same generation as Granovsky. This dislocation of chronological strata is, nevertheless, inevitable; for the very essence of the Byronic nobleman is that he is young; whereas the liberal of the forties can only be depicted as middle aged if he is to be seen in confrontation with his own intellectual offspring – the nihilist of the sixties. In the novel Stepan Trofimovich is Stavrogin's tutor, but it is significant that Dostoyevsky seeks to blur this relationship of teacher and pupil: 'It somehow came about quite naturally that there was not the slightest distance between them.'

Similar attempts to narrow the gap between these two characters are observable elsewhere in the novel. Thus at the very beginning (Pt I, Ch. I, 3) we are told that Stepan Trofimovich had become the son of Stavrogin's mother ('flesh of her flesh') and at the end she herself pronounces after the death of Stepan Trofimovich that she has no son ('as though prophesying'). On this occasion she is insisting on adopting Stepan Trofimovich's 'woman' – Sofya – just as earlier she had suggested adopting Marya, the 'woman' of her own son. The sense of parity between the two figures is further strengthened by the fact that it is Stepan Trofimovich who is chosen as a substitue for Stavrogin in the proposed marriage to Dasha 'for another man's sins'. As we shall see in the next chapter the substitution of Stepan Trofimovich for Stavrogin is valid on yet another level.

But, on the level of the 'pamphlet novel', if it is as 'sons' that the parity of the two characters is established, it is nevertheless as 'fathers' that this parallelism comes into its own; for just as Stepan Trofimovich is responsible for Petr Verkhovensky, so too Stavrogin is the intellectual 'father' of Kirillov and

Shatov. It is typical of the dualism which everywhere informs the writing of this novel, that the reader should thus be presented, not with one theme of 'fathers and children', but with two.

Shatov is a Slavophile, but his obsessive preoccupation with 'the nation' and with the Orthodox faith leads him into making such pronouncements as: 'He who is not Orthodox cannot be Russian', and this, he says, is no longer a Slavophile idea. Shatov's Slavophilism, in fact, is so extreme that it is virtually a caricature: the Russian nation has become God. In pushing assumptions latent in Slavophilism to their extreme, Dostoyevsky exposes its weakness; for Shatov has reached a point where he can believe in Christ and Orthodoxy, but the only God in whom he can believe is the Russian nation.

Kirillov, in contrast, is a Westerniser. He bears the imprint of Western technology (he is an engineer) and he comes to Russia from Switzerland; moreover, although he is Russian by birth, he speaks his native language in a disjointed way as though he were a foreigner. His central belief is the thesis of Feuerbach, that man is God, and this is tempered by a certain amount of Darwinian theory on the possibility of further physical evolution for the human race. Here again, these ideas are developed to the point where they become absurd; for the only way in which Kirillov can achieve his new-found godhead is to commit suicide. The terms he finally chooses for his signature on the suicide note (with the cry of Eureka) are also revealing; for *'gentilhomme russe et citoyen du monde civilisé'* seems to be a reference to Herzen,[18] and the addition of 'séminariste' (a word synonymous with nihilist in the sixties) shows that in the figure of Kirillov Westernism has developed into self-destructive nihilism.

The fact that Stavrogin, at one and the same time, has implanted two entirely different systems of ideas in the minds of his two disciples makes much sense in terms of Russia's cultural history; for it was the figure of the Byronic nobleman, and the ideas behind the Decembrist movement, which ultimately gave birth in the forties to the two opposing factions of the Westernisers, and the Slavophiles.[19] This metaphor holds good, even if 'the last of the nobleman's sons' be identified more directly with Bakunin; for Bakunin presided over that young body of Russia's intellectual élite, known as The Stankevich Circle, and at the very end of its existence – at that very moment, in fact, when it split up into Westernisers and Slavophiles.

The reason for the extreme conclusions reached by Shatov and Kirillov is that in them Slavophilism and Westernism have been updated so as to reveal the full extent of their development: Shatov is the last word in Slavophilism; just as Kirillov is the ultimate in Westernism. Here again Dostoyevsky is polemicising with Turgenev, as can be seen from the following words of Karmazinov:

'Yes, of course', lisped Karmazinov, 'in the figure of Pogozhev, I have exposed all the weaknesses of the Slavophiles, and in the figure of Nikodimov – all the weaknesses of the Westernisers.'

'Just fancy, *all* their weaknesses', whispered Lyamshin quietly.

(Pt II, Ch. x, 3)

The reference is to Turgenev's novel *A Nest of Gentlefolk*, and the self-congratulatory author is no other than Turgenev himself.

Turgenev is such a pervading presence behind 'the pamphlet novel' that it should come as no surprise that he himself figures in it as yet another polemical portrait. The 'eminent author' Karmazinov has been given certain of Turgenev's physical and moral characteristics: like Turgenev he has a querulous voice, and he walks with a mincing action (Turgenev was a tall man who had disproportionately short legs, so that when he walked he appeared to mince). The narrator speaks of Karmazinov's pride, and the way he would court highly-placed personages; he would even disown his friends in the company of the great: such were the criticisms frequently voiced about Turgenev's behaviour. When the narrator first meets Karmazinov, he is made to feel inferior, in the incident of the dropped bag. Dostoyevsky himself complained of Turgenev's habit of pretending to be about to embrace one on first meeting, only to offer his cheek to be kissed; this characteristic trait of condescension is given to Karmazinov in *The Devils*.[20]

It is, however, Dostoyevsky's portrait of Karmazinov as the man of letters which is the most spiteful. The narrator claims to have been a devoted reader of Karmazinov in his youth; for Karmazinov's early works were poetical; but the narrator says that his enthusiasm waned once Karmazinov started writing tendentious novels, and his very latest works he does not like at all. Here is a parallel with Turgenev's own literary career. Turgenev began as a poet (when Dostoyevsky first made his acquaintance he was chiefly known as the author of the poem 'Parasha') and poetic qualities permeate his early masterpiece in prose *The Hunter's Sketches*. Then there followed a series of novels on social themes (*Rudin, A Nest of Gentlefolk, On the Eve, Fathers and Children*) culminating in 'his latest work' *Smoke*, a novel whose anti-Russian theme incensed Dostoyevsky, and which more than anything led to their final break.

Particularly wounding is the narrator's criticism of an article written about a shipwreck, in which Karmazinov is accused of being more concerned with his own feelings than with the fate of the victims of the disaster. This corresponds to criticism which Dostoyevsky had expressed privately about Turgenev's article 'The Execution of Traupman' (1870).[21] But the fact that the subject of Karmazinov's article is a shipwreck adds another barb to Dostoyevsky's shaft; for it evokes rumours, then current in literary circles, of how Turgenev had disgraced himself in a similar incident at sea. As a young man Turgenev had travelled by sea to Germany. The ship had caught fire and Turgenev's rush for the boats and his desire to save himself before all others had become a matter for literary tittle-tattle.

In the opinion of the narrator 'the great writer' is not as great as he himself obviously thinks he is. He is, after all, only a middle-brow talent who has written himself out. Evidence for this artistic bankruptcy is provided by Karmazinov's literary reading: his farewell piece 'Merci' (or rather this evidence is provided by the hostile account of it given by the narrator himself). The piece is a parody of at least three of Turgenev's works: *Apropos of 'Fathers and Children'* (in which Turgenev talks about laying down his pen); *Enough* (with its emphasis on personal experiences and thoughts) and *Spectres* (with its rambling and fantastic theme). That *Spectres* is one of the works parodied lends added piquancy to the fact that the manuscript is lent to Petr Verkhovensky, who returns it quite negligently without having read it; for Turgenev had first handed the manuscript of *Spectres* to Dostoyevsky to be considered as a possible contribution for the journal *Vremya* [*Time*]. Dostoyevsky on this occasion was in Baden with Pauline Suslova and could think of nothing else but gambling; he returned the piece to Turgenev unread.[22]

When Dostoyevsky had next visited Turgenev at his home in Baden in 1867, Dostoyevsky had been in a hostile mood partly caused by reading *Smoke*. Dostoyevsky's version of this encounter seems to have furnished certain details for the character of Karmazinov.[23] At this meeting Turgenev declared himself an atheist, as Karmazinov does in the novel; he also claimed to consider himself a German and not a Russian, and to be proud of it. In the novel Karmazinov echoes these sentiments: 'I have become a German and regard this as an honour.' Indeed he professes to be more concerned about the water system in Karlsruhe than about all the reforms introduced in Russia during the sixties. Karmazinov's disparagement of Russia is in keeping with ideas voiced by Turgenev in *Smoke*, yet at the same time he shows a certain apprehensive toadying to the new generation of revolutionaries. He concedes that Europe will be destroyed; nevertheless, he thinks it will last his own lifetime, whereas in Russia there is nothing to be destroyed: nothing but wooden buildings.

When *Fathers and Children* appeared, Turgenev was accused by critics of the Right of attempting to win favour amongst the younger generation. Certainly Pisarev, one of the most extreme of the leaders of the younger generation openly welcomed Bazarov. In *The Devils*, Dostoyevsky renews the attack: Karmazinov is represented as trying to curry favour with the young people in general and with Petr Verkhovensky in particular. Thus he not only regards the various scandals committed by the young people as very amusing, but treats the younger Verkhovensky with a surprising amount of deference. His very name is significant; for Karmazinov is derived from a Russian version of the French word *cramoisi*: Karmazinov is a 'pink' – a secret sympathiser with the revolutionaries.

Many of the other characters in the novel have prototypes in real life. Shatov, within the 'Fathers and Children' framework of the novel, is the out-and-out Slavophile, but he is also Dostoyevsky's refurbishing of Ivanov – the victim of the Nechayev plot. Nevertheless, Dostoyevsky seems to have given him many autobiographical characteristics. Thus he is a man who has left the revolutionary movement, and is in search of God, though his faith is, as yet, shaky, and under the close questioning of Stavrogin he admits that belief in God is only a possibility for the future: 'I shall believe in God.' Shatov has become the mouthpiece for many of Dostoyevsky's own ideas, and it is obvious that, like many other characters in the novel, he is far removed from his original prototype.

There are prototypes, too, for the minor revolutionaries. The inspiration for Liputin, the ardent Fourierist and petty domestic tyrant was A. P. Milyukov, a minor literary figure of Dostoyevsky's own generation who was on the fringes of the Petrashevsky circle. The name Liputin is comic and seems to be derived from Swift's 'Lilliputians' (at the beginning of the novel, Stepan Trofimovich is likened to a Gulliver, who thinks of his fellow men as Lilliputians). Shigalev, the doctrinaire theorist, first figured in the notebooks under the name Zaytsev, an extreme nihilistic journalist of the sixties, who had fled abroad and at the time of the novel's conception was associated with Bakunin in the First International.

The others, as we should expect, are derived from the participants in the Nechayev affair. Virginsky has characteristics of two of the accused (P. G. Uspensky and A. Kuznetsov), Erkel is derived from another Nechayevist, N. Nikolayev, whilst the comparative late-comer into the novel,

Tolkachenko ('the expert on the common people') is based on I. G. Pryzhov, a minor *littérateur* and collector of folk-lore, who was also implicated in the trial.

So far we have mentioned five of the group of conspirators, but there is yet a sixth: the 'little Jew', Lyamshin. Before the murder they all meet at Erkel's, and Dostoyevsky tells us: '"Our people" met in full force – all five of them.' The 'five' prove to be six: Erkel, Liputin, Virginsky, Lyamshin, Shigalev and Tolkachenko. Moreover this number is to be increased by their leader Petr Verkhovensky. It is the same 'five' who commit the murder, although Dostoyevsky does attempt to redress the balance somewhat by having Shigalev leave before the act is accomplished. Nevertheless, if Petr Verkhovensky is to be included as the leader of the cell, then the 'five' must really be seven, and if the reason for Shatov's murder is that he is a defecting member of this cell, then the 'five' reaches the total of eight. This tendency towards the proliferation of characters has much in common with the phenomenon of 'doubling'.[24]

Other, even more minor, characters have real-life prototypes, like the sister of Virginsky who is interested in helping poor students; and the 'third reader' at the literary fête, the madman who brings the scene to its chaotic culmination with his violent denunciation of Russia.[25] The scenes in which both these characters occur are in themselves comic highlights of the novel. The first, 'Amongst Our People' (i.e. at Virginsky's), ridicules the petty-mindedness and ineptitude of the would-be revolutionaries; the second, the occasion of the literary readings, exposes the established figures (both literary and political) who appear to be the pillars of local society.

It is interesting that the revolutionaries and nihilists are not the only butts for Dostoyevsky's satire; established authority is made to appear just as ridiculous. This is true of the ex-governor who has his ear bitten by Stavrogin, and who, it is gently hinted, is having an affaire with a widow in the district. It is true too of the police inspector with the comic name of Flibusterov who was renowned for his 'immoderate zeal' and his 'congenital drunkenness'. But all this is mild compared with Dostoyevsky's treatment of the Von Lembkes. They are members of the German echelons of the Russian civil service, for whom Dostoyevsky has nothing but hostility and contempt. The governor himself is weak and incompetent, more fitted for his leisure pursuits of making elaborate toys out of paper and writing third-rate sentimental novels. Real power lies in the hands of his wife who is scheming and ambitious. It is because of her liberal pretensions that the couple come to such grief. When, as a result of their public humiliation, Von Lembke loses his last shred of mental equilibrium, he reveals himself as the weak man turned reactionary: he orders that the Shpigulinsky workers,[26] who have come peacefully to present a petition, should be beaten.

Dostoyevsky's tendency towards the creation of 'doubles' shows even here; for, as if the character of Von Lembke were not stupid enough, he is closely associated with a particularly obtuse German civil servant named Blum, who is protected by Von Lembke as though he were a brother (Blum bears the same Christian name and patronymic as Von Lembke himself). It is this comic 'double' who is responsible for Von Lembke's most misguided actions.

The reduction of a provincial civil service hierarchy to comic absurdity is strongly reminiscent of Gogol (particularly Gogolian is the supposed beating of the non-existent Tarapygina). Yet this ridicule of the ruling classes, taken in conjunction with Dostoyevsky's treatment of the revolutionaries, suggests a quite unexpected comparison; for this same double attack is the very substance of a novel which Dostoyevsky himself deeply detested: Turgenev's *Smoke*. Dostoyevsky's intention was not to write an 'anti-Russian' novel – indeed quite the reverse; yet the fact remains that there is not one social group in *The Devils* which has positive values, so that the overriding effect is inevitably one of pessimism; the same sort of pessimism about Russia which permeates *Smoke*. The presence of Turgenev, it seems, is never far away from the pages of the pamphlet novel.

THE PAMPHLET NOVEL: 'THE DEVILS'

From what we have seen earlier of Dostoyevsky's polemical writing, it is obvious that no 'pamphlet novel' which came from his pen would be complete without an attack on that father-figure of nihilistic thought, Chernyshevsky. Stepan Trofimovich reads *What is to be Done?* To find out what it is which inspires the behaviour of the younger generation. As we have seen, he comes to the conclusion that although Chernyshevsky's basic idea is the same as that of the men of the forties, his development of this idea is entirely different. Petr Verkhovensky, however, seems contemptuous of his father's choice of reading, and tells him he will bring him something better. The implications of this are clear: the men of the late sixties, the 'Nechayevs', have gone beyond even the nihilism of Chernyshevsky. Indeed the new theorist, Shigalev, is pointedly dismissing Chernyshevsky's dream of utopian palaces of glass and aluminium, when he says that aluminium columns are for sparrows not for men.[27]

Despite this, there are other nihilists in the novel who still uphold the ideals of *What is to be Done?* Thus Marie Shatov comes back to the town to have her baby, and intends to support herself by opening a bookbinding business on 'rational, principles of association' (shades of Vera Pavlovna's famous dress-making commune). But the influence of *What is to be Done?* is most noticeable in the Virginsky household; here can be seen a parody of the rational sexual relationships depicted by Chernyshevsky in his novel. Mrs Virginsky 'dismisses' her husband during the first year of marriage and takes in his place (of all people) Captain Lebyadkin. At this new turn in his personal affairs, Virginsky, so one rumour goes, said to his wife: 'My friend, up till now I have only loved you – now I respect you.'[28] Such selfless magnanimity does not last long, however; about a fortnight later they all go out on a picnic as a family group, and the idyll is shattered, when Virginsky suddenly attacks Lebyadkin and pulls him by the hair. The Virginsky/Lebyadkin triangle, and their rational attempts to square it, recall the situation of Vera Pavlovna and her two husbands Lopakhin and Kirsanov. The picnic too is a parody of a similar idyllic event at the end of *What is to be Done?*, but the inclusion of a hair-pulling incident is Dostoyevsky's own comment on such marvellously rational behaviour. Given their attitude to sexual relationships, the name Virginsky is an added touch of irony; and, as if to add emphasis, Mrs Virginsky is by profession a midwife (one of the occupations which female nihilists often took up in their championship of women's rights).

What is to be Done? is not the only work by Chernyshevsky which is parodied in *The Devils*. Stavrogin's mother vies with the governor's wife in professing to adhere to the fashionable ideas of the younger generation, and she treats Stepan Trofimovich to a lecture on aesthetics, derived from Chernyshevsky's doctoral thesis 'The Aesthetic Relationships of Art to Reality'. She attacks the aestheticism of the 'men of the forties', in particular she challenges Stepan Trofimovich on his championship of the Sistine *Madonna*. Such a work of pure art is out of fashion, she claims, and cannot be compared with simple objects like mugs and pencils, the beauty of which inheres in their usefulness. Here is a garbled version of the theory of utility as the chief criterion in aesthetic judgements, and Varvara Petrovna proceeds to give her own interpretation of Chernyshevsky's dictum that the creations of art are on a lower aesthetic plane than those of reality:

Try and draw an apple and place a real apple next to it. Which one will you take? There's no fear of you making a mistake. This is what all your theories are reduced to, as soon as they are illuminated by the first ray of free investigation.[29] (Pt II, Ch. v, 3)

Varvara Petrovna goes on to propound the teachings of the younger generation on charity, and accuses Stepan Trofimovich of having deliberately kept her in ignorance about all these new ideas. Nevertheless, she must have come across them before; for at the beginning of the novel we are told of Varvara Petrovna's trip to St Petersburg with Stepan Trofimovich during the intellectual ferment of the early sixties, and of their disheartening attempts to enter the literary world of the young radicals. We are told that Stepan Trofimovich even managed to penetrate to the Olympian heights of the leaders of the whole movement (this must surely mean Chernyshevsky, Dobrolyubov, etc.) and even invited them once or twice to the salon held by Varvara Petrovna.

Indeed, one of the reasons why Stepan Trofimovich rapidly fell out of favour with the young radicals on this occasion, was his solid defence of the aesthetic ideals of his own generation:

> He readily agreed about the useless and comic nature of the word 'Fatherland', even agreed with the idea of the harmful nature of religion, but he loudly and firmly declared that boots were lower than Pushkin, and very much lower at that. (Pt I, Ch. I, 6)

Now when he has to face the onslaught of these same anti-aesthetic ideas from the lips of Varvara Petrovna herself, he counters by asserting that he will once more speak out about beauty to the nihilists; he will speak about the Sistine *Madonna*[30] at the proposed literary reading.

In his argument with his old friend and benefactress, Stepan Trofimovich casts himself in the role of the knight true to his lady; and the 'lady' here, it seems, is not the Sistine *Madonna*, but Varvara Petrovna herself: 'You have always despised me, but I shall finish like a knight true to my lady.' (Pt II, Ch. v, 3.) This reference to 'the knight' is taken up in the culmination of the scene: Stepan Trofimovich threatens to go off on some new quest – 'But to the road, to the road, to a new road:

> Full of pure love,
> True to a sweet dream.'

The quotation is one we have encountered before: it is from Pushkin's 'Poor Knight': the poem which in the *The Idiot* identified Myshkin with the theme of 'beauty saving the world'. Here the effect of the quotation is comic, but behind it lies a serious idea: the foolish Stepan Trofimovich has something in common with the 'idiot' Prince Myshkin – he too is about to become the bearer of a great message.

Of all the ideas associated with 'the men of the forties', there is one which Dostoyevsky cannot ridicule for long: the cult of beauty. Earlier in the novel Stepan Trofimovich expressed the difference between the ethical preoccupation of the younger generation and his own cult of the aesthetic in such hyperbolical utterances as: 'I would give the whole of the Russian peasantry in exchange for one Rachel.' Here outré westernism fuses with veneration for the art of a great actress, and the utterance itself is grotesquely comic. But at the literary fête, even though elements of comedy are still strongly present, Stepan Trofimovich proclaims the same idea with the urgency and stridency of a man explaining a fundamental article of faith; the primacy of the aesthetic is now to be taken seriously:

'But I declare that Shakespeare and Raphael are higher than the Emancipation of the Serfs; higher than the concept of nationality; higher than socialism; higher than the younger generation; higher than chemistry; higher, almost, than the whole of mankind; for they are indeed the fruit, the real fruit of the whole of mankind, perhaps, the highest fruit that ever can be. Beauty's form already achieved, without the achievement of which, I would perhaps not even agree to live ... Good Lord!' he cried throwing up his arms. 'Ten years ago I shouted exactly the same from a stage in St Petersburg, exactly the same thing, in the very same words, and just like you, they did not understand anything, but laughed and hissed as you are doing now. Dull-witted people, what do you need to enable you to comprehend? Do you know, do you know that humanity could get along without Englishmen, could get along without Germany, and, of course, without the Russians. It could get along without science, without bread, but only one thing, and one thing alone, it could not get on without, and that is beauty; for there would be nothing to do on earth. All mystery is here; all history is here. Science itself could not last a moment without beauty. Do you know this, you who laugh? It would turn into clumsy philistinism. You would not be able to invent a nail! ... I shall not yield!' He yelled absurdly by way of conclusion, and banged his fist on the table with all his might.

(Pt III, Ch. I, 4)

Earlier in his speech Stepan Trofimovich had spoken of the need for mutual forgiveness [*vseproshcheniye*] between the generations, interpreting the gulf between them as the differ-ence between two ideals of beauty; but his audience is in no mood for forgiveness, nor is their ideal an aesthetic one as Stepan Trofimovich supposes; it is, rather, ethical. One of their number, a seminarist, asks 'the gentleman aesthete' an awkward question about his own moral responsibility for the crimes of his former serf, Fedka. Stepan Trofimovich is crushed by these jibes; and the idealist who had expressed the earnest hope for mutual forgiveness ends by renouncing his audience with a curse.

But if this is the failure of the old Stepan Trofimovich, it nevertheless marks the birth of the new. From now on the elder Verkhovensky is a humbler and at the same time more positive figure: he becomes a more substantial counter-weight to the negative ideas of the nihilists. His championship of beauty is the reverse of their anti-aestheticism; his desire for mutual forgiveness, which later finds expression in the dictum: 'all are to blame', is a bold inversion of 'no one is to blame' – a slogan current amongst young materialists who sought to explain human misery entirely in terms of environment and material conditions. 'All are to blame' is a theme implicit in the pamphlet novel itself, in which the central thesis is that 'Granovsky' is responsible for 'Nechayev'; but in the early stages of the novel the theme is worked out in a purely polemical way. Now with the sudden realisation of universal responsibility by both Stepan Trofimovich and Shatov (who is the first person in the novel to utter the words 'all are to blame') the polemical theme has acquired a new moral content; indeed the implications of this slogan go far beyond the confines of the pamphlet novel – it is one of Dostoyevsky's most challenging ideas.

In the argument between the generations, an argument which resolved itself crudely into a choice between Pushkin and a pair of boots, Dostoyevsky's own position seems clear. He chose to give his novel the title of a poem by Pushkin (*The Devils*, 1830), and a quotation from it forms his first epigraph. The second epigraph which expands this theme of 'the devils' comes from Luke viii. 32–3, and it is the new Stepan Trofimovich who takes up this passage of Scripture and points to its relevance for the novel itself:

You see it's exactly like this Russia of ours. These devils leaving the sick man and entering into swine – these are all the sores, all the stinks, all the filth, all the devils and their offspring which have been accumulating for centuries and centuries in our dear, great sick man, our Russia! Oui cette Russie, que j'aimais toujours. But there is a great idea and a great will which will protect her from above, as was the case with that madman who was possessed; and out will come all these devils, all this filth, all these abominations festering on the surface; and they themselves will cry out to enter into swine. Perhaps they have even entered into them already. Such ones as we, we and they, and Petr ... et les autres avec lui, and I perhaps first of all, at their head. Deranged and frenzied we will throw ourselves from the cliff into the sea and all will drown; and it will serve us all right for that is all we are fit for. But the sick man will be healed, and 'will sit at the feet of Jesus' ... and all will look at him in amazement.

(Pt III, Ch. VII, 2)

All the ills which have been tormenting Russia for centuries are thus to be purged in the urge towards self-destruction exhibited by the 'men of the forties' and 'the men of the sixties'. After elucidating the parable Stepan Trofimovich loses consciousness for three days, and when he regains it he looks out of the window and is surprised: '"tiens, un lac", he said. "Good Lord! I hadn't even seen it until now".' The solver of the riddle is himself dying on the shores of a lake.[31]

The parable of the Gadarene swine is the very kernel of the 'pamphlet novel', and as a result the associated themes of self-destruction and madness permeate the whole of its fabric. Kirillov is supposed to be collecting material relating to the question why people commit suicide: the novel itself would provide him with many answers. Thus there is the little girl Matresha (in the banned chapter) who commits suicide out of shame and despair; there is, by way of contrast, the youth in the hotel who commits suicide as the fitting climax to an ephemeral orgy of pleasure-seeking; by way of contrast again, there is the claim of Stavrogin that he understands the attraction of committing suicide after deliberately perpetrating a vile act which would be remembered for a thousand years. At the level of the pamphlet novel, his own suicide and that of Kirillov may be interpreted as the self-destructive urge of the two 'devils' of 'Pechorinism' and 'nihilistic westernism' plaguing the body of 'Holy Russia', but the motives behind these two acts are more complicated than this: they will be examined more fully in the next chapter.

One of the young people, crowding in to see the body of the youth in the hotel, asks a pertinent question:

Why is it that with us people have started hanging themselves and shooting themselves so frequently; just as though they have gone off their rockers, as though nobody any longer has anything firm to stand on? (Pt II, Ch. v, 2)

The novel provides much evidence for such an epidemic of madness. Thus mental derangement is presented as a possible explanation for the enigmatic acts of Stavrogin described at the beginning of the novel. Yet the author is at pains to disassociate Stavrogin's act of self-destruction from any taint of madness, and the novel ends on a typically ironic note of enigma: 'After the post mortem our doctors insistently denied any possibility of madness.' There is less doubt, however, about Kirillov, the other chief suicide in the novel; he is constantly referred to as mad by the other characters – and with good reason.

Perhaps nihilism itself is a form of madness. In Part II, Chapter VI, 2, we are introduced to a second lieutenant who suddenly acts in a way somewhat reminiscent of Stavrogin himself: he strikes his commanding officer and bites him on the shoulder. We are told that there was no doubt that he had gone mad; for instance he had thrown out his landlady's icons and put in their place the works of German materialist writers (Vogt, Moleschott and Büchner) even lighting a candle before each one. Another of the revolutionaries, Lyamshin, participates in the murder of Shatov, and as a result of his experiences goes mad. The 'detractor of Russia' at the literary fête is also depicted as a madman.

Madness, however, affects all levels of society. The governor, Von Lembke, loses his sanity under the pressure of events. He drives out into the country to pick flowers, mistakes the

Shpigulin factory workers for 'filibusters' and in general behaves like a man at his wits' end. He visits the scene of the fires caused by the 'nihilists' and in his fuddled ramblings delivers himself of a phrase, which once more points to a general epidemic of madness: 'The fire is in people's minds and not on the roofs of houses.' (Pt III, Ch. II, 4.) Madness in the novel finds a poetically tragic expression in the simple-mindedness of Marya Lebyadkin (her utterances at times recall those of Ophelia). Madness is presented in a comic light in the figure of Semen Yakovlev, the *yurodivyy* seer of the district, who throws potatoes at his visitors and uses unprintable words in the presence of ladies. As the mad visionary he provides a comic counterweight to Marya Lebyadkin, who is also a *yurodivyy* and a seer, and who sees her own death in the face of Stavrogin. But Semen Yakovlev has another function in the novel: he must be taken as a portrait of 'the holy man' to be set beside that of Tikhon (in the banned chapter): one utters nothing but nonsense: the other speaks only sense. Semen Yakovlev[32] is thus Tikhon's comic shadow; another manifestation of the ever present device of 'the double'.

Madness, it appears, is everywhere, but if it is to be equated more specifically with nihilism, then Petr Verkhovensky must be the most deranged of all. His behaviour seems to reveal the workings of a masterful mind, yet his ingenuity is misapplied; for the goal to which he is driving is sheer folly. When he finally explains his plans in the chapter 'Ivan, the Crown Prince', Stavrogin listens in amazement to what he thinks are the ravings of a lunatic.

Petr Verkhovensky seeks to appeal to the religious fanaticism and superstitious ignorance of the mass of Russian peasantry. He wishes to use Stavrogin as a god-like figurehead for his revolution, yet in order that the essential mystery of Stavrogin may be preserved, he must be as inaccessible as a god:

Do you know what this phrase 'he is concealed' means? But he will appear. He will appear. We will spread a legend better than those of the Castrates. He exists but no one has seen him. Oh what a legend we could spread ...

Listen, I shall not show you to anybody, not to anybody, that is how it must be. He exists, but no one has seen him. He is concealed. You could perhaps be shown to one man in a hundred thousand, for example. Then a rumour would sweep throughout all the land: 'He has been seen, he has been seen'. The God Savaof, Ivan Filippovich, was seen too, as he rose before the people in his chariot to heaven. They saw him with their 'own' eyes. But you are not Ivan Filippovich; you are beautiful, proud as a god, not looking for anything for yourself, 'in concealment', with a halo of a victim.   (Pt II, Ch. VIII)

So Petr Verkhovensky wants to present Stavrogin to the Russian people as a second Danila Filippov – the semi-legendary father-figure of the most extreme of the religious sects: the Flagellants and the Castrates.[33] Now, it becomes clear why Petr Verkhovensky had earlier told the lame teacher that a new religion was coming in Russia to replace the old one, and the oblique innuendo linking Stavrogin with the Castrates takes on a new light.

The identification of Stavrogin with the sects is not just a whim of Petr Verkhovensky. In a letter of 1870 Dostoyevsky himself explained that the hero of his projected novel, 'The Life of a Great Sinner' was, at one stage of his life to have become a member of the sects.[34] His notebooks are even more explicit. Here, discussing the kind of figure he wishes to portray in Stavrogin, he specifically dismisses the type of nobleman depicted by Tolstoy in favour of a more fundamentally Russian type (a character from the root – *tip iz korennika*): 'Such fundamental types frequently become either Stenka Razins or Danila Filippovichs, or take things to the extremes of the Flagellants or the Castrates.'[35] Stavrogin himself has already claimed that Petr Verkhovensky wants him to be his Stenka Razin: 'because of an unusual aptitude for crime'; now Petr Verkhovensky reveals to him that he also wants him to be his Danila Filippov.

We have already encountered a similar mixture of the trappings of religious dissidence with the ideas of political revolution – in *Crime and Punishment* and *The Idiot*. In *The Devils*, however, these two elements are more marked, for the novel itself is an amalgam of two other works: one political, the other metaphysical. Yet it is a measure of the integration of these two strands that it is scarcely possible to examine one without, of necessity, implying the other. Thus Stavrogin's two disciples, Kirillov and Shatov, have both been connected with the revolutionary movement in Switzerland, yet both, in their different ways, are men taxed by religious problems. It is therefore highly significant that the house which they share is called 'The House of Filippov' (the sects themselves had a tradition of calling the residence of their semi-divine leaders by such names as 'The House of David', 'The House of God', etc.). 'The House of Filippov' is situated on 'Bogoyavlenskaya' street. This name is usually translated 'Epiphany Street', and literally it means 'Appearance of God Street'. The name obviously links it with the metaphysical preoccupations of the inhabitants of 'The House of Filippov', and through them its significance refers back to Stavrogin himself. By way of contrast the house in which the *political* revolutionaries meet is situated in 'Muravinaya Street' – 'Ant Street': a name which recalls Dostoyevsky's symbol of the ant-hill for the type of society towards which, he considered, such people were striving.

But the name 'Bogoyavlenskaya' is connected with the figure of Filippov in a more direct way; for it was in the monastery of this name that Filippov himself was imprisoned, after he had declared himself by throwing the holy books into the Volga.[36] The name 'Bogoyavlenskaya', therefore combines the hint of concealment with the hope of manifestation: 'he is concealed but he will appear'. These words linking Stavrogin with Filippov are the nub of Petr Verkhovensky's attempt to present Stavrogin as a political figure, and they are also valid on the metaphysical plane itself; for, as we shall see in the next chapter, the dark enigma which Stavrogin represents is always promising to break out into the clear light of day.

Shatov[37] and Kirillov are not the only inhabitants of 'The House of Filippov'; before the advent of Stavrogin, the Lebyadkins had also lived there. In them, too, can be seen the same association of political dissidence with religious dissidence. The brother, Captain Lebyadkin, is a hanger-on of the revolutionary movement: his sister, on the other hand, is characterised by elements of religious unorthodoxy. She is described as *yurodivaya* [holy fool], and although she has spent some time in a convent, it was nevertheless there that she came into contact with religious extremism. Thus she is impressed by the extreme asceticism of another *yurodivaya*, Elizaveta Blazhennaya, and confesses that she would like to follow her example. It was in the convent that she formed the idea that God is nature, and met an old woman who had been sent to the convent as a penance for uttering prophecies. This woman could well be a schismatic, for she is certainly the bearer of heretical ideas: 'The madonna is the great mother, the raw earth, and in this there is a great joy for men.' (Pt I, Ch. IV, 5.) Under the influence of this false prophetess, Marya kisses the ground and weeps whenever she makes full obeisance. This cult of the earth seems pagan, but the sects also adored 'mother earth' in their songs;[38] indeed Marya herself is something of a mother-figure; thus she rambles incoherently about a baby she has had, though Stavrogin dismisses the possibility that this could have happened, as she is a virgin. This hint of 'the virgin mother' is continued in her name: Marya is the Russian form of Mary. If therefore Marya Lebyadkin is to be taken as a schismatical madonna-figure, she can be related to a phenomenon of some importance among the sects; for besides their 'christs' the Flagellants and Castrates also had their madonnas [*bogoroditsy*].[39]

It later transpires in the course of the novel that Fedka too is an inmate of 'The House of Filippov'; he hides there in the apartment of Kirillov. Here again the double warp is apparent; for Fedka is the chief instrument of Petr Verkhovensky's political action, yet at the same time he exhibits an unorthodox religious sensibility. Formerly he must have played an active part in church life; for he tells Stavrogin that he gave up his books and his bells and his church affairs when he went to penal settlement. Now it appears that he can rob churches and steal from icons, even commit murder, and still retain intact both his religious feelings and his soul.

All the inhabitants of the house, therefore, show to some degree these two aspects of political revolution and religious dissidence: the confusion of Stenka Razin with Danila Filippov. So it is not surprising that Petr Verkhovensky should seek to attribute all the troubles which have beset local society to this one source. Thus he comments with satisfaction on the implications to be drawn from Kirillov's suicide note: 'And so, everything has come from here, from the house of the Filippovs.' (Pt III, Ch. VI, 2.) This conclusion is correct; for 'The House of Filippov' is a symbol for Stavrogin himself, and Stavrogin is at the centre of the whole novel.

Although Petr Verkhovensky wants to present Stavrogin to the people in the manner of Danila Filippov, he really seeks to identify him with Ivan, the Crown Prince (Ivan tsarevich), the wonder-working hero of Russian folk-lore. This figure is obviously more in keeping with the aristocratic nature of Stavrogin himself, but it seems odd that a left-wing revolutionary should seek to rule through such means as aristocracy, folk-myth and religious fanaticism. The political theories of Petr Verkhovensky must be looked at more closely.

Dostoyevsky seldom presents ideas in a flat, one-sided way, and it is typical of his method that the political thought of Petr Verkhovensky does not always come from his own lips. He is given an ideological alter-ego, Shigalev, with whom he is basically in agreement, although this does not prevent him from arguing with him, even ridiculing him. In the exposition of these ideas the lame teacher and Lyamshin also play their part.

Shigalev is a theorist who has given great attention to the problem of the future society; his conclusions are bold and unexpected: 'starting from the idea of unlimited freedom, I ended up with unlimited despotism'. This view of the society of the future seems to have much in common with the crystal palace described in *Notes from Underground*: in both, man's happiness can only be achieved through the restriction of his freedom of action and choice. One of the underground man's chief objections to the perfection of the crystal palace is that it would be terribly boring. Shigalev, in his system, anticipates this. Petr Verkhovensky explains:

[There will be] absolute obedience, absolute lack of individuality. But once every thirty years Shigalev sets everything in turmoil, and everybody begins to fall on everyone else; that is, up to a certain limit, just so that it should not be boring. Boredom is an aristocratic experience. In Shigalev's system there will be no desires; desires and suffering are for us: but the Shigalev system is for the slaves.

(Pt II, Ch. VIII)

Petr Verkhovensky himself is a firm believer in an aristocracy supported by slavery. In Shigalev's system nine-tenths of humanity is to be turned into a herd, whilst the remaining tenth enjoys absolute freedom and unrestricted powers over the rest. Shigalev would even be prepared for a 'final solution' in the manner of Hitler: the herd-like nine-tenths of humanity could be blown up, if he thought this were possible.

Petr Verkhovensky's appeal to folk mythology, in order to weld together a society composed of a privileged élite supported by brutalised slaves, seems to project the aspirations of that political theory known as 'National Socialism' rather than Socialism itself. Verkhovensky himself is quite explicit on this matter: 'Everything for me must have discipline. You see I am a rogue, not a socialist.'

Three times during this scene with Stavrogin he affirms that he is no socialist; but is, on the contrary, a rogue. In order to achieve his ends he requires that society should be steeped in vice for one or two generations, and he sees the onset of this in the liberalism of the courts and the lack of religion in the country. Only when society has collapsed will they consider how to erect an edifice in stone, and this edifice will not be a socialist one:

What is there in Socialism: it has destroyed the old forces, but has not brought in any new ones. But we are a force, and what a force, a force unheard of! All we need is a lever for the moment to lift the earth, and all will be lifted.

(Pt II, Ch. VIII)

In view of this, the opinion of certain Soviet critics that in

The Devils Dostoyevsky had predicted the advent of Fascism[40] seems hardly far-fetched, though one might expect that certain passages could have a familiar ring in their ears:

Shigalev has spying, every member of society watches each other, and is obliged to inform. Each belongs to all, and all to each. All are slaves and are equal in slavery. In exceptional cases there will be slander and murder, but the chief thing is equality.   (*ibid.*)

The system of Shigalev looks forward to *The Brothers Kara-mazov* and the type of society ruled over by The Grand Inquisitor. The Grand Inquisitor makes use of the name of Christ to effect his 'Roman' tyranny, just as Petr Verkhovensky wishes to make use of Stavrogin. Here it is significant that Verkhovensky has himself toyed with the idea of using the pope as his figurehead but has rejected him in favour of Stavrogin.

The ship of state which Petr Verkhovensky desires to command is a slave galley sailing under a gilded figure-head.[41] As such, its course runs counter to the ideas of the younger generation; for in it aesthetic considerations very clearly predominate over ethical ones. Although Petr Verkhovensky himself uses the terms 'aesthete' and 'aesthetic' as cant words of abuse, he nevertheless knows where the mainspring of his political ideology lies:

'Stavrogin, you are beautiful!' exclaimed Petr Stepanovich almost in rapture. 'Do you know that you are beautiful? One of the most priceless things about you is that sometimes you do not even realise this yourself. Oh, I have studied you thoroughly. I frequently watch you unnoticed, from the side. You are even not without simplicity and naivety. Do you know this? It is true, it is true. You must suffer, and suffer genuinely, from such simplicity. I love beauty. I am a nihilist but I love beauty. Do you think that nihilists cannot love beauty? It is only idols they do not love, but I love an idol. You are my idol!'   (*ibid.*)

Yet as an embodiment of beauty, Stavrogin is more than Petr Verkhovensky's idol: he is his very inspiration; for at the end of this chapter Verkhovensky confesses that it is through watching Stavrogin that the political ideas which he here propounds came to him in the first place.

But Stavrogin himself has a dream of beauty, and beauty moreover which presents itself as a political ideal: it is the dream of paradise on earth which he has in the banned chapter ('At Tikhon's'). The people he sees are 'beautiful people' living in a primeval idyll of innocence. Everything about this dream is steeped in the aesthetic, including its inspiration; for it is based on the well-known painting by Claude Lorrain, *Acis and Galatea*, which Dostoyevsky himself thought of as a depiction of the golden age.

It is significant that it is in terms of the golden age that Shigalev seeks to present his own society: 'What I am suggesting is not something disgusting: it is paradise – earthly paradise, and there can be no other on earth.' (Pt II, Ch. VII, 2.) And the idea is defended by the lame teacher: '...his earthly paradise is very nearly the real one, the very one over whose loss humanity sighs, if, of course, it ever existed.' (*ibid.*)

In Stavrogin's confession, his optimism about mankind is shattered when he again closes his eyes and the dream does not return: it is blotted out by the tiny red spider which he watched as Matresha was committing suicide. This spider is obviously connected with his own criminal act of the will, and perhaps the message which may be drawn from the dream and its obliteration is that complete freedom for man to do exactly as he pleases cannot be reconciled with earthly paradise. Shigalev, after all, can only attain his idyll by the alienation of every man's right to exhibit free will:

One-tenth is granted personal freedom and limitless rights over the remaining nine-tenths. They, on the other hand, must lose all individuality and become something like a herd, and given their boundless obedience, through a long process of regeneration, they will achieve original innocence, something like original paradise, though, nevertheless, they will work. (*ibid.*)

The ideas of Petr Verkhovensky and Shigalev scarcely reflect the true political aspirations of the younger generation. Just the reverse: through them Dostoyevsky seems to be preoccupied with a problem which is peculiarly his own – the enigma of beauty. He has now come a long way from the assertion that beauty will save the world: beauty, in fact, might be a force which could enslave the world. For Verkhovensky, the would-be world dictator, Stavrogin embodies beauty as a political ideal; nevertheless the nature of Stavrogin is just as enigmatic as that of beauty itself: is he a force for good, or is he a force for evil? In the next chapter we must attempt to unravel this mystery.

7
THE GREAT SINNER:
'THE DEVILS'

This little word 'Why?' has covered the whole of the universe like a flood ever since the first day of creation, madam, and every minute all nature cries to its creator; 'Why?', and for seven thousand years it has received no answer. (Pt I, Ch. v, 4)

In these enigmatic terms Captain Lebyadkin replies to Stavrogin's mother when she tries to probe the mystery of the relationship between Lebyadkin's sister and her own son. 'Why?' is a question which the reader himself must often feel tempted to ask when confronted by Stavrogin's behaviour, and he may even suspect that Lebyadkin's comic evasiveness is the only answer he is likely to get.

Stavrogin has something in common with Svidrigaylov in *Crime and Punishment*, and like Svidrigaylov his entry into the narrative proper is preceded by a penumbra of enigmatic, tantalising facts and rumours. In particular, an image of Stavrogin is created by three incidents relating to an earlier stay in the town. These are the seizure of Gaganov's nose; the assault on the lips of Liputin's wife; the biting of the governor's ear – three anatomical assaults which serve to project Stavrogin as a man of violent whim, who has a taste for pretty women. Yet these three acts are really mirror images for three incidents to be related in the narrative proper. Then the apparently gratuitous insult will be turned against Stavrogin himself, when Shatov strikes him and he refuses to return the blow; the chaser after other men's pretty wives will declare that he himself is married, and to the least desirable of brides; and the malicious joker who bit the governor's ear when summoned to explain himself, will be called upon to 'give satisfaction' to Gaganov's son and will do so by allowing himself to be shot at without any convincing attempt at retaliation. On the one hand – expressions of what appears to be wilful self-assertiveness: on the other – parallel but contradictory expressions of seeming self-effacement. The pattern is one which we have met before.

The depiction of Stavrogin reveals duality at every point; every facet reflects a great enigma. On the one hand he seems almost a Christ-figure; Shatov exclaims: 'Why am I condemned to believe in you for ever?' and Kirillov accuses him of being a man in search of a burden. Indeed the symbol of Christ's burden is hinted at in his very name: Stavrogin (from *stavros* – the Greek word for a cross). Yet on the other hand he seems also be be a satanic figure (a Byronic or Lermontovian role in keeping with his identification as the 'last of the noblemen's sons') and if his surname hints at suffering, his other names Nikolay Vsevolodovich hint at ruthless power (Nikolay = conqueror of nations; Vsevolod = master of all). In the novel much of his behaviour, whether real or attributed, provides strong evidence for this latter view of Stavrogin; indeed, Petr Verkhovensky claims he is drawn towards him because of his 'great capacity for crime'.

As we have seen, Stavrogin entered *The Devils* from the framework of another novel which was never written: 'The Life of a Great Sinner' ('*Zhitiye velikogo greshnika*') and the word for 'life' in this title is very illuminating; for *zhitiye* is a term usually reserved for the 'life' of a saint. Thus Stavrogin embraces within himself both the sinner and the saint; he is both Raskolnikov and Myshkin. This is why, at one and the same time, he can implant in the minds of his two disciples two systems of ideas which seem so diametrically opposed.

If the portrayal of Stavrogin is steeped in enigma, there is nevertheless one thing which is certain – he is the undisputed centre of the novel. All the characters revolve around him, and for some – Kirillov, Shatov, Lebyadkin – he is an object of veneration; each in turn echoes the phrase that Stavrogin has meant much in his life, and Petr Verkhovensky, who bows down before no man, acknowledges Stavrogin as his idol: he wants him as a god-like figure-head for his own anarchic revolution.

It is not for nothing that, on a political level, Petr Verk-hovensky treats Stavrogin as divine; nor yet, on a lower comic plane, that Stavrogin's brother-in-law, Lebyadkin, replies to the little word 'why' in terms which reach out towards the meta-physical; nor indeed is it surprising that, on yet another level, Stavrogin's two intellectual offspring, Shatov and Kirillov, are both obsessed in their different ways with the problem of god-head; for Stavrogin *is* a god-figure; and, whether he be Christ or Satan, he is nevertheless remote from mere human concepts of good and evil. Shatov challenges him on this very point:

Is it true that you asserted that you knew of no aesthetic distinction between an act of bestial lasciviousness and any heroic deed, whatever it may be, were it even the sacrifice of one's life for humanity? Is it true that in both these poles you found an identity of beauty and the same sort of enjoyment? (Pt II, Ch. I, 7)

Stavrogin refuses to answer this question, but the evidence of the novel seems to suggest that the charge is true; for him the satanic act ('of bestial lasciviousness') and the Christ-like act ('the sacrifice of one's life for humanity') have some sort of bizarre identity.

We have already seen that the inference to be drawn from the incidents which first introduce Stavrogin to the reader is contradicted by a later series of events; but if we examine the first set of incidents in isolation, it is obvious that the motivation for each one is in itself an enigma. Is Stavrogin playing cynical, insolent jokes, or is he to be pitied as a man in an abnormal mental state, who is not responsible for his actions? The reaction of public opinion to these events swings now one way, now the other, like a barometer reacting to unsettled weather; but like a barometer it points to probabilities rather than to certainties.

There is a similar ambivalence of motive surrounding the second series of incidents, but here we are dealing with events which are central to the main body of the novel, and corres-pondingly they shed more light on the basic dichotomy of Stavrogin's character. Why does Stavrogin marry a poor, half-demented cripple girl? Is this merely the latest cynical escapade

of a decadent rake? This explanation, according to Petr
Verkhovensky, is the one that Kirillov offers:

It was the latest experiment of a man sated with life, who wanted to
know to what a pass he could bring a mad cripple. 'You', he said,
'have purposely chosen the least of human beings, a cripple eternally
abused and beaten, and knowing, moreover, that this creature was
dying of a comic love for you, you have suddenly set about deceiving her, merely in order to see what will come of it!'

(Pt I, Ch. v, 6)

This explanation seems to be corroborated by Stavrogin himself, when he admits to Lebyadkin that he married his sister
after a drunken banquet in order to win a wager of wine.

Yet in contrast to this, we have Stavrogin's claim that he feels
respect for Marya Lebyadkin. Again the source of information
is Petr Verkhovensky:

'You suppose, Mr Kirillov, that I am laughing at her. Disabuse yourself of this. I do, in fact, respect her, because she is better than all of
us.' And you know, he said this in such a serious tone.   (*ibid.*)

Again corroboration for this view can be found in Stavrogin's
own behaviour. Indeed, in the scene which precedes these
partial and confusing 'explanations' offered by Petr Verkhovensky, Stavrogin's respect for Marya Lebyadkin is clearly
shown. We are told that when he addressed her his eyes lit up
with unusual tenderness, and we also read: 'He stood before
her in the most deferential attitude, and his every movement
revealed the most genuine respect.' (Pt I, Ch. v, 5.) Is this
marriage of the god-like Stavrogin to the least of human beings
a satanic exercise of the will, or is it, on the contrary, a Christ-
like burden of self-identification with 'the insulted and the
injured'?[1] By this act is Stavrogin revealing himself a sinner or
a saint? This is the crux of the mystery surrounding Stavrogin
(as he is presented in the censored version of the novel), and it is
from this central enigma of the marriage that the other enigmatic events flow.

Thus at the Sunday gathering at which Stavrogin first
appears, Shatov suddenly gets up, and for no apparent reason

strikes him in the face. It is only later we learn that it is the nature of the relationship between Stavrogin and Marya Lebyadkin which lies behind this act; for Stavrogin had just denied that he was married to her. The reason for the blow puzzles local society, but an even greater riddle is posed by Stavrogin's refusal to retaliate; is this weakness on the part of 'the strong man', or is it a mark of even greater strength? It was noticed, for instance, that Stavrogin made a conscious effort to restrain himself. Shatov, the cause of the trouble, interprets this restraint as strength; but others, notably the son of Gaganov, take it to be weakness, and thus we come by an indirect chain of causality to the third of the enigmatic acts of 'self-efface-ment', by which Stavrogin perplexes the gossips of the town.

Gaganov feels emboldened to write an insulting letter to Stavrogin in which he mentions his 'slapped face'. Stavrogin has no alternative but to challenge him to a duel; and here, once more, Stavrogin's behaviour becomes a matter for speculation; for although he bravely presents himself for Gaganov's bullets, he himself, quite deliberately, shoots to miss. Again the little word 'why?' inevitably presents its simple monosyllabic question only to receive a complicated and enigmatic answer: Stavrogin claims that he wished to spare Gaganov's life; but as Kirillov points out, he has, in effect, mortally wounded him.

All these three acts are thus linked together and each reveals Stavrogin in a dual and contradictory light. His actions might be Christ-like: they might be interpreted as self-sacrifice for suffering humanity (Marya): as turning the other cheek (Shatov); as the refusal to take life (Gaganov). Alternatively all three acts could be mere attempts to prove his strength; empty exercises revealing the supremacy of his will in a challenge to common sense.

These two interpretations of Stavrogin's motives find their contradictory expression, not so much in what he says in the novel, but in ideas attributed to him by his two disciples. Thus Shatov seeks corroboration of Stavrogin's overwhelming belief in Christ:

But was it not you who told me that if it were mathematically proved to you that the truth lay elsewhere than in Christ, then you would prefer to remain with Christ rather than with the truth? Did you not say this? Did you not say it? (Pt II, Ch. I, 7)

Shatov is a fanatical Christian because of Stavrogin's teachings. His faith in Christ, in God made man, far exceeds his belief in God Himself; for under Stavrogin's probing Shatov reveals that belief in God is a future goal, rather than a present reality. Hence the significance of his name (*shatkiy* – unfirm, wavering).

It is the human will, on the other hand, which Kirillov elevates at the expense of God:

If God exists then all will is His, and because of His will I am powerless. If God does not exist, then all will is mine, and I am obliged to proclaim my wilfulness. (Pt III, Ch. VI, 2)

Kirillov, therefore, under the influence of Stavrogin, proclaims man made god through the supremacy of his will. He is the prophet of a new religion, hence his name evokes St Kirill, the missionary who first brought the new gospel to the Slavs.

Yet although these two characters are poles apart ideologically, their lives are inextricably bound together. In the plot the murder of Shatov is conditional on the suicide of Kirillov and *vice versa*. When Marie Shatov learns of the death of Kirillov, she knows instinctively that her own husband must be dead too, but the only explanation she gives for this feeling is: 'they lived together'. This is true; for not only are we told that Kirillov and Shatov lay side by side for a long time in America, but here in the town they live side by side in the same house, though each virtually ignores the presence of the other. This symbolic 'co-habitation' in The House of Filippov, tells us much about them; for we have already seen the same device in *Crime and Punishment*: Shatov and Kirillov are more than mere disciples of Stavrogin – they are the two halves of his divided self, the 'man of Christ' in harness with the 'man of the will'.

A key section of the novel is the sequence entitled 'Night', in which Stavrogin sets out through the darkness armed with an umbrella. It is a decisive moment in his life: he has to fight a duel and certain arrangements must be made.[2] But his journey is really a symbolic pilgrimage of self-questioning, during which he attempts to discover his true self and his real attitude to his marriage. His ultimate destination is the house across the river to which the Lebyadkins have been relegated, but first he must visit Kirillov to arrange the details of the duel. It is as though, in visiting The House of Filippov, Stavrogin needs to commune with the two halves of his own nature before deciding on the fate of Marya Lebyadkin.

Shatov answers his summons and opens the gate; Stavrogin steps over the high threshold as though symbolically entering into himself. Scarcely acknowledging Shatov, Stavrogin makes his way to the apartment of Kirillov. Here all is laughter and light; Kirillov himself is happily playing ball with a child. This is a good omen; it seems as though, despite his self-destructive philosophy, the apostle of the apotheosised will is full of the enjoyment of life. Indeed, throughout the whole of this interview, it is the positive aspects of the will which are stressed.

The way of the will leads to self-destruction: this is the parable expressed by Kirillov's suicide. Yet when Stavrogin takes up with him the question of his suicide, Kirillov refuses to admit that there is such a thing as death; what he is trying to achieve, he claims, is a state of mystical timelessness, an eternal present. Perhaps he means that inasmuch as the will can conquer time, it can also conquer death; for he tells Stavrogin that time is an idea, not an object, and as an idea it can be extinguished in the mind.

A similar triumph of mind over matter has given Kirillov the happiness which is now so evident; he persists in seeing everything as good. The origin of this attitude lies in an aesthetic experience: the beauty of the world is epitomised for him in the beauty of an old half-rotting leaf, which he has seen blown about by the wind. It is as though Kirillov, struck by the beauty of that which is apparently dead and rejected goes on to draw the conclusion that everything must be beautiful, indeed everything must be good. The inevitable shift from aesthetic to ethical criteria we have already seen in Myshkin's 'quietism', it is therefore not surprising to learn that Kirillov, too, is an epileptic. Moreover it is to his epileptic experiences that his notions on timelessness must ultimately be attributed.

There is, however, a basic difference between Kirillov and Myshkin: Kirillov places the emphasis of his thought upon the human will. Like time and death, beauty too is an idea in the mind, and can be created by an effort of the will. Once again its symbol is a leaf:

When I was ten years old, I used to close my eyes in winter, on purpose, and imagine a leaf, green and bright with veins and the sun shining. I would open my eyes and would not believe what I had seen, because it was very beautiful [good³] and I would close them again. (Pt II, Ch. I, 5)

Beauty for Myshkin was synonymous with happiness, and for Kirillov this too is a state of mind which man can create within himself: 'Man is unhappy because he does not realise that he is happy. This is the only reason.' (*Ibid.*) Like Myshkin's 'quietism', Kirillov's philosophy of willed optimism rises above pain, death and destruction. He knows that the mother of the little girl with whom he has just been playing is ill and will shortly die, but he stresses that the little girl herself will remain alive. 'Everything is good! I have suddenly just discovered it.' If everything is good, then the self-willed man himself must be good. This point is of some interest to Stavrogin. He questions Kirillov and receives the reply: '"I am good." "With this I agree", mumbled Stavrogin scowling.' There is, however, a certain ambiguity about Stavrogin's agreement; for the phrase: 'I am good' ['*Ya khorosh*'] may be taken ironically to mean: 'I am a queer sort of fellow.' Stavrogin shows further scepticism about Kirillov's ideas, when the latter's arguments seem to be drifting towards Christianity, and he leaves him with a parting remark on the subject, which Kirillov objects to as a 'society witticism', begging Stavrogin to remember what he has meant in his life. The scene ends with a minor affirmation of the power of Kirillov's will (he claims to be able to wake up at any time he desires) and this Stavrogin greets with the ambiguous: 'You have remarkable powers.'

The ironical way in which Stavrogin listens to Kirillov is understandable; for his philosophy has one serious defect: it ends in self-destruction. Moreover, Kirillov's positive endorsement of the will not only smacks of the Christ-like quietism of Myshkin, it even leads him to an ambiguous attitude towards the figure of Christ himself. It is fitting therefore that Stavrogin, having detected elements of religious equivocation in the prophet of 'man-god', should move on through the dark and empty house towards the quarters of the apostle of 'God-man': Shatov, the ardent proclaimer of Christ.

Shatov hears him coming and opens the door to give a little light. Before entering, Stavrogin pauses on the threshold, as he had done when visiting Kirillov.

The contrast in atmosphere between Kirillov's apartment and Shatov's is striking. There, all was light and laughter, there were even visitors and health-promoting games: here, there is loneliness, suspicion and ill health. Both begin by showing Stavrogin their firearms, but Shatov's attitude to the revolver which he has bought out of fear of Stavrogin is in sharp contrast to the loving pride of Kirillov for his revolver and, above all, for his expensive duelling pistols. Shatov has not even bought powder and bullets, and his first impulse, when he realises that Stavrogin has come in peace, is to throw the revolver away.

Both Kirillov and Shatov readily acknowledge that the ideas they are advancing are far from new, that they might even be clichés. Nevertheless these two sets of ideas stand in parallel: each is a commentary on the other. This is true of the central issue of man-god versus God-man, but it is also true of their aesthetic ideas. Shatov talks of 'the aesthetic principle, as the philosophers call it, the moral principle with which they themselves identify it' and so it would seem that Kirillov and Shatov are at one in confusing aesthetics with ethics. But in *his* aesthetic outlook, Shatov strives to distinguish between 'madonna' and 'Sodom': he accuses Stavrogin of confusing the two poles of beauty – the 'heroic act' and the 'bestial deed'. In other words, his charge is that Stavrogin has succumbed to the 'aesthetic nihilism' of his Kirillov side; for earlier, in his determination to see everything as good/beautiful, Kirillov had been prepared to acknowledge even the rape of a little girl as 'good'.

The most pressing instance of Stavrogin's apparent confusion of 'the two poles of beauty' is to be seen in his marriage to Marya Lebyadkin. Shatov takes a protective interest in her (although, somewhat ominously, Kirillov, along with Petr Verkhovensky, had been a witness at the wedding). We now learn that it is Shatov's protectiveness towards Marya Lebyadkin which was responsible for his striking Stavrogin at the Sunday gathering; he struck Stavrogin because of his 'falseness', because of his refusal to acknowledge Marya as his wife.

When, however, Stavrogin tells him that he now intends to acknowledge his marriage publicly, Shatov launches into an attack, questioning his motives: '"Do you know, do you really know," he shouted "why you have committed all this, and why you have made up your mind for such a punishment now?"' (Pt II, Ch. I, 6.) Shatov's phrasing seems ambiguous: does he mean punishment for Stavrogin, or punishment for Marya Lebyadkin? Stavrogin himself feels the sting in the question and replies:

Your question is intelligent and biting. But I intend to surprise you too. Yes, I almost know why I got married then, and why I have made up my mind for such a 'punishment' now, as you put it.

(*ibid.*)

Thus in the course of his communion with his two halves Stavrogin appears to be coming to some conclusions about himself and his motives: he 'almost knows' why he married Marya Lebyadkin and why he has decided on 'such a punishment now'. But whatever may be the true significance of this, Shatov suspects his worst motives:

You got married because of your passion for torment, because of your passion for remorse, because of your moral lasciviousness. There was behind this some irrational upsurge...the challenge to common sense was far too alluring. Stavrogin and a wretched, half-witted, destitute cripple girl!   (Pt II, Ch. I, 7)

Stavrogin's reply is evasive and does not absolutely rebut this charge. He merely says that Shatov is 'partly wrong' about his motives and he suspects that Kirillov has given him this information.

Perhaps Shatov even suspects what 'punishment' Stavrogin has in mind:

You have come to warn me about danger, you have allowed me to speak. Tomorrow you want to announce your marriage publicly. Do you think that I do not see from your face that a new and ominous idea is gaining a hold on you?   (ibid.)

One of Stavrogin's ostensible motives in visiting Shatov is indeed to warn him of danger, to tell him that the revolutionaries are planning to kill him, but a second reason is to ask him henceforward not to leave Marya Lebyadkin. Yet in spite of the protectiveness he has already shown towards her, Shatov now seems as unconcerned about the safety of her life as he is about his own. Stavrogin begins his request twice during the course of their meeting, but each time he is interrupted by Shatov. It is only at the third attempt, at the very end of the scene, that Stavrogin finally manages to convey his request. Even then Shatov's reply hardly shows concern: '"All right, all right. You mean Marya Timofeyevna", Shatov dismissed it with a wave of his hand, holding the candle in the other. "All right. Later, of course."' (Ibid.)

This hardly augurs well for the fate of Shatov's protégée. Moreover the arguments of Shatov himself have had very little effect on Stavrogin other than to annoy him. It is true that he does agree to visit Tikhon, but we are lead to believe that this will be from curiosity rather than for any other reason. Stavrogin tells Shatov quite plainly that he is sorry but he cannot bring himself to like him, and when Shatov had spoken disparagingly of Kirillov, Stavrogin had reminded him that Kirillov was happy and good. As he leaves he tells Shatov that he will not visit him again. The omens for Stavrogin 'the saint' look bad, but the final decision has not yet been made, and the words which end the chapter seem to reflect Stavrogin's spiritual state: 'The darkness and the rain continued as before.'

After communing with Kirillov and Shatov, Stavrogin now strides out through the night, armed with his umbrella, to visit the Lebyadkins: another pair of sibling figures living side by side in disharmony. If Kirillov and Shatov represent the divided subject, then Marya Lebyadkin and her brother may be taken as symbols of the divided object; for it is through his decision on his attitude to Marya Lebyadkin and her brother that Stavrogin will achieve self-knowledge; the subject will be defined by its relationship to the object.

In Captain Lebyadkin we have a manifestation, however comic, of the object's will. In the forthcoming encounter he will remind Stavrogin of this: 'For all the same, I am spiritually independent. Do not take this last of my possessions away from me.' (Pt II, Ch. II, 2.) Yet in his wilful behaviour Lebyadkin is always the pawn of others, despite the fact that 'pure exercises of the will' attract him greatly:

Of all your sayings, Nikolay Vsevolodovich, there is one in particular which I have remembered. You uttered it during the time that you were in St Petersburg: 'One must indeed be a great man in order to be able to withstand common sense.' (*ibid.*)

Stavrogin's scathing reply: 'Or by the same token a fool', puts the pretensions of Lebyadkin in their true perspective.

In Marya Lebyadkin, on the other hand, we have a manifestation, however befuddled, of the object's spirituality. Shatov's Christianity was not unmixed with a strange cult of the earth: he had told Stavrogin to fall on the earth and water it with his tears, and that he would find God by working as a peasant. Marya Lebyadkin too talks about the need to water the earth with her tears. She is the *holy fool* who in a convent has learned the heretical doctrine that the mother of God is none other than mother earth.

Formerly the Lebyadkins used to live in The House of

Filippov, and it seems somewhat ominous that they have now been moved to a house across the river. Yet it is on the one way across this physical barrier that something even more ominous occurs: Stavrogin is accosted on the bridge by an escaped convict and cut-throat: Fedka – the agent of destruction.

Fedka merely asks for shelter from the rain, but as he walks along under Stavrogin's umbrella, his words become ambiguously insinuating, and he seems convinced that he can be of service to Stavrogin. He asks for money but all he receives is the shelter of Stavrogin's umbrella, for which, in his parting words he expresses eternal gratitude: 'Happy journey, Sir; for all the same, you have taken a poor deprived man under your umbrella. For this alone I shall be grateful to you until my dying day.' (Pt II, Ch. II, I.) These words, as we shall see, have ironically sinister implications for what is to follow.

Fedka's offer is to kill Marya Lebyadkin, and he is acting under instructions from Petr Verkhovensky, who had earlier hinted to Stavrogin that Fedka might be useful in getting rid of any obstacles in his way to a marriage with Liza Tushina. But if Fedka is an agent of the political machinations of Petr Verkhovensky, he is also, in a sense, an emissary of Stavrogin's own will; for later in the novel it transpires that Fedka lives in the apartment of Kirillov. Thus the protégé of Kirillov is prepared to murder the protégée of Shatov. The political and the metaphysical strands of the novel are, once again, closely bound together.

Having left Fedka on the bridge, Stavrogin now arrives at the Lebyadkins' house, and, as earlier at The House of Filippov, he interviews each of the inhabitants separately, beginning with 'the representative of the will'.

In view of all that has gone before, this encounter with Lebyadkin is full of grim irony. The captain takes the umbrella, which only a moment before sheltered Fedka, and confesses that he has been waiting patiently for the arrival of Stavrogin in order 'to hear his own fate'. Like Kirillov before him, Lebyadkin offers his guest tea, and, typically his comic phraseology reaches out to embrace the cosmic: 'The samovar has been boiling since eight o'clock, but...it has gone out like everything on earth. Even the sun, they say, will go out in its turn.' (Pt II, Ch. II, 2.) Here there is a macabre note which seems the very reverse of Kirillov's joy in timelessness. When Kirillov suddenly realised that everyone was happy he stopped his watch; Lebyadkin, on the other hand, has no watch at all.

There is grim irony in all that Lebyadkin says. He tells Stavrogin that he has made his will. The details are pure black comedy; for Lebyadkin's sole estate is his body, and although he would like to follow the example of a rich American and bequeath his hide for a drum-skin on which the national anthem would be beaten out day and night, he knows that in Russia this would be considered liberalism. He will, therefore, confine himself to leaving his skeleton to medical science, with the proviso that a label be gummed to his skull 'for all eternity' bearing the words 'A Repentant Freethinker'.

There is always a serious note behind the comic speeches of Lebyadkin. We have already seen this in his answer to the 'little word why' at the Sunday gathering, and the continuation of that earlier comic outburst tells us a great deal about him:

'Madam', the captain went on without listening to her. 'I would perhaps have liked to have been called Ernest, but am obliged to bear the coarse name of Ignat. Why is this, do you think? I would like to have been called Prince de Montbard, but am only Lebyadkin, a name derived from a swan. Why is this? I am a poet, madam, a poet in my soul, and could receive a thousand roubles from a publisher, but instead I am forced to live in a slop bucket, Why? Why? Madam, in my opinion Russia is a jest of nature, nothing more.'

(Pt I, Ch. V, 4)

Here is the protest of the will at the mercy of circumstances (the very reverse of Kirillov's will, which can overcome all conditions, even death). Lebyadkin takes exception to that most readily changeable of attributes – his Christian name, and this is significant; for he has just referred to his sister as 'Mary Unknown' and now he reveals that his own name is 'Unknown' (i.e. Ignat).[4] Marya is 'unknown' because of the enigma of her relationship to Stavrogin, and this is an enigma in which Ignat himself has a part. The epithet 'unknown' is an essential attribute for the object; for it is only by defining his attitude to the Lebyadkins that the subject (Stavrogin) will achieve self-knowledge.

But 'unknown' may be taken, in another sense, as signifying 'obscure', 'insignificant'. This quality too is represented by the Lebyadkins; it is this that gives their relationship with Stavrogin its piquancy. In the speech quoted above, Lebyadkin is rebelling against this role of insignificance in which he has been cast, and he is about to take up the reference to the 'slop bucket' by quoting one of his own 'poems', in which he compares his lot to that of a cockroach.

It is with verses such as these that Lebyadkin pesters Liza Tushina, and in a letter accompanying one such 'poem' he again compares himself to the lowest form of life: an infusorian in a drop of water, writing a poem to the sun:

Even the 'Philanthropic Club for the Larger Animals' in St Petersburg society, whilst it feels compassion for the rights of dogs and horses, despises the tiny infusorian, does not mention it at all, because it is not large enough. I too am not large enough. The thought of marriage would seem ludicrous. (Pt I, Ch. IV, 2)

Lebyadkin's desire to marry Liza ('Stavrogin's woman') is a mirror image of Stavrogin's marriage to his crippled sister. The object is claiming the same right to will as the subject. If Stavrogin from his godly heights can marry the lowliest of creatures, then the lowliest of creatures too has a right to reverse the process. Lebyadkin brings this out now during this fatal interview with Stavrogin: 'Nikolay Vsevolodovich, even a louse, even a louse can be in love. The law does not forbid even a louse.' (Pt II, Ch. II, 2.) He is then induced to quote a poem addressed to Liza: 'If she should break a leg.' Here the parallel between his own marital aspirations and the marriage already contracted by Stavrogin is further hinted at; for the hypothetical lameness of Liza, it seems, could place her on some terms of parity with the brother of the lame Marya. Indeed behind

Lebyadkin's comic demands for the right to love lie the more tragic claims of Marya herself. She too has rights in respect of Stavrogin (for 'even a louse can be in love'). Lebyadkin himself says he feels a slur has been cast on his family by Stavrogin's treatment of his sister.

Captain Lebyadkin's attitude expresses the rebellion of the object; the object is claiming that it too should be considered as a subject in its own right. Lebyadkin feels justified in sending Liza his insulting verses, because, as Liputin has explained to him: 'every human being is worthy of the right to correspondence'. He feels too that he has rights in respect of Stavrogin; he is, after all, his brother-in-law. But Stavrogin reminds Lebyadkin that everything lies within his own will, and bluntly reveals that the motive of will is dominant in his relations with Marya:

I married your sister, when I took it into my head after a drunken dinner, for a wager of wine, and now I shall make this news public if it pleases me to do so. (*ibid.*)

After this declaration of wilfulness by the subject, we see now what the 'rights' of the object itself amount to:

'Surely you are not going to discard me like an old worn-out boot?'

'I shall see', laughed Nikolay Vsevolodovich. 'Well, let me go.'

'Why don't you tell me to stand on the verandah, Sir, so that I don't accidentally overhear something. The rooms are tiny.'

'That's a good idea. Stand on the verandah. Take the umbrella!'

'Your umbrella. Am I worthy of it, Sir?' the captain said with exaggerated deference.

'Everyone is worthy of an umbrella.'

'At a stroke you define the minimum of human rights.' (*ibid.*)

'The minimum of human rights' is in fact a symbolic death sentence; for Stavrogin has pointedly handed over to Lebyadkin the umbrella which he has just shared with Fedka. Murderer and victim are thus linked, and the fate of the Lebyadkins now seems sealed.

After this Stavrogin goes to see Marya. He surprises her

194

sleeping, and, catching her like that, has perhaps little need to dissemble as he gazes at her:

Perhaps this gaze was unnecessarily stern, perhaps it expressed revulsion, even malicious enjoyment at her fear, or perhaps it just seemed like this to Marya Timofeyevna, on waking from her sleep.

(Pt II, Ch. II, 3)

Whatever the reason, Marya is frightened by Stavrogin's entry, and she is only a little reassured when his manner changes: 'But the visitor remembered himself. In a moment his face changed, and he approached the table with a most welcoming and most tender smile.' (*Ibid.*) Here, then, are the two Janus-like masks of Stavrogin's divided attitude to Marya Lebyadkin, and Marya seems convinced that the figure she sees before her is not the true Stavrogin; it is not 'The Prince': it is 'The Pretender'.

Stavrogin's attempt to ascribe her fright to a bad dream only increases her distress: 'How did you know that I was dreaming about that?' she asks and confesses: 'Of course, I have been tormented by nightmares, but why did I dream of *you* in that very form?' These nightmares, moreover, seem connected with the appearance of Stavrogin in the town; for she says: 'I have had nightmares because you have arrived.'

But Marya's vision of the other Stavrogin is not just a matter of dreams. Throughout most of the scene she studiously keeps her eyes averted; and when she does look at him, fear seizes her once more. She asks Stavrogin to get up and enter the room a second time: Stavrogin grows annoyed.

The words of Marya Lebyadkin, like some mad Ophelia, are disjointed and figurative, but her meaning is clear enough: she refuses to accept the man she sees before her as Stavrogin; for this is the man who was ashamed of her at the Sunday gathering, and is ashamed of her now. He is not a 'hawk' he is an 'owl' (earlier her brother had asked: 'Why does he come furtively at night when he himself wants to declare it openly?'). Indeed he who has supposedly come to claim her as a wife, who intends to announce the marriage publicly, is too ashamed to have her live with him in his mother's house. First of all he suggests that she might feel happier in a convent, and then proposes that they should live together in quiet seclusion in Switzerland.

But Marya has even worse allegations to make: he is not only an 'owl' he is also 'a worthless little merchant' – a concept which assumes great significance in the further course of the novel. Returning to the subject of her nightmare, she says that she is not afraid of Stavrogin's knife; for she knows that he has a knife in his pocket and that he took it out when he first entered the room. This allegation greatly disturbs Stavrogin. He pushes her away from him violently, and flees. The parting words of Marya, which follow him out into the night, are the curse put by the Church on the archetypal pretender of Russian history: 'Grishka Otrepev[5] – Anathema.' Marya has guessed that it is not by the monastery nor yet by a forty-year seclusion in the mountains of Switzerland that Stavrogin will seek to resolve the enigma of his marriage – it is by the knife.

Rushing out into the night, Stavrogin keeps repeating: 'knife, knife', in a mood of relentless anger, and coming to the bridge, he once more meets Fedka. It now becomes clear why Marya accused Stavrogin of carrying a knife – Fedka has been in his thoughts right up to that very moment:

He was suddenly struck by the thought that he had completely forgotten about him, [i.e. Fedka] and had forgotten about him at that precise moment when he himself had begun repeating 'knife, knife.'
(Pt II, Ch. II, 4)

Stavrogin vents his anger on the convict, and Fedka now shows his own knife. Yet it is a knife obedient to Stavrogin's command; for when ordered to put it away, Fedka does so immediately.

Stavrogin now appears to give him encouragement. He questions Fedka about his activities and then says: 'Carry on with your knifing! Carry on with your robbing!' These are the very words of Petr Verkhovensky, observes Fedka. Fedka brings the conversation round to Captain Lebyadkin ('whom you have just been visiting, sir') and says that formerly ('before your arrival, when they lived in The House of Filippov, sir') he has had many opportunities of murdering him for his money, but has waited his chance, because he believes that Lebyadkin is about to receive 1,500 roubles from Stavrogin ('I am telling you this, sir, as though you were my father or my brother'). Fedka then asks for three roubles and Stavrogin laughs out loud; he takes out his purse and throws him notes from it, one after the other, ending up by throwing the whole bundle at him (up to 50 roubles).

The true nature of this gesture is explained on the following day, when Stavrogin tells Dasha:

Yesterday on the bridge a certain minor devil offered to murder Lebyadkin and Marya Timofeyevna in order to bring my legal marriage to a conclusion and cover everything up. He asked for an advance of three roubles, but let it be clearly known that the whole operation would cost not less than 1,500. There's a calculating devil for you! A book-keeper! . . . I gave him all the money in my purse, and he is now completely convinced that I have given him an advance! (Pt II, Ch. III, 4)

This commercial transaction Stavrogin himself calls 'going to Fedka's shop'; and it now seems that Marya Lebyadkin was right when she hurled the insult of 'worthless little merchant' [kupchishka][6] at Stavrogin. Yet Stavrogin can still suggest to Dasha that his mind is not finally made up (in spite of the overwhelming evidence to the contrary); that it is still possible for him not to 'visit Fedka's shop'.

The explanation to Dasha comes at the end of the chapter entitled 'The Duel', and after this event the centre of activity shifts away from Stavrogin towards Petr Verkhovensky. There is, indeed, a kind of political pendant to 'Night'. Like Stavrogin before him, Petr Verkhovensky, in his turn, visits Kirillov and Shatov. From Kirillov he seeks confirmation that he will indeed commit suicide and will allow the act to be used for political ends. His aim in visiting Shatov is to prepare a trap for him by inviting him to a political meeting. At this meeting, which takes place in Ant Street, at Virginsky's house, Verkhovensky attempts to show the political unreliability of Shatov, just as Stavrogin, earlier, had exposed his wavering [*shatkost'*] on metaphysical issues.

The political exposure of Shatov accomplished, Verkhovensky now proceeds to bring forward a political motive for the elimination of Lebyadkin. This takes place back at Kirillov's apartment, and here Verkhovensky tries to repeat the bargaining in 'Fedka's shop', with Fedka himself lurking unseen in the wings.

The section ends with Petr Verkhovensky enthusing on the political role he has in mind for Stavrogin himself. Earlier, Marya Lebyadkin had anathematised Stavrogin as Grishka Otrepev, the pretender; now Petr Verkhovensky seeks to deify him in this very role, but as the fairy-tale hero: 'Ivan the Crown Prince'. He tells Stavrogin:

'The earth will cry for her old gods. Well, then we will launch ... whom do you think?'
'Who?'
'Ivan the Crown Prince'.
'Who?'
'Ivan the Crown Prince. You. You!'
Stavrogin thought for a moment.
'A pretender?' he suddenly asked in profound amazement, looking at the madman before him. 'Oh, so that's your plan is it?'
(Pt II, Ch. VIII)

The political 'pamphlet novel' now proceeds to its comic climax in the fiasco of the literary fête and ball, but it is a climax linked with a period of crisis in Stavrogin's life; for the celebrations are used as a cover for Fedka's murder of the Lebyadkins and for Stavrogin's own abduction of Liza.

We have already seen that Lebyadkin's marital ambitions place Liza in antithesis to Marya. Indeed 'Stavrogin's woman' has all the qualities which his 'wife' lacks: she is beautiful, rich, intelligent, the product of a Western education: in short, a highly desirable match. It is noteworthy that the murder of the one should serve as the occasion for his flight to the arms of the other. Yet the results of this night spent with Liza are the same as those of that earlier 'Night' during which Stavrogin had visited Marya: both women renounce him.

Marya had unmasked Stavrogin's pretensions to saintliness; now Liza sees through his claims to be a 'great sinner', and she does so at the very point in the novel where the evidence for Stavrogin's demonism would seem to be at its most glaring – the murder of the Lebyadkins and her own abduction. It is Stavrogin's aura of evil which has apparently attracted Liza to him:

I always thought that you would lead me to a place, where there lived a huge, evil spider the size of a man, and we would spend all our life there, looking at it and being frightened; our mutual love would be spent in this. (Pt III, Ch. III, 1)

Liza's image of the spider is strongly reminiscent of Ippolit's concept of the tarantula as the evil force of destruction which lies behind the world. But Stavrogin is incapable of realising her dream: he is neither one thing nor the other: neither hot nor cold. Stavrogin's spiritual impotence is unmasked by Liza in terms of sexual impotence. This has more than one connotation, but it may be taken as a symbolic statement of what he says about himself in his final letter to Dasha; for although Stavrogin has will, he has no desires, no passions: he is an emotional eunuch.

Liza tells him that he is the equivalent of any cripple, and that he only needs a woman in the capacity of a nurse. This jibe is particularly interesting in that it suggests a certain parity between him and the woman he has thought fit to marry (indeed, lameness is specifically mentioned in Liza's taunt). If Stavrogin is, after all, a cripple in need of a nurse (and he has such a person in Dasha) then his marriage to Marya assumes a new light: it is not only an act of self-knowledge – it is an act of self-identification; through it the subject is revealing an essential identity with the object. This is a logic which we have seen at work in another of Dostoyevsky's self-willed heroes;

199

for Raskolnikov comes to the realisation that he has not killed an old woman – he has killed himself.[7]

Here, too, as in *Crime and Punishment* the object is divided. Besides Marya there is also her brother; besides the tragedy of Stavrogin's situation there is also the comedy. When Lebyadkin had quoted back Stavrogin's words on the ability of a great man to withstand common sense, Stavrogin had pointed to another possibility – such a man might be a fool. Indeed the acts against common sense which first present Stavrogin to the reader, are not only enigmatic, they are also ludicrous; the reader laughs at the insolent irreverence of the pulled nose and the bitten ear. In these incidents, as in Lebyadkin's diatribe on 'the little word: "why?"', the metaphysical enigma is presented in comic terms; and Lebyadkin himself (the retired military man with a reputation for violence and for *amours*) cannot be wholly dissociated from the former guards officer – the 'Pechorin devourer of hearts': in accepting the comic Lebyadkin as his brother-in-law, Stavrogin is also revealing something of himself.

After the duel, Stavrogin had confessed to Dasha: 'Oh, what is my demon! It is simply a vile, minor little devil, with scurvy and a snivel. A failure.' (Pt II, Ch. III, 4). And now Liza in unmasking Stavrogin's demonism also suspects that it has certain comic aspects:

I must confess to you that even while we were in Switzerland, the idea took root that you had some terrible, vile and bloody matter on your mind, and at the same time that this was something which placed you in a terribly comic light. Make sure that you do not reveal this to me if it is true; I shall laugh at you. I shall laugh at you the whole of your life.   (Pt III, Ch. III, 1)

The demonic becoming the comic is a process which, as we have seen, is inherent in Dostoyevsky's treatment of the Nechayev theme from the beginning. In order to be able to write his 'pamphlet novel', the satanic Nechayev had to become the clownish Petr Verkhovensky. Now, after the *débâcle* of the night which Stavrogin has spent with Liza, Petr Verkhovensky senses that there is a possible reversal of roles and, as we have already seen, he tells Stavrogin that he does not want him to be a clown. Nevertheless Liza has revealed that Stavrogin is incapable of showing her the spider of evil, and if there is such a spider at all in the novel, it must surely be that weaver of intrigue – Petr Verkhovensky. This is certainly how the members of his own revolutionary group regard him towards the end of the novel:

They felt that like flies they had suddenly fallen as prey into the web of a huge spider. They were annoyed about it but they shook with fear.   (Pt III, Ch. IV, 2)

After the fateful night of the fires the roles of evil genius and clown do seem to be reversed. Verkhovensky reveals himself as the active perpetrator of evil: Stavrogin's passive impotence is exposed to ridicule.

This night marks Stavrogin's lowest point; indeed it really marks his spiritual destruction. The chapter heading is '*Zakonchenyy roman*' ('The End of a Love Affair', but literally: 'A Finished Novel'). It does mark the end of a novel; for after Liza's exposure of him, Stavrogin disappears from the pages of *The Devils*, and the final letter which he sends to Dasha is like a voice from a ghost: when it is read, Stavrogin is already dead, hanging in his attic.

But if the progress of Stavrogin through *The Devils* veers towards the comic, whereas that of Petr Verkhovensky is from the comic towards the satanic, there is yet a third and compensatory progress in the novel: the movement away from the comic towards the serious and the positive. We see this in the figure of Stepan Trofimovich Verkhovensky, who sets out as the butt of Dostoyevsky's satire and ends up as the bearer of his message.

We saw in the last chapter that there are many points which suggest a certain parity between Stavrogin and Stepan Trofimovich, and it is therefore not surprising that after the collapse of Stavrogin it should be Stepan Trofimovich who carries on the search for the truth. The representative of Dostoyevsky's own generation is to become the mouthpiece for some of the author's most cherished ideas.

'Stepan Trofimovich's Last Pilgrimage', when he sets out with his umbrella at daybreak, invites comparison with the earlier pilgrimage of Stavrogin, when he strides out, armed with his umbrella, through the night. For Stavrogin this had been a night of self-questioning: a metaphysical night, and these metaphysical implications are once more brought to the reader's attention at the outset of Stepan Trofimovich's daylight pilgrimage:

Although he had left when it was already daylight, when a nervous man already becomes a little more courageous (the major, who was Virginsky's relative, would even cease believing in God once the night had passed), nevertheless I am convinced that he could never formerly have conceived of himself, alone on the high road and in such a situation, without fear.[8] (Pt III, Ch. VII, 1)

Here, then, is a contrast between the boldness of Stavrogin stepping out through the night, and the timidity with which Stepan Trofimovich undertakes his daylight journey. Nevertheless there is the same idea of a quest. Stepan Trofimovich thinks of himself as raising the standard of 'a great idea': the very road itself is a symbol: 'The high road is something which goes on and on; something without visible end, like human life, like human dreams. The high road contains an idea...' (*ibid.*)

The ultimate goal of Stavrogin's pilgrimage had been the house of Marya Lebyadkin, but its end had, in fact, been 'Fedka's shop'. The goal of Stepan Trofimovich is ostensibly 'ce marchand', about whom he keeps babbling, but instead he finds Sofya Ulitina. Here again is a parallel of contrary motion.

As if to emphasise that Stepan Trofimovich is taking over the quest from Stavrogin, the author interferes with the chronological sequence of his new hero's 'last pilgrimage'. Stepan Trofimovich is dramatically presented already 'on the road', at the very point where Stavrogin has reached the end of his. Liza, fleeing from her night of disillusionment, encounters the unexpected figure of Stepan Trofimovich trudging along through the rain.

But Liza is more than just a link between the two heroes, she is in herself the embodiment of an ideal. Stepan Trofimovich falls on his knees before her explaining the gesture as follows:

'...in saying farewell to the world, I want, in your image to part with all my past!' He burst out weeping and raised both her hands to his tear-stained eyes. 'I am kneeling before all that was beautiful in my life. I kiss it and am grateful! Now I have broken myself in half. There, there is the madman, who dreamed of flying to heaven, vingt deux ans! Here there is a broken, frozen old man, a tutor chez ce marchand, s'il existe, pourtant, ce marchand...' (Pt III, Ch. III, 3)

In the person of Liza, Stepan Trofimovich is saying farewell to the Westernism of the generation of the forties: he is to find another ideal of beauty in Sofya Ulitina – the embodiment of a religious temperament which is essentially Russian. It is this very ideal which Stavrogin, through the murder of Marya, has just rejected, only to find that the ideal of beauty represented by Liza cannot be his either. Thus the crisis in Stavrogin's life coincides with a crisis in the life of Stepan Trofimovich, and, in his suggestion that a humble teacher has now left behind a fallen Icarus, Stepan Trofimovich is alluding, not merely to the outcome of his own personal crisis; his words also point to the solution of the crisis now reached by the novel itself – he, Stepan Trofimovich, will go on where Stavrogin has fallen.

In view of the role played by the umbrella in the section entitled 'Night', there is grim irony in the fact that Stepan Trofimovich now offers Liza his own umbrella. But Stepan Trofimovich is not Stavrogin: the offer of protection is genuine. Liza, however, refuses it, and goes off to see for herself what has happened beyond the river. By the inevitable logic of Dostoyevsky's symbolism, she is murdered on the very spot where a few short hours before Marya Lebyadkin had been disposed of. Liza is killed by the crowd because she is 'Stavrogin's woman'. She is thus the last of Stavrogin's victims.

After the meeting with Liza, Stepan Trofimovich sits down

to rest, and, like Stavrogin on that earlier occasion, Fedka comes
into his thoughts. Indeed, he thinks that if he should meet Fedka
he will have to give him his purse. Here, again, is a reference to
Stavrogin's behaviour in 'Night'; but at the thought of
surrendering his purse to Fedka, Stepan Trofimovich makes a
sudden symbolic gesture: 'For some unknown reason he shut
his umbrella in terror, and laid it down beside him.' (Pt III,
Ch. VII, I.) Thus the good intentions of Stepan Trofimovich
seem to be vindicated: his pilgrimage through the day will be
quite different from Stavrogin's journey through the night.
It is at this very moment that Stepan Trofimovich perceives
the vehicle which is to lead him to his salvation: the peasant
cart which will carry him to the Russia of the common people,
and, in particular, bring him to Sofya Ulitina. The name of
this humble bible-seller is not without significance: Sofya is,
of course 'wisdom' (which is presumably what Stepan Trofimovich finds); whereas the surname, Ulitina, evokes *ulita* – a
snail, and is thus suggestive of her lowly status and her humility.
Ulitina does not presume to teach Stepan Trofimovich, rather
she acts as a catalyst by which he himself might find faith.

The positive ideas at which Stepan Trofimovich arrives are
not unlike those of Myshkin. Before undertaking his pilgrimage
he had even likened himself to Pushkin's 'Poor Knight', as we
have seen: the aestheticism of the 'man of the forties' has now
become a passionate endorsement of beauty. Like Myshkin too,
Stepan Trofimovich proclaims human happiness.

Every minute, every moment of life ought to be a state of bliss for
man. It must be so, it absolutely must be so! It is the obligation of
man himself to arrange it so. It is a human law, which is hidden but
which definitely exists.   (Pt III, Ch. VII, 3)

Universal forgiveness, another of Myshkin's virtues, has now
been taken over by Stepan Trofimovich:

Oh, let us forgive, let us forgive before all else. Let us forgive everyone; forgive always; and let us hope that we too shall be forgiven.
Yes, because each and everybody is to blame in respect of others. All
are to blame!   (Pt III, Ch. VII, 2)

Yet all these ideas we have encountered earlier in *The Devils* itself. Kirillov, at his most positive, had expressed a philosophy of beauty and happiness; and the idea of 'forgiving everybody because all are to blame' had first been uttered by Shatov. So the final philosophy of Stepan Trofimovich reveals an attempt to synthesise all that is positive in the two halves of Stavrogin.

But, if this is true, Stepan Trofimovich's new-found religious faith has something of the uncertainty of Shatov himself. He undertakes to sell bibles with Sofya Ulitina, so that he can 'be useful on the high road'; but then qualifies this by offering to correct the mistakes of 'this wonderful book'. He accepts the last rites of the Church, and claims that he has a need for God 'because He is the only being capable of being loved eternally'. Yet for all this, his final words on the eternal Great Idea seem more in keeping with some vague theism of the forties than with true Christianity. The narrator himself seems unsure about the reasons for his friend's apparent conversion:

Whether, indeed, he had found faith, or whether the impressive ceremony of administering the mystery had overwhelmed him and aroused the artistic responsiveness of his nature, whatever the reason, he nevertheless uttered firmly, and, it is said, with great feeling, several words completely at variance with his former convictions.

(Pt III, Ch. VII, 3)

Moreover, despite Stepan Trofimovich's new seriousness, his comic aura has not entirely deserted him. Even on his death-bed he is attended by a doctor with the comic name of Salz-fisch, and the priest who administers the last rites is a patently comic character.

Perhaps after all, Stepan Trofimovich offers merely a hope for faith rather than its full realisation. Symbolically he dies by the side of a lake separating him from the goal to which Sofya Ulitina had directed him – 'The Village of The Saviour': *Spasovo*.

If the positive side is still somewhat in doubt, there are nevertheless two negative ideas expressed by Stepan Trofimovich which place him firmly at the centre of the novel as the author's mouthpiece. The first of these: the application of the parable of the Gadarene swine to the revolutionaries, is the motto theme of the 'pamphlet novel'; the second points the moral of 'The Saintly Life of The Great Sinner' – it is the quotation from the Apocalypse on the fate of those who are neither hot nor cold, and originally, in the banned chapter, was applied to Stavrogin.

Both these quotations have relevance, too, for Stepan Trofimovich. He counts himself among the Gadarene swine, and is himself perishing at the lakeside. He too is 'neither hot nor cold'. For most of his life this typical liberal of the forties has shunned all real commitment and now he is separated by the water from his real goal of Spasovo. In the letter to Dasha, Stavrogin himself will present his own 'lukewarmness' in similar metaphorical terms: 'One can cross a river on a log of wood but not on a chip.'

We have already seen that Dostoyevsky interferes with the normal narrative sequence of 'Stepan Trofimovich's Last Pilgrimage' in order to show that the elder Verkhovensky is taking over the 'quest' from Stavrogin. But this is not all: the narrative is broken up in such a way as to provide a frame round other events: incidents which are crucial to the plot – the death of Shatov and the suicide of Kirillov.

It is inevitable that Stavrogin's ideological 'death' during the night of the fires should be further expressed in the deaths of Shatov and Kirillov, but by encompassing these events within the narrative of Stepan Trofimovich's quest, Dostoyevsky is providing the disintegration of the old illusions with a framework of new hope.

Yet even here, in the deaths of Shatov and Kirillov, hope is not finally abandoned. It is as though the author is making a desperate last attempt to vindicate the fallen Stavrogin. Thus on the day following the murder of the Lebyadkins a new Mary appears. She is, as it were, a restatement of 'the object'; for her Christian name is Marya and her patronymic is Ignatevna (cf. Ignat – Lebyadkin's Christian name). Marya Ignatevna is another of 'Stavrogin's women', but, significantly, she is the legal wife of Shatov. The new Mary calls herself 'Marie' and is Western in outlook and of nihilistic beliefs – the very antithesis of Marya Lebyadkin. Thus in the reunion of *this* Mary with Shatov there is contained a promise for the reconciliation of the two disparate halves of Stavrogin himself.

The new Mary differs from the old in yet another important respect. Marya Lebyadkin had talked to Shatov about her baby, but when Shatov had challenged Stavrogin on this during their nocturnal interview, he had replied that this was impossible: his wife was a virgin. Now Marie has come home to Shatov because she is about to bear a child, and a child, moreover, of which Stavrogin is the father. Thus the charge of Stavrogin's impotence is here refuted: the Shatov side is fertile and productive.

Shatov is elated by the news, and the unexpected blessing of 'parenthood' is presented in stark contrast to the self-acknowledged sterility of Kirillov. In 'Night' Kirillov had been discovered playing with a child, whereas Shatov was lonely and ill. But the presence of a child in Kirillov's apartment is a ray of false optimism: the way of the will is unproductive and sterile – the ultimate outcome of its logic is self-destruction.

'It's a great pity that I don't know how to give birth,' replied Kirillov pensively. 'That is, not that I do not know how to give birth, but do not know how to bring birth about, or rather, no...I don't know how to say it.' (Pt III, Ch. v, 3)

Shatov interprets these incoherent words as Kirillov's regret at not knowing how to be of assistance in the delivery of his child. But Kirillov's inability to comprehend goes deeper than this: he does not seem able to distinguish clearly between the fertile and the sterile. Thus he confuses Shatov's wife with the old woman who is to look after her, and then attempts a philosophical justification of his own impotence:

I think that man must cease giving birth. What need is there for children, what need is there for development, if the goal has been reached? The Gospels say that in the Resurrection, men will no

longer give birth but will be like God's angels. Here is a hint. Your
wife is giving birth, isn't she?   (Pt III, Ch. v, 5)

The Kirillov side is sterile and self-destructive: but the Shatov
side gives hope for the future. The advent of Marie is a promise
of reconciliation, reconciliation not only of the God-seeking
Shatov and his nihilist wife, but reconciliation even of Shatov
and Kirillov; for it is only after the advent of Marie that any
real, friendly contact is established between these two occupants
of The House of Filippov. Shatov, now, is even prepared for
reconciliation with the revolutionaries: 'Perhaps I am greatly
to blame in respect of them! Every one is to blame, everyone
is to blame, and...if only everyone would realize this!' (Pt III,
Ch. v, 3.)

Yet the tragic irony of Shatov's new-found hope is that at
this very moment the revolutionaries are plotting his death.
The dice are loaded against him. It is not merely that Marie's
response to his love and concern is so capricious and ungrateful:
her very arrival in the town seems surrounded by ill omens.
She gives the cabman the name of the wrong street, instead of
Epiphany Street [*Bogoyavlenskaya*] she gives the address (ominous in view of her own name) of Assumption Street [*Vozne-
senskaya*]. There is moreover, an omen of impotence; for it is
pointedly stressed that the horse which brings her is a gelding
(the word is repeated in quotation marks).

The last flicker of hope for Shatov comes to nothing: the
arrival of his wife 'saves the blackguards', and he is murdered
by them. His death drags in its train the suicide of Kirillov, and
this is followed by the death of Marie and the child she has just
borne. The Lebyadkins have been murdered; Liza has suffered
the same fate; and even Stepan Trofimovich is dying by the
lakeside. Stavrogin had promised not to outlive Liza and the
novel now reaches its foregone conclusion.

A letter like the insubstantial voice of a ghost arrives for the
nurse-figure Dasha. In it Stavrogin tries to explain himself:

I have tried my strength everywhere. You advised me to do this 'in
order to know myself'. In the tests I conducted for myself and for

exhibition, my strength proved boundless, as earlier and throughout my whole life. Before your eyes I bore the slap in the face from your brother; I publicly acknowledged my marriage. But to what purpose can this strength be applied? This is what I have never been able to see, and cannot see now, in spite of your encouragements in Switzerland, though I believed them. I can still wish to do good and feel pleasure from this, as I always could; at the same time I wish for evil, and also feel pleasure. But, as before, both these feelings are always too shallow; they are never strongly felt. My desires are much too weak, they cannot guide me. One can cross a river on a log of wood but not on a chip. (Pt III, Ch. VIII)

Thus the will, shorn of all else, is revealed in all its impotence: it lacks direction. Even to undertake an experiment in self-knowledge it has to be prompted and encouraged. This lack of direction is the absence of any ethical code, and Stavrogin, in this letter, says he has even looked on with envy at the revolutionaries. He himself is neither hot nor cold; he is uncommitted either to evil or to good; the two poles of beauty are equal for him, and he has no means of distinguishing between them. Like the Angel of the Laodiceans he will be spewed out – he will be rejected.

The letter reveals what has been apparent throughout the course of the novel: of his two selves, Stavrogin has chosen the Kirillov side. Yet even Kirillov can be envied because he is an extreme; he is a pole of Stavrogin's own personality, and as such he is a point of direction towards which Stavrogin's compass veers, but is not constantly set; for what Stavrogin lacks above all is a sense of real direction:

One can argue about this for ever, but from me there has only come negation, without any real nobility, without any real strength. Not even negation has been the result. Everything has always been shallow and languid. The noble Kirillov could not withstand an idea, and he shot himself, and I regard him as noble because he was not in his right mind. I could never lose my reason and could never believe in an idea to the same extent as he. I could not even be interested in an idea to that extent. I could never, never shoot myself! (*ibid.*)

Yet despite this claim, Stavrogin knows that he must finish in some form of suicide:

I know that I ought to kill myself, to wipe myself off the face of the earth like a vile insect, but I fear suicide, because I am afraid of showing nobility. I know that this would be still further deceit, the last deception in an endless series of deceptions. What use is there in deceiving one's self, merely in order to play at being noble? (*Ibid.*)

This 'final deception in an endless series of deceptions' is nevertheless inevitable. Half an hour after the receipt of this letter, Dasha and his mother are preparing to pay him a visit, when the old servant, Aleksey Yegorych, comes to tell them of the strange and unexpected arrival of his master at Skvoreshniki: 'He went through all the rooms and locked himself up in his own quarters.' The word for 'quarters' is in fact 'half' [*polovina*] and as, in the ensuing description of the discovery of Stavrogin's body, this word is repeated in quotation marks, it is safe to assume that it is being used with special emphasis; i.e.: 'In "his half" all the doors were open, but Nikolay Vsevolodovich was nowhere to be seen.' And again: 'It was remarkable that several servants followed Varvara Petrovna into "his half".'

Stavrogin then has locked himself up in 'his own half' – the Kirillov side of his nature: the will that leads ultimately to self-destruction. But unlike Kirillov, Stavrogin has specifically rejected the noble act of shooting himself; instead he hangs himself ignominiously in his loft.

It is perhaps significant that the details of this death (by hanging and in a garret-like room) reproduce those of another suicide, that of Matresha: the little girl whose fate is related by Stavrogin in 'the banned chapter'. If this is so, Stavrogin's suicide may be interpreted as an act of oblique contrition for her death. Stavrogin, the emotional eunuch, cannot directly feel the promptings of conscience; nevertheless 'the banned chapter' reveals what the novel itself hints at more deviously: that his marriage to the cripple, Marya, is an attempt to cripple his own life because of Matresha. He wishes to take on a burden to assuage some vague, unformulated sense of guilt:

The incident in Gorokhovaya Street, I would have forgotten completely, once the danger was past, as I forgot everything else from that period, if I hadn't still kept on remembering all the details with malice. I poured out my malice on everyone I could. It was precisely at this time and for absolutely no reason at all, that the thought came to me of crippling my life in some way or other, any way, provided it were the most objectionable possible. I had already thought a year ago of shooting myself, but something better presented itself.

('At Tikhon's', II)

This 'something better' is his marriage to Marya Lebyadkin:

The thought of Stavrogin marrying this, the least of human beings, played on my nerves. Nothing more hideous than this could be imagined; no, nothing. But it was at that particular time; it happened at that time, and is therefore understandable. At any rate, I did not get married merely 'to win a wager of wine after a drunken banquet'.

(*ibid.*)

Thus like a Russian doll (Matreshka) the little girl Matresha lies concealed but implicit within the larger figure of Marya Lebyadkin.

The banned chapter, 'At Tikhon's', was to have followed immediately after the disclosure of Petr Verkhovensky's political ambitions for Stavrogin ('Ivan the Crown Prince'). Its exclusion not only disturbs the balance of the novel, it also withholds essential information about Stavrogin.[9]

Stavrogin's confession is presented to Tikhon in the form of a pamphlet, which he has had printed in large numbers. The 'crime' involves a little girl against whom Stavrogin may, or may not, have committed an offence, but whether he has or no, he was certainly present in the apartment when she committed suicide. This equivocation over facts arises because Tikhon is not permitted to read the second of the five sheets of Stavrogin's pamphlet. The document purports to reveal the depths of Stavrogin's wickedness, but it is not seen by Tikhon altogether in this light. He thinks, rather, that the confession places Stavrogin in a comic position, and makes him vulnerable to the laughter of his readers. This observation is clearly an anticipation of Liza's later unmasking of Stavrogin.[10]

Stavrogin himself seems concerned about the ambivalence of his own character; for, towards the beginning of their interview, he specifically asks Tikhon about the quotation from the Apocalypse on the fate of those who are 'neither hot nor cold.' Yet towards the end of their meeting Tikhon offers hope for the good side of Stavrogin: 'It has always turned out that the most shameful of crosses has become a great glory and an enormous strength if the humility of the act is genuine.' ('At Tikhon's', III.) But Stavrogin has already accidentally broken a small ivory crucifix on Tikhon's desk, as though symbolically destroying the 'cross-like' implications of his own name, and Tikhon's final words predict that he will commit a new crime to avoid making his pamphlet public: Tikhon has sensed the murder of the Lebyadkins.

The figure of Matresha refuses to leave Stavrogin's imagination; the vision of the little girl raising her fist to him haunts him daily. On one occasion, abroad, he had even bought a photograph of a girl who looked like her. Indeed Matresha is a presence lurking behind the nocturnal interview with the two halves of himself. Thus when Kirillov points out that the little girl with whom he has been playing will remain alive, even though her mother is about to die, and goes on to pronounce that everything is good, it is as though a memory stirs within Stavrogin: '…and a man who insults and dishonours a little girl, is that good?' (Pt II, Ch. I, 5.) Kirillov's reply is enigmatic but reassuring:

Yes, it is good; and the man who blows his brains out for a child, that is good too. And the man who doesn't blow his brains out, that also is good. (*ibid.*)

It is a mark of the conscious nature of his actions that during the suicide of Matresha, Stavrogin is constantly looking at his watch. But Kirillov has stopped his watch,[11] and says he did so when he first realized everyone was so happy. When Stavrogin now goes on to ask him whether the stopped watch symbolises his discovery of timelessness, the reply he receives is merely a qualification of the earlier answer:

'They are bad,' he suddenly began again, 'because they do not know that they are good. When they realise this, they will not rape little girls. They must realise that they are good, and immediately they will all become good, every single one of them.'   (*ibid.*)

For Kirillov, consciousness is the key to good and evil, and the consciousness of evil can be turned off just as simply as stopping a watch; when Stavrogin realises that he is good, then he *will be* good.

Stavrogin's account of the suicide of Matresha provides yet another symbol of his consciousness of evil: the little red spider which he watches on the geranium plant. But when, on the other hand, he suddenly becomes aware of goodness and beauty in the dream he has of the golden age, it is this same little red spider which returns to blot it out. Kirillov, however, has the ability to see goodness and beauty everywhere around him, and this vision is not marred by anything, not even a spider: 'You see? A spider is crawling up the wall. I watch him and am grateful to him for crawling.' (*Ibid.*)

In the 'case' of the crime committed against Matresha, Kirillov appears as the counsel for the defence: Shatov conducts the argument for the prosecution. Thus, after the death of Matresha, Stavrogin comes to the conclusion that there is no right and no wrong: it is amoralism such as this which Kirillov seems to be supporting, whereas Shatov attacks such a confusion of 'the two poles of beauty', and specifically questions Stavrogin about acts committed against children:

Is it true that in St Petersburg you belonged to a secret society of bestial-like voluptuaries? Is it true that the Marquis de Sade could have learned something from you? Is it true that you enticed and corrupted children?   (Pt II, Ch. I, 7)

Stavrogin's reply: 'I said these words, but it was not I who molested children' suggests that his guilt is one of words rather than deeds. Perhaps this is the conclusion to be drawn too from that piece of literary bravado which he calls his 'confession'.

The evil in Stavrogin is not symbolised by 'a spider the size of a man', as Liza soon discovers: its real symbol is the tiny red spider on the geranium plant. This spider, observed by Stavrogin during Matresha's suicide, represents evil in an ambiguously passive form; the same sort of evil which is at work in the murder of the Lebyadkins, and the abduction of Liza; for here, too, Stavrogin has not acted, he has merely allowed himself to be implicated in evil by the real spinner of intrigue – Petr Verkhovensky.

Stavrogin's moral neutrality is in essence a religious problem. When Kirillov says: 'If Stavrogin believes, then he does not believe that he does believe; but if he doesn't believe, then he doesn't believe that he doesn't believe,' (Pt III, Ch. VI, 2) the statement is not as absurd as Petr Verkhovensky thinks; for Dostoyevsky himself characterised the theme of 'The Life of a Great Sinner' in the following terms:

> The chief problem, which will be developed in all parts [of the novel] is the very one, over which, consciously and unconsciously, I have been tormented all my life – it is the existence of God.[12]

In *The Devils* this religious turmoil is symbolically portrayed in 'The House of Filippov'.

In the simple view Kirillov, the nihilist, represents the atheism of the will: Shatov, the Slavophile, represents the religion of Christ. On examination, however, the differences between them prove to be not so clear cut. The 'nihilism' of Kirillov is not a denial of religion; on the contrary he is obsessed by religious values. During the section 'Night' Stavrogin had sensed a religious undertone in Kirillov's arguments and had told him that he would probably be religious the next time he saw him. Indeed when Kirillov next expounds his ideas on suicide a new and unexpected argument does emerge. He tells Petr Verkhovensky:

> God is necessary and therefore must exist ... But I know that he does not exist and cannot exist ... You must surely realise that a man with two such ideas cannot remain alive.   (Pt III, Ch. VI, 2)

Again during this same scene, Kirillov points to an icon of the Saviour hanging in his room, and says: '"There is no secret that will not be made known" that is what *He* said.' Petr

Verkhovensky accuses him of believing like any priest, but Kirillov takes him up on this:

'In whom? In *Him*? Listen,' Kirillov stopped and gazed before him with a fixed but frenzied stare, 'Listen to a great idea. There was a certain day on earth, and in the middle of the earth stood three crosses. One man on a cross believed so much that he said to another: "Today you will be with me in paradise." The day finished; they both died; they departed...and found neither paradise not resurrection: the words did not come true. Listen, that man was the most perfect man on all the earth. He represented that for which the earth lived. The whole planet and everything it contains is sheer nonsense without that man. There has never been anyone like him either before or since – never; and this in itself is a miracle: it is a miracle that there has not been anyone like him and never, in fact, will be. But if this is so, if the laws of nature did not spare even this man, did not spare even their own miracle but made him live amongst lies and die for a lie, then it follows that the whole of the planet is a lie, is based on lies and stupid mockery; it follows that the very laws of the planet are lies and a satanic farce. What is there to live for? Answer me that if you are a man!' (*ibid.*)

In this scene Kirillov seems to be explaining his suicide as an act of religious despair, and Verkhovensky is quick to see the shift in his thought: 'This is another twist to the matter. It seems to me that here you have confused two different reasons.'

Indeed such veneration for Christ seems odd in an atheist. Striking too is the fact that Kirillov has been given many of the traits of Dostoyevsky's own Christ-figure: Prince Myshkin.

Yet, for all his veneration, Kirillov sees Christ as a failure, and in this he is at one with Myshkin's chief critic, Ippolit. Kirillov's speech on Christ, quoted above, is very close to the train of thought which Rogozhin's picture inspires in Ippolit: both see the laws of nature, death and destruction as ultimately stronger than Christ. Moreover in the lives of both, death is a central preoccupation. Suicide for Ippolit is an act of despair and defiance, and although Kirillov, too, has this motive, his suicide has yet another aim: it represents the means whereby he can offer himself as a new saviour for mankind:

215

But I shall declare my will [i.e. *svoyevoliye* = wilfulness]. I am obliged to believe that I believe. I shall begin and I shall end. I shall open the door and save. It is this alone which will save all mankind, and in the next generation man will change physically, for in his present physical form, as I see it, he cannot do without the old god. For three years I have been seeking the attribute of my godhead, and I have found the attribute of my godhead: it is will.   (*ibid.*)

Death conquered the old Saviour, so Kirillov, the new saviour, must now conquer death, or more precisely the *fear* of death so that a new generation of Darwinian supermen may follow him; for man in his present state has elevated the fear of death itself into a god (or in Kirillov's own formula: 'God is the pain of the fear of death'). Kirillov like a second underground man is pitting his own will against 'the laws of nature', the inevitability of $2 \times 2 = 4$ and the ultimate, impenetrable 'wall' of death itself.

Nevertheless, Kirillov's symbol for man's fear of death is not a wall, it is a boulder the size of a house suspended over man's head. Shatov, too, is under a similar 'boulder': 'Stepan Trofimovich was right when he said that I am lying under a boulder, squashed, though not finally crushed, merely writhing. It is a good comparison.' (Pt I, Ch. IV, 4.) But the religious problem which crushes Shatov is in many ways the very obverse of that suspended over the head of Kirillov. Kirillov sees Christ as 'living among lies and dying for a lie', he therefore rejects Christ for the 'truth', (i.e. the divinity of man). Shatov, on the other hand, is prepared to accept Christ even if it means rejecting the truth:[13] the ideal of one is that of 'man-god', the ideal of the other is that of 'God-man'.

But the very fact that Shatov can concede the possibility of an antithesis between Christ and the truth, in itself reveals the presence of religious doubt. Even more fundamental is his apparent inability to believe in God; for in spite of his fanatical faith in Christ, Shatov's belief in God is insubstantial, and under Stavrogin's constant probing, he can only assert: 'I shall believe in God.' Shatov realises that in order to make hare-gravy he must first catch his hare, and God is the hare which eludes him.

If he is ever to influence Stavrogin, the catching of this hare is crucial: 'Listen, I can set it all to rights. I will get you the hare.' Yet in spite of this promise, the only hare he seems able to produce has more the appearance of a rabbit pulled out of a slavophile hat: 'God is the synthesised personality of the whole nation from the beginning of its existence right to the end.' (Pt II, Ch. I, 7.) At this Stavrogin accuses him of having reduced godhead to a simple attribute of nationality, but Shatov corrects him: 'On the contrary, I am raising the nation to the status of God.' Shatov's idea of the nation as god is not dissimilar from Kirillov's concept of 'man-god' – both end by attributing divinity to man. Moreover both look with hope to a future generation. Kirillov, as we have seen, thinks in terms of their physical evolution, whereas Shatov seems to be thinking of a new moral and social force:

A new generation is coming straight out of the heart of the people, and neither you nor the Verkhovenskys, father and son, nor even I – none of us will recognise it. (Pt II, Ch. I, 7)

Shatov and Kirillov represent two different attempts to resolve a religious dilemma – the contradiction between the truth of Christ and the existence of evil – yet their antithetical solutions are not contained in idea-proof shells; their arguments touch at many points, and the atheism of Kirillov veers towards religion whilst the religious philosophy of Shatov drifts towards atheism.

The two poles of this religious dilemma are thus in reality not very far apart; they meet, as do the two poles of beauty and the antithetical principles of 'sinner' and 'saint', in the central figure of Stavrogin. Yet the man who can reconcile the warring elements of fire and ice is fated to be spewed forth as one who is 'neither hot nor cold'. This is the tragedy of Stavrogin: in him boundless potential has become the impotence of an existence without aim.

8

PARRICIDE:
'THE BROTHERS KARAMAZOV'

In the summer of 1871 Dostoyevsky returned with his family to Russia, and thus entered on the final decade of his life: a period of relative stability. He devoted himself to journalism (the *Writer's Diary*), and wrote two full-length novels. The first of these: *A Raw Youth*, is a manifest failure, and will not be discussed here; the second: *The Brothers Karamazov*, represents, perhaps, the very peak of his achievement: it is a work which must be examined in some detail.

The action of *The Brothers Karamazov* is pivoted on one central event – the death of a father. Many commentators have related this to an event in Dostoyevsky's own life; for his own father was murdered – not by one of his sons, it is true, yet nevertheless the circumstances surrounding his death could hardly have left them with an easy conscience. The sons did not get on well with their father, and any feelings of guilt bred in their minds by the consciousness of this hostility must surely have been further nourished by the way in which they acted after his death. Dostoyevsky's father was killed by his own peasants in dubious circumstances, and whether it was to avert scandal or whether it was for the less creditable reason that the very peasants, who had been the instrument by which the sons could inherit, were also the inheritance itself (at this time serfs were still counted as chattels), it is nevertheless a fact that the murder was hushed up and none of those guilty was sent to Siberia.[1]

A second link between biography and novel can be seen in Dostoyevsky's interest in the fate of a fellow prisoner in the Omsk Penal Settlement. Ilinsky was a retired second lieutenant who had lived a very profligate life until he had been brought to trial for the murder of his father. His character is described by Dostoyevsky at the beginning of *Notes from the House of the Dead*; but after the publication of that work Dostoyevsky learned that Ilinsky had been released from penal servitude, his innocence fully vindicated. This tragic figure, wrongly accused of parricide, interested Dostoyevsky greatly, and an early sketch clearly shows that Ilinsky served as a prototype for Dmitri Karamazov.[2]

The tiny estate of Dostoyevsky's father, so closely associated with his own murder and the unease of the sons who inherited it, contained the village of Chermashnya. This name occurs in the novel as a village on the Karamazov estate.[3] But Chermashnya is more than a village: as we shall see it becomes, for both Ivan and Dmitri, a symbol of their guilt in the death of their father. Alongside this, it is an interesting fact that the local priest who represents the interests of the elder Karamazov in Chermashnya is always referred to as 'the Ilinsky father'. Thus allusions to the two inspirational germs of the plot are to be found side by side in the symbol which Dostoyevsky uses to show apparent complicity in the crime of parricide.

Yet a third incident in Dostoyevsky's life has left its imprint on the novel. In 1878 Dostoyevsky's three-year-old son Aleksey died from an epileptic fit, and the father, shattered by this tragedy, sought consolation in a pilgrimage to the Optina Monastery. This is the period of the novel's inception, and the prominence of monasticism in *The Brothers Karamazov* is clearly traceable to this experience. Not only does the portrayal of Zosima owe much to Ambrosius, the Elder who so impressed Dostoyevsky at the Optyna Monastery, but the words of comfort spoken by Zosima to the peasant woman who has lost a child are those by which Ambrosius sought to console Dostoyevsky's own wife.[4] Significant too is the name of this three-year-old child – Aleksey. But Aleksey is also the name of the youngest of the Karamazov brothers, the one designated by Dostoyevsky as the hero.

If, for Dostoyevsky, the name Chermashnya is charged with the guilt of the sons, the name Aleksey, on the other hand is charged with the guilt of a father, for grief at the death of his baby son was not unmixed with torment over yet another guilt-ridden inheritance: Aleksey had died of his father's affliction – epilepsy. It is as though Dostoyevsky's feelings of guilt as a son and his feelings of guilt as a father have found artistic expression in his last novel, for the reciprocal guilt of fathers and sons is the very substance of *The Brothers Karamazov*; the novel about parricide is in fact another *Fathers and Children*.

Dostoyevsky had been obsessed by this theme for some years. It can be already remarked in *The Devils*, and later in 1876 Dostoyevsky wrote in the *Writer's Diary*:

When Nekrasov, eighteen months ago, invited me to write a novel for *The Fatherland Notes*, I was on the point of beginning my *Fathers and Children*, but I held back, and thank God I did. I was not yet ready. So for the time being I wrote *A Raw Youth* as the first trial of my idea[5].

In *The Devils* the theme had been important in a politically schematic sense; *A Raw Youth* was an artistic failure, but the *Fathers and Children* theme, lifted now on to a new moral plane, was to be saved for the last great novel: *The Brothers Karamazov*.

If in *The Devils* Dostoyevsky had gone beyond Turgenev in suggesting that the fathers *were responsible* for the children, he now takes up with renewed force the message proclaimed in *The Devils* itself that 'everyone is to blame', and uses it to carry the theme one stage further. In *The Brothers Karamazov* it is not only the father who is responsible for his sons: the sons must also answer for the father.

Yet in spite of this, the title of the novel itself singles out not the relationship of fathers and children, but that of brothers. It would be as well to look at this relationship before proceeding further.

One of the problems which the title poses is the position of the brothers in the architecture of the novel. All Dostoyevsky's major novels up to this point had been constructed round one central figure; but here, it seems, we are witnessing a new departure – the emergence of a collective hero. The plot appears to be developed in such a way as to give almost equal prominence to each of the three legitimate brothers. Even so, it might be felt that Dmitri is nearer to the centre of the action than Ivan, and Ivan himself is more prominent than Alesha. Yet the author, for his part, is quite clear on this issue: the hero, he tells us in his introduction, is Alesha.

But the introduction was obviously written to apologise for the 'heroic pretensions' of Alesha. He will come into his own, we are told, in a second novel, the sequel to *The Brothers Kara-mazov*. There is, indeed, much that is unfinished in the novel as it stands. The fate of Dmitri is left suspended; a whole new novel (so we are told) could be written about Ivan and Katerina Ivanovna; the final scene between Alesha and the children looks forward to a future time when they will all meet again after some twenty years have elapsed – the theme has grown and grown under Dostoyevsky's pen.

In Dostoyevsky's further plans for Alesha he seems to have had in mind his cherished project for 'the life of a great sinner'. Alesha was to fall to the temptations of the world and would only find his faith again, strengthened and renewed, after many adverse and tempering experiences. But the fact that the Alesha of *The Brothers Karamazov* does not compel the imagination to the same extent as his brothers should not blind us to his central position in the novel. There is scarcely one important scene (leaving aside the events surrounding the murder itself) at which Alesha is not present. His role is more often that of an observer, even a catalyst; less frequently that of an active participant.

The first major set scene in the novel is the scandal scene in the monastery. Here are two worlds in antithesis; we witness the invasion of the peaceful monastic retreat by all the strife and pettiness of the world outside. It is Alesha who links these two worlds. But more than this, throughout the further course of the novel he attempts to reverse this process of invasion; for in following the injunction of Zosima that he must go out into the world, he seeks to penetrate it with the values he has learned within the monastery walls.[6]

Through Alesha the reader looks deep into the souls of the other characters. It is as though Alesha, in the world, is carrying on a tradition of Zosima within the monastery: the tradition of confessing the brotherhood aloud.

The first confession Alesha hears is that of his brother Dmitri. In three chapters ('The Confession of an Ardent Heart in Verse', 'The Confession of an Ardent Heart in Anecdotes' and 'The Confession of an Ardent Heart Head over Heels') Dmitri pours out his soul. From the beginning we are made aware of the poetic qualities of this 'ardent heart':

> Glory to the highest on the earth.
> Glory to the highest within me   (Bk III, Ch. 3)

a couplet which, Dmitri later acknowledges, he has himself composed. Its sentiments are not Christian: they are humanistic, and a preoccupation with *man* lies at the heart of Dmitri's attitude to life. He quotes much poetry, all of it humanistic in spirit, much of it classical and pagan in setting.

Dmitri says he wishes to begin his confession with Schiller's ode to joy; '*An die Freude*', and this is understandable for in Dmitri there is primitive exultation at the sheer joy of being alive. Instead of this, however, he begins to quote from another poem by Schiller, '*Das Eleusische Fest*'.

This poem has great significance for Dmitri. The very name 'Dmitri' means 'belonging to Demeter' – the goddess of agriculture, otherwise known as Ceres, and the verses he now quotes describe the civilising influence of Ceres on savage, rapacious man. Ceres descending from Mount Olympus in search of her daughter Proserpine is confronted by the abject misery of man's state: – 'And wherever Ceres looks/Her sad eye sees man/Everywhere in deep degradation.' At this point in the verse Dmitri breaks off in tears: this degradation is still relevant for contemporary man – it is still relevant for Dmitri himself:

God grant I do not talk nonsense now, and do not praise myself. I think about this man for the very reason that I myself am just such a man:

> 'For man to rise spiritually/From his baseness/Let him enter
> into union for ever/With ancient mother earth.'

But this is the real trouble: how shall I enter into union with the earth for ever? I do not kiss the earth. I do not plough her. What shall I do, become a peasant or a shepherd? I go on without knowing whether I have fallen into filth and shame, or into joy and light. This is where the trouble lies, for everything on earth is a riddle. And whenever I have chanced to sink into the deepest, deepest shame of debauchery (and this is all I have ever managed to do) then I have always read this poem about Ceres and man. Has it ever corrected me? No, never. Because I am a Karamazov.   (Bk III, Ch. 3)

In a pejorative sense, the epithet 'earthy' is more than once applied to this surname Karamazov, but his baptismal name, Dmitri, 'belonging to Demeter', stands as a pledge of his ultimate redemption.

Before he is to 'rise spiritually', however, he must suffer the consciousness of even greater degradation. After the incident in his father's garden his 'wildness' is commented on by Perkhotin. Dmitri obsessively takes up his remark in words which suggest that the personal message of the Schiller poem is ever present in his mind: 'I am wild, you say. Savages, savages! I keep on repeating just one word: savages!'[7] (Bk VIII, Ch. 5.)

His brother Alesha will find this bond with the earth before him; will find it, it seems, at the very moment when Dmitri is about to plumb the depths of his own abasement in that decisive last night at Mokroye:

It was that very night, perhaps even that very hour, when Alesha fell on the earth and 'swore in ecstasy to love her for ever and ever'. But the soul of Dmitri was troubled, very troubled, and although much tormented him inwardly, at that moment all his being was yearning implacably for her alone, for his queen, to whom he was flying in order to look at her for the last time.   (Bk VII, Ch. 6)

It is this 'queen', Grushenka, who later during that same night will speak to him like a second Ceres:

What do we want money for? We would just squander it on riotous living. We're just the folk for that. But rather let us both go and till the earth. I want to scratch the earth with these hands of mine. We must work, do you hear. Those are Alesha's orders.   (Bk VIII, Ch. 8)

These words are spoken in a moment of hope before the final blow falls on Dmitri. Later that same night he is to experience the full extent of his degradation, epitomised in the state of complete nakedness which his tormentors require of him. The Dmitri who stands before them naked, embarrassed by his own feet, ashamed and yet enraged, seems to invite the epithets which open 'Das Eleusische Fest': 'Shy, naked, and wild' – the description of man, the savage, unredeemed by eternal union with the earth. Thus Dmitri's confession to Alesha reveals themes which are important for the whole of his future life.

When Alesha next goes to his brother's look-out post, it is not Dmitri he finds but Smerdyakov. The bastard brother is unaware of Alesha's presence and talks freely. This may be seen as an indirect confession on the part of Smerdyakov, and certainly the comparison between this scene and Alesha's earlier meeting with Dmitri is quite explicit. Thus Alesha mechanically sits in the very place assigned to him the day before by Dmitri, when he had wanted him to hear his confession:

Empty, useless thoughts came into his mind, as always during a boring wait. For example, why had he, on entering, sat down in the very same place that he had sat yesterday; why nowhere else?

(Bk v, Ch. 2)

But the indirect nature of Smerdyakov's self-revelation stands out in complete contrast to the frank outpourings of Dmitri. This in itself is emblematic of the devious reticence which characterises Smerdyakov, and which becomes markedly manifest again once Alesha tries to approach him openly.

The lofty poetic declamations of Dmitri are here replaced by the banal stanzas of a 'lackey's' song: Dmitri's passion for women is reduced to the condescending association which Smerdyakov apathetically carries on with Marya Kondratyevna, and when she complains that he has altered the words of his song and it is not as gently amorous as before, Smerdyakov's retort reveals a more fundamental point of contrast with Dmitri:

As regards verse, it is just absolute nonsense. Think yourself, who in this world speaks in rhymes? And if we all did begin to speak in rhymes, at the command of the authorities say, well would we really say anything at all? Verses are not practical, Marya Kondratyevna.

(*ibid.*)

Whereas Dmitri, in his poetic effusions, sings out his joy at being alive, Smerdyakov complains to Marya Kondratyevna about the conditions of his birth and wishes he had been killed in the womb. This is the only time in the novel that Smerdyakov mentions his mother, and his words reveal not so much hostility towards her as towards those who talk about her.

The name Smerdyakov is derived from that of his mother, 'Stinking Liza' [*Liza Smerdyashchaya*].[8] Smerdyakov himself is extremely fastidious and the implications of his name are purely moral. It is in this sense that Rakitin jibes at Alesha that there is something which stinks in his family, and that the elder Zosima has smelled out a crime. This crime, as it later transpires, will be committed by Smerdyakov.

After his interview with Smerdyakov, Alesha goes to the inn where Ivan is vainly waiting for Dmitri. The three chapters which follow ('The Brothers Get Acquainted', 'Rebellion', 'The Grand Inquisitor') stand in parallel to the three chapters in which Dmitri had unburdened his soul to Alesha: they are Ivan's 'confession'.

From what we have seen of Ivan earlier, we might expect the dry scholarly essay to be the mode of expression nearest to his heart, and indeed much of his *profession de foi* here is concerned with facts. But there has already been a hint of another side of Ivan, a poetic side; and when his emotions are aroused he too is capable of quoting from Dmitri's favourite poet. The provocation is the behaviour of Katerina Ivanovna ('Heartache in the Drawing-room'):

'*Den Dank, Dame, begehr ich nicht*',

he added with a contorted smile, proving moreover, and quite unexpectedly, that he too had read enough Schiller to know it by heart. Alesha would not have believed this before.　(Bk IV, Ch. 5)

Nor is Alesha alone in his surprise on this occasion: Mrs Khokhlakova thinks the quotation worthy of Alesha himself.

Now in the final chapter of Ivan's 'confession' his interest in poetry is revealed a second time, and once more Alesha greets it with surprise:

'You have written a poem?'

'Oh, no, I haven't written it', laughed Ivan, 'I have never composed as much as two verses in my life. But I have thought of the idea for a poem and have remembered it. I conceived it with great passion. You shall be my first reader, that is to say listener.'

(Bk v, Ch. 4)

Poetry is a touchstone by which the brothers are judged. For Smerdyakov, poetry is senseless and without value; for Dmitri, it is the outpouring of 'an ardent heart'; for Ivan, it is largely cerebral: an idea 'conceived with great passion', but not given full artistic form. It is, however, not an antithesis of heart and head alone which distinguishes the 'poetry' of these two brothers; there is also a difference of poetic universe: Dmitri draws his symbols from a pagan classical world; Ivan draws his from Christianity.

Ivan's attitude to Christianity (as revealed in the discussion of his article in Zosima's cell, and the ensuing arguments with his father 'over the brandy') seems ambivalent and contradictory. Why this should be is more clearly seen from his 'confession' to Alesha; here he reveals himself, not as an apologist of the ways of God to man, but as a religious philosopher arguing the case of man against God – Ivan is an inverted theologian, and this is the very figure he projects as the hero of his poem: 'The Legend of the Grand Inquisitor'.

Ivan's preoccupation with man links him with Dmitri; both are concerned at the abject unredeemed state of man. But the only salvation which the inverted theologian can offer is not the pagan 'eternal union with the earth', it is an ecclesiastical formula of 'miracle, mystery and authority'. Yet, for all that Ivan ends with 'The Legend of the Grand Inquisitor', his rebellion had nevertheless begun with quite a different figure:

I somewhere happened to read about 'John the Merciful' (one of the saints) about how, when a passer-by, who was starving and frozen, came to him and asked him to warm him, he lay down in bed with him, took him in his arms and began to breathe into his mouth – a mouth decaying and evil-smelling from the effects of some disease.

(Bk v, Ch. 4)

Such utter compassion serves as a constant reproach to his own behaviour in the novel; for the name of the saint is significant: John (Ioann/Ivan) is his own name.[9] Thus throughout most of the novel Ivan is alienated from his guardian saint, just as Dmitri is separated from his cult-identity as 'one belonging to Demeter'.

Both brothers need Alesha's help; both turn away from him:

Ivan suddenly turned and set off on his way, without turning round any more. It was similar to the way in which his brother Dmitri had left him yesterday, although yesterday's meeting was of an entirely different nature. This strange fleeting observation flashed like an arrow through the despondent mind of Alesha, for his mind for the moment was despondent and sad. He waited a little, watching his departing brother. For some reason he suddenly noticed that his brother Ivan walked with a sort of swaying motion, and that his right shoulder, viewed from behind, seemed lower than the left. He had never noticed this before.

(Bk v, Ch. 5)

The gait of Ivan seems to hint at his intellectual shuffling; it is in obvious contrast to the bold, firm strides which characterise the directness of Dmitri's nature.[10]

After leaving Ivan, Alesha returns to the monastery where his spiritual father is on his death-bed. Alesha takes down the reminiscences and teachings of the dying elder, and this testament forms the substance of Book vi: 'The Russian Monk'. Thus once more Alesha is the instrument by which one of the chief characters of the novel chooses to lay bare his soul, and it is obvious that the three chapters of 'The Russian Monk' are to be taken as a pendant to the three chapters of Ivan's 'confession': they are its refutation. To Ivan's nihilism is opposed the teaching of the elder on the positive aspects of life, and his name, Zosima (strong in life), is highly appropriate.

We have already seen that Alesha's name (Aleksey) has deep personal significance for the author; but the passage which makes this explicit (Zosima's words of consolation to the bereaved peasant woman) also gives an added resonance to the very name itself:

'I shall pray for the soul of your little child to be at rest. What was he called?'

'Aleksey, Father'.

'It is a nice name. Was he called after Aleksey the man of God?'

'Yes, after the man of God, Father, after Aleksey the man of God'.

'What a saint he was! I shall pray for him...'   (Bk II, Ch. 3)

Alesha himself, then, is walking in the footsteps of a saint. More than once he is referred to in the novel as an angel; but the reference to Aleksey the man of God is taken up in annoyance by Rakitin as a gibe after their visit to Grushenka ('An Onion'). The name Aleksey literally means 'helper', and this would appear to fit in with his attitude to the other characters in the novel. But the relationship of Alesha to his elder is not just that of a 'helper'; the part he plays in the 'confession' of Zosima is more than that of a mere scribe. It is Zosima himself who explains the symbolic importance of Alesha in his life:

'My fathers and teachers', he addressed his guests with a benign smile, 'until today I have never told anyone, why the face of this youth has been so dear to my soul; I have not told even him. Only now will I tell you: his face has been a sort of reminder and a prophecy to me. At the dawn of my days, whilst still a little child, I had an elder brother who died before my very eyes, a youth of seventeen. Later as I went through life, I gradually became convinced that this brother was, as it were, a signpost of what was preordained in my life from on high; for, I think, if he had not appeared in my life, if he had never existed, I, perhaps, would never have become a monk, would never have set foot on this path so dear to me. He first appeared to me in childhood, and now in my declining years there has appeared before my very eyes a repetition of this. It is odd, fathers and teachers, that although Aleksey is not like him so much facially – only a little, perhaps – he nevertheless seems to me to be spiritually so like him, that I have many times thought of him as being that very youth, my brother, mysteriously come to me at the end of my road as a reminder and an inspiration, so much so that I have wondered at myself and at this strange dream of mine.' (Bk VI, Ch. 1)

Thus we are confronted with an interesting fact: the inspiration of Zosima's life and teachings is identified with Alesha himself; Alesha is both pupil and mentor. It is therefore doubly fitting that it should be Alesha who is Zosima's chronicler, for in a sense this is his own *profession de foi*. Alesha, having allowed the reader to see deep into the souls of his brothers, now through the words of Zosima reveals what is in his own.

But the role of Alesha in the novel is not limited to that of 'confessor' to his brothers alone. It is through contact with Alesha that Rakitin, Katerina Ivanovna, Grushenka, Liza Khokhlakova, Snegirev, Kolya Krasotkin – in short all the characters of any importance – reveal their true natures. The claim that Alesha is at the centre of the novel is fully justified; yet the novel is not dominated by him; its hero is not one man; it is a brotherhood. It is as though the central figure so typical of Dostoyevsky's previous writing is ultimately unable to withstand its own dichotomous inner tensions and has here broken apart into separate and distinct facets; in Alesha we have *the soul*; in Dmitri *the emotions*; in Ivan *the intellect*: but behind them all lurks Smerdyakov – the devious, unlit recesses of man's psyche.

This interpretation is obviously schematic, but the brothers seem to invite such assessments; thus a sociological interpretation is placed on their characters by the public prosecutor at Dmitri's trial. Ivan, he says, represents Russian Europeanism; Alesha, on the contrary, represents *national principles*; whereas Dmitri stands for the ingenuous spontaneity of the Russian temperament.

But the fact that the brothers can be viewed schematically does not mean that they are presented as characters in a medieval morality play; there is much more than allegorical significance alone in the way each brother is portrayed. Indeed the striking fact is not the narrowness of their portrayal, but its broadness.

It is Dmitri who complains that man is too broad; for he himself is aware of his own contradictory nature. Like the underground man, both lofty ideals and base ideals can motivate him at one and the same time. His confusion is apparent in his confession to Alesha; he wishes to open his confession on a note of human exultation with Schiller's '*An die Freude*', instead he begins on a note of human despair with '*Das Eleusische Fest*'.

When, however, Dmitri does begin to quote 'The Hymn to Joy' (in Tyutchev's version) it is significant that he chooses the two verses in which joy is specifically linked to the beauty of nature. Such exultation in the joyous harmony of a beautiful world ('Joy has coaxed the blade of grass up towards the light') is reminiscent of Myshkin surrounded by 'the feast of nature' ('Each blade of grass grew and was happy'). But the personal reproach implied in Ippolit's 'little fly in the sunlight' marred the beauty of nature for Myshkin, and in Dmitri's quotation another insect – the insect endowed with lasciviousness – is just such another fly in beauty's ointment. In order to bring out this point more forcibly, Dmitri (although in other respects he quotes accurately) has transposed the original sequence of these two verses, and thus from a state of joy he returns to a state of despair; for he recognises himself in this insect to whom God has given lasciviousness.

The very existence of this insect of lasciviousness seems to cast doubt on the ideal of beauty itself; man's yearning for beauty might not be wholly pure and good:

Beauty is a terrifying and awful thing! Terrifying because it is indefinable. It cannot be defined because God has set us nothing but riddles. Here two shores meet, here all contradictions live together. I am very uneducated, brother, but I have thought a lot about this. There are a terrible number of mysteries. Too many riddles oppress man on earth. You have to unravel them as best you may and try to come off unscathed. As for beauty, I cannot bear the fact that a man, most noble of heart and with a noble mind, begins with the ideal of the Madonna and ends with the ideal of Sodom. Even more terrible is it when a man already has the ideal of Sodom in his heart and does not renounce the ideal of the Madonna, but rather his heart burns with this ideal, burns in all sincerity, as in the innocent years of youth. No, man is broad, too broad even; I would narrow him. The devil knows what he really is, in truth. What the mind sees as shame, the heart sees as sheer beauty. Is there beauty in Sodom? Believe me; it is, in fact, in Sodom that beauty resides for the great majority of people. Did you know this secret? What is awful, is that beauty is not only a terrifying but a mysterious thing. Here the devil struggles with God, and the battle ground is the hearts of men.

(Bk III, Ch. 3)

Dmitri ends this tirade with the admission that he is speaking of his own problems. The truth of this is obvious: his behaviour reflects both love for the 'ideal of the Madonna' and yearning for the 'ideal of Sodom'. The dilemma of Dmitri recalls that of Prince Myshkin, in that this double ideal of beauty appears to confront him in the shape of two women. However, we saw that in *The Idiot* Aglaya and Nastasya Filippovna could only be equated with these two ideals of beauty at a superficial level, and that the reality of their characterisation was much more complex. The same is true for Katerina Ivanovna and Grushenka: each of these two women (by the Dostoyevskian law of the endless division of idea-cells) contains within herself both a pole of good and a pole of evil. Thus the virtue of Katerina Ivanovna (Yekaterina = 'pure', 'innocent') turns out in fact to be her vice: 'She loves her virtue and not me' claims Dmitri with justification. Indeed such virtue is in itself suspect; for the patronymic Ivanovna seems to contain a hint that she is in reality 'Ivan's woman', and it is ultimately to Ivan that her affections will go.

As for the 'fallen woman' Grushenka (grushenka = juicy little pear) her vice is really her virtue. Old man Karamazov defends her in these terms: 'She has loved much, and the woman who loved much was forgiven by Christ.' This identification of Grushenka with Mary Magdalene is hinted at once more when Alesha tells Rakitin that: 'she is greater in love than we', and, in Grushenka, Alesha even thinks he has found a treasure to compensate him for the loss of Zosima. At the end of the novel her influence on Dmitri promises to be for the good. Dostoyevsky 'has set us nothing but riddles'.

Dmitri's relationship to the two women is expressed in terms of a very important symbol – money. Dmitri himself tells us what emotional and dramatic significance he ascribes to it: 'With me money is a theatre prop, fire of the soul, a stage set.'[11] It is with money, on the one hand, that he pays tribute to honour: he hands Katerina Ivanovna a 50,000 rouble bill to save her father from disgrace, attaching no conditions. On the other hand, with money entrusted to him by Katerina Ivanovna he buys himself shame: he spends it on debauchery with Grushenka.

These two incidents are taken up at the trial by the Public Prosecutor; his words offer us a new image for Dmitri's dilemma:

What then are we to believe? The first legend, the impulse of noble generosity of a man who surrendered all the money he had to live on, and bowed down before virtue? Or that other side of the medal which is so repulsive? Usually in life, when presented with two extremes, one must search for the truth in the middle. In the present case this is categorically not so. The most likely explanation is that in the first incident, he was genuinely noble; and in the second incident, just as genuinely base. And why? Precisely because we have broad natures, Karamazov natures – and this is what I am leading up to – natures capable of containing all manner of contradictions and of contemplating at one and the same time both abysses: the abyss above us, the abyss of high ideals; and the abyss beneath us, the abyss of the lowest and most vile-stinking degradation.

(Bk XII, Ch. 6)

But in Dostoyevsky such obvious polarisation never proves to be quite so simple on analysis. Thus, if we take the first incident, Dmitri's motives had not originally been as 'genuinely noble' as the prosecutor supposes: he had offered money to lure Katerina Ivanovna to his room for ends which were far from honourable (much as later his father will try the bait of 3,000 roubles to lure Grushenka). In the event, of course, Dmitri's cynical plan does turn out as 'an impulse of noble generosity', but it is nevertheless plain that here the ideal of the Madonna lies side by side with the ideal of Sodom.

Moreover the first incident is more directly linked with the second than the prosecutor suggests. After receiving the money in this way, Katerina Ivanovna is less concerned with Dmitri's magnanimity than with her own humiliation; she seeks revenge by humiliating Dmitri, as he had humiliated her, with money:

I knew that he needed money, and I knew for what: he wanted it just for the purpose of enticing that baggage and taking her off with him. I knew at that time that he had already deceived me and wanted to desert me, and I, I myself gave him that money then, offered it on the pretext that he should send it to my sister in Moscow, and as I handed it to him, I looked him straight in the face and said, that he could send it whenever he liked; 'even in a month's time'. Well, then, how could he fail to understand that I was saying straight to his face: 'you want money to be unfaithful to me with this baggage of yours. Well then, here is your money. I myself am giving you it. Take it, if you are so lacking in honour as to take it!'

(Bk xii, Ch. 5)

Thus it appears that Dmitri is almost provoked into the second incident; that plunge into the abyss which is beneath his feet. Yet, here, too, the ideal of Sodom cannot rid itself of the ideal of the Madonna. Dmitri does not spend the whole of Katerina Ivanovna's money on Grushenka; he sews half the sum into an amulet to wear around his neck. This he can always pay back to Katerina Ivanovna to prove that he is not a thief.

The Public Prosecutor not only challenges the credibility of this story, but argues that even if it were true, the character of Dmitri is such that he would soon have spent the bulk of what remained in dribs and drabs:

'For what', he might say, 'is the point of half the money, that is of 1,500 roubles? 1,400 roubles would be enough; the result would be the same – I am a rogue, but not a thief; for I have brought you something back, if only 1,400 roubles, and a thief would have taken everything and returned nothing.'

(Bk xii, Ch. 6)

But the point of keeping half the money is precisely that it is *half the money* – its value is symbolic. In paying tribute to the ideal of Sodom, Dmitri is still capable of reserving half of his offering for the ideal of the Madonna. Thus both these incidents, interpreted by the Public Prosecutor as illustrations of the poles of Dmitri's character, are in themselves subject to further polarisation; it is a phenomenon we have encountered before in Dostoyevsky's writing.

But this process does not stop even here; that very *half* which Dmitri wears round his neck takes on an ambivalence of its own. In Dmitri's replies to the examining magistrate on his reasons for retaining half the money, the motive of vindicating his honour before Katerina Ivanovna is given only second; the first reason Dmitri gives is one entirely incompatible with it: he wanted to have money laid by should Grushenka be prepared to marry him. Moreover this 'double reason' is again put forward by Fetyukovich in his defence.

There is, however, another point which must be taken into account here. Twice before the murder Dmitri had beaten his breast to the accompaniment of vague hints at the existence of the amulet and its contents; the reader could be forgiven for thinking that Dmitri is really talking about his heart. In a sense this is true: the amulet is a symbol for Dmitri's heart. But this heart, as we know, is divided, and this is why the money which the amulet contains is a pledge to both Katerina Ivanovna and Grushenka at one and the same time – Dmitri's heart is torn between two ideals.

This same 'broadness', although at its most extreme in Dmitri, nevertheless characterises other members of the family too. There is a certain ambiguity about Ivan. Zosima detects religious equivocation in his article, and his own brothers look on him as something of a mystery. Alesha tells him that Dmitri regards him as 'a grave', whereas he himself thinks of him as a riddle. The expression: 'a grave' refers to Ivan's reticence, but it might also hint at his nihilism. Yet the broadness of Ivan lies precisely in this: there is something at work within him running counter to his nihilism:

I was sitting here just now, and do you know what I was telling myself: were I to lose faith in life; were I to become disillusioned in a woman I hold dear; were I to become disillusioned in the order of things and become convinced on the contrary that everything was an unordered, damned, perhaps even satanic, chaos; were even all the horrors of human disillusionment to overwhelm me – I should still nevertheless wish to live; and, having so greedily taken to this cup, I shall not be torn away from it, until I have drained it completely. But doubtless I shall throw the cup away by the time I am thirty, and even though I may not have drunk it to the bottom, I shall go off, I know not where. (Bk v, Ch. 3)

Thus Ivan, intellectually convinced of the pointlessness of existence, is nevertheless intoxicated by life. The metaphor he uses is 'the cup of life' [*kubok zhizni*], and it is a phrase we have encountered before:

> [Joy] With the secret power of ferment
> Enflames the cup of life [*kubok zhizni*]

These are the words declaimed by Dmitri in 'The Hymn to Joy'.

Already in the novel Ivan's knowledge of Schiller has been greeted with surprise. Now, it appears, there is even more which links him with Schiller and with Dmitri's joy at being alive. Dmitri proclaims that joy 'has coaxed the blade of grass up towards the light', and for Ivan there is a similar emblem for life: 'for all that I have no faith in the order of things, I nevertheless love the sticky, little leaves of spring as they unfold.' The nihilism of Ivan, like that of Kirillov, has been defeated by the beauty of a leaf:

It is the sticky little leaves of spring, it is the blue sky that I love. There you have it. In this there is no question of intellect, no question of logic. In this case you love with your inside, with your belly. (*ibid.*)

Thus there is in Ivan an emotional side to his nature which his intellect is scarcely able to understand: his dilemma is that of 'loving life rather than the meaning of life', whilst his intellect demands meaning. This love of life stems from the earthy

Karamazov within him, and he too wishes to fall down on the earth in ecstasy, but, unlike his brothers, his veneration is that of a westerniser:

I want to make a trip to Europe, Alesha, I shall leave from here, but I know I shall be going merely to a graveyard, yet to the most precious of all graveyards – yes, indeed! Dear are the dead who lie there. Each stone over them proclaims such an ardent life, such a passionate faith in their achievements, in their truth, in their struggles and in their knowledge, that I know in advance that I shall fall down on the earth, and kiss, and kiss those stones, and cry over them, being at the same time deeply convinced that this has long been a graveyard and nothing more. (*ibid.*)

Alesha sees this emotional and aesthetic side of Ivan as the other half of his nature which will save him:

'Half your job is done, Ivan, half is gained: you love living. Now you must strive for your other half, and you are saved'.
   'Here you are, already saving me, and perhaps I haven't even perished. But what does it consist in, then, this other half of yours?'
   'It consists in resurrecting your dead, who perhaps have never even died.' (*ibid.*)

The contradictions of Ivan's character may still pose a riddle, but his self-revelation to Alesha proves that, in neither sense, is he fully 'a grave'.

Ivan reminds Alesha that the Karamazov trait is in him too, and, indeed, perhaps Alesha is not the pure angel he seems. Rakitin had already taunted him with his likeness to the rest of his family:

You yourself are a Karamazov. You are wholly Karamazov. Breeding and natural selection mean something after all. You are a sensualist like your father and a *holy fool* like your mother.

(Bk II, Ch. 7)

Here then are the two sides of Alesha's nature – the sensual and the holy. Dmitri, too, tells Alesha that he cannot escape from family characteristics, that the 'insect of lasciviousness' in 'The Hymn to Joy' is as relevant for Alesha as it is for himself:

We Karamazovs are all the same; even in you, angel that you are,
this insect lives and raises storms in your blood. They are storms,
because lust is a storm, worse than a storm!   (Bk III, Ch. 3)

When Dmitri begins to relate incidents which illustrate his
own sensuality, Alesha blushes; but not on account of Dmitri,
he blushes because he recognises himself in Dmitri's anecdotes.
Not that he has done what Dmitri has done, but he explains
that sensuality is like a ladder:

'I am on the lowest rung, and you are somewhere above on the
thirteenth. That's how I look at it, but it amounts to the same thing;
it is all of a piece. He who has stepped on the lowest rung will
nevertheless undoubtedly step on the top rung too'.
  'One should not, therefore, put a foot on the ladder at all?'
  'If one is capable of not doing so'.
  'Are you capable of this?'
  'It seems not.'   (Bk III, Ch. 4)

Temptation is placed before Alesha in the person of Liza
Khokhlakova, who behaves with him very much as Grushenka
and Katerina Ivanovna behave with other members of the
Karamazov family. When Alesha, clad in his monk's habit,
kisses Liza, we have what is perhaps the most striking illustration of Alesha's 'broadness', we see 'the insect' at work within
'the angel', and for all that Alesha claims to stand only on the
first rung of the ladder of sensuality, it is nevertheless a vice
which leads to other sins. Alesha does not wish to surrender
the love letter he has received from Liza, so he shamelessly lies
to her about its whereabouts, as he will later himself confess
to her.
  'Broadness', then, is a characteristic shared by all the legitimate brothers; the only one to suffer from 'narrowness' is the
bastard brother Smerdyakov. His nature is not open to beauty;
he does not know the thirst for life; he does not know the
torments of sensuality. But it is, above all, in the father that
these earthy Karamazov traits are writ bold and large.
  Superficially the father has much in common with his eldest
son, Dmitri. There is the same propensity for causing scandal;

there is the same overt sensuality (and this is thrown into even starker relief by a passion for the same woman). The outpourings of the elder Karamazov 'over the brandy' seem to invite comparison with the earlier confessions of 'an ardent heart' also inspired by a bottle of brandy. Yet Dmitri makes a pun about his drinking which seems to hint at the difference between himself and his father: 'I'm not Silenus, I'm strong [*ne Silen a silën*], because I've made a decision for all time.' (Bk III, Ch. 3.) There is, after all, a certain strength of character in Dmitri, which is totally lacking in the lewd old man who sired him.

According to Smerdyakov, however, it is Ivan who of all the brothers is the most like his father – they have the same soul. This judgement is reinforced at the trial by the public prosecutor who refers to this opinion of Smerdyakov. Yet this is a similarity which the old man himself does not acknowledge; he tells Alesha that he does not own Ivan: Ivan is not a Karamazov. Perhaps Smerdyakov regards the free-thinking nihilism which leads the elder Karamazov into such indefensible behaviour as the quality linking him spiritually with his son. Certainly when Dmitri questions Ivan on his theory that everything is permissible, Ivan remarks that for all that their father was a pig he nevertheless thought along the right lines.

It is less easy to see in the elder Karamazov any of the spiritual qualities of Alesha. Perhaps there are glimmerings in the more solicitous attitude he shows towards Smerdyakov, once he learns that he is an epileptic. But such promptings are usually perverse; thus on the death of his second wife, when shamed into some response by the actions of his servant Grigory, he himself gives money for prayers to be said, yet not for the wife who has just died, but for his first wife who used to beat him.

However disgusting the behaviour of Fyodor Pavlovich may be, we are told that he always stops short of actual crime, and it is perhaps with his own murderer that he has least of all in common. The fastidious, taciturn, sexless Smerdyakov bears a name, Pavel Fyodorovich, which reverses the order of his own. The elder Karamazov is guilty before all his children, and the extent of this guilt is clearly shown at the beginning of the novel. The theme of the responsibility of parents for the sufferings of their children is taken up again during Ivan's 'Rebellion' in the cases of child cruelty he has culled from the newspapers. The guilt of Fyodor Pavlovich as a father is emphasised once more towards the end of the novel during the trial of Dmitri. Here Fetyukovich is very concerned to link the concept, 'father' to a sense of responsibility: 'Merely to beget is not to be a father, a father is he who begets and deserves to do so.' (Bk XII, Ch. 13.)

Fyodor Pavlovich is much to blame for the behaviour of his sons, and he himself has largely created a situation which could end in parricide. Yet Dostoyevsky's treatment of the *Fathers and Children* theme here is consonant with his formula: 'all are to blame' – each one of the sons, too, must bear his share of responsibility for the death of the father.

As we know, it is Smerdyakov who commits the murder, but he persists in regarding himself as a mere instrument: the real murderer, he says, is Ivan. During the course of three interviews with Smerdyakov, Ivan gradually becomes aware of the degree of his own complicity, that he is guilty on three counts.

First and foremost, in the eyes of Smerdyakov, it is Ivan who provides the theoretical justification for the crime with his teaching that 'if God does not exist, then everything is permissible'. Ivan, the intellect, is Smerdyakov's inspiration.

Secondly, as Smerdyakov tells him during the second interview, Ivan had secretly wished for the death of his father. This is undoubtedly true. At the end of the chapter, 'The Sensualists' (where Dmitri bursts into the house and beats his father), Ivan, speculating on the possibility of a murder taking place, had remarked: 'I reserve full freedom for myself as regards my desires in the present case.' The night before his departure for Moscow, Ivan had eavesdropped on his father from the staircase, and after the murder the recollection of this act comes back to torment him time and time again; he regards it as evidence of his desire for the death of his father. At the trial he will give open expression to such desires when he exclaims: 'Who does not wish the death of his father?' and goes on to accuse everyone of entertaining such desires.

The third point of Ivan's guilt is his passivity in the face of a situation which he knows can only have a violent end, unless by his continued presence in the house he were to prevent this happening. But his guilt, in fact, amounts to conscious connivance; for it is not merely that Ivan seeks to flee from the situation by leaving for Moscow, he suddenly yields to the exhortations of his father and Smerdyakov, and quite unexpectedly agrees to stop off at Chermashnya. For Smerdyakov this is the signal he needs:

'Well...I am going to Chermashnya', Ivan Fyodorovich suddenly blurted out. Just as yesterday the words seemed to rush out themselves and were accompanied, moreover, by a kind of nervous laugh. For long afterwards he remembered this.

'Then it's true what people say, that it's interesting to have a chat with an intelligent man', Smerdyakov replied firmly, looking in a penetrating way at Ivan Fyodorovich.   (Bk v, Ch. 7)

Thus it seems that against Ivan's better judgement, the desire for the death of his father wells up within him and forces him to come to a tacit understanding with Smerdyakov. Although, in the event, he does not go there, Chermashnya is, nevertheless, the symbol of Ivan's complicity in the death of his father; and Smerdyakov, during the second interview, tells him as much: 'Everything came about through that very same Chermashnya.'

However, the full consciousness of his guilt is brought home to Ivan only during the third interview with Smerdyakov, and this interview itself is enclosed within the framework of another incident which we may regard as a second 'Chermashnya'. Ivan, on his way to Smerdyakov's house, encounters a little peasant who is very drunk. Ivan has a terrible feeling of hatred for him, and the reason for this is obvious: the peasant keeps singing two lines of a song about a certain Vanka (the diminutive form of Ivan), who has gone off to St Petersburg:

> Akh, Vanka has gone off to Petersburg,
> I shall not wait for him.   (Bk XI, Ch. 8)

The refrain could almost be a reproach to Ivan for his own flight before the murder, it reminds him of Chermashnya; but worse is to follow. The peasant violently lurches into Ivan and in anger he pushes him away. The peasant falls to the frozen ground and loses consciousness. Ivan walks over to him, looks at him and decides that he will freeze to death. He then walks on to the house of Smerdyakov.

Such callousness is in stark contrast to the compassion of St John the Merciful, with whose fleeting image Ivan had begun his 'Rebellion'. But more than this, there is here a parallel situation to the one in which Ivan found himself at the time of the murder – another 'Chermashnya'. Ivan cannot be held actively responsible if the peasant should die; the blame lies more in the situation in which the peasant finds himself at the time – very drunk, in a snow-storm. The push with which Ivan gets rid of the peasant can be interpreted as an act of self-defence; for he has done no more than the peasant has done to him. But yet this is not true; for the circumstances in which the peasant finds himself are such that a push is sufficient to bring about his death. The same is true of his father's situation before the murder. For all that his father neglected him as a child, Ivan cannot retaliate by neglecting him now. By deserting him with the promise that he would go to Chermashnya, Ivan has delivered the same sort of push to events as he has now given the peasant. In both cases he has gone away to escape the consequences of an outcome he can predict.

Now in Smerdyakov's overheated room, having left the peasant to die outside in the cold, Ivan is confronted with the truth about the murder, and once more the refrain which the peasant had sung flashes through his mind, like a reproach for his own complicity in the crime. He leaves, knowing that Smerdyakov committed the murder but that he himself is just as guilty. As a result of this knowledge he has now taken a firm resolve. But, stepping out through the snow-storm, he stumbles over the prostrate form of the peasant, whom earlier he had left to freeze to death. Now, however, his attitude is quite different; he spends an hour of his time and a certain amount of money in making sure that the peasant will recover. This new-found compassion is directly linked to his interview with Smerdyakov:

'If my decision for tomorrow had not been taken so firmly', he suddenly thought with pleasure, 'I would not have stayed for a whole hour to make sure that the peasant was all right. I would have passed him by, and would not have cared a damn about the fact that he would freeze to death.' (Bk XI, Ch. 8)

The decision of which he speaks, is that he will save his brother at the trial by accusing himself; for the rhetorical question of Cain with which he had earlier dismissed any solicitude for Dmitri has now received an unexpected answer. From now on he *is* to be his brother's keeper. This new-found compassion for his neighbour begins with the little peasant and will continue with his own brother. The two are linked in Ivan's rambling self-denunciation in court, in which he contrasts the motif which reminds him of his own guilt with Dmitri's 'Hymn to Joy':

Well, set the monster free … He has sung a hymn, that is because it is easy for him to do so, just like any drunken ruffian will yell out 'Vanka has gone off to Petersburg' but for two seconds of joy I would give a quadrillion quadrillions. (Bk XII, Ch. 5)

Yet, if Ivan bears the intellectual guilt for the death of his father, the emotional guilt nevertheless falls squarely on Dmitri; by his violent behaviour and openly expressed hostility towards his father Dmitri has created a situation which makes murder possible. The direct emotional response, which is the dominant trait of Dmitri's character, leads him into making open vows that he will kill his father – leads him even to assault his father physically. The 'emotional' evidence for Dmitri's guilt is so great that his trial and conviction for the murder seem almost inevitable.

Dmitri himself knows that he must answer for the blood of

'the old man', but the old man of whom he is thinking is not his own father: it is the servant Grigory, whom he has laid low by his father's fence. When Dmitri is told that Grigory is alive, it is as though the burden of guilt has been lifted from his shoulders:

Oh, how you have brought back life to me. How you have resurrected me from the dead in a single moment. That old man used to carry me in his arms, Gentlemen, used to wash me in a pail when I was three years old and deserted by everybody. He was a real father to me.   (Bk IX, Ch. 3)

Grigory[12] has indeed been a father to him, when his real father had shirked the responsibility of parenthood; and, if Grigory is to be taken as a father substitute, it is significant that, on the two occasions when Dmitri breaks into his father's house, Grigory also suffers from the intrusion along with the elder Karamazov. Moreover, Grigory seems to regard the assault on his own person as a greater crime than the assault on the real father:

'He dared to strike me', Grigory pronounced sullenly and with emphasis.
'He dared to strike his father, never mind you!' Ivan observed, his mouth writhing.
'I used to wash him in a pail ... he dared to strike me!' Grigory repeated.   (Bk III, Ch. 9)

Thus Dmitri has physically attacked two fathers, but his guilt is somehow transcendental – his crime is that of assaulting the very concept of fatherhood itself; for there is yet a third father who suffers at Dmitri's hands – Snegirev: the father of Ilyusha. Here it is not the violence committed against the worthless Snegirev which constitutes Dmitri's crime: it is rather that Dmitri's vengeance takes the form of publicly humiliating a father in the eyes of his own child. The effect on Ilyusha is overwhelming: the humiliation of his father is his own humiliation, and this is more than he can bear. We can see now where the true guilt of Dmitri lies: he breaks the bond of respect which the son should feel for his father; he is the profaner of a sacred taboo. This is Dmitri's real crime; it is in fact the only crime which he commits, and it is therefore fitting that he finally comes to understand the nature of his guilt through a dream about the suffering of a child.

We have already seen that Chermashnya is a symbol of Ivan's guilt in the murder of his father. But, in the event, Ivan does not go to Chermashnya: it is his brother Dmitri who goes there instead. Dmitri's journey to the village on the eve of the murder seems out of keeping with the ever-suspicious and ever-alert jealousy which appears to rule his actions at the time. The public prosecutor hints as much as Dmitri's trial. But however flimsy the reasons for Dmitri's absence from the town at that precise moment may be, there is nevertheless good justification for this visit at a symbolic level: through Chermashnya Ivan and Dmitri are linked in a common guilt.

This link is further strengthened by events at Chermashnya itself. Dmitri is sleeping in an overheated hut with the drunken Lyagavyy, when suddenly he awakens to the realisation that they are being poisoned by fumes from the stove. He acts at once, sparing no effort to save his drunken companion. Although it could be argued that Dmitri has a strong interest in preserving the life of Lyagavyy, his concern, nevertheless, stands out in stark contrast to the attitude of the peasant owner of the hut, who is completely indifferent to the fate of his drunken guest. This whole situation seems to invite comparison with the episode of Ivan and the drunken peasant, which occurs later in the novel.[13] Having just left a drunken man to his fate, Ivan will find himself in an overheated hut too, and here he will be confronted by the evidence of his own guilt. But the symbol of Chermashnya, which links the brothers in a common guilt, also points to the difference between them; on the one hand spontaneous compassion, on the other calculating indifference; for the guilt of Dmitri springs from the warmth of the emotions – the guilt of Ivan from the coldness of the intellect. When Dmitri, through his dream about a child, comes to recognise his own guilt too, this warmth is repaid in kind; for some solicitous hand has placed a cushion beneath his sleeping head.

For Ivan 'Chermashnya' is an apparent act of compliance with his father's wishes, but in reality it is the signal for his father's murder. By assenting to the trip, Ivan tacitly agrees to act as pander to his father's lust; not only will his absence leave the old man alone when Grushenka comes for the bait of 3,000 roubles, but the object of Ivan's journey is to provide this very 3,000 roubles itself. Ivan's task at Chermashnya is to confirm the price offered by Lyagavyy, a price which his father claims is 3,000 roubles higher than local merchants will pay:

Just think, eight and eleven – that's three thousand difference. It is as though I had found three thousand roubles. It's not all that easy to find a buyer and I need the money very badly.   (Bk v, Ch. 7)

For all that Ivan ultimately decides against the trip, his initial assent has nevertheless confirmed another bargain – the 3,000 roubles, for which Smerdyakov will murder his father.

For Dmitri, on the other hand, 'Chermashnya' is an apparent attempt to thwart his father, but in reality it is a desperate effort to avert the inevitability of tragedy. The fateful sum of 3,000 roubles has a different significance for Dmitri – it is the price of his honour in the complicated relationship with the two women who are close to his heart. Three thousand roubles is accordingly the price which he too places on Chermashnya. If he can get this sum from Lyagavyy for the village which he regards as his own, he will have no need to look elsewhere, and the lengths to which Dmitri might go to find this sum are clear from his letter to Katerina Ivanovna.

Three thousand roubles, as we have seen, is the price of the old man's murder, and it is the sudden appearance of money estimated at 3,000 roubles in the hands of his son which constitutes one of the most telling pieces of evidence against him. Yet the money which Dmitri takes on his second excursion to Mokroye is, as we know, not 3,000 roubles at all, it is only half this sum: the remaining half of that other 3,000 roubles which represents his debt of honour to Katerina Ivanovna.

Dmitri opens up his amulet at a very crucial moment in the novel. In spending the second half of Katerina Ivanovna's

3,000 roubles in the same manner as he had squandered the first (in entertaining Grushenka), Dmitri is symbolically acknowledging himself to be *fully* a scoundrel. Yet it is more than coincidental that this very act which epitomises his 'plunge into the abyss beneath him' should, at the same time, seem to proclaim to the world his guilt in another and more terrible act. For by the same symbolic process whereby the price of the old man's lust for Grushenka becomes the fee for his own murder, so that other 3,000 roubles, by which Dmitri expresses his own yearning for Grushenka, turns into the very sum which indicts him as the murderer: half guilt is taken for full guilt.

But what of Alesha? His father senses that Alesha is the only person who does not judge him, and even half guilt scarcely seems to taint the purity of Alesha's filial duty. Yet the message which the novel proclaims is: 'all are to blame', and in the death of his father Alesha must bear his share of responsibility too.

Early in the novel Rakitin extracts a significant admission from Alesha:

'I will wager that you yourself have thought of it. That's interesting. Listen, Alesha, you always speak the truth, although you always fall between two stools, have you thought of this or not? Answer me.'

'Yes, I have,' Alesha replied quietly. Even Rakitin was taken aback.

'What do you say? Have you really thought of it?' he cried.

'I haven't exactly thought of it,' mumbled Alesha, 'but when you started to talk about it in such a strange way just now, it seemed to me as though I myself had thought of it.'

'You see (and how clearly you have expressed it), you see? Today, looking at your dear father and your dear little brother Mitya, you thought of a crime. So, I am right, am I not?'

(Bk II, Ch. 7)

There is, perhaps, more here than the barely conscious awareness that a crime is possible, there is a hint almost at a suppressed wish. In the light of this, Aleksey's behaviour the day after Dmitri's violent irruption into his father's house seems pregnant with meaning; for this is to be the last occasion that Aleksey will see his father alive, although he has no consciously held reason to suppose that this will be so:

> Alesha came up to him to take his leave, and kissed him on the shoulder. 'What did you do that for?' the old man showed some surprise. 'We shall see one another again, you know, or do you think we won't?'
> 'Oh not at all. I don't really know why I did it. I didn't mean to.'
> 'Well I didn't mean anything either. I was only saying this ...' the old man looked at him. 'Do you hear, do you hear?' he shouted after him 'Come again sometime as soon as you can. Come and have some fish soup. I will cook you a fish soup, a special one, not the sort we had today. Come, without fail! Yes, tomorrow, do you hear, come tomorrow!' (Bk IV, Ch. 2)

Alesha makes no reply to this invitation, but the next time he eats fish soup it is at the invitation of Ivan during that revealing conversation at the inn, which does so much to undermine Alesha's religious faith.

It is indeed Alesha's attitude to religion which lies at the root of his guilt; for Alesha is no ordinary young man: he is the novice of an elder. The strength of this bond of obedience, which binds him to Zosima, is emphasised early in the novel by the story of the much venerated martyr, whose coffin was miraculously rejected by the tomb, because he had broken his vow of submission to his elder. Alesha firmly believes the story, and so Zosima's injunctions to his novice must be seen as having a peculiarly binding force.

After the incident of Zosima's obeisance before Dmitri, the elder instructs Alesha to leave the monastery for the world outside, where it is more important for him to be. These are his parting words: 'Go quickly. Be with your brothers, and not just with one of them but with both.' (Bk II, Ch. 7.) Later in this same chapter Rakitin tells Alesha that Zosima has sniffed out a great crime which is about to be committed in the Karamazov family.

Faithful to the elder's instructions, Alesha does try to be with his brothers, but what he sees disturbs him. Not only is he a

witness to Dmitri's violence against his father, but later that
same evening Dmitri again causes him further anguish, when
he waylays him with the joke: 'Your purse or your life!' and
goes on to hint obliquely at his own purse of shame, which he
wears round his neck. There and then Alesha resolves to look
out Dmitri on the following day at all costs.

When the following day comes, we find Alesha pondering
the respective attitudes of Dmitri and his father, and again he
resolves that he must at all costs find Dmitri ('He gets involved
with schoolboys'). But Dmitri proves to be elusive, and Alesha
has another matter on his mind: Zosima is dying and he feels
that he must return to the monastery. Yet to find Dmitri is a
prior duty, and he persists in his search, thinking of his obligation towards Dmitri in terms which recall the parable of the
good Samaritan ('Smerdyakov with a guitar').

Instead of Dmitri he finds only Smerdyakov and Ivan, both
of whom tell him bluntly that they do not consider themselves
to be Dmitri's keeper. Having failed in his search, it is now a
different Alesha who returns to the monastery; for Ivan has
deeply disturbed him with his 'Rebellion' and his 'Legend of
the Grand Inquisitor', and this, the first blow against Alesha's
faith, is also a blow against his duty towards Dmitri:

Later, several times in his life, he would wonder in great perplexity,
how it was that, after he had left Ivan, he could so suddenly forget
about his brother Dmitri, whom, that morning, only a few hours
ago, he had determined to seek out at all costs, and not leave without having done so, even though it might mean not returning to the
monastery that night.   (Bk v, Ch. 5)

But he does return to the monastery, and there he finds
Zosima on his death-bed. Once more the elder emphasises his
earlier injunction to Alesha, but now his meaning is even more
clear:

'Get up, dear boy,' the elder continued speaking to Alesha. 'Let
me look at you. Have you been with your family, and have you seen
your brother?' It seemed strange to Alesha that he should ask so
firmly and precisely about only one brother. But about which? It

must mean that it was for this very brother perhaps, that he had sent him away both yesterday and today.

'I have seen one of my brothers,' Alesha replied.

'I am talking about the one who was here yesterday: the eldest, to whom I made a low bow.'

'I saw him only yesterday, but I couldn't find him at all today,' said Alesha.

'Hurry, find him. Go again tomorrow and hurry. Leave everything and hurry to him. Perhaps you will be in time to avert something terrible. Yesterday, I bowed down before the great suffering which awaits him.' (Bk VI, Ch. 1)

Before he can do this, Alesha is to receive a second and even greater blow to his faith: Zosima dies and his body begins to decompose with unseemly haste. In his anguish Alesha forgets everything:

(He himself recalled later, that during that difficult day he had completely forgotten about his brother Dmitri, about whom he had felt such concern and anguish the day before ...) (Bk VII, Ch. 2)

His loss of faith is such that now he is even prepared to fall for the temptations of the world offered to him by Rakitin. But Rakitin, too, reminds him of a danger: Ivan is leaving his father's house. At the mention of this, there immediately comes into Alesha's mind the fleeting image of Dmitri, together with a vague sense of urgency and duty. Yet he does not act upon his premonition; instead he goes off to drink champagne with Grushenka.

But Alesha's faith returns; and, during the reading of the miracle at Cana in Galilee, Alesha muses on the elder's teaching on happiness: the name of Dmitri again comes into his mind. But, although Alesha seems to hesitate at Dmitri's name, he is too caught up in his mystical experience to remember where his duty lies, and by this time it is too late; for Dmitri, we are led to believe, is already speeding on his journey to Mokroye.

Thus each of the three brothers bears a different degree of guilt in the circumstances surrounding the death of his father; but crucial to the guilt of each is his capacity for showing towards his neighbour what Zosima describes as 'active love'. In Ivan this quality is absent; in Dmitri its promptings are confused and contradictory; and even in Alesha 'active love' is not capable of surmounting all the obstacles placed before it. But there is yet a fourth brother, an illegitimate one – Smerdyakov; and if blame is to be apportioned, he cannot be left out of the reckoning: it is he who commits the murder.

Yet for all this, the author to a remarkable degree contrives to persuade the reader that the crime was committed, not by Smerdyakov, but by Dmitri. It is not merely the incriminating evidence of the money, it is also the way in which the events surrounding the murder are related. Thus Dmitri in the garden watches his father, leaning out of the window, with loathing and hatred. He takes the pestle from his pocket, and...At this crucial point the narrative is interrupted by a row of dots. With apt ambiguity this chapter is entitled 'In the Dark'. Moreover, the same significant lacuna occurs in Dmitri's own narration of these events to the examining magistrates:

Having come at last to that moment when he had seen his father leaning out of the window, and boiling with hatred, he had grabbed the pestle from his pocket, he suddenly stopped, as though on purpose. (Bk ix, Ch. 5)

The difference between truth and appearance is of crucial importance in the events surrounding the murder. The word 'reality' is constantly on Dmitri's lips during this crisis in his life, and yet, in going to Chermashnya; in entering his father's garden; in opening up the amulet, his actions smack more of symbol. The same is true of Ivan's behaviour; for in saying that he will go to Chermashnya, he is making a symbolic statement which will be taken by Smerdyakov as a signal for action. The actions of the old man himself reveal an inordinate trust in signs as the emblems of truth. Thus in dispatching Ivan to Chermashnya he tells him that the only way to be sure whether Lyagavyy is genuine is by watching his beard; and, for his own part, the old man has invented a system of knocks, by which Smerdyakov is to warn him, either of the arrival of Grushenka, or of the presence of Dmitri. It is through these knocks that Smerdyakov gains access to the old man to commit the murder; for although he will not believe the evidence of Smerdyakov's words, he is, nevertheless, prepared to trust the message communicated by knocks. The murder, then, seems so hedged about by ambiguity and symbol that by the time the reader comes to the culmination of Fetyukovich's defence at Dmitri's trial: 'And there was no murder either',[14] he is almost prepared to accept this as a true statement.

In a sense, of course, it is a true statement: the death of the father stands as a giant metaphor, which implicates each one of the sons in some form of symbolic parricide. An examination of their behaviour will reveal this quite clearly.

The transcendental nature of Dmitri's rebellion against 'fatherhood' has already been noted; the text affords much evidence to show that Dmitri's hatred for his father is something primal, almost inexplicable, and that, as a motivating force, it is even stronger than his love for Grushenka. It is particularly revealing that the jealousy which Dmitri feels over Grushenka is a jealousy he feels *in respect of his father alone*. Thus Dmitri pays little attention to the possibility that Grushenka's former Polish lover could be a serious rival, even when she shows him the letter she has received:

but to her amazement, he attached almost no significance to this letter, and it would be very difficult to explain why. Perhaps it was because he himself was tormented by all the hideousness and horror of the battle he was having with his own father over this very same woman, and he could not imagine anything more terrible and dangerous for himself than this, at least at that particular time.

(Bk VIII, Ch. 1)

As if this were not explicit enough, the point is reinforced almost immediately afterwards:

He thought only, that whatever might happen, however the matter turned out, the imminent and final clash with his father was far too near, and must come to a conclusion before all else.   (*ibid.*)

After the 'murder', Dmitri, searching for Grushenka, is told

251

that she is in Mokroye with her officer. It is only then that he asks himself an intriguing question:

But how could he, how could he have ignored him? Why was it that at that time he had just forgotten about this officer, forgotten immediately after being told about him? Here was a question which confronted him like some monster, and he contemplated this monster in real terror, numb with terror. (Bk VIII, Ch. 5)

But for all that these questions themselves cause terror in the heart of Dmitri, the object of the questions, the Polish officer, appears to arouse no jealousy. The narrator naively comments on this, as Dmitri flies off to Mokroye to catch them both together:

I will not be believed, perhaps, if I say that this jealous man did not feel the slightest jealousy towards this new man, this 'officer', this rival, who had sprung up out of nowhere. Had it been anyone else, he would immediately have felt pangs of jealousy, and perhaps once more would have stained his terrible hands with blood. But for this man, this 'her first one', he felt now, flying in his troyka, neither jealous hatred, nor even feelings of hostility ... (Bk VIII, Ch. 6)

At Dmitri's trial, the Public Prosecutor, too, calls attention to the fact that Dmitri, who was 'jealous of everybody to the point of madness' should pay no attention to his Polish rival (Bk XII, Ch. 9). But yet the notion that Dmitri is insanely jealous of everybody, with the exception of this one overlooked rival, does not fit the facts: there is, for instance, Samsonov.

Samsonov is another of Grushenka's former lovers, yet Dmitri apparently feels so little jealousy towards him, that he can escort Grushenka to his house and feel that she is safe there (i.e. safe from his father). It is even more surprising that Dmitri is prepared to humble himself before Samsonov, and ask for the 3,000 roubles he so needs. Once more such extraordinary behaviour calls forth a naive explanation from the narrator:

Perhaps to many readers of our tale it will seem that it was far too crude and insensitive on the part of Dmitri Fyodorovich to count on help of this kind, and intend to take his bride, as it were, from the hands of her protector. I can only add that Grushenka's past was regarded by Mitya as over and done with once and for all.

(Bk VIII, Ch. 1)

Once more, too, the Public Prosecutor drives the point home:

And he himself accompanies her to the house of her protector Samsonov. (It is a strange thing, we are not jealous of Samsonov, and this is a psychological peculiarity entirely characteristic of this affair!) (Bk XII, Ch. 7)

What is therefore noteworthy about Dmitri's attitude to Grushenka is not his indiscriminate jealousy of rivals: it is his lack of it. At the beginning of the novel, during 'The Confession of an Ardent Heart Head over Heels', Dmitri tells Alesha something highly significant – he intends to marry Grushenka, but if lovers should come to visit her, he will go into another room out of the way. Is this a jealous man?

Both the Polish rival and Samsonov are older men. Both, in a sense, are father figures (this is particularly true of the aged paterfamilias Samsonov). This lack of jealousy towards these older men throws into sharp relief Dmitri's one and only jealousy; the jealousy he feels towards his own father. It seems that the only rival he can treat seriously is the one rival who could turn Grushenka into a second mother for him:

For him personally the whole problem which tormented him resolved itself into two propositions: 'either him, Fedor Pavlovich; or me, Mitya'. Here, by the way, one firm fact must be noted: he was completely convinced that his father would propose marriage to Grushenka (if he had not indeed already done so), and not for one moment did he believe that the old lecher was hoping to escape merely with the payment of his three thousand roubles.

(Bk VIII, Ch. 1)

Once more we come to that fateful sum of 3,000 roubles, so closely identified with the village of Chermashnya. It is even more significant that this is regarded as the son's inheritance from his mother:

The most important thing is this: an insane old man entices the object of his passion and lures her by the very three thousand roubles which his son regards as his birthright, his inheritance from his mother, the very money over which he bears a grudge against his father. Yes I agree that this was very hard to bear, that it could even give rise to an obsessive madness. The real point lies not in the money, as such; but in the fact that it was this very same money which was being used with such disgusting cynicism to destroy his happiness. (Bk xii, Ch. 7)

In keeping with this 'disgusting cynicism', of which the old man is here accused by the Public Prosecutor, is the information that he has concealed this money in his bed. It does not matter that Smerdyakov has misled Dmitri on this point; Dmitri believes it to be true, and the sexual symbolism surrounding the money is thereby reinforced.

The rivalry of Dmitri and his father over Grushenka, it seems, is less straightforward than might at first appear. In a sense, Grushenka is merely a pawn in the struggle between father and son; and the origin of the love which she inspires in both is worthy of note. Dmitri's love for Grushenka is born out of violence, and this violence is, in essence, directed against his father; for Dmitri suspects Grushenka of acting against him as his father's agent. Yet the father's love dates from the very same time; and so a passion, conceived in violence, continues in violence, and apparently ends in violence. The Public Prosecutor's analysis of the situation is most revealing:

Here Ippolit Kirillovich developed at length the whole story of the accused's fatal passion for Grushenka. He began from the very moment when the accused set out for the house of that 'young person', in order 'to beat her up' – his very own words, as Ippolit Kirillovich explained. But instead of beating her up, he fell under her spell. Here is the beginning of this love. At the same time the old man, the accused's father, cast a glance in the direction of this very same person. An amazing and fatal coincidence, for both hearts were suddenly set aflame at the same time, even though both of them had known this person previously, had met her before; and both hearts were set aflame with the most unbridled, the most Karamazovian of passions. (Bk xii, Ch. 7)

Here, indeed, we have a very interesting state of affairs. It seems as though both father and son have *simultaneously* seized on Grushenka as a juicy bone of contention: she is an emblem of their mutual hatred rather than its cause. Dmitri himself, in his replies to the examining magistrate, reveals that jealousy over Grushenka is not a prime cause for the 'parricide':

'What was it that prompted your feelings of hatred at that time? It seems that you announced publicly that it was a feeling of jealousy?'
'Well, yes, jealousy, but not just jealousy.'
'Quarrels over money?'
'Well, yes, that too.' (Bk IX, Ch. 3)

Dmitri seems just as unsure of his real motive as was Raskolnikov of his. But perhaps the most revealing passage of all occurs during the 'parricide' scene itself:

'He is alone, alone!' he repeated again. 'If she were here, his face would be different.' It was a strange thing: there suddenly boiled up in his heart a kind of senseless, weird anger at the fact that she was not present. 'Not at the fact that she's not here,' Mitya explained in reply to himself at once, 'but at the fact that there is no way I can know for sure, whether she is here or not.' (Bk VIII, Ch. 4)

Here the initial emotional response of Dmitri tells us all: the immediate rationalisation of this response is designed to conceal.

If Dmitri *were* to murder his father, the one thing which would drive him to the act is an overwhelming sense of physical revulsion. Now, in the garden, he recalls the words he had uttered to Alesha at the end of his 'Confession of an Ardent Heart Head over Heels':

I am afraid that he will suddenly inspire me with hatred *by his face at that very moment*. I hate his Adam's apple, his nose, his shameless sneer. I feel personal revulsion. This is what I fear; I shall not restrain myself then. (Bk III, Ch. 5)

Here is something dark and primitive. Fetyukovich, in seeking to prove that 'There was no murder, either' claims that Dmitri experienced a mental 'blackout' induced by the sight of his father: '…a temporary state of insanity brought about by nature avenging her eternal laws, unconsciously and without restraint, like everything in nature'. (Bk xii, Ch. 13.) Fetyukovich is more right than he knows: Dmitri did not commit the murder, but yet his behaviour was prompted by eternal laws of nature of which he himself was not consciously aware.

The roots of Dmitri's antagonism towards his father lie deeper than the wrangling over money; deeper even than the wrangling over Grushenka: these are but symptoms and symbols. Dmitri is 'the savage'; Dmitri is 'emotional man', and the crime with which he is tainted is 'parricide' in this context: the context of primitive emotion. It is Ivan who provides the key to this at Dmitri's trial, when he suddenly blurts out: 'Who does not wish for the death of his father?'

The theme of sexual jealousy as a motive for parricide in *The Brothers Karamazov* aroused the interest of Freud.[15] The appropriateness of this interest is clear. On analysis, the sexual jealousy of Dmitri towards his father proves to go beyond their rivalry over Grushenka: it is connected, however indirectly, with Dmitri's mother. Just as enlightening as the causes prompting him to murder is the reason Dmitri gives for his restraint: 'I suppose my mother must have been praying for me.' (Bk xii, Ch. 12.) This sexual jealousy finds its most concentrated expression, not in Dmitri's attitude to Grushenka, but in the sheer physical revulsion he feels for his father, and it is this which leads him to the symbolic act of parricide. The guilt of Dmitri is unmistakeably an Oedipal guilt.

In contrast to the emotional crime of Dmitri, the 'parricide' of Ivan is a crime of the intellect: the father whom he attacks is God. The first clear statement of Ivan's atheism occurs in the scene 'Over the Brandy', but a fuller exposition of his views is contained in the chapter called 'Rebellion'. Here Ivan purposely restricts his evidence against God to the narrow field of crimes which involve children. It is significant that this testimony consists entirely of acts perpetrated by parents or those in authority, and although this hardly constitutes *direct* evidence against God himself, it is nevertheless presented as such by Ivan.

The transference of blame from earthly 'fathers' to a heavenly one is striking. Yet the charge that God is ultimately responsible for the crimes of sadistic 'fathers' is based not on God's own actions, but rather on his lack of action: his apparent indifference to the lot of his earthly children. Indeed, Ivan's 'God' shows the same perverse negligence in fulfilling his parental responsibilities that Ivan's own father has always shown in his treatment of him and his brothers: if the 'God' of Ivan is cast in the image of his own father, then, inevitably, his destruction of God implies the destruction of his father. He asserts that: 'If God does not exist, then everything is permitted': Smerdyakov puts this doctrine to the test and kills the old man.

But if Ivan's father becomes a sort of sacrificial substitute for God, he also stands as a political emblem. The features which inspire such loathing in Dmitri, he himself looks on with pride as the features of a Roman patrician during the period of Rome's decadence. That the old man is a representative of *the fathers* in a political sense is later reinforced at the trial, when the public prosecutor not only claims that the Karamazov family reflects certain traits of contemporary society as a raindrop mirrors the sun, but also identifies the old man as a typical contemporary father: an idea which is greeted with a certain amount of dismay by the 'fathers' sitting in the public gallery.

The chapter 'Over the Brandy' begins with Ivan and his father discussing political revolution. Such people as Smerdyakov will be useful when the 'rocket goes up', Ivan claims: they will be 'front-rank cannon fodder'.[16] But when the old man takes an anti-clerical stand and talks about a dissolution of the monasteries, Ivan has to remind him that he himself is the established order:

'Why get rid of them?'
  'In order that truth should shine forth all the sooner. That's why.'
  'But if that truth were to shine forth, you would be one of the first to be plundered, and then got rid of.'   (Bk III, Ch. 8)

The 'truth' about which Ivan here speaks links political revolution with atheism (shortly after this, his father asks him whether he believes in God, and Ivan replies unequivocally: 'No'). But whether the rebellion be religious or political, the drift of Ivan's arguments is nevertheless clear: it is towards 'parricide', and the chapter ends with another threat of parricide: Dmitri breaks in and physically assaults his father. The 'parricide' of Ivan and the 'parricide' of Dmitri are thus placed side by side.

But the ambiguity of Ivan's position reasserts itself; there is another father-figure obsessing his mind. In the absence of God, Ivan has had to find his substitute in a figure who will embody that authoritarian paternalism, both religious and political, which man so much craves. This nightmare of Ivan's rebellious intellect is The Grand Inquisitor. The Grand Inquisitor is *man* – the proud usurper of God's authority, and as a Machiavellian father-figure of the intellect, he stands in direct contrast to Zosima, the humble servant of God and spiritual father of Alesha.

We have already seen that Alesha's failure to carry out Zosima's command implicates him in the guilt surrounding the death of his father, and the nature of the metaphorical 'parricide' committed by Alesha is underlined by the fact that the murder of his father is made to coincide with the death of Zosima. The 'parricide' of Alesha is, therefore, not unlike that of his full brother Ivan: it is rebellion against God. Alesha's inability to carry out Zosima's command is, as we have seen, connected with a crisis of faith, brought on by the arguments of his elder brother. But Ivan's words fall on prepared ground; for Alesha, as he tells Liza Khokhlakova, is only too aware of the Karamazov within him:

'I know only that I myself am a Karamazov ... Am I a monk? A monk? am I a monk Lise? You said, just now, I think, that I was a monk?'
    'Yes I did say that.'
    'But perhaps I do not even believe in God.'   (Bk v, Ch. 1)

Later in the novel Liza herself tells Alesha of a dream she keeps on having:

'Sometimes I dream of devils. It is as though it is night. I am in my room with a candle, and suddenly there are devils everywhere; in all the corners; and under the table; and opening doors; and there is a whole crowd of them on the other side of the door, wanting to come in and seize me. They approach me; they seize me. But suddenly I cross myself, and they shrink back, afraid. But they do not go away altogether; they stand by the doors and the corners, and wait. Suddenly, I have a terrible desire to begin cursing God out loud. I begin to curse him, and they suddenly crowd towards me again; but I at once cross myself again, and they retreat. It is terrifyingly amusing; your heart goes to your mouth.' 'I too have had this same recurrent dream', Alesha said. (Bk XI, Ch. 3)

This experience, although it is presented as Liza's dream and so is at one remove from Alesha, is nevertheless acknowledged by him as his own. It is a clear indication of the struggle between faith and scepticism which, throughout the novel, is being waged within his soul: the dreamer curses God, and the devils approach to seize him; he crosses himself, and the devils recede. Alesha, at a barely acknowledged level, is a prey to the same religious ambivalence that besets Ivan; but whereas the rebellion of the intellect is clearly formulated and explicit, the 'dark night of the soul' is obscure and circuitously expressed. Nevertheless both intellect and soul are, to different degrees, capable of religious 'parricide'.

Parricide, of course, is not only a metaphor it is also an established fact: the murder *is* committed by one of Fyodor Pavlovich's own sons. At first sight Smerdyakov's motives seem straightforward and prosaic: he kills for money. Earlier, however, when he had returned the three 100-rouble notes which he had found, Smerdyakov had shown a surprising lack of interest in the old man's money. But this was before the advent of Ivan; now he is not only prepared to steal from the old man, but to murder him as well. In this Smerdyakov claims that he is merely the agent of Ivan's ideas, that it is Ivan who is the real murderer: whereas he is but Ivan's 'Servant Licharda'.[17] But Smerdyakov's relationship with Dmitri is also justified by the same phrase. Dmitri, he claims, has appointed him his 'Servant Licharda' in the war he is waging with his father.

That Smerdyakov, in committing the murder, is acting as Ivan's agent is explicit in the novel; perhaps less obvious, though just as true, is the fact that he is acting as a substitute for Dmitri; for when at the very last moment Dmitri balks at the murder of his father, it is Smerdyakov who acts in his place. Moreover it is odd that Dmitri should climb over his father's fence exactly where he does:

Here he selected a place, and, it seems the very place where, according to a tradition of which he himself was aware, Stinking Liza had clambered over on a previous occasion. 'If she were able to get over, then why shouldn't I get over', flashed through his brain for no apparent reason. (Bk VIII, Ch. 4)

After the murder, Grigory's wife, awakened by the feigned epileptic wailing of Smerdyakov, goes into the garden in search of her husband. Here she hears moans; they are those of Grigory on whom Dmitri has vented his violence instead of his father, yet these groans suggest to her, not the sufferings of a father, but those of a mother: '"Lord, exactly like Stinking Lisa that other time" flashed through her fuddled head.' (Bk IX, Ch. 2.) It is significant that, amidst all the metaphor surrounding the murder, Dmitri's actions should be linked with the death of Stinking Liza; for these references to the circumstances of Smerdyakov's birth hint not only at the true murderer but also provide him with a motive: revenge on the father for violation of the mother – the motive, indeed, of Dmitri himself. Thus in 'getting over the barrier' round his father's garden, Dmitri is linked in a significant way with the agent who will carry out his Oedipal promptings. The brother turned servant is, indeed, the 'Servant Licharda' for his two legitimate brothers: he is the agent of the emotions as well as that of the intellect.

Nevertheless the portrayal of Smerdyakov has its own significant overtones. Smerdyakov is adopted by Grigory, and the night of his birth coincides with the burial of Grigory's own child – an infant born with six fingers, branded by Grigory himself as 'a dragon' which should not be baptised. The adopted child, too, grows up in the role of 'monster'; one of the young Smerdyakov's favourite occupations is hanging cats; and later in life he teaches young boys to feed starving dogs with bread in which pins have been concealed.

But the cats which Smerdyakov hanged were also buried with a parody of religious pomp, and this note of religious deviation is a dominant motif in his characterisation. His mother was a 'holy fool', and his adopted father, Grigory, after the death of his six-fingered child, plunges into greater asceticism. He spends his time reading The Lives of The Saints, The Book of Job, and the writings of St Isaak the Syrian,[18] and he even becomes very interested in the sect of the Flagellants, although in the end he does not join their faith.

As a youth, Smerdyakov shows a tendency to dispute with Grigory on religious matters, but after he returns from Moscow a significant change seems to have taken place:

He had suddenly and quite unexpectedly grown older, had become wrinkled out of all proportion to his age. He had grown yellowish, and had begun to look like a Castrate. (Bk III, Ch. 6)

He is also compared to The Contemplator, a portrait of a peasant by the Russian artist Kramskoy. This, we are told, is the face of a man who could either leave everything and make a pil-grimage to Jerusalem, or just as easily burn down his native village – who could, perhaps, even commit both acts at the same time. This is obviously the portrait of a religious fanatic, and the title The Contemplator [Sozertsatel'] confirms this; for the term 'Contemplative Sects' [Sozertsatel'nyye sekty] was used to designate those extreme religious fanatics – the Flagel-lants and the Castrates. Smerdyakov does not burn down his native village, but he does murder his natural father, and when he makes oblique references to this as a possibility, the identi-fication with the sect of the Castrates is again revealed in Ivan's reaction: 'He looked with anger and revulsion at Smerdyakov's haggard, Castrate-like features.' (Bk V, Ch. 6.)

Smerdyakov is very fastidious about food and clothing, and although we are told that he despises women, he nevertheless has a girl friend – a neighbour's daughter who greatly admires him. Yet when Alesha surprises them together ('Smerdyakov with a Guitar') the most noticeable feature of their relationship is the condescending attitude of Smerdyakov, plus the falsetto voice in which he serenades her.

At the end of the novel Smerdyakov, it appears, is about to marry this girl, but this should cause no surprise in view of the girl's name; for Marya Kondratevna is a name with special connotations. Marya not only suggests the Madonna figure important to both Flagellants and Castrates, but the patronymic Kondratevna (daughter of Kondratiy) seems to imply that Kondratiy Selivanov,[19] the founder of the sect of the Castrates, is her spiritual father. The figure of Marya Kondratevna therefore hints at a 'Castrate madonna', and when after the murder Smerdyakov goes to live with her, he occupies a separate part of the house which she refers to as 'the white hut'.[20] This name, which in the text is given quotation marks, is another significant indication of Smerdyakov's true nature, for white had particular importance for the Castrates, who referred to themselves as 'The White Doves', dressed in white, and called the process of castration itself 'whitening' [*ubeleniye*].[21]

It is to 'the white hut' that Ivan comes for the last two of those interviews with Smerdyakov at which he is to learn of his own guilt in the murder. By the third visit Smerdyakov has grown thinner and more yellow-looking. Instead of the French vocabulary which he was reading on the occasion of Ivan's second visit, he now has a large book which turns out to be the writings of St Isaak the Syrian (a book which had earlier been associated with Grigory's promptings towards greater asceticism after the death of 'the dragon'). To prove that he has committed the murder, Smerdyakov produces the money, but first he has to roll up his trouser-leg to reveal the long white stocking in which the money is concealed. The effect on Ivan is astonishing, and the violence of his reaction seems out of all proportion to its cause; for what appears to terrify him is not the money itself, but the white stocking. This is, indeed, the explanation he gives to Smerdyakov: '"You frightened me... with that stocking..." he said, strangely smirking.' (Bk XI, Ch. 8.)

To help Ivan over his shock, Smerdyakov offers him lemonade. Before the second interview Smerdyakov had apparently been drinking tea, but now the offer of lemonade is perhaps significant – the sects regard tea as an abomination.

Smerdyakov tells Ivan that he had taken the money from behind the icons (a holy place; not his father's mattress as he had told Dmitri). Now its hiding place, the white stocking,[22] is associated with religious fanaticism. Moreover, once the money is out in the open, Smerdyakov thinks of covering it a second time with the volume of the writings of St Isaac the Syrian.

The money is Smerdyakov's motive for the murder, and it seems that this symbol of 3,000 roubles takes on now a new significance, which suggests that the murder itself has strong overtones of an act of religious fanaticism. Throughout this interview Smerdyakov appears to be insinuating a similarity between himself and Ivan, and this is, perhaps, what disturbs Ivan most of all; for he now realises that he, the rebel against God, is just as much an heretical extremist as Smerdyakov – he himself is a monster, a self-crippler, a 'castrate'.

But during this interview Smerdyakov makes one other significant admission: he would not have carried out the deed if it had not been for Dmitri. Here again we return to the idea that Smerdyakov is just as much the agent of Dmitri as he is of Ivan.[23]

There is one final point to be made about Smerdyakov. Dostoyevsky has not only given him his own affliction of epilepsy, but has made the very possibility of murder depend on Smerdyakov's epileptic state. It is no accident that in Dostoyevsky's novel on the *Fathers and Children* theme it should be the epileptic who is the murderer. In the figure of Smerdyakov we have a self-abasing expression of the artist's own guilt both as a son and as a father.

JUSTICE AND PUNISHMENT: 'THE BROTHERS KARAMAZOV'

A striking feature of *The Brothers Karamazov*, and one which marks it off from Dostoyevsky's other novels, is the extent to which the characters are obsessed by hell; each, it seems, has his own ideas on the subject. The hell of old Karamazov has a ceiling and devils with hooks. Grushenka's hell is a burning lake from which an old woman might be saved by an onion. In the name of 'harmony', Ivan renounces hell altogether, yet hints that his 'Legend of the Grand Inquisitor' owes something to the medieval poem 'The Holy Virgin's Journey through Hell': he seems unduly interested in the concept of hell it describes. Dmitri, riding to Mokroye, is told by his cabman that hell is only for the rich and the important, but finds a hell of interrogation there which is consciously likened to Ivan's medieval poem (cf. Bk IX, Chs. 3, 4 and 5: 'The Journey of the Soul through Hell'). Nor, indeed, can Ivan escape hell himself. Before his brother's trial he is tormented by the devil, who mocks him with a made-to-measure hell, ordered on liberal lines, with reforms extending to the introduction of the metric system and an enlightened view of punishments. This by no means exhausts the references to hell in the novel, but most important of all is Zosima's conception of hell; the last section of his teachings: 'About Hell and Hell fire, A Mystical Discourse' constitutes the longest treatise on this subject in the novel. The prominence of hell in *The Brothers Karamazov* is not fortuitous: it is a symptom of that theological debate which is carried on throughout the whole novel; a debate which has as its principal concern the question of punishment.

The first fruits of this theological debate are to be seen in the argument which develops, early on in Zosima's cell, around the question of ecclesiastical courts. The subject may seem appropriate, in as much as the Karamazovs have met to compose their differences before a small gathering of monks headed by the elder, but the discussion arises not so much from the occasion, as from an article written a short time before by Ivan. This article is the seed from which the great preoccupation with punishment springs; it has the same germinal significance for *The Brothers Karamazov* as Raskolnikov's article has for *Crime and Punishment*. In that novel the centre of interest had been focussed on the crime and the motives for the crime; a preoccupation which had emanated from the very subject-matter of Raskolnikov's article. In *The Brothers Karamazov*, on the other hand, Ivan's article on ecclesiastical courts raises another but related issue: the nature of justice and the punishment of the criminal; it points the direction which the novel itself must take, and it sets a new emphasis: not *Crime* but *Punishment*.

Before going on to discuss the ideas of this article, it would be as well to look at the way in which they are presented. Ivan, as we have seen, is a divided man, and it is not clear whether he is for or against the propositions he is advancing in his article; this leads Father Iosif, the librarian of the monastery, to call it: 'an idea with two ends'. There are no direct quotations from the article, but its contents are related, first by Iosif, and then by Ivan himself. Ivan as the expounder of his own article is concerned to establish what was actually written, rather than to join in disputation. This produces the curious effect of Ivan presenting the points of his own argument as if he were an uncommitted third person, a mere narrator; while the disputation itself is carried on by two other voices representing, as it were, his own divided self. These are, on the one hand Miusov, the cultured free-thinking 'Westerner', and on the other Father Paisiy, the scholarly monk. The clash of contrary opinions is presented through them, and this frees Ivan from any obligation to be other than the cool expounder of the ideas of his article; it also releases Zosima from the burden of minor disputation, so that, when he does enter the discussion, his words have particular emphasis and importance.

Ivan's article appears to make two points: the first of which serves as a premise for the second. His first concern is to synthesise the two apparently diverse principles of Church and State; and this, he argues, could be achieved in two ways. Thus it is possible for the Church itself to become a State which is the Roman solution to the problem; for whereas the Roman Church appeared to conquer the Old Roman Empire, in reality it was the old Roman Empire which took over the Church. This idea we have already met before in the mouth of Myshkin,[1] and in *The Brothers Karamazov* it has the approval of Zosima himself; for when he enters the argument he supports the words of Ivan: 'In Rome a State has been proclaimed instead of a Church for a thousand years at least.' (Bk II, Ch. 5.) It is an idea which, in the future course of the novel, will take on flesh.

The other solution to this problem of synthesis is that the State itself become the Church: that the civil element become completely absorbed into the body of the Church. This is what Zosima himself believes in, and he proclaims it will happen: 'It will be! It will be!' – an expression of fervent faith which serves as the title for the chapter in which this whole discussion takes place.

Ivan's arguments on Church and State, however, are an introduction for his main theme: the diverse elements of Church and State in the sphere of justice (i.e. ecclesiastical courts versus civil courts). Justice as conceived by the State, Ivan argues, is a purely mechanical process; the cutting off of an infected limb. The justice prescribed by the Church, on the other hand, is entirely different; it is not physical, but spiritual:

'If everything became the Church, then the guilty and disobedient would be excommunicated by the Church, and no heads would be cut off', Ivan continued. 'Where, I ask you, would the excommunicated man go? For in this situation, he would not only have to go away from men as he does now, but from Christ too; for, by his crime, he would have rebelled not merely against men but against Christ's Church as well.' (Bk II, Ch. 5)

If there were only ecclesiastical courts, argues Ivan, even the nature of crime itself would change.

When Zosima enters the discussion it is to corroborate much of what Ivan has said:

'It is like this', began the elder, 'sending people to penal servitude in Siberia (and formerly this was accompanied by beating) does not correct them, and most important of all it does not really frighten any criminal. Not only does the number of crimes not decrease – it grows yearly. You must agree about that. It is obvious, therefore, that society is not in the least protected by this; for although a harmful limb is mechanically cut off, and put far away – out of sight, out of mind – nevertheless another criminal immediately springs up in his place; perhaps two – more, even. If there is anything which, even today, protects society and corrects the criminal himself, turning him into a different person, it is but one thing – the law of Christ revealing itself in the awareness of the individual conscience. Only by recognising one's guilt as a son of Christ's society, that is the Church, does one recognise one's guilt in respect of society itself: that is in respect of the Church. Therefore the criminal of today is capable of recognising his guilt only in respect of the Church, not in respect of the State.' (*ibid.*)

But in his teaching on the Church's attitude to punishment, Zosima is not in full agreement with Ivan. He stresses, not excommunication, but the suffering of the individual conscience. This, he claims, is real punishment: 'The only real punishment, the only one which deters and which reconciles, and it consists in the awareness of one's own conscience.' (*ibid.*)

For all that there appears, on the surface, to be a large measure of agreement between the ideas here expressed by Ivan and those of Zosima himself, the elder is not taken in by them; and in the next chapter ('Why does such a Man Live?') he tells Ivan plainly that he has not yet decided the question of faith. In acknowledgement of the truth of this observation Ivan comes up to the elder for his blessing.

Ivan is, indeed, a divided man, and in the next stage of his theological debate he reveals the other side of his thought. This is the occasion of his 'confession' to Alesha at the inn – the proclamation of his 'rebellion'. At first he talks generally about Turkish atrocities in Bulgaria; the plight of the Swiss 'savage',

Richard (i.e. the theme of the condemned man); and the Nekrasov poem about a peasant beating a horse. But, in order to strengthen the case for his 'rebellion', Ivan says that he will restrict his argument to documented acts of cruelty committed against children. There is the banker Kroneberg who sadistically birched his seven-year-old daughter; there are the parents who locked up their five-year-old daughter at night in a privy, and made her eat excrement. Both these incidents were taken from contemporary newspaper accounts; the third took place at the beginning of the nineteenth century, and concerns a child hunted by dogs.[2]

What is significant in Ivan's evidence is that all the incidents he quotes – from the Turkish reprisals in Bulgaria to the boy hunted for wounding a dog – all without exception illustrate the grotesque cruelty of human punishments: all are examples of human justice at its most vile. Nor can these incidents be dismissed as rough justice operated without reference to the law; for the case of Richard illustrates the workings of a sophisticated legal system of the civilised West, whereas the Kroneberg affair provides an additional commentary on the Russian judiciary: the Kronebergs are brought to trial, and their actions are vindicated by a Russian court.

Ivan, however, does not stop here: on this evidence of human notions of punishments he goes on to pass judgement on divine justice itself; he cannot see how any form of ultimate harmony can compensate for the sufferings which human beings inflict on each other:

Oh, Alesha, I am not blaspheming. I do understand what a cataclysm of the universe there must be when everything in heaven and under the earth will fuse into one voice of praise, and everything that lives and has lived will cry out: 'Thou art just, Oh Lord, for Thy ways have been revealed!' When the mother embraces the torturer, who had her son torn to pieces by dogs; and all three, in tears, cry out loud: 'Thou art just, Oh Lord' – then, of course, the crown of knowledge will have been gained, and everything will be explained. But here is the rub; this is just what I cannot accept, and whilst I am on earth I hasten to take my own measures. You see, Alesha, when I live to see this moment, or am resurrected to see it, perhaps it really will happen that I myself will cry out with all the rest: 'Thou art just, Oh Lord!' But I do not want to cry out, and whilst there is still time, I hasten to guard myself against it. I therefore renounce higher harmony completely. It is not worth one little tear of one suffering child; a child such as the one who beat her breast with her little fist, and, with her tears unredeemed, prayed in her stinking privy to 'Good, kind God.'   (Bk v, Ch. 4)

The argument in Zosima's cell on civil justice versus ecclesiastical justice has now developed into a debate on human justice versus divine; and, when Alesha tries to solve Ivan's dilemma by bringing in the figure of Christ, Ivan counters with his own 'anti-christ' – The Grand Inquisitor. Here again the references go back to the debate in Zosima's cell. Father Paisiy had commented on the notion of Church turned into State: 'This is Rome and its dream. It is the Devil's third temptation of Christ', and now the Grand Inquisitor proudly acknowledges this in his own words to Christ:

It is exactly eight centuries ago that we took from him, that which you had angrily refused: that last gift which he offered you, showing you all the kingdoms of the earth. We took from him Rome and the sword of Caesar, and proclaimed ourselves merely kings of the earth.[3]   (Bk v, Ch. 5)

Yet the figure chosen by Ivan to represent the 'Church turned State' is, significantly, not the pope – it is the Grand Inquisitor: the dispenser of terrible punishments and crude mechanical justice.

We can now see how closely Ivan's 'confession' is related to the earlier discussion of his article. Ivan's arguments in Zosima's cell had had as their premise the desirability of the State becoming the Church; they had culminated in an examination of the true nature of punishment. Now, however, it is as though Ivan is picking up Zosima's theory of ideal punishment, and countering it by concrete examples of punishments as they exist. The reality of human 'justice' is so barbaric, he appears to argue, that it negates any possibility of an ideal higher justice; there is no divine harmony which is capable of reconciling man's injustice to man, and so, in the absence of eternal harmony, man is thrown back on a purely temporal solution: the ecclesiastical justice of the Grand Inquisitor – the enforced 'harmony' of the Church turned State.

Thus Ivan's argument is the very reverse of the argument in the cell; the movement is not from ideal theocracy to ideal justice, but from concrete justice of an appalling nature to an equally appalling concrete theocracy – that very solution to the problem of synthesis which had been so vigorously rejected in the argument in the cell. The convictions which Ivan appeared to share with Zosima have been stood on their head, and the assertion that Ivan's article was 'an idea with two ends' is now seen to be true.

But Ivan's equivocation goes deeper than this; for if his 'rebellion' inheres in his refutation of divine justice, the attack, as we have seen, is hardly direct. Ivan is no Voltaire moralising on the senseless tragedy of the Lisbon Earthquake[4] – indeed it is remarkable that the evidence on which he indicts divine justice does not contain even a single 'act of God' – nor yet is he a second Ippolit railing against the dark force behind the world. Ivan says he wishes to restrict his evidence to the sufferings of children, but even so he does not, like Ippolit, rebel against the existence of disease which can torment children just as cruelly as birches, can kill them just as mercilessly as a pack of hounds. This omission seems particularly remarkable in view of the fact that Dostoyevsky had the death of his own child Aleksey so much on his mind when he was writing the novel. Indeed it is striking that the author not only does not turn the dying Ilyusha into a second Ippolit, but actually presents a refutation in the figure of Markel, the dying boy who is Zosima's brother and inspiration.

Ivan's evidence is obsessively centred on man, and his rebellion is that of a humanist: 'I do not want harmony. I do not want it out of love for humanity.' Nevertheless, he himself admits that he does not fully reject God: 'It is not God that I don't accept: it is the world he has created.' This is true;

for his evidence indicts not God, but man. Ivan as a humanist is a very disillusioned one: the Devil seems to have more reality for him than does God. Thus after his description of the Turkish atrocities he says: 'I think that if the Devil does not exist, and has therefore been created by man, then man has created him in his own image and likeness.' (Bk v, Ch. 4.) Ivan acknowledges that a beast lurks in every man. Even in his saintly brother Alesha there is a devil thirsting to mete out punishment, and capital punishment at that (a practice that the Russian State had in theory abandoned). Ivan gets Alesha to agree that the general who hunted down the little boy should be shot:

'Shoot him,' Alesha uttered quietly, raising his eyes towards his brother with a pale contorted smile.

'Bravo!' yelled Ivan in something like rapture. 'Well, if you say so, then ... and you a monk! So that's the little devil that sits in your heart, Alesha Karamazov!' (*ibid.*)

By centring his rejection of universal harmony so firmly on man, Ivan, far from limiting the scope of his argument, is in fact widening it; for all this evidence of the devil in man is just as relevant for harmony of another kind: socialist utopia – the *Crystal Palace*. The argument in the cell had ended with Miusov implying that the Christianity of the monks was really socialism, and Ivan, in his 'confession' to Alesha seems to acknowledge a degree of interchangeability between the two ideologies, when he mentions the topics discussed in taverns by Russian youths:

[They talk] About universal problems, how could it be otherwise? Does God exist? Is there immortality? And those who do not believe in God will talk about socialism and anarchism, about remaking the whole of humanity in accordance with some new order. So it turns out to be the same old devil in disguise, the same old problems, only the other way round. (Bk v, Ch. 3)

As 'harmony' might therefore be seen in purely human terms, Ivan's criticism is all the more valid for being restricted to man in disharmony with man; and, as if to show the wider implications of his point, he invites Alesha to assume the role of architect of universal harmony:

'Imagine that it is you yourself who are erecting the edifice of human destiny, with the aim of finally making people happy, of giving them, in the end, peace and rest. But in order to do this (there would be no other way) you would have, of necessity, to torture just one insignificant little being, let us say that little child who beat her breast with her tiny fist; let us say you had to found this edifice on her unavenged tears. Would you agree to be the architect on these conditions? Tell me, speak the truth!'

'No, I would not agree,' said Alesha quietly.   (Bk v, Ch. 4)

Alesha's reply expresses a moral principle which runs through the whole of Dostoyevsky's mature work. In *Crime and Punishment*, Raskolnikov had discovered that he could not found human happiness on the destruction of another human being; and at the end of his life, in the famous *Pushkin Speech*, Dostoyevsky himself will make much the same point, when he maintains that the reason for Tatyana's final rejection of Yevgeniy Onegin (in Pushkin's novel of the same name) is that she realises the impossibility of founding happiness on the unhappiness of another. Ivan, therefore, is applying the same humanistic yardstick, by which Raskolnikov was measured, to the architect of universal harmony himself – both Raskolnikov and God are found wanting.

Such a conclusion is obviously absurd; it can only mean that the laws of man are not the laws of God. The rationalistic mind of Ivan grasps at a mathematical analogy. In 1833 the Russian mathematician Lobachevsky had challenged Euclidian geometry, and had proved that parallel lines can meet in infinity. The difference between human justice and divine justice is therefore seen by Ivan as the difference between a lower Euclidian truth and a higher Lobachevskian truth. Yet even so he cannot be reconciled:

Let me explain myself. I am convinced, like a child, that suffering will be healed, will be as though it never was, that human contradictions in all their offensively comic aspects will disappear, like a pitiable mirage, like some disgusting invention of a puny human mind, a Euclidian mind as insignificant as an atom. I am convinced that finally, at the end of the world, at the moment of eternal harmony, something so precious will occur, and be made manifest, that it will satisfy all hearts, will suffice to assuage all indignation, will be enough to redeem all human crimes and all human blood shed by human beings themselves. It will suffice not only for forgiveness to be possible, but for everything that has happened to man to be justified, I grant this... I grant that all this will be so, and that it will be made manifest, but this is the very thing I can not accept, do not wish to accept. Even though parallel lines meet, and I myself see them, and I myself say they have met, nevertheless I shall not accept it. This is my fundamental point, Alesha, this is my thesis.

(Bk v, Ch. 3)

Ivan is no underground man for whom twice two can equal five, nor is he a Shatov/Stavrogin refusing to desert the image of Christ for the reality of mere truth. Ivan's position is the very reverse of this: he cannot renounce common, everyday logic for the sake of some higher revelation; and yet this logic is obviously not sufficient:

Oh, my mind, this pitiable, earthly, Euclidian mind of mine tells me only that there is suffering, and that no one is to blame; that everything, in a quite simple and straightforward manner, is the result of something else; that everything flows and finds its level. But this after all is mere Euclidian nonsense. I do know all this, but what I cannot do is to agree to live by it. What difference does it make to me that no one is to blame, and that I know this? I need retribution otherwise I shall kill myself, and retribution, not in eternity, at some time or other and some place, but here on earth, so that I myself can see it.

(Bk v, Ch. 4)

The ideas of Ivan's 'Rebellion' are not allowed to stand unchallenged; a positive refutation is advanced through the figure of Zosima. The gulf between human truth and divine truth, which so perplexes Ivan, is bridged for Zosima by revelation: by the message preached in The Book of Job:

But what is great is that here is a mystery – that the transient face of the earth and eternal truth have here come into contact together; the process of eternal justice fulfils itself before earthly justice. Here the Creator, as in the first days of creation, bringing every day to its culmination with words of praise: 'that which I have created is good',

273

looks at Job, and is again proud of his creation. And Job praising God serves not only Him, but will serve the whole of His creation from generation unto generation and for all eternity. For he was pre-ordained for this. (Bk VI, Ch. 2(b))

God's world, which Ivan specifically rejects, is accepted whole-heartedly by Zosima, who in his short autobiography describes how he once spent a night on the bank of one of the great Russian rivers in the company of a simple peasant lad:

we fell to talking about the beauty of God's world and about its great mystery. Every blade of grass, every little beetle, every ant, every golden bee, everything so amazingly knows its own course, even though it has no mind: it witnesses God's mystery and is itself continually fulfilling it. And I saw the heart of the dear youth was filled with enthusiasm; he confessed to me that he loved the forest and the forest birds. He was a bird-catcher; he understood all their calls and could bring to him any bird he wanted. 'I know of nothing better than to be in a forest', he said, 'everything is good'. 'That is true', I replied. 'Everything is good and wonderful, because everything is the truth'. And I said to him, 'Look at a horse, a great animal which is close to man, or at an ox which feeds man, and works for him, an animal that is bowed down and pensive. Look at their faces: what gentleness! what attachment to man who frequently beats them mercilessly! What lack of malice there is in their faces! What trust and what beauty! It is touching, even, to realise that they are without sin; for everything is perfect; everything, apart from man, is sinless, and Christ was with them even before he was with us'. 'But surely', asks the boy, 'how can it be that Christ is with them?' 'How can it be otherwise', I tell him, 'for the word is for all, for all creation and all creatures. Every little leaf strives towards the word, sings praises to God, weeps to Christ unknown to itself, fulfils this by the mystery of its sinless existence.' (*ibid.*)

Zosima has here made explicit many of the ideas tentatively broached by Myshkin in *The Idiot*; it is obvious that it is the *beauty* of God's world which convinces the elder of its *justice*; for him, as for Myshkin, aesthetic criteria have become identi-fied with ethical criteria; and for both, happiness is an essential element in this quietist philosophy. Thus Zosima says: 'people are created for happiness, and he who is completely happy certainly deserves to say to himself: "I have fulfilled God's commandment on this earth".' (Bk II, Ch. 4.)

In *The Devils* Kirillov, too, is capable of achieving this state of happiness, and of concluding, like the peasant lad here, that ' everything is good'. Kirillov is obsessed by a leaf, and in *The Brothers Karamazov* there is another nihilist who is susceptible to the beauty of God's world as epitomised in the miracle of the leaf; for, in spite of his dark thoughts, Ivan Karamazov, as we have seen, tells Alesha that he loves 'the sticky little leaves of spring'; it is this half of his brother, the aesthetic half, which Alesha claims will ultimately save him.

Yet in his present state of doubt and torment, Ivan's aesthetic susceptibilities only inhibit his progress towards salvation. He is alienated from his namesake, St John the Merciful, because of his revulsion at all those hideously ugly aspects of human suffering which the saint so readily embraced. If only human suffering could be presented more aesthetically, Ivan might be prepared to make some effort towards compassion:

One can love one's neighbour in the abstract, and sometimes even from a distance, but almost never from close at hand. If everything were as it is on the stage, in a ballet, where beggars, when they appear, enter in silk rags and torn lace, and beg for alms in a graceful dance, one could then admire them; admire them, but all the same, not love them.   (Bk V, Ch. 4)

But Ivan's objections have already been anticipated earlier in the novel. Zosima has already told Mrs Khokhlakova ('A Lady of Little Faith') that there is a love for humanity which is more concerned with theatrical effect; this he calls 'imagined love' [*lyubov' mechtatel'naya*]. Moreover the theatricality of Khokhlakova's professed love seems to owe much to the example of St John the Merciful; for she claims that she is even prepared to kiss the putrefying wounds of her fellow human beings. But such love on the part of Khokhlakova is only in the imagination, whereas the love of St John the Merciful found concrete expression in action, and it is 'active love', which Zosima preaches, not only as his positive answer to the doubts of Khokhlakova, but ultimately to those of Ivan as well.

Yet if Ivan begins his 'Rebellion' with the legend of St John the Merciful, he ends it with another legend – 'The Legend of the Grand Inquisitor'. Here we have another 'saintly' figure who also claims to love humanity, but like Ivan himself he can only do so from a distance, and through devices worthy of the theatre; for the reality behind this professed love for humanity is nothing other than contempt.

The living refutation of what the Grand Inquisitor represents can be seen in Zosima himself. Both are old men on the verge of death; both are monks and ascetics; but whereas the Grand Inquisitor embodies the legend of the Church turned State, Zosima is the prophet of the State turned Church ('It Will Be, It Will Be'). The Grand Inquisitor rules by 'mystery, miracle and authority', but for Zosima mystery is not an instrument of rule, it is nature; it is life itself. Miracles too, he teaches, only stem from faith: they cannot inspire it. Moreover authority for Zosima is spiritual authority – the voluntary submission of a novice to his elder – it is not the physically imposed will of a despotic 'benefactor'; for the mainspring of Zosima's authority is not pride but humility. On the central question of punishment the attitude of the State/Church is diametrically opposed to that of the Church/State. The Grand Inquisitor solves the problem of crime by eliminating the criminal with incarceration, torture and fire – this is the external and purely mechanical form of justice deplored by Zosima in the discussion in the cell. To the *autos da fe* of the Grand Inquisitor are opposed the open confessions of Zosima; for he points to the individual conscience as the only true instrument of punishment.

The Grand Inquisitor is but a figment of Ivan's mind, a mind which is essentially mathematical and 'Euclidian', and the logic of his 'Rebellion' is that a minus cancels out a plus; that the negative evidence of human suffering is stronger than the most positive sign of human happiness. Zosima's non-Euclidian logic is the very reverse of this: for him a plus is always stronger than a minus; so in justifying the ways of God to man he emphasises the beauty and goodness of the created world.

But if Zosima expounds the positive side of life, the existence of the negative side, dwelt on in Ivan's rebellion, still demands explanation. This is supplied by another figment of Ivan's imagination – the devil himself. He, according to his own words, is 'the indispensable minus sign'. Indeed, everything about this devil is negative. In the first place he does not really exist; he is merely the hallucination of a fevered brain. His arguments, too, are inconclusive and are ultimately as insubstantial as he is himself. Negative, too, is his method of argument, which is mocking and destructive; he taunts Ivan not merely with his very own arguments, but jeers at his competence even to reason at all. Still more insulting is the fact that this devil is a distorted image of Ivan himself – the ironic proof of his own contention that man has invented the devil in his own likeness. Because of this, the devil's mockery of Ivan is far-reaching and fundamental: it is an attack on the whole of his personality, but the chief target is nevertheless Ivan's rationalistic mind.

He accuses Ivan of being concerned only with the mind, and in words which parody Ivan's own mathematical reasoning he hints at the limitations of human rationality:

You see, I too, like you yourself, am a prey to the fantastic, and therefore I love this earthly realism of yours. Here, with you, everything is delineated, here there are formulae, here there is geometry. But with us everything is vague indeterminate equations.

(Bk XI, Ch. 9)

The jibe here is at Ivan's perplexity over the 'two truths', and the devil drives home his attack by mocking Ivan's love of parable; for just as Ivan had told Alesha the 'Legend of the Grand Inquisitor', the devil now recounts another legend to Ivan.

This concerns a learned atheist who refuted the possibility of an after-life. When he died he found himself confronted by just such an after-life, and grew very annoyed; for, he said:

'This contradicts my beliefs'. Accordingly he was condemned to walk in the darkness a whole quadrillion kilometres before the gates of paradise could be opened for him. But he lay down and refused to walk, for again the principles of a rational, free-thinking liberal had been insulted: 'I do not wish to go. I will not go on principle.' He lay there until in the end he decided it would be better to walk his quadrillion kilometres. Then the gates of heaven were opened and he was allowed in; and he had not been inside more than two seconds, before he exclaimed that these two seconds were not only worth a quadrillion kilometres, but a quadrillion of quadrillion kilometres, even, indeed, a quadrillion kilometres to the power of a quadrillion.

Ivan recognises this as his own 'legend' – it is a story which he had made up as a schoolboy in Moscow. But it is his own 'legend' in a more direct sense; for the intellectual, who here tries so stubbornly to reject the after-life, has much in common with that other intellectual who, on principle, returns the ticket to eternal harmony. Indeed, the story is a moral tale directed at Ivan; it is a devil's parable on the dangers of intellectual arrogance and on the inability of the intellect to reconcile the 'two truths'.

But the devil himself is caught in that very same gulf which separates the 'two truths'; he, too, is in the position of the man condemned to walk a quadrillion kilometres:

I know in the end I shall be reconciled. I shall come to the end of my quadrillion, and I shall learn the secret. But until this happens I sulk and grudgingly carry out my appointed job of ruining thousands so that one shall be saved. How many souls, for instance have had to be ruined, how many honourable reputations discredited, in order to gain the righteous Job alone, over whom I was so cruelly duped in times of yore! No, until the secret is revealed, there exist for me two truths: one of that world, their truth, one that for the time being is completely unknown to me; and another truth, my truth, and I do not know yet which is the better. (Bk xi, Ch. 9)

The enigma of 'the two truths' is thus exemplified in the devil himself, who through the workings of his own mysterious destiny is that 'indispensable minus', the ultimate product of which is a plus. The figure the devil points to as a positive achievement is Job, and here he is in agreement with Zosima; for he too sees in the story of Job a reconciliation of 'the two truths' – 'the process of eternal justice fulfilling itself before earthly justice'. Yet as the devil here confesses, the devil himself is ultimately as perplexed as is Ivan. There is, indeed, nothing he can tell Ivan, and Ivan reacts to his words in annoyance:

Everything that in my own nature is stupid, everything that I have passed through long ago, thrashed out in my mind, then thrown away like carrion, this you offer to me, to me of all people, as if it were something new.   (*ibid.*)

The devil cannot resolve Ivan's doubts; he can only exacerbate them; for the devil is only Ivan himself, or rather one part of him – he is Ivan's intellect mirroring itself in destructive self-mockery.

At the same time, however, the devil is also a manifestation of a non-rational function of Ivan's mind – conscience; for this hallucination is symptomatic of a growing inner awareness of his own complicity in the death of his father. That this instrument of conscience should be a mirror mocking his intellect is only just, since the guilt of Ivan is the guilt of the intellect. It is fitting too that its outward form should be seen to resemble that of the devil; for, as we have seen in the last chapter, the crime of Ivan is in essence theological parricide.

The culmination of Ivan's hallucination clearly reveals the true nature of his crime. The devil contends that, to gain its ends, nihilism need destroy only one thing: the idea of God in the minds of men. He then goes on to taunt Ivan with the concept of 'man/god', and with his own theory that everything is permitted. Ivan, in a rage, throws a glass at his tormentor, but he cannot be disposed of so easily; he only disappears on the arrival of Alesha. Now, from Ivan's rambling words, Alesha ultimately comes to realise the true nature of Ivan's hallucinations:

He began to understand Ivan's illness: 'the torments of a proud decision, a profound conscience'. God, in whom he did not believe, and God's truth were conquering a heart which did not want to submit. (Bk XI, Ch. 10)

Ivan's decision is that he will publicly confess his guilt at the trial. This is the final stage in the acknowledgement of his guilt, and even there the devil reappears to haunt him. The mental suffering experienced by Ivan is his punishment; he is being punished in the only possible way that a man may be punished, according to Zosima; he is tormented by the consciousness of his own guilt.

From the very first, from their meeting in Zosima's cell, the elder had sensed the troubled mind of Ivan, and when Zosima had offered him his blessing, Ivan acknowledged the justice of the elder's penetrating insight, by going up to him himself and kissing his hand. But if this little scene had caused a stir of surprise among the onlookers in the cell, an even greater sensation is created shortly afterwards, when Zosima bows down low before the eldest brother Dmitri. The key to these two enigmatic acts is to be found in the chapter immediately preceding them – the discussion on the nature of punishment. Ivan, as we have just seen, is to undergo spiritual punishment. Zosima, therefore, offers him his blessing. But the punishment which lies in store for Dmitri is to be both spiritual and temporal; he is to suffer not only from the consciousness of his own guilt, but is also to be cut off like an infected limb by the mechanical justice of the State, even though legally he should not be held responsible for the crime.

Zosima makes his obeisance to Dmitri because he senses that Dmitri will undergo both forms of punishment of which he himself had been speaking shortly before. The following day, on the eve of his death, he offers an explanation of his action: 'I bowed down yesterday to the great suffering that awaits him in the future.' This in itself, of course, is not absolutely explicit, but it must be taken in conjunction with the highly significant terminology in which Zosima had chosen to couch his disquisition on punishment. The word here used for 'punishment' is not *nakazaniye* (the word which figures in the title: *Crime and Punishment*) it is *kara*[5] [punishment, retribution] and when this word next occurs in the novel, it is during the trial of Dmitri:

The majority of the men positively wished for the punishment [*kara*] of the offender, except perhaps the lawyers, who were concerned, not with the moral side of the case, but only with, as it were, its contemporary legal significance. (Bk XII, Ch. 1)

The thirst of the men for the *kara* of Dmitri is, of course, only one aspect of the polemical way in which Dostoyevsky presents the trial: the lawyers are not concerned with the moral aspects of the case; the eloquence of the public prosecutor is motivated by considerations of personal prestige; and even the defence counsel is given the comic name Fetyukovich (*fetyuk* = a ninny). In fact the presentation of Dmitri's trial is such that it might be taken as an illustration of Zosima's pronouncements on human justice:

Remember particularly that you can be the judge of no man. For there can be no judge of a criminal on earth, until that very judge himself recognises that he himself is just such a criminal as the man standing before him, and that, perhaps, he himself is most of all to blame for the crime of the man standing before him. When he has realised this then he can become a judge. However absurd this may seem, it is nevertheless the truth. (Bk VI, Ch. 3(h))

The human conception of justice is such a travesty of the word, that all that Dmitri can expect from the outcome of his trial is *kara*, even though the summing up of Fetyukovich contains a plea for justice of another kind, a kind that could even be accepted by Zosima himself:

Is it for me, unworthy as I am, to remind you that Russian justice is not punishment [*kara*] only, but the saving of a fallen man? Let other nations have the letter of the law and punishment [*kara*] but let us have the spirit of the law, its sense: the saving and regeneration of those who have fallen. (Bk XII, Ch. 13)

The word '*kara*', therefore, seems to be particularly associated with Dmitri. He is 'Karamazov' – 'punishment-daubed' (the second element of his surname, '*maz*' suggests *mazat'* – 'to daub',[6] 'to smear'). It is, of course, a name which he shares in common with his brothers and his father; they too, in their different ways, undergo punishment, but it is in Dmitri that the full implications of *kara* are worked out.

Dmitri is condemned by the State to a purely 'external' form of punishment for a crime he has not committed, but he also suffers his own 'inner' spiritual punishment for a guilt of which he has suddenly become acutely aware. It is because of this inner torment that he can accept the outward manifestations of punishment as, in some sense, just:

I accept the torment of my accusation and my public shame. I want to suffer and by sufferng I shall cleanse myself. Perhaps I shall succeed in cleansing myself, gentlemen, what do you think? But hear me, however, for the last time. I am not guilty of the blood of my father. I accept punishment not because I have killed him, but because I wished to kill him, and even, perhaps, was capable of killing him. (Bk IX, Ch. 9)

The realisation of the true nature of his guilt comes to him through a poignant dream. He is driving through slush on a cold November day, and he passes a burned-out village with its peasants, hungry and suffering, lined up beside the road. The whole of their plight seems summed up in the crying of a cold and hungry child in the arms of its mother. Dmitri keeps asking stupid and obvious questions about the plight of the 'bairn' [*ditye*], as his peasant driver calls it; questions which seem to emphasise Dmitri's lack of comprehension of the problems of human suffering, as well as his own impotence before them:

He inwardly felt that although he was stupidly asking questions that had no sense, these were questions which he absolutely must ask: they were the questions which had to be asked. He felt, moreover, a kind of tenderness welling up in his heart, the like of which he had never experienced before. He felt that he wanted to cry, that he wanted to do something for everybody, to do something so that the bairn would not cry any more, so that the black, dried-up mother of the bairn would not cry any more, so that there would be no more tears at all for anybody from that moment on. And he wanted this to happen at once; he wanted to do this immediately without delay and in spite of everything, with all his Karamazov impulsiveness.

(Bk IX, Ch. 8)

Thus for Dmitri, as for Ivan, the terrible enigma of the existence of evil is epitomised in the suffering of a child. Moreover Dmitri's dream, like Ivan's hallucination, reveals him to himself; it is a turning-point in his life. From now on Dmitri is a different man. On awakening, he immediately feels gratitude for the unknown person who has thoughtfully provided him with a pillow while he slept, and in spite of the dream's poignancy, he nevertheless thinks of it as a good dream. Indeed it reveals to him a truth, a truth preached by Zosima, and therefore a central message of the novel: 'everyone is to blame'.

Gentlemen, we are all cruel; we are all monsters; we all force others to weep, mothers and the children at their breasts. But of all, let it be decided now, of all I am the worst abomination. So be it. Every day of my life I have promised, beating my breast, to mend my ways, and every day I have gone on doing the same vile things. I understand now that what is necessary for such people as me is a blow, a blow of fate.

(Bk IX, Ch. 9)

The dream confronts Dmitri with the far-reaching implications of his own actions; for his crime is a crime against the father yet the haunting image of his guilt is here portrayed as the suffering mother and her child, and this is why he feels himself to be 'the worst abomination of all'. This greater complexity of guilt has already been illustrated in the novel; Dmitri in assaulting the father, Snegirev, is responsible for the tears of the son, Ilyusha. But Oedipal crime is a boomerang which returns to strike the hand which aimed it. The tragedy of Oedipus inheres not in the murder of a father but in the inevitable sufferings of the son and his mother as a result of this murder, and so the suffering child in Dmitri's dream is also a symbol for himself; his perplexed questions on the plight of the child are a dream-projection of his own perplexity over 'the blow of fate' which has suddenly struck him down. Here, indeed, is a Dmitri far removed from the declaimer of the

'Hymn to Joy', and this contrast is emphasised in the dream by his questions on why the peasants are not singing joyful songs. Nevertheless the dream ends on a hopeful note for he hears the voice of Grushenka telling him that she is with him and will not desert him.

The dream, therefore, is an expression of Dmitri's parricidal guilt, and it is significant that it reproduces elements of his 'plunge into the abyss beneath his feet' – that mad ride to Mokroye. On that occasion the evidence of Dmitri's parricidal guilt had appeared overwhelming, and it seems only natural that he should have asked his coachman Andrey whether he thought he would go to hell. The reply was reassuring: hell, according to Andrey, is only for important people, whereas: 'We all think of you, sir, as a little child. That is how we consider you.' But a kind of hell does await Dmitri in Mokroye. This is made clear both by the chapter-heading, 'The Journey of a Soul through Hell' (a reference to the medieval poem which so fascinates Ivan) and is implicit in the very name of the place itself. *Mokroye*[7] means 'wet' and it is thus connected with the idea of 'the lake' as a symbol for hell (the lake figures prominently in the medieval poem and in Grushenka's story of the old woman and the onion; moreover Dmitri himself lives not far from Lake Street).

It is after the three infernal 'ordeals' of the preliminary investigation that Dmitri has his revealing dream, and in it are reproduced the fast ride, the questions to the coachman, and above all the figure of the child – the child whose plight Dmitri cannot understand; for in spite of the assurances of Andrey, the child has suffered an ordeal of fire. It is this image of the child which haunts Dmitri and will influence the whole of his future life:

Why did I dream of the 'bairn' then at such a critical moment? 'Why is the bairn poor?' It was a prophecy for me at such a moment! I shall go to Siberia for the 'bairn'; because everybody is to blame for everybody else, for all 'bairns'; because there are little children and big children. All people are 'bairns'. I shall go for them all, because it is necessary for someone to go for all. (Bk XI, Ch. 4)

The plight of the child demands sacrifice; Dmitri is going to accept suffering for all. In this he is a Christ-figure, and it is therefore not surprising that it is Christ's prophecy of his own death and resurrection (St John xii. 24) which serves as an epigraph for the whole novel, and is applied more particularly to the fate of Dmitri. Thus Zosima quotes this passage of Scripture to Alesha in explaining the reason for his obeisance to Dmitri. The quotation occurs again in Zosima's testament, where it is a turning point in the account of his relations with 'the mysterious visitor'; a story which is a parable about the terrible power of conscience, and as such sheds light on the inner torments of both Dmitri and Ivan.

But the quotation is particularly striking for its imagery: 'Verily, verily, I say unto you, Except a corn of wheat fall into the ground and die, it abideth alone: but if it die, it bringeth forth much fruit.' These are the terms in which Christ expresses the prophecy of his own resurrection; but they could well be those of a pre-Christian dying-god-cult of an agricultural people – the cult of Ceres and Demeter, with whom, as we have seen, Dmitri himself is closely identified.

In Christ's prophecy an ancient pre-Christian assertion of renewal is fused with a new Christian message of resurrection, and it is significant that this particular passage of Scripture should be a favourite quotation of Zosima; for the Christian teachings of this saintly man are firmly wedded to a cult of the earth:

If all should desert you, and drive you out by force, then, when you remain alone, fall on the earth and kiss it; water it with your tears, and the earth will yield fruit from your tears, even though no one has seen you or heard you in your loneliness. (Bk VI, Ch. 3(h))

This expression, through agricultural symbolism, of the miracle of hope springing out of despair can be compared in general terms with the verse from St John, but its pagan emphasis is more obvious. It is, moreover, reminiscent of certain ideas of Marya Lebyadkin in *The Devils*; heretical ideas which she, too, learned in a convent.

Zosima's mystical teaching on 'other worlds' is also presented in terms of this earth and its cultivation:

God took seeds from other worlds and sowed them on this earth and cultivated his garden, and everything came up which could come up. But that which grew only lives and is kept alive by the sense of its contact with other mysterious worlds. If this feeling grows weak or is destroyed within you, then that which has grown up within you dies. Then you will become indifferent to life, will even hate it.

(Bk vi, Ch. 3(g))

When the time comes for him to leave the earth for the mystery of the 'other worlds', he is faithful to his own teachings:

He suddenly felt a kind of violent pain in his chest. He turned white and firmly pressed his hands to his heart. At this, everyone got up from his place and rushed towards him; but although he was suffering he nevertheless looked at them smiling, and gently sank from the armchair to the floor, and knelt down. Then he bent down with his face lowered towards the earth, spread out his arms, and, as though in joyous ecstasy, kissing the earth and praying (as he himself had taught), quietly and joyfully he gave up his ghost to God.

(Bk vi, Ch. 3)

In view of Zosima's cult of the earth, the obeisance to Dmitri during which he actually touches the earth with his forehead, seems to take on added significance: he is bowing down to one whose name links him with Demeter and who, like Zosima himself, will be regenerated by a cult of the earth; for there is perhaps yet another reason for Zosima's obeisance – in the wild young officer, he recognises a former self.[8]

It is old Karamazov who first intimates to the reader that Zosima might not be all he seems; that there is something of the Lermontovian guards officer about him, and that moreover he is prey to the Karamazov vice of sensuality. The old man's words are, in fact, little more than drunken nonsense; he himself finally admits that he has confused Zosima with someone else. But in Dostoyevsky, idle gossip is seldom entirely gratuitous; a doubt has been sown in the mind of the reader, and the early life of Zosima, as he himself relates it, gives some substance to Karamazov's empty words. Zosima has, in fact, been a guards officer, whose behaviour was not unlike that of Lermontov's heroes, nor, indeed, that of Dmitri Karamazov himself; for Zosima, too, has been cruel, he too has been a monster, he too has had a shock which has pulled him up and brought him to the realisation that 'we are all to blame' – the very experience which the future holds for Dmitri. The relationship between the two men is not simply that of sinner and saint, each in himself represents the sinner turned saint, but at different stages of this development.

Dmitri had wished to begin his 'Confession of an Ardent Heart in Verse', by proclaiming 'The Hymn to Joy', instead he had quoted *Das Eleusische Fest* and identified himself with man's abject state before he had linked himself in an eternal bond with the earth. Zosima in the exhortations of his testament shows no such equivocation over joy. Joy at the whole of creation will come to those who venerate the earth:

Love falling down on the earth and kissing it. Kiss the earth, and love ceaselessly, tirelessly. Love everyone; love everything; search for this rapture, this frenzy. Water the earth with the tears of your joy and love these tears of yours. Be not ashamed of this access of emotion, but treasure it; for it is a gift of God, a great gift, and it is not given to many, only to the chosen. (Bk VI, Ch. 3(h))

If Dmitri has not yet found his bond with the earth, he is nevertheless at one with Zosima in his striving for joy. Alesha is suddenly struck by the comparison:

'He who loves people, loves their joy', this is what the late elder used to repeat constantly. This was one of his most important ideas ... 'Without joy it is impossible to live', is what Mitya says ... Yes Mitya ... (Bk VII, Ch. 4)

These thoughts come to Alesha during the funeral rites performed over the body of the dead elder, and if Zosima is a crucial figure for an understanding of both Ivan and Dmitri, how much more is this true for his own novice Aleksey. The funeral itself reveals to Alesha the truth of Zosima's favourite biblical quotation, that fruit springs from the corn of wheat that has perished, the miracle of hope born out of despair. This experience *is* a miracle in the sense in which the elder himself understands the word; for unlike the Grand Inquisitor, Zosima sees miracles not as phenomena inspiring faith, but as phenomena springing from faith. During his lifetime, the credulous had ascribed miracles to Zosima himself, but by his death he disabuses them. Instead of the miraculous happenings which everyone expects, there takes place merely an unpleasant natural phenomenon – with unseemly haste the body begins to smell.

This is a test of his followers' faith, not a strengthening of it, and for no one is this more true than for Alesha. He is quite shaken by the event; it is not so much that he himself expected a miracle, but that what has taken place is the very reverse of a miracle – it is unjust. This yardstick of 'justice' shows how deeply the words of Ivan have affected his thinking, and now in the depths of doubt and despair he echoes the words of Ivan, in which he expresses his rejection of God's world.

Yet Alesha's faith returns; a miracle does after all occur, but one which is nevertheless presented in terms of ordinary everyday existence; for it is typical of Dostoyevsky's treatment of the supernatural that this miracle should take the form of a dream – Alesha is present at Christ's first miracle: the turning of the water into wine at Cana in Galilee. This, the dream of the miracle, is the miracle itself; for in the heart of Alesha the very same process is at work – water becomes wine; despair is turned into joy; the dead husk of Zosima's rotting body yields a marvellous new fruit; the funeral rites merge into the celebrations of the wedding feast; and at this wedding feast Zosima himself is present and alive, just as Alesha has always known him. He has been resurrected to this miracle of joy, because like Grushenka's old woman he has given an onion, and now he is drinking the new wine, the wine of a new and great happiness. The dream unites in one great reassuring synthesis the positive elements in all that Alesha has experienced since the death of his elder; the desire for a miracle; the story of Grushenka; and the holy text read over the body of the beloved monk.

The real miracle here is the renewal of faith, and now, true to the elder's precepts, Alesha goes outside to embrace yet a further mystery:

Alesha stood, looked, and suddenly, as though his legs were cut from under him, threw himself on the earth.

He did not know why he embraced it, he did not try to account for the fact that he so irresistibly felt like kissing it, kissing the whole of it. But he kissed the earth weeping, sobbing, covering it with his tears, and in ecstasy he swore to love it, to love it for all eternity. 'Water the earth with the tears of your joy and love these tears of yours' rang out in his soul. What was he crying about? Oh, in his rapture, he was even crying about those very stars which were shining to him out of the abyss, and 'he was not ashamed of this access of emotion'. It was as though threads from all these countless worlds of God had come together all at once in his soul, and his soul trembled 'in contact with other worlds'. He wanted to forgive everyone for everything and to beg forgiveness, oh, not for himself but for everyone and everything. 'Others will ask forgiveness for me' rang out again in his soul. But with every moment he felt clearly, almost tangibly, that something firm and unshakeable, like that heavenly dome above him, was entering into his soul; something almost in the form of an idea was being enthroned in his mind and was there for the whole of his life, for all eternity. He fell on the earth a callow youth: he arose a warrior, doughty for the rest of his life. He realised this; he felt it suddenly at the moment of his ectasy, and never, never, throughout the whole of his life could Alesha forget that moment. 'Someone visited my soul at that moment', he said later with firm belief in his words. (Bk VII, Ch. 4)

The frequent quotations within this passage show how closely Alesha is following the ideas of his spiritual father. Yet the elder is not merely a father; Zosima himself recognises in Alesha the spiritual reincarnation of his own brother; and brotherhood, the brotherhood of all men, is one of Zosima's most cherished concepts. Besides The Book of Job, his favourite reading includes the story of Joseph; a story which points to the possibility of reconciliation between brothers, in spite of all that has passed between them. But the larger brotherhood of all men is just as possible if men will only act as brothers:

In order to refashion the world anew, it is necessary for people psychologically to turn to a new road. Until you do indeed make yourself the brother of everyone, no brotherhood will be achieved.

(Bk VI, Ch. 2 (d))

Brotherhood, of course, is a concept present in the very title of the novel itself, and it is as central to the work as is the theme of fatherhood. The sub-plot with Snegirev, so illustrative of that theme, is at the same time a vehicle for Alesha's attempts to follow the teachings of Zosima on universal brotherhood. Snegirev is reluctant to accept money for the injury he has sustained at the hands of Dmitri, but Alesha represents Katerina Ivanovna's offer of 200 roubles as 'a sister coming to a brother with help'. Indeed, for Alesha, the whole fate of universal brotherhood seems to hang on whether Snegirev will accept the money or not:

Otherwise it would mean that everyone has to be the enemy of everyone else on this earth, but there is also on this earth such a thing as brotherhood. (Bk IV, Ch. 7)

But the 'active love' demanded by universal brotherhood must overcome many difficult obstacles, as Alesha finds out, not merely in his relations with Snegirev, but in his dealings with his own blood brothers. Indeed, from the lips of one of these, Ivan, he hears the classic rejection of brotherhood: 'Am I my brother's keeper.' Yet the way has been shown to him by Zosima, who has himself learned the truth of brotherhood by bitter experience. As a young impetuous officer he had struck his servant Afanasiy; and the fact that the servant had accepted the blow without retaliation or complaint precipitated a crisis in his master's life. The young officer realised for the first time how badly he behaved to his fellow men; and in order to proclaim the brotherhood of all men, he joined another brotherhood, the brotherhood of a monastery. When next he meets Afanasiy there is a new bond between them: 'there took place between us a great human union.'

In the Karamazov household, however, there is a figure who

embodies the very antithesis of Zosima's relationship with Afanasiy and his revelation that his servant is his brother: that figure is Smerdyakov – the brother turned into a servant. Zosima, who has such a strong connection with all the other brothers, hardly seems to touch Smerdyakov at any point, yet the logic of Dostoyevsky's novels is such that the saint and the sinner, the Christian and the heretic, are never far apart. If Smerdyakov does provide an antithesis for Zosima, he also stands as some sort of dark commentary.

In *The Brothers Karamazov* Smerdyakov is the figure identified with heresy, the character who is given the attributes of the Castrates; but the ascetic, celibate Zosima is himself not without a taint of heresy. The idea is first mooted by the elder Karamazov, who pretends to be offended by the monks' 'heretical practice' of confessing aloud (by 'the monks', of course, he means only Zosima):

It is indeed a scandal! No, Holy Fathers, with you one might even get caught up in the heresy of the Flagellants. I shall write to the Synod about this on the first occasion, and I shall take my son Aleksey home.

(Bk II, Ch. 8)

This outburst is comic but, like Karamazov's ramblings on Zosima as a Lermontovian hero, such nonsense is not without its grain of truth: the old man is merely giving his own typically exaggerated version of something he has heard; for within the monastery itself there is much criticism of Zosima on this very point. Indeed, the very 'Orthodoxy' of the function of elders is called into doubt by several of the monks.

The condemnation of Zosima's teachings comes to a head after his death, when the sudden decomposition of his body seems to lend validity to the denunciations of his critics. They remember that he taught that life was a great joy and not a vale of tears; that he did not believe literally in hell-fire; that he did not strictly observe the fasts; that he allowed himself to be adored as something holy; that he abused the mystery of the confessional. The scene reaches its final culmination when Zosima's arch enemy Ferapont enters the room where the body is resting, and sets about exorcising the devil, as though the smell were the stench of ungodliness.

All this, again, is comic,[9] but there is a fundamental element in Zosima's teaching which is never presented in a comic light, but which is certainly heretical – this is Zosima's cult of the earth. This teaching seems to be something pre-Christian; as we have seen it links Zosima, as does his teaching on joy, with the pagan Dmitri Karamazov, but also it looks back more explicitly to the heretical ideas which Marya Lebyadkin (in *The Devils*) had picked up in a convent. Its literary antecedents, therefore, link it to the Russian sects.

In *The Idiot* Myshkin had been impressed by religious ideas on the soil, which he had heard from the lips of an Old Believer, and in that novel Dostoyevsky had made his saint the spiritual brother of the 'Castrate' heretic, Rogozhin. In *The Brothers Karamazov*, on the other hand, these two figures of saint and heretic are poles which never touch, but the name Smerdyakov [stinker] seems nevertheless to suggest that into his portrait of the bastard brother, Dostoyevsky has distilled all the negative aspects of his saint, all that odour of corruption which the monk Ferapont tried to exorcise as the stench of ungodliness.

The figure of Zosima is thus central to the whole novel; he is a father-figure in apposition to the elder Karamazov, yet at the same time he is also a kind of brother-figure for all his sons: he is the spiritual hub around which all the characters revolve.

The future of Zosima's ideas lies with Alesha, but their implementing is far from easy. In his dealings with Snegirev, for example, Alesha's patience can be sorely tried, yet, as always the teachings of the elder come to his aid. On the subject of Snegirev, he tells Lise Khokhlakova: 'Do you know, Lise, my elder once said: people must be looked after exactly as though they were children, and some as though they were sick in hospital.' (Bk v, Ch. 1.) Lise greets this idea with enthusiasm, and cries: 'Let us look after people as though they were sick.' It is not difficult to see why she is so enthusiastic; for this precept has more direct relevance for her than for Snegirev. She is, indeed, one of the most difficult people with whom Alesha has to deal, and in her own person she combines both the child and the invalid. She therefore becomes a symbolic goal of Alesha's 'active love', and in spite of all the obstacles she places in its path, this love is unfaltering, and Alesha's intention of marrying her is unchanged.

As a cripple, Lise obviously invites love and consideration, yet she is spoilt and wayward, and she has a strong desire to subject other people to the suffering of which she herself is a victim. Her relationships with those around her, notably her mother and Alesha, are all tormented relationships. She even strikes a servant, then later begs her forgiveness; but this incident scarcely seems to have the same regenerative effect that Zosima experienced in a similar situation.

The most frank expression of her desire to see others suffer and enjoy it occurs in a conversation with Alesha towards the end of the novel. She recounts the story she has read of a four-year-old boy who has first had his fingers cut off, and then been crucified:

I sometimes think that I myself crucified him. There he is hanging and groaning, and I sit down beside him and eat stewed pineapple. I love stewed pineapple very much. Do you? (Bk xi, Ch. 3)

This love of torment which she expresses so vividly here is itself designed to torment Alesha, whom she is torturing, not merely with this loathsome self-revelation, but also with hints of a relationship between herself and Ivan. At the end of this chapter this sadism is turned in on herself: as soon as Alesha has left she purposely traps her finger in the door.

It is not merely that Alesha looks after people as though they were children: he treats children as though they were adults, and this is the secret of his success with them. He becomes the elder brother of all the children in the novel. Yet he is not the only Karamazov for whom children are important. We have seen that for Ivan children are the embodiment of innocence, and that he purposely restricts his arguments on eternal harmony to the suffering of children. We have also seen that Dmitri, who has been likened to a child by the cabman Andrey, decides to take on suffering for the sake of a child. Nevertheless, children are not all they seem. The crippled adolescent Lise Khokhlakova is perverse and tiresome: she seems bent on destroying Ivan's myth of the innocence of children. For not only does she offer herself to Ivan; she also reveals to him the same sadistic reverie of the crucifixion of a child with which she had tormented Alesha: the crimes committed against children by children, it seems, might almost be more terrible and bizarre than those perpetrated by adults.

The sub-plot of 'the boys' begins with Ilyusha, whose sufferings, as we have seen, serve as a commentary for the actions of Dmitri, but this sub-plot grows in importance as the novel progresses, and it is responsible for some of the least satisfactory passages in the work. The chapters 'At Iluysha's Bedside' and 'Little Ilyusha's Funeral' are mawkish; they seem merely to be catering for a nineteenth-century taste for bizarre sentimentality – for stewed pineapple and crucified children. Nevertheless, both these chapters are related to central themes in the novel.

After the incident with his father, Ilyusha turns from being one of the injured into being one who injures: he gives a stray dog, Zhuchka, a piece of bread with a pin in it. Here as in the main plot the actions of Dmitri have prepared the ground for Smerdyakov; for it is the bastard son who teaches Ilyusha to do this. After this incident no one, it appears, has been able to find the dog, but in fact Kolya Krasotkin has found Zhuchka alive and well; has taught him a variety of tricks and renamed him Perezvon. Kolya not only refuses to have anything to do with Ilyusha after the incident with Zhuchka, but purposely hides the fact that he has found the dog; his aim is to punish Ilyusha by developing in him the consciousness of his own guilt. He hopes to intensify the effect by producing the dog as an un-expected gift at the bedside of the dying boy.

The consciousness of one's own guilt is, of course, the only form of punishment which Zosima will recognise as such, but Krasotkin, who is a natural leader for the children, has here abused his moral influence: he has caused Ilyusha too much suffering over Zhuchka. Indeed his behaviour is reminiscent of the way in which Lebedev torments his friend General Ivolgin in *The Idiot* over the matter of the stolen money; but here the effect is not comic – it is tragic.

And if Krasotkin, who suspected nothing of the sort, had only known what a fatally tormenting effect such a moment could have on the health of the sick boy, then not for anything would he have ventured to play such a trick. Perhaps in the whole room there was only Alesha who understood this.   (Bk x, Ch. 5)

Here then, through the actions of a child, is a perverse commentary on one of Zosima's most cherished ideas.

Later in the same chapter ('At Ilyusha's Bedside') Krasotkin provides another commentary, not this time on punishment, but on guilt. The boy relates how he had induced a twenty-year-old errand-lad to drive a cart over a goose's neck, and how when the two had been apprehended and brought before a magistrate, the town lad had pointed to Kolya as the chief culprit:

'It wasn't me', he said. 'It was him who set me on to it', and he points to me. I reply quite calmly, that I had not set him on to it at all, but I had only given expression to a basic idea, and had spoken only in theory.   (Bk x, Ch. 5)

The character of Kolya is presented as that of any embryo nihilist, and the incident with the goose is another expression of the guilt of the theorist who provides the intellectual inspiration for a crime: it is a minor illustration of the guilt of Ivan.

'The Funeral of Little Ilyusha' again has implications for the wider framework of the novel itself. This is the final chapter and it ends on a note of hope for Alesha and the children of the novel. The innocence of children once more seems vindicated. Ilyusha has died and his saintliness seems confirmed by the fact that his body does not smell. Alesha asserts in his funeral speech that all the children will be better for having known him; the memory of his last days will fortify them even when they become men; for such is the edifying power of a memory like this:

You must realise that there is nothing better, more powerful, more wholesome and beneficial for the life that lies ahead than a pleasant memory; particularly one from childhood, from the parental home. People tell you a great deal about your education, but just such a beautiful and holy memory as this, preserved from childhood, is perhaps the very best education there is. (Epilogue, Ch. 3)

Aleksey Karamazov whose own parental home was so lacking in edifying memories is only too conscious of the sins of the fathers which are visited on the children, but nevertheless, the *Fathers and Children* theme is positively re-emphasised at the end of the novel; there is hope that the sons will succeed where the fathers failed. Alesha, whose own spiritual regeneration began with a funeral, is sending his young disciples out into the world fortified by the uplifting experience of another funeral; and this ending, from the point of view of the author's own biography, is psychologically convincing; for the spiritual crisis which gave birth to that great affirmation of life which is the novel itself – that crisis was the death of a child: the death of the author's baby son Aleksey.

10

CONCLUSION

The typical Dostoyevskian novel may be described as centripetal, in that it is built round one central figure on whom everything revolves and to whom everything ultimately points. Yet with each successive novel the effect diminishes: it can be observed at its most concentrated in the self-obsessed hero of *Notes from Underground*, who is at once narrator, commentator and chief protagonist in his own chronicle; with Raskolnikov in *Crime and Punishment*, the all-consuming nature of the central character is still very obvious; but with Myshkin in *The Idiot* the cohesiveness of this centripetal effect is noticeably weaker; and when we reach the elusive and enigmatic Stavrogin in *The Devils* the centre seems to have lost much of its substance. The crisis is reached with *A Raw Youth*: in spite of Dostoyevsky's attempt to strengthen the central position of Dolgoruky by making him both hero and narrator, he is nevertheless too weak to exert a cohesive influence; the plot keeps shooting off eccentrically in different directions, and the novel disintegrates into chaos. But from defeat stems even greater victory. The last novel, *The Brothers Karamazov*, although paying lip-service to the idea of a central figure (Alesha), abandons this device, in fact, for a new type of 'hero', a collective one – the brothers. Nevertheless, 'there is still a terrible amount of centripetal force in our planet': these are the words of one of the 'heroes', Ivan Karamazov, and if such a force is at all relevant for the novel itself, it is to be found, not so much in any one character as in a central event – the death of the father.

The progression towards a collective hero is perhaps inevitable, given that the dynamism of all Dostoyevsky's central figures results from a certain inner dichotomy which is so strong that it is almost as though within each character lurk two quite disparate people. In simple terms the central figures show both weakness and strength, are both good and evil, and the struggles of each are a search for self-identity. A similar alternation may be detected, broadly speaking, in the chronological portrayal of these figures. Thus Raskolnikov is superseded by Myshkin, who in turn is followed by Stavrogin: it is as though the author himself is engaged in a search – a quest for a hero, who will combine both strength of will with purity of soul.

Replying in his *Writer's Diary* to the charge that he was too interested in 'morbid manifestations of the will', Dostoyevsky claimed that in his novels he had had some success in *exposing* such manifestations.[1] Certainly the infinite possibilities of the will and its limitations constitute an important theme in Dostoyevsky's work. An examination of the problem first begins with the underground man, who, in challenging the primacy of reason, sees a more important counter principle in his own volitive urges. But, unlike that other anti-rationalist, Rousseau, he cannot give his will a moral direction by basing it upon the inherent goodness of instinctive feelings. On the contrary, the emotion which principally directs the will of the underground man is malice: he is the victim of his own self-destructive feelings.

Raskolnikov seeks to solve the problem by turning his back on the emotions altogether; he attempts to base his acts of will on reason and on reason alone. Yet he fails: he is unable to purge himself of the 'emotional' man who lurks within him. Finally in Stavrogin we have the rejection of both reason and emotion: Stavrogin is the embodiment of the will in its purest form, but as such, there is nothing which can give him direction. His sense of futility is marked finally by the pointlessness of his suicide. The lack of a central hero in *The Brothers Karamazov* means that, in this novel, Dostoyevsky's central preoccupation with the will has also disappeared. Instead we are presented with the emotions and the intellect divorced from the will; for although Dmitri and Ivan have each a motive for killing their father, they have not the will to carry it out – the act is left to their 'faithful Servant Licharda'.

The Brothers Karamazov has been called a great synthesis of all Dostoyevsky's work: there is much truth in this view.

Thematically, in its obsession with a central murder, the novel is another *Crime and Punishment*, in which, however, emphasis is placed on punishment rather than on the crime. Here, too, can be seen a restatement of both the positive and the negative ideas of *The Idiot*; for the quietest philosophy of Myshkin achieves its most confident expression in the life and teachings of Zosima; whereas Ippolit's rebellion against God's ordering of the world is taken up again in the figure of Ivan Karamazov; moreover Ivan's perplexity over the 'two truths' is a further development of the attack on the infallibility of human reason first launched by the underground man. The theme of the generations, so prominent in *The Devils* is reworked again, and in a new light, in this last novel. Indeed both these works share a common indebtedness to the projected novel 'The Life of a Great Sinner', and many of 'the great sinner's' acts which were presented so ambiguously in *The Devils* are given a positive interpretation in *The Brothers Karamazov*. Thus the motives for Zosima's behaviour at the duel may be taken as a comment on those of Stavrogin in his encounter with Gaganov, whereas Alesha's betrothal to the crippled girl Liza Khokhlakova is a positive restatement of Stavrogin's marriage to Marya Lebyadkin. In *The Brothers Karamazov* this element of synthesis is so strong that it even contains a synthesis of itself; for the lengthy trial scene recasts in concentrated form all that has gone on in the first part of the novel.

A constant thread running through Dostoyevsky's major writing is that of polemics with the nihilists. The brunt of this attack is borne by Chernyshevsky; in novel after novel Dostoyevsky feels the need to join issue with this publicist of the early sixties. Even at the end of his life when the period of the sixties was far behind him, Dostoyevsky was still pouring out his scorn on Chernyshevsky's followers. Thus Rakitin, 'the seminarist careerist' in *The Brothers Karamazov* is a polemical portrait of Yeliseyev, who became an editor of the *Contemporary* after Chernyshevsky's arrest.[2]

This polemical theme is very important in Dostoyevsky's work; for it is this which gives him his positive ideas. Chernyshevsky propounded the philosophy of monism and saw man as an uncomplicated creature capable of solving all his problems rationally: Dostoyevsky replied by emphasising dualism in man's nature and by revealing the overwhelming role played by non-rational and irrational factors in human behaviour. The young extremists of the sixties proclaimed the primacy of social justice and utilitarian values over the aestheticism of the older generation ('A pair of boots is better than Pushkin'): Dostoyevsky's reaction was to claim that 'beauty could save the world'. Yet again, the crude materialism of the times had given rise to the slogan: 'No one is to blame!' Dostoyevsky countered with another slogan: 'We are all to blame!' Moreover, throughout the nineteenth century the radicals were struggling for political and social freedom, but in his 'Legend of the Grand Inquisitor' Dostoyevsky dealt the most insidious blow of all by suggesting that it was not freedom that man desired but the lack of freedom offered by a ruthlessly 'benign' despotism. With the inspired perverseness of a Rousseau, Dostoyevsky stood all the fashionable assumptions of his own time on their head and created his own 'philosophy'.

Nevertheless these ideas are not presented as static eternal truths; they themselves have been engendered by a process of antithesis, and here is a force which, once unleashed, Dostoyevsky is unable to halt. Thus we have constantly seen that in his treatment of the theme of dualism, the 'poles' of this dualism in themselves frequently undergo further polarisation; antithesis begets antithesis. Nor can Dostoyevsky assert that beauty will save the world, without at the same time entertaining doubts about a dark side to beauty: the ideal of Sodom which might be found in parallel with the ideal of the Madonna. Yet again the phrase: 'We are all to blame' can easily revert to its opposite. Thus Dostoyevsky comments in his *Writer's Diary*: 'When everybody is to blame *en masse*, then individually there is no one to blame.'[3] If, too, 'The Legend of the Grand Inquisitor' seems to deny man's hope for utopia, there is, nevertheless, another legend – that of the golden age – which seems to reaffirm it.

It might seem that this eternal pull of warring opposites must leave Dostoyevsky in the position of one 'who is neither hot nor cold', in the position of his own hero Stavrogin. But here again is paradox; for the overriding impression created by his novels is certainly not neutrality, it is rather that of a passionate and ill-contained urgency; for he is committed to both sides and thus is ultimately saved by what Henry Gifford has called the 'the dialectic of resistance'.[4]

Yet there is the danger that 'the inevitable antithesis' might ultimately produce an effect close to that of cancelling out, might perhaps, be symptomatic of a form of nihilism, and certainly Dostoyevsky's attitude to the so-called 'nihilists' he attacks is not without its ambivalence. As a young man he had flirted with the revolutionary movement embraced by Petrashevsky and his circle: an illicit liaison which had cost him exile in Siberia. Even after this ordeal, when he had returned to the literary life, to all intents chastened and more of a reactionary, he had nevertheless resumed this flirtation, and in a far less metaphorical sense, first in his liaison with the young nihilist girl, Pauline Suslova, and later through his infatuation with the young radical, Anna Korvin-Kryukovskaya. There is, too, the evidence of his writing. When he ostensibly set himself the task of pillorying nihilism in *The Devils* he also, at the same time, pilloried established authority, and allowed Petr Verkhovensky to expose himself not as a socialist, but as a right-wing élitist. In commenting later on his portrayal of Verkhovensky (in the *Writer's Diary*) he again stresses that his arch-nihilist is not a socialist.[5] It is almost as if the word 'Socialism' is one which he does not wish to taint, and at the end of his life he even brands his own pet theory of the unification of mankind through the Russian Christ as 'Russian Socialism'.[6] Indeed several of his most jingoistic utterances he seeks to justify by 'democratic' arguments.[7] Like his own Karmazinov, Dostoyevsky too was concerned not to lose touch with the younger generation, and his novel *A Raw Youth* was published in Nekrasov's *Fatherland Notes*, the leading progressive journal of the day, as a gesture of conciliation towards left-wing opinion.

In the major novels, Raskolnikov, Ippolit, Kirillov, Ivan Karamazov are all tainted by the ideology of nihilism, yet the author's portrayal of these figures shows deep sympathy and understanding.

The theme of beauty is an important one for Dostoyevsky. Beauty is a motivating force, it is a pledge of something greater; it is an ideal. Thus the young hero of *A Raw Youth* says: 'Blessed is he who has an ideal of beauty even though it be a wrong one.' Myshkin, Stepan Trofimovich, Dmitri Karamazov, all are searching for an ideal of beauty, but the fact that wrong ideals of beauty are possible complicates the quest. Beautiful women are frequently presented as embodiments of such ideals: Myshkin must choose between Nastasya Filippovna and Aglaya; Dmitri between Katerina Ivanovna and Grushenka.

Although poetry in Dostoyevsky's novels occupies an important place, especially the poetry of Pushkin and Schiller, it is nevertheless true that for him beauty is primarily visual. The 'icons' of this beauty are paintings such as the Sistine *Madonna*, with which Stepan Trofimovich seeks to fight the philistinism of the times, or *Acis and Galatea* – the promise of the golden age.

Yet the whole world is beautiful; it contains a pledge of harmony and happiness for man: this is the message proclaimed by Myshkin, Kirillov and Zosima. But, of course, the pledge is flawed. Raskolnikov whenever he contemplates one of St Petersburg's most beautiful views, always feels an ominous and inexplicable chill within him (Pt II, Ch. 2). Myshkin feels despair when he contemplates the idyllic beauty of a Swiss mountain scene (Pt III, Ch. 7); and almost the same type of scenery and the same despair is described by Marya Lebyadkin in *The Devils* (Pt I, Ch. IV, 5). But the proclaimers of the message are themselves flawed. Myshkin and Kirillov are both epileptics, and this affliction, which affords them a mystic insight into beauty and harmony, is associated in both cases with madness. Zosima alone is sane and healthy. Flawed too is the 'picture' of the golden age. The vision is destroyed for Stavrogin by the 'little red spider' of his own guilt. For Versilov in *A Raw Youth* the painting offers, not the beginning of hope, but its end: this sun setting on the first day of European man turns into the sun setting on the last. The most interesting development of all is in *The Dream of the Comic Man* (1877); for the hero dreams that he lives among the people of this golden age. Yet despite his strong desire to immerse himself completely in their idyll, it is nevertheless he – the civilised man of nineteenth-century Europe – who, on the contrary, communicates his values to them: he ends by corrupting them. This is a dream which the hero experiences instead of committing suicide; for 'the comic man' is a nihilist, convinced of the futility of carrying on with life. The story is thus a further comment on the predicament of Kirillov – he, too, is a nihilist who might have been saved from suicide by his vision of beauty.

It is a curious fact that in each of the four novels, murder is quite closely associated with the Russian religious sects. In *Crime and Punishment* it is Raskolnikov who commits the murder, whilst the true schismatic [*raskol'nik*] Mikolka, is held on suspicion. Rogozhin, the instrument of destruction in *The Idiot*, is linked with the sect of the Castrates, as is that other murderer in *The Brothers Karamazov* – Smerdyakov. In *The Devils* the murders and suicides are all centred round the figure of Stavrogin, so that Petr Verkhovensky is right when he attributes everything to the 'House of Filippov'. The warped image of sectarianism lies at the heart of each novel.

In *A Raw Youth* there is no murder, and this is perhaps one of the factors contributing to the novel's weakness. Instead there is the theme of general disintegration, and an important symbol for this is an Old Believers' icon which Versilov breaks in two (the symbolism is reinforced by a double verbal play on the words '*raskol'nichiy*' = 'schismatic's', and '*raskolot'*' = 'to split in two'; and '*obraz*' = 'icon', and '*blagoobraziye*' = 'harmony'). This icon belongs to Makar, and in him we have a milder and more positive sectarian figure: he is a *strannik* or a wandering holy man, a penitent.

The very existence of the sects casts a dark shadow on

Dostoyevsky's hopes and aspirations for the Russian people. If it is Russia's mission to save the world through her greater spirituality, and the ideal of this spirituality is to be seen in the 'Russian Christ' – the true image of Christ preserved in the hearts of the Russians alone, then the existence of such warped recesses of the Russian soul as the sects of the Flagellants and the Castrates must cast strong doubts on the saving qualities of the Russian religious temperament. Hence the figure of Myshkin is dogged by his 'brother in Christ' Rogozhin: the 'ideal of the Madonna' exists side by side with 'the ideal of Sodom'.

Inevitably, of course, there is a further polarisation: this 'ideal of Sodom' might after all prove to have within itself an even greater power of salvation. In the *Writer's Diary* (1873) Dostoyevsky recounts the story of Vlas, the peasant who committed the ultimate sacrilege of shooting at Christ's body, represented by the host. Like Makar in *A Raw Youth*, Vlas becomes a wandering penitent. Dostoyevsky concludes:

I am still of the opinion that the last word will be uttered by them, by these Vlases of various sorts, the repentant and the unrepentant. They will speak and they will show us a new road, a new way out of all our problems, which appear to be so insoluble.

Here is the theme of the ultimate saintliness of the great sinner, which is implied in all Dostoyevsky's work from *Crime and Punishment* to *The Brothers Karamazov*.

The hint of heresy is never far away, even when Dostoyevsky is putting forward his most positive endorsement of the Christian message, as in the teachings of Zosima. Thus his saint lays great stress on a strange cult of the earth, not unlike the heresy acquired by Marya Ledbyadkin in a monastery, or the ideas learned by Myshkin from the lips of an Old Believer.[8] Indeed, the 'Christianity' of the author is itself heretical: its basic premise is that everything must start with Russia; hence the insistence on such concepts as the 'Russian soil', the 'Russian Christ' and 'the brotherhood of mankind achieved through Russia's messianic mission'. For Dostoyevsky is at one and the same time intensely parochial, yet undeniably cosmopolitan: he embodies that very paradox he claimed to see in Pushkin – the most Russian of writers, yet the most universal.[9]

Dostoyevsky's veneration of 'the soil' [*pochva*] links him with Grigorev and the *pochvenniki*,[10] but it also takes on strangely Tolstoyan overtones (another major novelist who was interested in the Russian sects). Thus Shatov exhorts Stavrogin to find God by toiling as a peasant, and Grushenka suggests that Dmitri will find a new life and a new happiness through tilling the soil. For these two noblemen, cut off, as they are, from the common people, this bond with the soil is prescribed for reasons which are both mystical and sociological.

A constant thread running through Dostoyevsky's work is 'consciousness' [*soznaniye*] – a concept which might be better described as 'heightened awareness'. The underground man is a victim of his own heightened awareness, yet it is this very quality which marks him out from his fellow men and enables him to look down on them. A somewhat similar state of mind is experienced by Raskolnikov; he too feels himself a man apart; he, too, locks himself up in his room and surrenders himself to extreme conclusions. But his imagination, strained to fever pitch, finally yields place to a trance-like state, which is the very reverse of heightened awareness; it is a state unknown by the underground man, in which action becomes possible. Yet once this action has been committed, the floodgates of consciousness are opened again and Raskolnikov is finally swept away.

The hero of *The Idiot* suffers from epilepsy, which induces in him brief but excruciating states of heightened consciousness, during which he feels he has penetrated the secret of the universe: it is this elevated state of awareness which he tries to recapture when he urges that people should look at the beauty of nature. This idea is further developed in the later novels in the portrayal of Kirillov and more positively in the teachings of Zosima. Heightened awareness is, indeed, so fundamental to Dostoyevsky's art, his philosophy and his life itself, that if one were looking for a quality which, more than any other, marks him out as a writer, it must surely be this. Dostoyevsky is the poet of heightened awareness.

As a condemned man returned to life, a convict restored to the world, Dostoyevsky knew only too well the profound significance invested in ordinary everyday things. In *The Idiot* Myshkin describes the last moments of a man about to be executed. The shock of what is about to happen makes him see everything with new eyes; he becomes intensely conscious of time, and of the importance of not wasting a single moment. In the same novel Ippolit, who is dying of consumption, cannot understand how a man who is alive and well does not realise the value of something which he himself is unable to take for granted. Another dying boy, Markel in *The Brothers Karamazov*, suddenly becomes aware of the beauty, goodness and happiness of everything in the world. The message is always the same: man does not realise what he has got.[11] Perhaps what is needed, indeed, is a shock, which will throw him out of the rut of his normal existence in order that he may see reality as it is.

Dostoyevsky himself had had such a shock in the ordeal of the mock-execution and the incarceration in Siberia, and if a doctrine of 'heightened awareness' was the direct result of such punishment, then punishment itself was reinterpreted in the light of the doctrine; for it is in 'consciousness', and in consciousness alone, that Dostoyevsky sees the only possibility of true punishment: the sinner's awareness of having done wrong is the only form of punishment which Zosima will dignify by the name.

Dostoyevsky is frequently accused of advocating suffering for its own sake. This is not true. The positive message of Myshkin, Stepan Trofimovich, Zosima is that man is born for happiness. Throughout the whole of his life Dostoyevsky abhorred suffering; there is no more eloquent testimony to this than Ivan's horror at the suffering inflicted on innocent children. This is human justice at its crudest, to this Zosima opposes only that suffering which has been freely and consciously accepted as a mark of atonement – the suffering inflicted by the consciousness of guilt.[12]

In the eyes of Dostoyevsky the greatest crime is the infliction of suffering on children, and for this view he has good authority:

But whoso shall offend one of these little ones which believe in me, it were better for him that a millstone were hanged about his neck, and that he were drowned in the depth of the sea.[13] (Matthew xviii.6)

It is in this sense that Stavrogin's 'crime' against Matresha and Svidrigaylov's crime against the fourteen-year-old deaf-mute must be taken. These acts, hedged about as they are by rumour and ambiguity, are more emblematic than real – they mark the very nadir of human depravity. Yet if children bear the image of innocence, this quality, by a now familiar process, may also be inverted. Thus Svidrigaylov dreams of a child prostitute, and Liza Khokhlakova not only offers herself to both Alesha and Ivan, but also reveals to them her fantasy of the crucified child. Nevertheless children are the future, in them lies the great hope. In his novels Dostoyevsky tentatively holds out the promise that the 'children' might succeed where the 'fathers' have failed.

A question which has concerned us more than once in this study is the degree to which Dostoyevsky may be considered a 'realistic' writer. This is a problem which, as we have seen, also taxed the author himself; his chief concern seems to have been about the typicality of his characterisation. The behaviour of Dostoyevsky's characters is, on many occasions, extreme and irrational, but, with few exceptions, his figures are fully-rounded and convincing. Moreover, Dostoyevsky's grasp of human psychology is such that behind their actions the reader can often see the barely conscious motives of his own behaviour. Yet, for all that, there is a heightening of typicality.

In part, this 'heightening' is a device by which Dostoyevsky achieves his drama, but it is nevertheless true that his characters often strike the reader as 'not normal', as though they are drunk or in a state of delirium – indeed these are often the very terms which the author chooses to describe them. But it happens, too, that such 'abnormality' may be synonymous with a 'state of heightened awareness'; that one is the direct result of the other; for, as we have seen, an abnormality such as Myshkin's fits or Ippolit's consumption is a means of bringing this state about.

Yet if Dostoyevsky is the poet of heightened awareness, we might expect that detail in his novels would be sharply observed and invested with particular significance. In *A Raw Youth* Versilov tells the hero:

Do not forget the insignificant details. The main thing is not to forget the insignificant details. The more insignificant a feature is, sometimes the more important it is.

This insistence on detail is the very stuff of realism. The street and tavern scenes in St Petersburg, the Karamazov house with its rats and its icons[14] – it is details such as these which give Dostoyevsky's world its sense of tangible reality.

But detail has two faces; it may also, and at the same time, form a counterpoint of symbolism within the realistic fabric of the plot. Thus *Crime and Punishment* and *The Brothers Karamazov* are probably the most 'realistic' of all Dostoyevsky's novels, yet to regard them purely as works of social or psychological realism is obviously inadequate: there are many incongruities which cannot be easily accommodated to such a view (the 'contrived' nature of chance encounters, relationships and shared living quarters in *Crime and Punishment*; the role played by the village of Chermashnya, by money and the amulet in *The Brothers Karamazov*). Improbable coincidences and incongruities abound in all Dostoyevsky's novels, but the reader accepts them without demur because in the framework of symbolism within each novel such details are right and true. Rarely does this framework itself crudely and glaringly obtrude into the reader's conscious mind. The novels have all the feel of reality: it is only on closer scrutiny that the outlines can be discerned of the shadowy bulk which keeps the lofty tip afloat.

A significant role in Dostoyevsky's novels is played by dreams. Through them the reader is frequently given illuminating psychological insights into the inner world of the characters. Dreams add a new dimension to the realistic perspective of the writing, often imparting to the narrative a fantastic, supernatural quality. But for all that Dostoyevsky flirts with the supernatural, he never transgresses that thin line which marks it off from the natural world he portrays. The supernatural is introduced into his novels in a 'naturalistic' way, through such realistically acceptable devices as dreams, anecdotes, hallucinations.

In these novels reality frequently merges into dream, dream into reality: there is, indeed, a certain vivid but dream-like quality about the writing itself. In Chapter 5 the idea was advanced that the central character of a Dostoyevsky novel is undergoing an experience akin to the nature of a dream, the varied phenomena of which have peculiar relevance for that character himself. This again is the centripetal effect, and at its most extreme it becomes a form of solipsism. Thus the 'comic man' says about the everyday reality he sees about him: 'perhaps all this world and all these people are just me alone'. Shortly afterwards he himself plunges into the greater reality of his own marvellous dream. Perhaps the dream-like quality of Dostoyevsky's realism may be attributed to three main factors: in the first place reality is often perceived in a heightened state of awareness; secondly this reality itself is allowed to merge with dream states; and thirdly there is an ever-present hint that 'all this world and all these people' are but aspects of the central character himself.

Dostoyevsky has perhaps suffered too much from the inflexible yardstick applied by the great realistic tradition in Russian criticism. He himself complained in his *Writer's Diary* about what he called the 'straightforwardness' [*pryamolineynost'*] of the times:

But the worst thing is that, the more we go on, the more this 'straightforwardness' reigns supreme. For example, the flair for adaptation, for indirect means of expression, for allegory – this is noticeably beginning to be lost. It is noticeable that we have ceased (generally speaking) to understand humour, and this, as one German thinker has observed, is one of the most glaring signs of the intellectual and moral decline of an age.' (1876, Dec., Ch. 1, 2)

Dostoyevsky's own use of 'indirect means of expression' [*inoskazaniye*] and allegory has been examined at some length during the course of this work; what has received less attention is his use of humour. Humour is one of the great motive forces in Dostoyevsky's art. It does much to sustain the momentum of such novels as *The Idiot* (cf. the role of Ivolgin and Lebedev) and *The Devils* (cf. the portrayal of Stepan Trofimovich and that of the nihilists). Yet, as we might suspect with Dostoyevsky, humour has its dark side too, and it is this use of humour which the English reader often finds the most perplexing. Thus, as Ronald Hingley has pointed out, some of the most harrowing scenes in *Crime and Punishment* (those involving the Marmeladov family) are also potentially the most comic.[15] One of the most serious moments in *The Brothers Karamazov*, the death of Zosima, is suddenly swamped by unexpected comic elements (the smell, the complete change of attitude amongst his followers, the irruption of Ferapont). Only Dostoyevsky could turn the death of a saintly monk into comedy, and then, through a sheer artistic miracle, turn this same water into wine by making it the beginning of a mystical experience.

The other great motive force in Dostoyevsky's work is his gift for drama. This is so strong that under his pen even ideas can take on a dramatic intensity. At his best Dostoyevsky is a master of suspense and tension who is capable of creating within the minds of his readers the expectancy that almost anything may happen on the very next page. But it would not be Dostoyevsky if the reverse were not also true. At his worst he is capable of flat uninteresting writing with thin characterisation and jumbled, chaotic plots. It is also fair to say that in general the conclusions of his novels scarcely live up to the promise contained in the works themselves. This is more true at the level of ideas than at the level of art. Thus the final scene of *The Idiot* is among the best Dostoyevsky ever wrote, yet it marks the failure of the 'great idea'. In this sense both *The Idiot* and *The Devils* are 'failure' novels; for the turn taken by Stavrogin also marks the end of a great idea. Yet, in both these novels, Dostoyevsky fights a rearguard action through the symbolism implicit in each work. The figure of Vera Lebedev and baby Lyubov' in *The Idiot*; the last pilgrimage of Stepan

Trofimovich and the arrival of Marie Shatov in *The Devils* – these represent a desperate attempt to save a great idea, if only at the level of symbol.

It is perhaps inevitable that Dostoyevsky should have had difficulty with the endings of his novels; for his is an art which does not lend itself to conclusions in either sense of the word. Throughout the whole of his work there beats an incessant and merciless dialectic. The analogy is perhaps with chess. The underground man maintains that chess is not played for its ending, which is merely a dead formula, but that the game is played for the game itself. It is the process, not its conclusion, which is the important thing. Just such a struggle between competing forces, as in chess, makes Dostoyevsky the great writer he is. When, however, his ideas are shorn of their dialectic, when he is attempting to present firm precepts and irrefutable conclusions, as in much of the *Writer's Diary*, the result is merely bizarre dead formulae. The novels, on the other hand, are not only dynamically alive: they have the very quality of life itself. The last word must be with Ippolit: 'It is life that matters, life alone. The continuous process of discovering it, and not the discovery itself.'

NOTES

CHAPTER I. EARLY WRITING AND 'NOTES FROM UNDERGROUND'

1 The story has a happy ending with Foma reinstated as a reformed character.

2 Sleet (lit. 'wet snow') is a climatic condition particularly associated with the seaboard capital of St Petersburg. It was a motif common to the writings of the 'natural school', and was recognised as such by the critics of the day. See P. V. Annenkov, 'Zametki o russkoy literature 1848 goda', *Sovremennik*, no. 1 (1849); also F. M. Dostoyevsky, *Sobraniye sochineniy v desyati tomakh* (Moscow, 1956), Vol. 4, p. 599 (hereafter this work will be referred to as *D.1, D.2* etc.).

   Sleet is a persistent feature of Dostoyevsky's own story *The Double*.

3 The theme of the redemption of the 'fallen woman' is also treated by Chernyshevsky in *What is to be done?* in the relationship between Kirsanov and Kryukova.

4 This work serves as a commentary on *Notes from Underground* at many points. Like his underground man Dostoyevsky himself, in this work, complains of a liver condition. There is the same playful attitude of author to reader and Dostoyevsky's tone at times anticipates that of *Notes from Underground* (cf. the opening of Ch. 5 of *Winter Notes*). But whereas in the earlier work Dostoyevsky puts forward the possibility of founding utopia on feelings and human nature rather than on reason, the implications of *Notes from Underground* refute such optimistic *Rousseauism*; for the instinctive reaction of the underground man (Rousseau's '*le premier mouvement*') is not the innate goodness of *l'homme de la nature et de la verité*, it is malice.

5 *Podpol'ye* is literally 'the space beneath the floorboards'. The symbol appears to derive from the underground man's comparison of himself to a mouse (Pt I, Ch. 3).

6 See F. M. Dostoyevsky, *Pis'ma*, edited and with commentary by A. S. Dolinin (Moscow/Leningrad, 1928), Vol. 1, p. 353 (hereafter referred to as *Pis'ma*).

7 *Umyshlenny* (lit. 'intentional'). Cf. *Winter Notes*, Ch. 3, where Dostoyevsky refers to St Petersburg as 'the most fantastic city with the most fantastic history of all the cities of the earth.'

   Shortly before his death, for reasons such as these, Dostoyevsky declared himself against St Petersburg (*Writer's Diary*, 1881, Jan., Ch. 3). See F. M. Dostoyevsky, *Dnevnik Pisatelya za 1877 god* (YMCA Press, Paris, n.d. *c.* 1950), p. 579 (hereafter referred to as *Dnevnik*).

8 Dostoyevsky, paying tribute to George Sand on her death, called her: 'one of our contemporaries, an idealist of the thirties and forties'. (*Writer's Diary*, 1876, Dec., Ch. 1, sect. 3.) (*Dnevnik*, 1876, p. 229.)

9 *Zhivaya zhizn'* (lit. 'living life'), a term which later Dostoyevsky would use to mean a belief in immortality. See *Writer's Diary*, 1876, Dec., Ch. 1, sect. 3 (*Dnevnik*, 1876, p. 476).

10 See *Pis'ma*, Vol. 1, p. 365.

CHAPTER 2. THE ETHICAL REAPPRAISAL: 'CRIME AND PUNISHMENT'

1   See Fyodor Dostoyevsky, *The Notebooks for 'Crime and Punishment'*, edited and translated by Edward Wasiolek (Chicago and London, 1967), p. 23.

2   At the beginning of *The Insulted and the Injured* Dostoyevsky had already observed: 'In a narrow room one even thinks narrowly' (see *D.3*, p. 7). The link between Raskolnikov and the figure of 'the dreamer' is brought out by Svidrigaylov, who taunts Raskolnikov with being a 'Schiller' (see *D.5*, pp. 492 and 507).

3   On hearing the full details of his friend's behaviour in 'The Crystal Palace', Razumikhin repeats the idea that Raskolnikov has been 'sticking his tongue out' at Zametov (see *D.5*, p. 200).

4   Razumikhin jokingly says that his name is 'Vrazumikhin' (i.e. from *vrazumit*' = 'to knock sense into someone'): see *D.5*, p. 125. Luzhin, unable to remember Razumikhin's name correctly, calls him 'Rassudkin' (i.e. from *rassudok* = 'reason', 'intellect'): see *D.5*, p. 313. Svidrigaylov carries on this idea when he says that Razumikhin's name suggests that he is 'a man of reason' (i.e. *rassuditel'nyy*), and that he must be a seminarist: see *D.5*, p. 496.

5   See Leonid Grossman, *Dostoyevsky*, in series 'Zhizn' zamechatel'nykh lyudey' (Moscow, 1962), p. 351 (also pp. 353, 356 ff where Grossman relates *Crime and Punishment* to contemporary reforms).

6   E.g. Philip Rahv, 'Dostoevsky in *Crime and Punishment*', *Dostoevsky; A Collection of Critical Essays* in series 'Twentieth Century views', edited by René Wellek (Englewood Cliffs, N.J., 1962), p. 34.

7   See V. V. Danilov, 'K voprosu o kompozitsionnykh priemakh v *Prestuplenii i nakazanii* Dostoyevskogo', *Izvestiya ANSSSR., Otdeleniye obshchestvennykh nauk*, No. 3 (1933). See also K. N. Polonskaya's commentary to *D.5* (p. 582); also M. Gus, *Idei i obrazy F. M. Dostoyevskogo* (Moscow, 1962), pp. 275–8.

8   See Georg Lukács, 'Der russische Realismus in der Weltliteratur', *Probleme des Realismus*, Vol. II (Neuwied and Berlin, 1964), pp. 164–5: also Rahv, 'Dostoevsky in *Crime and Punishment*', p. 29. The argument on the 'Chinese mandarin', however, is essentially different from the justifications given by Raskolnikov for his crime, in as much as it hinges upon the idea of a great distance separating the murderer and his victim and their complete dissociation. Dostoyevsky himself discusses the influence of distance on human concepts of morality when examining the motives of Levin in *Anna Karenina* (see *Writer's Diary*, 1877, July/August, Ch. 3, sect. 4) (*Dnevnik*, 1877, p. 307).

9   See Grossman, *Dostoyevsky*, p. 349. The translation of *Eugénie Grandet* appeared unsigned and in an abridged form in *Repertuar i Panteon* (1844), Bks 6 and 7.

10 See *Pis'ma*, Vol. 1, p. 418.

11 Dostoyevsky advances similar ideas himself in his *Writer's Diary*, 1877, Feb., Ch. 1, sect. 3 (*Dnevnik*, 1877, p. 57).

12 See N. G. Pomyalovsky, *Polnoye sobraniye sochineniy* (Leningrad, 1935), Vol. 2, p. 214.

13 According to Strakhov himself, Dostoyevsky told him: 'You alone have understood me.' See N. N. Strakhov, 'Vospominaniya o Fedore Mikhayloviche Dostoyevskom' in *F. M. Dostoyevsky v vospominaniyakh sovremennikov* (Moscow, 1964), Vol. 1, p. 316 (this collection will hereafter be referred to as *Vosp.*).

      For a contrary view of Raskolnikov, see Henri Troyat, *Dostoïevsky; L'Homme et Son Oeuvre* (Paris, 1940), p. 383.

14 I.e. 'G-n Shchedrin, ili raskol v nigilistakh', *Epokha*, Bk 5 (1865). For an account of these polemics, see S. S. Borshchevsky, *Shchedrin i Dostoyevsky* (Moscow, 1956), pp. 107 f.

15 See N. A. Dobrolyubov, 'Svatovstvo Chenskogo, ili materializm i idealizm – "O neizbezhnosti idealizma v materializme" Yu. Savicha', *Sobraniye sochineniy* (Moscow/Leningrad, 1962), Vol. 5, pp. 178-9. (For an English translation, see N. A. Dobrolyubov, *Selected Philosophical Essays*, translated by J. Fineberg (Foreign Languages Publishing House, Moscow, 1956), p. 375.)

CHAPTER 3. MOTIVE AND SYMBOL: 'CRIME AND PUNISHMENT'

1 The 'realism' of Pushkin has also particular relevance for *Crime and Punishment*. Dostoyevsky was extremely enthusiastic about Pushkin's story, *The Queen of Spades*, valuing it both for the element of the fantastic and for its treatment of the inner struggles and final collapse of the hero. (See M. A. Polivanova, 'Zapis' o poseshchenii Dostoyevskogo 9 Iyunya 1880 goda', in *Vosp.* Vol. 2, pp. 361 and 363.)

      The story, set in St Petersburg, concerns a ruthless young man with a Napoleonic profile, who plays with people as though they are cards (so the 'realism' of the story is rich in symbol). To gain a gambling secret from an aged countess he poses as the lover of her companion. He unwittingly kills the old woman and is saved by Liza (the companion). The central core of both works is strikingly similar: a tyrannical old woman who bullies a meek Elizaveta Ivanovna is killed by a young man with Napoleonic aspirations. (See also K. Mochul'sky, *Dostoyevsky, Zhizn' i tvorchestvo* (Paris, 1947), p. 238.)

      Elsewhere in Pushkin we read: 'We all aim at being Napoleons/The millions of two-legged creatures/Are merely tools for us.' (*Yevgeniy Onegin*, Ch. 2, stanza xiv.)

2 Thus the 'miracle' of Raskolnikov's unexpected meeting with Svidrigaylov in Pt. VI is explained by the latter as a quirk of memory.

3 E. J. Simmons takes this as a sign of bad writing. See E. J. Simmons, *Dostoevsky. The Making of a Novelist* (New York, 1962), pp. 169-70.

4 I.e. *yurodivyy*. The 'holy fool' is a constantly recurring figure in Dostoyevsky's novels, and here the comparison is particularly significant in view of the traditional role of the *yurodivyy* as the voice of conscience speaking out against the tyrant (cf. Nikolka in Pushkin's *Boris Godunov*, or the historical figure of Nicholas Salos, who put Ivan the Terrible to shame when he was about to sack the city of Pskov).

5   By this italicised *she* Raskolnikov appears to be referring to Alyona and
    not to his mother (see *D.5*, p. 286), but the apparent continuity of thought
    between an expression of hatred for his mother and hatred for Alyona is
    interesting. For a theory on the role played by the mother in the motives
    for the crime, see Wasiolek's commentary to *The Notebooks for 'Crime
    and Punishment'*, p. 186. It might also be added that Alyona was the name
    of the faithful peasant nurse who brought up the Dostoyevsky children.
    See A. M. Dostoyevsky, 'Iz "Vospominaniy"', *Vosp.* Vol. 1, p. 42.

6   It is perhaps significant that during the ensuing conversation with Ras-
    kolnikov the reappearance of the dead in the form of ghosts is one of
    Svidrigaylov's main themes.

7   The full force of *perestupit'* is lost in English: the verb evokes its variant
    prestupit' = 'to commit a crime' (cf. Eng. 'transgress'). The title of the
    novel itself, *Prestupleniye i nakazaniye*, contains this root.

8   Even this pledge proves to be in two pieces: one of metal, the other of
    wood (see *D.5*, p. 75).

9   Thus we are told that Porfiry has contemplated becoming a monk (though
    this is presented as one pole of an enigmatic nature; for on the other hand
    Porfiry also claims that he intends to marry) (see *D.5*, p. 267).

10 Svidrigaylo spent the eighty-odd years of his life fomenting trouble on
    Russia's borders. Although nominally a Roman Catholic, he allied him-
    self with Orthodox dissidents, Hussites and the Order of the Livonian
    Knights in his efforts to further his own political aims. In 1434, against the
    wishes of Muscovy, Svidrigaylo had Gerasim of Smolensk consecrated
    in Constantinople as Metropolitan of all Russia, only to have him execu-
    ted the following year. The Dostoyevskys themselves were conscious
    of being descended from noble Lithuanian stock, and in choosing this name
    perhaps the author is indulging in a device typical of his writing – self-
    identification with his worst characters (e.g. the murderer who is the tool
    of the nihilists in *The Devils* is called 'Fedka the convict', and in *The
    Brothers Karamazov* the murderer Smerdyakov suffers from Dostoyevsky's
    own affliction – epilepsy.

11 Cf. D. L. Fanger, *Dostoevsky and Romantic Realism: A Study of Dostoevsky
    in Relation to Balzac, Dickens and Gogol* (Harvard University Press, 1965),
    p. 23.

12 This idea will be taken up at length in the novel, *The Devils*, where once
    more it will be interwoven with the theme of heresy (see Ch. 6 of the
    present work).

    The schism [*raskol*] was a term loosely applied to all heretics within
    the larger Orthodox fold, although the origins of some of the more
    extreme sects (e.g. the Flagellants [*Khlysty*] and their offshoot the Castrates
    [*Skoptsy*]) appear to be largely pagan and have little, if anything, to do with
    the true schism in the Russian Church which took place in the seventeenth
    century.

    Interestingly enough there was even a more recent sect which hailed
    Napoleon as a new Messiah – the sect of the *Napoleonovy*. See K. K. Grass,
    Die russischen Sekten, (Leipzig, 1907), Vol. 1, pp. 562–3; also P. I. Mel'nikov
    (Andrey Pechersky) 'Pis'ma o raskole', *Sobraniye sochineniy v shesti*

tomakh (Moscow, 1963), Vol. 6, p. 238; and F. C. Conybeare, *Russian Dissenters* (Harvard University Press, 1921), p. 370.

13 This realisation is brought about, characteristically, through a certain linguistic ambivalence. The Russian *ty* = thou (cf. French 'tu') can convey both great intimacy and great contempt:

'"Leave me alone," Dunya implored.

Svidrigaylov shuddered: this *ty* had not been pronounced as it had been formerly.

"So, you do not love me?" he asked her quietly.' 　　　　(*D.5*, p. 520.)

14 The name Resslikh occurs in connection with her (*D.5*, p. 526) as it had in Luzhin's account of the supposed seduction by Svidrigaylov of a fourteen-year-old deaf-mute (*D.5*, p. 309). It is with this same Gertruda Karlovna Resslikh that Svidrigaylov claims to be staying, when he hires the apartment next to Sonya (*D.5*, p. 254).

15 Svidrigaylov, for example, has turned self-blame into a fine art, as a weapon to be used for the seduction of women (*D.5*, p. 497).

16 In his argument inducing Sonya to stay, Raskolnikov's final words seem charged with ironic ambiguity: '…for you will remain guilty' [*…ved' vy zhe ostanetes' vinovaty*] (*D.5*, p. 425).

17 Dostoyevsky's distinctive use of language for each character has been remarked on. See, for example, Grossman, *Dostoyevsky*, p. 355.

CHAPTER 4. THE TRIUMPH OF AESTHETICS: 'THE IDIOT'

1 See *The Notebooks for 'The Idiot'*, edited and with an introduction by Edward Wasiolek; translated by Katharine Strelsky (Chicago and London, 1967), *passim*.

2 *Pis'ma*, Vol. 2, p. 71. (Dostoyevsky also has great praise for *Don Quixote* in his *Writer's Diary*, 1876, March, Ch. II, 1; and 1877, Sept., Ch. II, 1: see *Dnevnik*, 1876, p. 129 and 1877, pp. 339–44.)

3 Towards the end of his life, Dostoyevsky himself commented on what he regarded as his own inability to present arguments and his fear of ridicule. See *Writer's Diary*, 1881, Jan., Ch. 1, 3 (in *Dnevnik*, 1877, p. 576).

4 The word, however, for beauty in the formula: 'beauty will save the world' (i.e. *krasota*) is unambiguous. *Krasota* contains no direct sense of 'good'.

5 See Dostoyevsky's article 'G. -bov i vopros ob iskusstve', *Vremya*, Feb. 1861 (included in *Dnevnik*, 1873, p. 58). For English translation, see *Dostoyevsky's Occasional Writings*, selected, translated and introduced by D. Magarshak (London, 1963), p. 97.

6 Similar ideas are put forward in the *Writer's Diary*, 1876, June, Ch. II, 4; and 1880, Aug., Ch. III, 3 and 4 (see *Dnevnik*, 1876, p. 254 and *Dnevnik*, 1877, pp. 549 and 561).

7 There is, perhaps, a hidden irony in the fact that Myshkin chooses to recommend himself by *propisi* [i.e. samples of beautiful writing]; for the word can also mean 'trite moral precepts', and to the critical the prince's positive ideas appear as little more. Thus in the ensuing scene with the

Yepanchin sisters (in which he is hailed as a philosopher) Myshkin says that one can find a great life even in prison, and receives the comment of Aglaya: 'That last praiseworthy thought I read in my "chrestomathy" when I was twelve years old.' (*D.6*, p. 68.)

For a use of '*propis*' in the sense of 'copy-book precept' see *Dnevnik*, 1873, p. 22.

8 This incident could well be added to those in the analogy between the life of Christ and that of Myshkin which Dolinin draws in his editorial foreword to *Pis'ma*, Vol. I, p. 14.

9 For Dostoyevsky's ideas on 'the Russian Christ', see *Writer's Diary*, 1873, ('Smyatennyy vid'); and 1876, June, Ch. II, 4; also 1877, May–June, Ch. I, I (*Dnevnik*, 1873, p. 258; 1876, p. 252; 1877, pp. 168–9).

10 *Pis'ma*, Vol. 2, p. 160.

11 I.e. love of children, attitude to creditors, love of calligraphy and of beautiful writing implements. See commentary of G. M. Fridlender to *D.6*, p. 707.

Another possible prototype for Myshkin may have been Dostoyevsky's nephew, A. P. Karepin. He had many of Myshkin's qualities and was even called 'the Idiot'. See Grossman, *Dostoyevsky*, p. 361.

12 See 'G. -bov i vopros ob iskusstve' (*Dnevnik*, 1873, p. 85): Eng. trans. in *Dostoyevsky's Occasional Writings*, p. 125.

13 The poem as quoted here is a censored version. The full text of 'The Poor Knight' was published in 1930 for the first time, but it is extremely interesting to compare the restored verses with Dostoyevsky's portrait of Myshkin. Thus from these we learn not only that 'the poor knight' had a vision of the Virgin Mary near Geneva (cf. the influence of Marie on Myshkin in Switzerland) but also it transpires that 'the poor knight' is a heretic – he is anti-trinitarian and does not fast and does not pray to God (Myshkin's relationship to Russian heretics is discussed later in this chapter pp. 84–95). See A. S. Pushkin, *Polnoye sobraniye sochineniy v desyati tomakh*, (AN SSSR, Moscow, 1957), Vol. V, p. 481 (it is just possible that Dostoyevsky knew of a manuscript version of the full poem).

If one accepts Grossman's identification of Rogozhin with 'the Moor' (see Grossman, *Dostoyevsky*, pp. 425–6) then the word 'Mussulman' may even take on a more precise meaning.

14 See Ch. 8 of the present work.

15 Aglaya's marriage to Myshkin is constantly linked with 'destiny' in this chapter.

16 E.g. E. H. Carr, *Dostoevsky* (London, 1962), p. 100.

17 The Flagellants [*Khlysty*] were supposed to take their name from *khlyst* (i.e. 'whip'). They themselves, however, called themselves *Khrysty* (i.e. 'The Christs'), and this should perhaps be their correct name; for they believed in many manifestations of Christ on earth. They organised themselves in communities known as 'ships' [*korabli*] often with a 'Christ' or 'Madonna' [*bogoroditsa*] at their head. Whether they did really indulge in the bouts of flagellation widely ascribed to them is open to serious doubt.

18 See *The Notebooks for 'The Idiot'*, p. 170. (*Three* kinds of love in the novel:

(1) Passionate and spontaneous love – Rogozhin. (2) Love out of vanity – Ganya. (3) Christian love – the Prince.)

19 See Mel'nikov-Pechersky, *Sobraniye sochineniy*, Vol. 6, p. 231 and p. 240.

Grossman also sees Rogozhin's aunt in Pskov as a person who is probably connected with schismatics; for Pskov, he argues, was a centre for the Old Believers: see Grossman, *Dostoyevsky*, p. 425.

20 See *D.6*, p. 689. The murder referred to is that of the jeweller Kalmykov by the Moscow merchant Mazurin (see *D.6*, p. 725).

21 On the subject of faith Myshkin himself seems afflicted by 'double thoughts'. Thus before reading his 'Necessary Explanation' Ippolit asks Myshkin: 'You are a zealous Christian, aren't you? Kolya says that you yourself call yourself a Christian...' Myshkin pointedly does not reply to this (see *D.6*, p. 433). This invites comparison with what Ippolit says at the beginning of his Confession, where he records the fact that he charged Myshkin with being a materialist, and goes on to comment: 'He replied with that smile of his that he had always been a materialist. As he never lies, these words must mean something.' (*D.6*, p. 439.)

22 The schismatic Mikolka in *Crime and Punishment* also sold his cross for vodka: see *D.5*, p. 144.

23 If this is Myshkin's spiritual inheritance, his actual inheritance appears to have much the same origins; for the relative from whom he inherits his money is also a merchant and an Old Believer: see *D.6*, p. 298.

24 In his *Writer's Diary*, 1880, Aug., Ch. 1, Dostoyevsky stresses that Pushkin had pointed to the beauty of the principle embodied in the Russian common people:

'"Believe in the national spirit [*dukh narodnyy*] and expect salvation from that alone, and you will be saved." It is impossible not to form this conclusion from a study of the works of Pushkin.' (See *Dnevnik*, 1877, p. 501.)

25 See *The Notebooks for 'The Idiot'*, p. 244; also Grossman, *Dostoyevsky*, pp. 425–6.

26 See, for example, words attributed to Versilov in *A Raw Youth* (*D.8*, p. 284).

27 Dostoyevsky repeats these ideas in his *Writer's Diary*, 1877, May–June, Ch. III, 3; and Nov., Ch. III, 1 (see *Dnevnik*, 1877, pp. 220 and 429).

CHAPTER 5. THE CONDEMNED MAN: 'THE IDIOT'

1 The murder of one Suslov by the peasant Balabanov. Myshkin gives his own version of this crime as the second of his anecdotes illustrating the state of faith in Russia (Pt II, 4) (see also *D.6*, p. 728). Balabanov came from the Myshkin District of the Province of Yaroslav – a district which is a possible source for Myshkin's own name. (See also Magarshak's introduction to his translation of *The Idiot* (Penguin, 1955), p. 13.)

2 Dostoyevsky himself expresses almost identical ideas in his *Writer's Diary*, 1876, March, Ch. II, 1 (see *Dnevnik*, 1876, pp. 127–8).

3 *Georges Dandin*, a comedy by Molière: Podkolesin is the hero of Gogol's comedy, *Marriage*.

4 A similar dream will be described by Dmitri Karamazov, and will be contrasted with 'realism' (see *D.9*, p. 583).

5 The Russian word is in fact *mera* (i.e. 'measure').

6 See N. N. Strakhov, 'Vospominaniya o Fedore Mikhayloviche Dostoyev-skom', *Vosp.* Vol. 1, p. 315.

7 See also *Pis'ma*, Vol. 2, p. 118, where Dostoyevsky expresses the fear that his step-son Pasha might turn into a Gorsky or a Raskolnikov.

8 Cf. the words of the student who outlines Raskolnikov's own projected crime in the tavern: 'and what does the life of this consumptive, stupid, evil old woman signify, when weighed in the general scales [*na obshchikh vesakh*]' (*D.5*, p. 71).

9 In preaching the possibility that all might achieve 'the golden age' *Writer's Diary*, 1876, Jan., Ch. 1, 4, 'The Golden Age in One's Pocket') Dostoyevsky exclaims: 'It surely, surely cannot be that the golden age exists only on china cups?' See *Dnevnik*, 1876, p. 16.

10 Cf. the reminiscences of Dostoyevsky's wife, *Vosp.* Vol. 2, p. 15.

11 Cf. the diary of A. G. Dostoyevskaya for 1867 (*Vosp.* Vol. 2, p. 118): 'The fear of death was a constant phenomenon after a fit.' See also the evidence of K. A. Trutovsky ('Vospominaniya o Fedore Mikhayloviche Dostoyevskom') on Dostoyevsky's fear of falling into a coma which might be mistaken for death (see *Vosp.* Vol. 1, p. 109).

12 In his *Writer's Diary*, 1876, Oct., Ch. 1, 4, Dostoyevsky printed a similar confession of a suicide under the title 'A Death Sentence' [*Prigovor*]. See *Dnevnik*, 1876, pp. 390–3 (and pp. 472–3 for Dostoyevsky's own explanation of the piece (i.e. in Dec., Ch. 1, 3).

13 Cf. 'G. -bov i vopros ob iskusstve', 'Beauty is normality, health' [*krasota est' normal'nost'*, *zdorov'ye*]. See *Dnevnik*, 1873, p. 96.

14 The student whom Ippolit consults instead of a real doctor bears the ironic name of 'Kislorodov' (i.e. from *kislorod* = oxygen). See *D.6*, pp. 440–1.

15 A famous French criminal. Dostoyevsky had published an article on Lacenaire in *Vremya*, no. 2, (1861).

16 Rogozhin is illuminated by the lamp as the tarantula had been by the candle, but it is significant that the lamp is one placed before an icon: for *obraz* ['icon', 'image', 'form'] is a key word in this passage. Thus Ippolit says about the Holbein picture: 'And if that teacher himself could have seen his *obraz* [image? icon?] on the eve of his execution, would he himself have gone on the cross as he did?' Moreover, these thoughts on the picture come to Ippolit in the form of *obrazy*, and he goes on to pose an intriguing question about them: 'Can that which has no *obraz* [form?] present itself as an *obraz* [image?]?'

   In this passage the confusion of 'images', of course, operates on more than the linguistic level: the device recalls Ippolit's earlier dream of the scorpion. In view of this, it is interesting that certain details of the hunt for the scorpion seem to reflect a real incident with a tarantula which Dostoyevsky experienced in Italy: though Dostoyevsky's own dating of this incident (which is by no means infallible) would seem to rule out the possibility of its having influenced the novel (*Writer's Diary*, 1876, Sept., Ch. 1, 1) (see *Dnevnik*, 1876, pp. 335–6).

17 On 1 May 1867 Dostoyevsky had visited Dresden and had been greatly impressed by another of Holbein's paintings – *The Madonna*, called the 'Meier *Madonna*', because it had been commissioned by Jacob Meier, burgomaster of Basle, and showed the Madonna with the Meier family group. The better-known Dresden picture was, in fact, a copy of the original held in Darmstadt, and differed from it in such details as the child's face, which the Dresden version presents as more sad and worn. Because of this a legend persisted that it had been painted as a thank-offering for the recovery from illness of Meier's youngest boy.

'The idea, and it is so graceful that one wishes it had been true, was that Holbein has represented the Madonna as taking the sick boy in her arms, while she restores to the Meier family their child in good health.' (Gerald S. Davies, *Hans Holbein The Younger* (London, 1903), p. 92.)

On 24 May 1868 Dostoyevsky's own baby daughter died in Geneva, and the author was plunged into anguish. The three chapters which Dostoyevsky wrote for the June number of *Russkiy vestnik* (i.e. Pt II, Chs. 6–8) mark the growing importance of Ippolit. Ippolit himself not only embodies the protest against the futility of death, but his confession also mentions dead and ailing children (cf. Surikov and the doctor's sickly three-week-old child). In giving the wall of Ippolit a specific name, Dostoyevsky is, perhaps, providing a bitterly ironic comment on his own personal 'wall' – his own ailing baby who, unlike Meier's child, did not recover.

18 Carr says this is one of the great answers in literature. See Carr, *Dostoevsky*, p. 168.

CHAPTER 6. THE PAMPHLET NOVEL: 'THE DEVILS'

1 A. G. Dostoyevskaya, 'Vospominaniya', in *Vosp.* Vol. 2, p. 74.
2 *Pis'ma*, Vol. 2, p. 294 (see also *D.7*, p. 722).
3 See *The Notebooks for 'The Possessed'*, edited and with an introduction by E. Wasiolek, translated by V. Terras (Chicago and London, 1968), p. 116 (see also *D.7*, p. 717).
4 Nozdrev – a bullying braggart in Gogol's *Dead Souls*.
5 I.e. A. N. Stankevich, *T. N. Granovsky* (Moscow, 1869).
6 See F. Venturi, *Roots of Revolution: A History of the Populist and Socialist Movements in Nineteenth Century Russia*, translated from the Italian by F. Haskell (London, 1960), p. 26.
7 Later, Dostoyevsky spoke highly of Granovsky (e.g. 'He was one of our most honourable Stepan Trofimoviches (the type of the idealist of the forties which I presented in the novel *The Devils*, and which was regarded as accurate by our critics. I love Stepan Trofimovich and deeply respect him)': *Writer's Diary*, 1876, July–Aug., Ch. II, 1 (*Dnevnik*, 1876, p. 276). See also *ibid*. Ch. II, 2, and Sept., Ch. II, 1 (pp. 281–6, and pp. 357–8); also 1877, May–June, Ch. II, 1 (*Dnevnik*, 1877, p. 187).
8 Dostoyevsky is obviously referring to Granovsky when he ascribes similar flattering views on the French people to 'a certain Russian pro-

fessor' in his *Writer's Diary* (*Grazhdanin*, no. 51 (1873)): see *Dnevnik*, 1873, p. 451. (Cf. also *Writer's Diary*, 1876, Sept., Ch. II, 1 (*Dnevnik*, 1876, p. 358).)

9 In a host of minor details the figure of Stepan Trofimovich parodies that of Granovsky. Such are: his gentle character; his bouts of melancholy and tendency to write long confessional letters (see remarks of F. I. Yevnin, *D.7*, p. 715). The scholarly interests of Stepan Trofimovich are also close to those of the famous professor. Thus the thesis on the Hanseatic town of Hanau, which was seen as an attack on the Slavophiles (*D.7*, p. 9) is a gibe at the subject matter and polemical slant of Granovsky's own thesis (see *D.7*, p. 737). The article on chivalry (*D.7*, pp. 9–10) and the 'Stories from Spanish History' (*D.7*, p. 79) also correspond to work published by Granovsky (see *D.7*, pp. 737–8 and p. 743).

Granovsky had been placed under surveillance because of a flattering reference to him in a letter from one member of the Petrashevsky circle to another (i.e. letter of Pleshcheyev to Durov). He had also been summoned before Filaret, Metropolitan of Moscow, to account for the allegedly anti-religious tendency of his lectures (see *D.7*, p. 10, 'Someone demanded of him some sort of explanations', and note *D.7*, p. 738). Moreover, Granovsky like Stepan Trofimovich was an obsessive card player, who constantly lost and got into debt (see Ch. Vetrinsky (V. Ye. Cheshikhin), *V. sorokovykh godakh* (Moscow, 1899), p. 89).

10 Students and lecturers were officially reproved for throwing laurel wreaths on the coffin at Granovsky's interment (see Vetrinsky, *ibid.* p. 89).

11 Dostoyevsky himself is not far from the central thesis of Dobrolyubov's influential essay, when in his *Writer's Diary*, 1880, Aug., Ch. III, 2, he discusses the dependence of the so-called 'superfluous men' on the system they attacked (*Dnevnik*, 1877, pp. 541–2).

12 For an account of this work, see Venturi, *Roots of Revolution*, pp. 366–7.

13 See 'Odna iz sovremennykh fal'shey', *Writer's Diary*, 1873 (*Grazhdanin*, 1873, no. 50) (*Dnevnik*, 1873, pp. 351–66; see esp. p. 357).

14 Cf. Pechorin as he is portrayed in *Princess Ligovskaya* and *Hero of Our Time*.

15 Cf. the words of Kirillov on Pushkin's letter to van Heeckeren, which link the duel of Stavrogin with the fatal duel of Pushkin (*D.7*, p. 248). The insolent behaviour of Stavrogin at this duel recalls a similar episode in Pushkin's story *The Shot* [*Vystrel*]. Shatov's charge that Stavrogin belonged to a secret society of voluptuaries in St Petersburg (*D.7*, p. 269) recalls the sort of rumours prevalent about the 'Green Lamp Club' of which Pushkin was a member.

16 See L. Grossman, 'Bakunin i Dostoyevsky', *Pechat' i revolyutsiya* (1923), Bk. IV, pp. 82–112.

17 ' "I am a clown, but I do not want you, my chief half, to be a clown. Do you understand me?"

Stavrogin did understand him. Perhaps he alone did so. For Shatov was astounded when Stavrogin told him that Petr Verkhovensky had enthusiasm.' (*D.7*, p. 566).

18 Cf. 'Staryye lyudi', *Writer's Diary*, 1873: 'Herzen was entirely different: he was the product of our gentry class, *gentilhomme russe et citoyen du monde* above all else, a type which has appeared only in Russia, and which could appear nowhere else except in Russia. Herzen did not emigrate, did not lay the foundation for the emigration. No, he was already born an *émigré*' (*Dnevnik*, 1873, p. 188).

19 In an article in 1861 Dostoyevsky had already broached this idea, when he ascribed the origins of the Slavophiles and the Westernisers to the Byronic figure of Yevgeniy Onegin. See 'Knizhnost' i gramotnost'': stat'ya pervaya', *Vremya* (July 1861) (in *Dnevnik*, 1873, p. 105). In the same essay Dostoyevsky sees Pechorin as the ultimate manifestation of the 'original Russian contradiction': egoism to the point of self-veneration and at the same time a malicious disrespect of self (i.e. qualities not unlike those of Stavrogin himself). See *ibid.* p. 108.

20 Cf. Dostoyevsky's letter to Maykov on his meeting with Turgenev in 1867, *Pis'ma*, Vol. II, p. 32.

21 See *Pis'ma*, Vol. II, p. 274 (also note *D*.7, pp. 743–4).

22 'Spectres' was published by Dostoyevsky in the first issue of his new journal *Epokha* (Feb. 1864). Turgenev himself recognised this parody. See his letter to M. A. Milyutina in I. S. Turgenev, *Polnoye sobraniye sochinneniy i pisem* (Moscow-Leningrad, 1965); *Pis'ma*, Vol. 10, p. 39. Turgenev here claims that Dostoyevsky had showered him with grateful and flattering letters about 'Spectres' (cf. *Pis'ma*, Vol. I, pp. 319–20, 337–8, 342–4; for Dostoyevsky's private opinion of 'Spectres', however, see his letter to his brother: *ibid.* p. 352).

23 See *Pis'ma*, Vol. 2, p. 32.

24 The murder of Ivanov, the defecting 'fifth' member, was carried out by Nechayev (as overall organiser) and the four other members of the group: P. Uspensky, A. Kuznetsov, I. Pryzhov and N. Nikolayev. By including the 'Petrashevets' Milyukov/Liputin in the group, Dostoyevsky is perhaps seeking to link Nechayev with his own implication in revolutionary activity ('I myself am an old Nechayevist'); whereas the inclusion of 'the little Jew' Lyamshin is probably a gesture in the contrary direction – to show the alien, non-Russian nature of such activity.

25 Virginsky's sister is based on A. Dement'yeva-Tkacheva, a young disseminator of propaganda among students, who was implicated in the Nechayev affair (see *D*.7, p. 752). The 'madman' is based on a liberal professor of history, P. V. Pavlov, who was arrested in March 1862 for what was considered a defamatory speech against Russia. (See M. Lemke, *Ocherki osvoboditel'nogo dvizheniya shestidesyatykh godov* (1908), pp. 9–13; also *D*.7, p. 754.)

26 The Shpigulinsky affair is based on a real strike which took place in St Petersburg in May and June 1870 at a cotton-spinning factory. It was Russia's first mass strike: see *D*.7, pp. 750–1.

27 These aluminium columns are a feature of the crystal palaces of the society of the future which Vera Pavlovna sees in her Fourth Dream in *What is to be done?*

The point that the younger revolutionaries had gone further than Chernyshevsky and Dobrolyubov has already been made in the figure of Lebezyatnikov in *Crime and Punishment*.

28 Cf. the words of Lebezyatnikov, *Crime and Punishment*, Pt V, Ch. 1 (*D.5*, p. 392).

29 Dostoyevsky's funniest comment on this theory is to be found in 'Iz dachnykh progulok Kuz'my Prutkova i ego druga' ('Poslednyaya stranichka,' iz zhurnala *Grazhdanina* za 1878 g.) where he says that instead of adorning rooms with classical statues of nude figures, it would be 'more natural' to have naked servants fulfilling this function (see *Dnevnik*, 1877, p. 495).

30 Stepan Trofimovich's choice of the Sistine *Madonna* has perhaps added significance, in as much as it was this very picture which for reasons of pure expediency Bakunin placed in jeopardy, when at the siege of Dresden in May 1849 he ordered it to be shown to the Prussian artillery, because he considered that the Prussians were '*zu klassisch gebildet*' to fire at Raphael.

31 The Russian text of Luke VIII. 32–7, which is given as the second epigraph of the novel, translates the Sea of Galilee by the word *ozero* = 'lake'.

32 He is, nevertheless, based on a real-life figure – Ivan Yakovlevich Koreysha, a *yurodivyy*, on whom one of the Nechayevists, I. Pryzhov, had written a pamphlet (see *D.7*, p. 343).

33 At some point in the seventeenth century Danila Filippov (his name may also be spelt both 'Danilo' and 'Filippovich') who was one of the disciples of Kapton, a leader of the schism, cut across the arguments then being waged on the virtues of the old books versus those of the new ones, and claimed that the only book was divine inspiration. Filippov collected all the books he could and placing them in a bag weighted with stones threw them into the Volga. For this he was imprisoned in the Bogoyavlenskiy Cloister by the Patriarch Nikon.

Shortly after the drowning of the books (some versions say before) Filippov appeared in the village of Starodub (Klyazemskiy) and there on a hill named after the village of Gorodina, the Lord Savaof himself descended in a fiery chariot in all his glory, with angels and archangels, cherubim and seraphim amid fiery clouds. The heavenly powers withdrew back to heaven, but the Lord Savaof remained on earth in human form in the body of Danila Filippov. From this time forth Danila Filippov was no longer a man but 'the living god', and his residence was 'The House of God'. Filippov gave his followers twelve commandments, and thirteen years after his apotheosis, there was born 'the son of god', the 'Christ' – Ivan Timofeyevich Suslov. Filippov summoned Suslov to Kostroma and there conferred upon him his divinity, carrying him up to heaven for three days. (See Mel'nikov-Pechersky, *Sobraniye sochineniy*, Vol. 6, pp. 261–4 and Conybeare, *Russian Dissenters*, pp. 358–9.)

Although variants of Filippov's name are possible it seems odd that Dostoyevsky should here refer to him as Ivan. Is he perhaps confusing him with Ivan Tsarevich or even with the Christ-figure Ivan Suslov? It could well be that this confusion over names stems from Dostoyevsky's epilepsy.

Thus he told Vsevolod Solovev: 'When I was finishing off *The Devils* I had to read everything over from the very beginning, because I had forgotten everything, even the names of the characters' (see Vs. S. Solov'ev, '*Vospominaniya o F. M. Dostoyevskom*' in *Vosp.* Vol. 2, p. 192). Nevertheless the form 'Ivan Filippovich' occurs elsewhere in Dostoyevsky. (See *Writer's Diary*, 1876, Jan., Ch. III, 2 (*Dnevnik*, 1876, p. 49).)

34 See *Pis'ma*, Vol. 2, p. 263.

35 See *The Notebooks for 'The Possessed'*, p. 67; also F. M. Dostoyevsky, *U Tikhona: Propushchennaya glava iz romana 'Besy'* introduced by A. Kozin (New York, 1964), p. 89.

36 See Conybeare, *Russian Dissenters*, p. 358.

37 A. S. Dolinin has advanced the theory that Shatov might himself be based on V. I. Kel'siev, one of the most famous chroniclers of the Russian sects. See the commentary to *Pis'ma*, Vol. 2, pp. 398–9.

38 See N. Tsakni, *La Russie Sectaire; Sectes Religieuses en Russie* (Paris, 1888?), p. 72. (Cf. also G. P. Fedotov, *The Russian Religious Mind* (Cambridge, Mass., 1966), Vol. I, pp. 11–15. 'In Mother Earth, who remains the core of Russian religion, converge the most secret and deep feelings of the folk', *ibid.* p. 12.)

39 In a story dating from the same period as *The Devils* (i.e. *The Eternal Husband*, first published 1870) Dostoyevsky says of one of the characters:

'Compared with Velchaninov himself, she was like a "Flagellant Madonna", who, to the highest possible degree, believes that she is in fact a madonna, and so to the highest possible degree did Natalya Vasilyevna believe in every single one of her actions.'

(See *D.4*, p. 463.)

40 Cf. R. Hingley, *The Undiscovered Dostoyevsky* (London, 1962), p. 136.

41 Petr Verkhovensky seeks to interest Liza in his political plans for Stavrogin by telling her about a ship [*lad'ya*] with oars of maple-wood in a Russian folk-song. Ships were important in the mythology of the Flagellants and Castrates. Thus both sects were organised in communities called 'ships' [*korabli*], and the Castrates had a legend that when their own 'Christ', Kondratiy Selivanov, reached Moscow, ships would arrive full of gold and precious stones. (See Conybeare, *Russian Dissenters*, p. 366.)

CHAPTER 7. THE GREAT SINNER: 'THE DEVILS'

1 Versilov (another version of 'the great sinner') in *A Raw Youth* marries an idiot girl and makes the last days of her life happy (see *D.8*, p. 527).

2 Stavrogin, striding out through the rain to make his arrangements, to some extent recalls the last hours of Svidrigaylov in *Crime and Punishment*, Pt VI, 6.

3 In the word *khoroshiy* the same ambiguity of 'good/beautiful' may be seen as earlier with the word *prekrasnyy* in *The Idiot*.

4 The other names with which Lebyadkin juggles in this passage are significant. He would like to be thought of as 'Ernest' (i.e. serious); he would like to bear the distinguished title of a European prince. 'Le Prince de

Montbard' is perhaps a reference to Georges Louis Le Clerc, Comte de Buffon (1707–88). Buffon was born at Montbard which became his ancestral seat. He was both a nobleman (the title 'prince' is perhaps a piece of exaggeration typical of Lebyadkin) and the author of the celebrated *L'Histoire Naturelle* and an acknowledged stylist. Natural History is relevant to Lebyadkin in view of his own name, and the fact that he too has pretensions to being a writer of style who draws much of his imagery from the animal kingdom. Dostoyevsky has a memorandum in his notebooks for *The Devils* to the effect that he must read Buffon on wild animals (see *The Notebooks for 'The Possessed'*, p. 156).

The 'swan' recalls the myth (mentioned by Buffon) of the swan singing before death. Lebyadkin himself is the 'poet' condemned to a bloody fate. But in Slavonic wedding symbolism the swan stands for the bride, the hawk for the bridegroom (cf. the opening of *Slovo o Polku Igoreve*). Marya Lebyadkin herself refers to Stavrogin as 'my hawk' [*sokol moy*]: see *D.7*, p. 294, also p. 293. There is therefore in the name Lebyadkin a hint at marriage in terms of predator and victim, and the only relationship which Lebyadkin himself has with Stavrogin is through his sister.

5 Grishka Otrepev claimed to be Dmitri the son of Ivan the Terrible. With Polish help he ruled from 1605–6.

6 N.B. the root of this word is *kupit'* = 'to buy'.

7 This identification of a murderer as a suicide is present in Dostoyevsky's attitude to the would-be regicide Karakozov. In a draft of the preface for *The Brothers Karamazov* he referred to him as follows: 'Even that unfortunate, blind suicide of the fourth of April believed at the time in the rightness of what he was doing.' (See Grossman, *Dostoyevsky*, p. 514.)

8 Cf. *The Eternal Husband*: '…the convictions of a lifetime have sometimes suddenly changed under the melancholy influence of night-time and insomnia' (*D.4*, p. 436).

It is perhaps significant that Tikhon says to Stavrogin: 'Reply to my question honestly, to me alone or as though to your own self in the darkness of night.' (See *U Tikhona*, p. 75.)

9 After the section 'Night' two more acts connected with it seem designed further to illustrate the divided nature of the hero. The first is the duel. Kirillov acts as second, and this may be taken as an act of the will; but, as we have seen, Stavrogin's motivation here is ambiguous. Moreover Kirillov explicitly tells him not to try to be a 'strong man' (*D.7*, pp. 306–7).

The second act would have been the visit to Tikhon on the suggestion of Shatov. This is ostensibly an act of self-humiliation before a man of God, but its implications are no less ambiguous: it is not clear whether Stavrogin is confessing genuinely, nor even whether there is really anything to confess.

10 'The incident in Gorokhovaya Street' in itself contains a hint of clowning; for although the street was a well-known one in St Petersburg, there may, nevertheless, have been the consciousness of a certain linguistic ambiguity in Dostoyevsky's mind; for the adjective '*gorokhovyy*' is one applied to jesters (cf. '*gorokhovyy shut*' = 'a clown' or 'jester').

11 *Chasy* means both watch and clock. In the case of Kirillov translators have chosen to render it 'clock'.

12 Letter to A. N. Maykov, 25 March 1870 (see *Pis'ma*, Vol. 2, p. 263). This is not unlike what Kirillov himself says ('God has tormented me all my life') (*D.7*, p. 125).

13 The words in which this is expressed are very close to those of the author himself in a letter from Siberia (i.e. letter to Mme N.D. Fon Vizin, February 1854) (see *Pis'ma*, Vol. 1, p. 142).

CHAPTER 8. PARRICIDE: 'THE BROTHERS KARAMAZOV'

1 These facts are recorded by Dostoyevsky's younger brother Andrey in his 'Recollections': see *Vosp.* Vol. 1, p. 89.

2 See *D.10*, p. 465-6; also *D.3*, pp. 403-4 and 651.

3 The village was apparently called Cheremoshnya, but Andrey in a note to his 'Recollections' does not hesitate to identify the two: see *Vosp.* Vol. 1, p. 71.

4 See *D. 10*, p. 492.

5 *Writer's Diary*, 1876, Jan., Ch. 1, 2 (*Dnevnik*, 1876, p. 8).

6 The other figure linking these two worlds is Rakitin and his role is the very antithesis of that of Alesha.

7 I.e. 'wild' = '*dik*'; 'savages' = '*dikari*'. Cf. the opening of Zhukovsky's translation of '*Das Eleusische Fest*' quoted by Dmitri (*D.9*, p. 136):

> 'Robok, nag i dik skryvalsya
> Troglodit v peshcherakh skal'

8 Andrey Dostoyevsky sees a prototype for Liza Smerdyashchaya in 'Foolish Agrafenya' [*Durochka Agrafenya*], another figure connected with his father's small country estate. See *Vosp.* Vol. 1, p. 73.

9 The saint in question is really St Julien (see *D.10*, p. 498). Dostoyevsky appears to have in mind Turgenev's translation of Flaubert's *La Légende de Saint-Julien l'Hospitalier*, which had appeared in 1877 (see I. S. Turgenev, 'Polnoye sobraniye sochineniy i pisem', *Sochineniya*, Vol. 13, pp. 221–50, esp. pp. 247–50). The fact that Dostoyevsky records the saint as John and not Julien underlines the significance of this figure for Ivan.

10 Cf. also the studied way in which Smerdyakov keeps shuffling his feet in the crucial interview with Ivan in Bk v, 6 ('As Yet a Very Obscure One').

11 A translation of: '*U menya den'gi – aksessuar, zhar dushi, obstanovka*' which strives to retain the theatrical terminology implied in '*aksessuar*' and '*obstanovka*' (see *D.9*, p. 139).

12 As the editors of *Vosp.* point out, Grigory's Christian name and patronymic correspond to those of a faithful retainer on the estate of Dostoyevsky's father (see *Vosp.* Vol. 1, p. 71, and note on p. 392).

13 When Lyagavyy asks Dmitri to show him the law which says it is permitted to do foul deeds (*D.9*, p. 471) the taunt seems more applicable to Ivan and his theory that everything is permissible.

14 The figure of Fetyukovich seems partly based on Spasovich, the defence counsel in the Kroneberg case. His words here seem to echo those of

Spasovich (as reported by Dostoyevsky): 'There was no torturing; there was no harm done the child.' See *Writer's Diary*, 1876, Feb., Ch. II, 2 (*Dnevnik*, 1876, p. 78). The evidence produced at the trial of the Kronebergs plays an important role in the 'Rebellion' of Ivan.

15 See Sigmund Freud, 'Dostoevsky and Parricide', in *Dostoevsky; Twentieth Century Views*, pp. 98–101.

16 I.e. '*peredovoye myaso*' (see *D.9*, p. 168). Magarshak translates this as 'first class material' (see *The Brothers Karamazov*, Vol. 1 (Penguin, 1964), p. 153).

17 *Sluga Licharda* is a figure from Russian folk-tales. In *Shazka o Bove koroleviche*, Licharda is the faithful servant of King Gvidon who helps him to gain the heroine Militrisa Kirbit'yevna. The name has passed into the language as the epitome of the faithful servant (see N. S. and M. G. Ashukin, *Krylatyye slova* (Moscow, 1955), p. 297).

18 A writer who preached extreme asceticism, and who was, in the strict sense, heretical as he was a Nestorian (i.e. a follower of the fifth-century Patriarch of Constantinople, Nestorius, who maintained that there were two Persons in Christ, one human and one divine). Dostoyevsky's own library contained a collection of his writings (see *D.10*, p. 494).

19 Although the Castrates acknowledged the divinity of Danila Filippov, their own true leader and 'Christ' was the historical figure Kondratiy Selivanov. (See Mel'nikov-Pechersky, *Sobraniye sochineniy*, Vol. 6, 331–40, *et passim*; and Conybeare, *Russian Dissenters*, pp. 365–7.)

20 I.e. '*belaya izba*' as a technical term is used to mean a hut with a properly constructed stove (Magarshak translates it 'parlour'), but the fact that the phrase is used in quotation marks seems to imply a special emphasis.

21 See Mel'nikov-Pechersky, *Sobraniye sochineniy*, p. 327.

22 A second hiding place is a hollow tree. In *The Devils* Petr Verkhovensky mentions a hollow tree as a post box for peasants who wished to contact the 'new Danila Filippov' – Stavrogin. (See *D.7*, p. 442.)

23 The fact that Smerdyakov is so strongly associated with the sect of the Castrates puts his role as Dmitri's servant in a new light; for Freud in his article 'Dostoevsky and Parricide' stresses that castration is the punishment meted out for the Oedipal crime (see *Dostoevsky; Twentieth Century Views*, pp. 103–4).

CHAPTER 9.
JUSTICE AND PUNISHMENT: 'THE BROTHERS KARAMAZOV'

1 See *D.6*, p. 615. The same ideas occur in the *Writer's Diary*, 1876, March, Ch. I, 5 (*Dnevnik*, 1876, pp. 124 and 126). Here Dostoyevsky mentions that he has also touched on these ideas in one of his novels.

2 Kroneberg – see Ch. 8, note 14. The incident with the dogs appears to be a reference to 'Vospominaniya krepostnogo', *Russkiy vestnik*, 1877, no. 9, pp. 43–4. The child was not harmed by the dogs, but the mother went mad and died three days later. (See *D.10*, p. 499.)

3 Cf. *Writer's Diary*, 1876, March, Ch. I, 5 (*Dnevnik*, 1876, p. 123).

4 In his journal *Vremya*, for February 1861, Dostoyevsky cites the Lisbon earthquake as an example of a human tragedy so overwhelming that any

poet of the day would ignore it at his peril. On the other hand a Dr Pangloss who told the stricken inhabitants that it was all for the best would be given a pension and proclaimed a friend of humanity. (See 'G. -bov i vopros ob iskusstve' in *Dnevnik*, 1873, pp. 54–5.)

It might be that the Lisbon earthquake was considered as the subject for another of Ivan's 'poems'; for later in the novel the Devil taunts him with an earlier composition entitled 'The Geological Upheaval' [*Geologicheskiy perevorot*]: see *D.10*, p. 178.

5 According to Andrey Dostoyevsky the peasants who murdered his father fell on him at the cry of: '*Rebyata, karachun yemu!*' ['Let him have it lads!'] See *Vosp.* Vol. 1, p. 89 (here again the word for 'violent retribution' contains the root *kara*).

'*Kara*' is in origin Turkish (cf. Kara Kum Desert) and means 'black'. The Russian adjective '*kariy*' has the meaning of dark (of eyes). Dostoyevsky appears to be playing with the ambiguity of the word, when he has the wife of Snegirev hail Alesha as '*Chernomazov*' instead of Karamazov (cf. *chernyy* = 'black' and *chernomazyy* = 'swarthy'). See *D.9*, p. 253.

6 Dostoyevsky appears to be playing with the sense of this other root in the Karamazov name in the following exchange between Lyagavyy and Dmitri, in which Karamazov is mistaken for a house-painter (*mazat'* = 'to daub', 'to paint')

> '*Ty krasil'shchik!*'
> '*Pomiloserduyte, ya Karamazov...*'

('You are a painter!' 'For goodness sake, I am Karamazov') (*D.9*, p. 471).

7 We also learn that the peasants of Mokroye are great inflicters of punishment: they like to have their girls birched by the young village lads. Old Karamazov calls them sadists (see *D.9*, p. 169).

Many of the physical aspects of the town of Skotoprigonevsk [Cattle Pen] take on symbolic and moral overtones. The word *pereulok* [narrow side street] is frequently found used in a double sense. Thus Dmitri talks about the 'moral side streets' of the town (e.g. *D.9*, pp. 139 and 150), by which term, on at least one occasion, he obviously means Grushenka (*D.9*, p. 151). He himself is described as living 'in a side street not far from Lake Street' (*D.9*, p. 246). In a metaphorical sense the idea of 'leaving the main road for a side street' is also applied to Rakitin (*D.9*, p. 449). The word *pereulok* has much prominence at the time of Dmitri's entry into his father's garden (cf. the opening of 'In the Dark'). Here it is perhaps significant that Dmitri leaves the street which bears his own name (*Dmitrovskaya ulitsa*) for a deserted side-turning which will give him access to the back of his father's house (*D.9*, p. 486).

The term 'backs' [*zady*] is another prominent feature of the town, which again seems to be used with a certain degree of metaphorical significance (cf. *D.9*, pp. 131, 135, 486, and *D.10*, p. 250).

The word for 'fence' [*zabor*] is used symbolically to denote a boundary which may not be crossed (i.e. the fence round his father's house). See *D.9*, p. 494. Later in the novel it takes on the connotation of 'stumbling block' (*D.9*, p. 595), and even 'line of defence' (*D.10*, p. 269).

8 This point is also made by P. M. Bitsilli. See his article in *O Dostoyevskom: Stat'i*, Introduction by D. Fanger (Brown University, 1966), p. 20.
9 Dostoyevsky himself speaks of the comic elements surrounding Zosima in a letter to Pobedonostsev. See *Pis'ma*, Vol. 4, p. 107.

CHAPTER 10. CONCLUSION

1 See *Writer's Diary*, 1877, Dec., Ch. I, 6 (*Dnevnik*, 1877, p. 462).
2 See V. S. Dorovatovskaya-Lyubimova, 'Dostoyevsky i shestidesyatniki', in *Dostoyevsky* (Moscow, 1928), pp. 14–17. See also *D.10*, p. 511.
3 See *Writer's Diary*, 1877, Oct., Ch. II, 1 (*Dnevnik*, 1877, p. 372).
4 See H. Gifford, *The Novel in Russia* (London, 1964), pp. 108–19.
5 See 'Odna iz sovremennykh fal'shey', *Grazhdanin*, no. 50, (1873) (*Dnevnik*, 1873, p. 356).
6 See *Writer's Diary*, 1881, Jan., Ch. I, 4 (*Dnevnik*, 1877, p. 585).
7 See *Writer's Diary*, 1876, Jan., Ch. III, 1; and April, Ch. II, 1; and May, Ch. II, 3 (*Dnevnik*, 1876, pp. 42–3; p. 173 and pp. 226–7) where Dostoyevsky appears to be basing arguments for the furtherance of Russia's imperial aims on a supposed Russian policy of universal education, and the even more bizarre idea that Russia is more democratic than the West.
   Dostoyevsky's thought is never fixed and settled enough for him to be a true conservative. Thus he claims: 'I consider myself the most liberal of all men, perhaps merely because I do not wish at all to be reconciled.' (See *Writer's Diary*, 1876, Jan. Ch. I, 1 (*Dnevnik*, 1876, p. 8).)
8 One of the most positive affirmations of such 'earth worship' comes from the atheist Versilov (*A Raw Youth*). In pursuing the ideas evoked by the painting *Acis and Galatea*, he describes a society in which religious values (i.e. the promise of immortality) have been replaced by love of nature and veneration of the earth (see *D.8*, pp. 518–19). Dostoyevsky himself obviously considered this passage to be a significant utterance; for he quoted it *in toto*, when discussing the concept of a 'Church of Atheists' in his *Writer's Diary*, 1876, March, Ch. II, 1 (*Dnevnik*, 1876, pp. 136–7).
9 I.e. in the famous *Pushkin Speech* of 1880 (see *D.10*, pp. 442–59).
10 Apollon Grigorev (1822–64) invented the theory of 'organic criticism', which examined art as an organic growth of the national soil. Grigorev was associated with Dostoyevsky's two journals *Vremya* and *Epokha*.
11 The idea is voiced, too, by Dostoyevsky the publicist. See, for example, 'The Golden Age in One's Pocket', in *Writer's Diary*, 1876, Jan., Ch. I, 4 (*Dnevnik*, 1876, pp. 15–16).
12 Against this, however, must be balanced such statements as that of the underground man that suffering is the sole source of consciousness (see *D.4*, p. 161) or that of Dostoyevsky himself, when he says that the deepest need of the Russians is to suffer (see 'Vlas', *Grazhdanin*, no. 6 (1873), (*Dnevnik*, 1873, pp. 225–6)).
13 Also quoted by Dostoyevsky in *A Raw Youth* (see *D.8*, p. 435).
14 The description of the house owes some of its details to the Dostoyevskys' *dacha* in Staraya Russa. See Grossman, *Dostoyevsky*, p. 473.

15 See Hingley, *The Undiscovered Dostoyevsky*, p. 100. In the *Writer's Diary*, 1877, March, Ch. III, 2, when describing a picture of squalor similar to that of the Marmeladovs, Dostoyevsky writes: 'One could even express here a great deal of humour, and it would be very much to the point; for humour is the wit of deep feeling. I very much like this definition of it.' (*Dnevnik*, 1877, p. 122.)

BIOGRAPHICAL TABLE

1821 Dostoyevsky born 30 October, second eldest of family of seven. Father a doctor at paupers' hospital in Moscow.

1837 Death of mother. Dostoyevsky and brother Mikhail go to St Petersburg.

1838 Dostoyevsky enters Military Engineering College in St Petersburg.

1839 Father murdered by peasants.

1843 Dostoyevsky finishes engineer's course, translates *Eugénie Grandet*.

1844 Retires from military service.

1845 Dramatic literary acclaim.

1846 Publication of *Poor Folk* and *The Double*.

1847 Dostoyevsky visits Petrashevsky Circle.

1849 April: Dostoyevsky arrested; December: subjected to mock execution.

1850 Dostoyevsky arrives at Omsk Penal Settlement.

1854 Dostoyevsky posted to Semipalatinsk as private in army.

1857 Marriage to first wife (Isayeva). *The Little Hero* allowed to be printed.

1859 Dostoyevsky allowed to leave military service.

1860 Dostoyevsky in St Petersburg. Publication of *Notes from the House of the Dead*.

1861 Launching of journal *Vremya* with *The Insulted and the Injured*.

1862 First trip abroad.

1863 *Winter Notes on Summer Impressions*. Closure of *Vremya*. Second trip abroad with Suslova. Gambling mania.

1864 Launching of second journal *Epokha* with *Notes from Underground*. April: death of wife; July: death of brother Mikhail.

1865 Friendship with Anna Korvin-Kryukovskaya. June: *Epokha* closed. Dostoyevsky flees abroad. In Wiesbaden works on *Crime and Punishment*.

1866 *Crime and Punishment* serialised in *Russkiy vestnik*. *The Gambler* delivered to Stellovsky.

1867 Marriage to second wife (Anna Snitkina). Flight abroad. Gambling.

1868 *The Idiot* serialised in *Russkiy vestnik*. May: death of daughter, Sof'ya.

1869 October: Dostoyevskys in Dresden visited by Anna's brother; November: Nechayev kills Ivanov.

1871 Parts I and II of *The Devils* serialised in *Russkiy vestnik*. July: Dostoyevskys return to Russia.

1872 November–December: third part of *The Devils* serialised in *Russkiy vestnik*.

1873 Dostoyevsky editor of *Grazhdanin*, contributes 'Writer's Diary'.

1874 Dostoyevsky leaves *Grazhdanin*.

1875 *A Raw Youth* serialised in *Otechestvennyye zapiski*.

1876 Dostoyevsky launches *A Writer's Diary* as a separate monthly paper.

1878 Son Aleksey dies from epileptic fit. Visit to Optina Monastery.

1879–80 *The Brothers Karamazov* serialised in *Russkiy vestnik*.

1880 June: Pushkin Celebrations in Moscow. Dostoyevsky's *Pushkin Speech*.

1881 28 January: Dostoyevsky dies.

INDEX

The following abbreviations are used: *C. and P.* for *Crime and Punishment*; D for Dostoyevsky; *The Bros K.* for *The Brothers Karamazov*.